Revitalising Audience Research

The revitalisation of audience studies is not only about new approaches and methods; it entails a crossing of disciplines and a bridging of long-established boundaries in the field. The aim of this volume is to capture the boundary-crossing processes that have begun to emerge across the discipline in the form of innovative, interdisciplinary interventions in the audience research agenda. Contributions to this volume seek to further this process though innovative, audience-oriented perspectives that firmly anchor media engagement within the diversity of contexts and purposes to which people incorporate media in their daily lives, in ways often unanticipated by industries and professionals.

Frauke Zeller is an Assistant Professor at Ryerson University, Toronto, Ontario, Canada.

Cristina Ponte is an Associate Professor at Universidade NOVA de Lisboa, Portugal.

Brian O'Neill is the Head of the School of Media at Dublin Institute of Technology, Ireland.

EUROPEAN COOPERATION
IN SCIENCE AND TECHNOLOGY

http://www.cost.eu

Action IS0906

Transforming
Audiences,
Transforming
Societies

http://www.cost-transforming-audiences.eu

This publication is supported by COST.

COST—European Cooperation in Science and Technology is an intergovernmental framework aimed at facilitating the collaboration and networking of scientists and researchers at European level. It was established in 1971 by nineteen member countries and currently includes thirty-five member countries across Europe and Israel as a cooperating state.

COST funds pan-European, bottom-up networks of scientists and researchers across all science and technology fields. These networks, called 'COST Actions', promote international coordination of nationally funded research. By fostering the networking of researchers at an international level, COST enables breakthrough scientific developments leading to new concepts and products, thereby contributing to strengthening Europe's research and innovation capacities.

COST's mission focuses in particular on

- building capacity by connecting high-quality scientific communities throughout Europe and worldwide,
- providing networking opportunities for early career investigators, and
- increasing the impact of research on policymakers, regulatory bodies and national decision makers as well as the private sector.

Through its inclusiveness, COST supports the integration of research communities, leverages national research investments and addresses issues of global relevance.

Every year thousands of European scientists benefit from being involved in COST Actions, allowing the pooling of national research funding to achieve common goals.

As a precursor of advanced multidisciplinary research, COST anticipates and complements the activities of EU Framework Programmes, constituting a 'bridge' towards the scientific communities of emerging countries. In particular, COST Actions are also open to participation by non-European scientists coming from neighbour countries (e.g. Albania, Algeria, Armenia, Azerbaijan, Belarus, Egypt, Georgia, Jordan, Lebanon, Libya, Moldova,

Montenegro, Morocco, the Palestinian Authority, Russia, Syria, Tunisia and Ukraine) and from a number of international partner countries.

The COST Action IS0906 'Transforming Audiences, Transforming Societies' (2010–2014) is coordinating research efforts into the key transformations of European audiences within a changing media and communication environment, identifying their complex interrelationships with the social, cultural and political areas of European societies. A range of interconnected but distinct topics concerning audiences are being developed by four working groups: (1) new media genres, media literacy and trust in the media; (2) audience interactivity and participation; (3) the role of media and Information and Communication Technology use for evolving social relationships; and (4) audience transformations and social integration.

COST is supported by the EU RTD Framework programme.

Routledge Studies in European Communication Research and Education

Edited by Nico Carpentier, Vrije Universiteit Brussel, Belgium and Charles University, Czech Republic, François Heinderyckx, Université Libre de Bruxelles, Belgium and Claudia Alvares, Lusofona University, Portugal.

Series Advisory Board: Denis McQuail, Robert Picard and Jan Servaes

ECREA
http://www.ecrea.eu

Published in association with the European Communication Research and Education Association (ECREA), books in the series make a major contribution to the theory, research, practice and/or policy literature. They are European in scope and represent a diversity of perspectives. Book proposals are refereed.

1 **Audience Transformations**
Shifting Audience Positions in Late Modernity
Edited by Nico Carpentier, Kim Christian Schrøder and Lawrie Hallett

2 **Audience Research Methodologies**
Between Innovation and Consolidation
Edited by Geoffroy Patriarche, Helena Bilandzic, Jakob Linaa Jensen and Jelena Jurišić

3 **Multiplayer**
The Social Aspects of Digital Gaming
Edited by Thorsten Quandt and Sonja Kröger

4 **Mapping Foreign Correspondence in Europe**
Edited by Georgios Terzis

5 **Revitalising Audience Research**
Innovations in European Audience Research
Edited by Frauke Zeller, Cristina Ponte and Brian O'Neill

Revitalising Audience Research
Innovations in European Audience Research

Edited by Frauke Zeller, Cristina Ponte and Brian O'Neill

http://www.cost.eu

First published 2015
by Routledge
711 Third Avenue, New York, NY 10017

and by Routledge
2 Park Square, Milton Park, Abingdon, Oxon OX14 4RN

*Routledge is an imprint of the Taylor & Francis Group,
an informa business*

© 2015 Taylor & Francis

The right of the editors to be identified as the author of the editorial material, and of the authors for their individual chapters, has been asserted in accordance with sections 77 and 78 of the Copyright, Designs and Patents Act 1988.

All rights reserved. No part of this book may be reprinted or reproduced or utilised in any form or by any electronic, mechanical, or other means, now known or hereafter invented, including photocopying and recording, or in any information storage or retrieval system, without permission in writing from the publishers.

Trademark Notice: Product or corporate names may be trademarks or registered trademarks, and are used only for identification and explanation without intent to infringe.

Library of Congress Cataloging-in-Publication Data

Revitalising audience research : innovations in European audience research / edited by Frauke Zeller, Cristina Ponte, and Brian O'Neill.
    pages cm. — (Routledge studies in European communication research and education)
    Includes bibliographical references and index.
    1. Mass media—Audiences—Research—Europe. I. Zeller, Frauke, editor.
II. Ponte, Cristina, 1956– editor. III. O'Neill, Brian, 1961– editor.
P96.A83R48 2014
302.23072′04—dc23
2014022355

ISBN: 978-1-138-78881-7 (pbk)
ISBN: 978-1-315-76282-1 (ebk)

Typeset in Sabon
by Apex CoVantage, LLC

Printed and bound in Great Britain by
TJ International Ltd, Padstow, Cornwall

Contents

List of Tables and Figures ix

Introduction:
Revitalising Audience Research: Innovations in
European Audience Research 1
FRAUKE ZELLER, CRISTINA PONTE AND BRIAN O'NEILL

PART I
Methodological Revitalisation and Innovation 11

1 Lost in Transition? Conducting a Hybrid
  Ethnography 'In' and 'Out' of Second Life 13
  KATLEEN GABRIELS AND JOKE BAUWENS

2 'If You Asked Me . . .': Exploring Autoethnography as a
  Means to Critically Assess and Advance Audience Research 29
  ALEXANDER DHOEST

3 Expanding the Reach of the Interview in Audience and
  Reception Research: The Performative and
  Participatory Models of Interview 44
  DAVID MATHIEU AND MARIA JOSÉ BRITES

4 Software Studies and the New Audiencehood of
  the Digital Ecology 62
  CRAIG HIGHT

5 Emergent Group Identity Construal in Online Discussions:
  A Linguistic Perspective 80
  BARBARA LEWANDOWSKA-TOMASZCZYK

6 Using Linguistic Ethnography to Study Techno
  Eliteness of Social Media Audiences 106
  JOKE BEYL AND YUWEI LIN

7 Exploring Landscapes of News Consumption
   Cross-Nationally: The Use of Q Methodology to
   Fuse Quantitative and Qualitative Approaches for
   Increased Explanatory Power in Comparative Research   123
   CÉDRIC COURTOIS, KIM CHRISTIAN SCHRØDER AND
   CHRISTIAN KOBBERNAGEL

PART II
New Fields of Research, New Challenges   143

8 From the Womb to the Tomb: Conceptual Similarities in
   Studying the Youngest and the Oldest of Audiences   145
   DAFNA LEMISH AND GALIT NIMROD

9 Grey Zones: Audience Research, Moral Evaluations and
   Online Risk Negotiation   159
   INGUNN HAGEN AND ANA JORGE

10 Using and *Not* Using Social Media: What Triggers
   Young People's Practices on Social Network Sites?   176
   CHRISTINE W. TRÜLTZSCH-WIJNEN, SASCHA TRÜLTZSCH-WIJNEN AND
   ANDRA SIIBAK

11 Audiences as Socio-Technical Actors: The 'Styles' of
   Social Network Site Users   195
   PIERMARCO AROLDI AND NICOLETTA VITTADINI

12 The Intermediality of Cross-Media Audiences:
   The Case of Digital Television   215
   TAISTO HUJANEN AND SEPPO KANGASPUNTA

13 Exploring Audience Activities and Their Power-Relatedness
   in the Digitalised City: Diversity and Routinisation of
   People's Media Relations in the Triply Articulated Urban Space 236
   SEIJA RIDELL

14 Big Data in Audience Research: A Critical Perspective   261
   FRAUKE ZELLER

   Contributors   279
   Index   287

Tables and Figures

TABLES

3.1	Tasks and Roles in the Participatory Process	53
3.2	Types of Interview and Features of the Interview	56
5.1	Type/Token Ratio	92
5.2	Selected Keywords	94
5.3	Keywords	94
5.4	Word Frequency List (Selection)	98
5.5	Frequencies of Selected Content Words	100
7.1	Fixed Q Grid with Nine Positions, Presented to the Participants	129
7.2	Danish and Flemish Q Results	132

FIGURES

5.1	Infomap 'Identity'	83
5.2	Interconnectivity Values for Sample 1	91
5.3	Visualisation of the Top User's Interconnectivity	95
5.4	Visualisation of a Ping-Pong Interaction	96
5.5	Visualisation of a Subordinate Thread Interconnectivity	97
14.1	Influences and Challenges	266
14.2	Big Data Dimensions	267

Introduction
Revitalising Audience Research: Innovations in European Audience Research

Frauke Zeller, Cristina Ponte and Brian O'Neill

According to the Oxford English Dictionary, the verb *revitalise* means "[t]o restore to vitality; to put new life or vigour into" (OED Online, 2013). Choosing this term for the title of this edited collection does not imply, however, that the current field of audience research is lacking vitality or activity or that it needed some kind of reanimation. Rather, revitalising is used here in an adjectival sense, describing emergent responses to the changes in audience behaviours, media landscapes and of course its inherent challenges and potential for academic research. *Revitalising Audience Research* therefore captures these dynamic processes, new approaches and affordances in audience research.

The book was inspired by the notion that, ultimately, the revitalisation of audience studies does not only mean developing new approaches and methods; it also requires a Kuhnian debate (Kuhn, 1996) regarding the introduction of new paradigms, methods or conceptual developments into the field of audience research. This entails both the need to cross disciplines (e.g. between the social science tradition and the critical/cultural tradition, or the computational tradition) and the need to bridge long-established boundaries in the field (e.g. between 'old media' and 'new media'; between mass communication and group communication; between content/production and audience/reception). The aim of this edited volume is therefore twofold: to capture these boundary-crossing processes that have already started to appear in different places such as project collaborations and conference panels, among others, and to promote or foster this process constructively by explicitly inviting contributions with an interdisciplinary background.

STRUCTURE OF THE BOOK

Our original call invited contributions to address *revitalisation* and *innovation* in the form of three interrelated questions:

1. What needs to be done in audience research in order to meet the challenges?

2. What needs to change academically, methodologically and regarding the underlying theories and concepts of audience research?
3. What needs to be kept? In other words, which of the traditional theoretical and methodological approaches in audience research are still valid and should be combined with additional approaches from other disciplines?

These three questions resulted into two broad frameworks of research which are represented within the collection: first, seven chapters relate to revitalisation and innovation in research methodology, whereby new or so far less established solutions in European audience and reception studies are proposed for challenges and affordances of researching audiences across diverse contexts and platforms. Second, new fields of research emerging from new configurations in audience reception and co-creation are discussed in the second part of this book, also comprising seven chapters.

PART I: METHODOLOGICAL REVITALISATION AND INNOVATION

The first part starts with two applications of ethnography which provide an innovative approach throughout their very different study objects and contexts. Starting with virtual world contexts, in which identities of the self are being created and represented through avatars, the second chapter brings the focus back on the very self and introduces autoethnography as a useful tool to enrich media and audience studies.

Katleen Gabriels and Joke Bauwens focus in "Lost in Transition? Conducting a Hybrid Ethnography 'In' and 'Out' Second Life" on an important emerging area of audience studies—virtual worlds and avatar studies. Offering a critical theoretical introduction to avatar studies as well as an innovative methodological discussion of the challenges and opportunities of virtual ethnography, the authors underscore the importance of the interrelation of actuality and virtuality, that is "the reciprocity between actual and virtual selves". Gabriels and Bauwens present what they term *hybrid ethnography* as a systematic approach to study these reciprocities but underscore the transitional aspect, which demands meeting participants not in a "one-off actual and one-off virtual situation, but hearing and seeing people recurrently in both realms". Beside the theoretical and methodological discussion, the chapter also provides practical insights as to how to conduct hybrid ethnographies by depicting a study they conducted with Second Life residents and their understanding of actual and virtual morality. Using the study, they also provide a critical discussion of the challenges of hybrid ethnography, ranging from ethical issues, trust and time management constraints.

Alexander Dhoest introduces autoethnography in his chapter "'If You Asked Me . . .'" and explores its application as a means to critically assess and inform traditional methods in audience research. His starting point is the notion of "how artificial audience research tends to be", acknowledging that the data we gather are actually "constructed" insofar as they are "created in the research context as a response to a particular stimulus". Autoethnography thus is seen here as a means to critically assess these stimuli, that is the assumptions and questions underlying audience research. Hence, if researchers conducted autoethnographies on their own media use, the insights gained from such studies would help them to reflect on their traditional method usage in relation to the "complexity and contextual nature of media uses and to indicate possible avenues for future research".

The third chapter discusses two advanced approaches to the traditional interview method that enable studies and goals that often fall beyond the reach of the interview method. David Mathieu and Maria José Brites take as their point of departure in "Expanding the Reach of the Interview in Audience and Reception Research". They state that despite the widely acknowledged important role of context in for example media reception studies, context is, however, rarely explicitly mentioned in methodological discussions relating to the interview method. The main reason for this lies in the complexity of the concept. The authors introduce two approaches to this problem—the performative and participatory interview design—illustrated by their use in two different studies. Knowledge about context is produced in the performative interview through its conceptualisation as a cognitive construct created in the online reception of mediated texts by the recipients. The participatory interview, in turn, empowers the study participants by asking them to capture themselves context as their everyday-life experience.

The need to re-conceptualise media engagement in relation to 'software culture' and the implications this has for the design of audience research is the subject of Craig Hight's chapter "Software Studies and the New Audiencehood of the Digital Ecology". Software culture now structures diverse forms of engagement through factors such as automation, algorithms, templates and interface settings. The challenge for audience researchers is to understand how these are understood and performed by different groups of users. The chapter provides an outline for a software-focused ethnography of user-generated content, centred on the key pieces of software which are integral to the ecology of online video (such as the software on image-gathering devices, the proliferation of video-editing tools, the online video sharing site YouTube, web browsers and media players). Attending to forms of 'software literacy', such studies examine the skills and knowledge which each user draws upon thereby empowering and constraining their performance of pieces of software, effectively serving to contextualize their agency within software culture. Audience research, then, Hight argues, needs to reorientate itself around the obvious research questions these assumptions generate.

The next two chapters cross boundaries in terms of their disciplinary outreach, combining traditional audience studies approaches with linguistic instruments for the analysis of computer-mediated communication and social interaction online. Barbara Lewandowska-Tomaszczyk introduces advanced linguistic analyses of language usage as a means to identify "Emergent Group Identity Construal in Online Discussions". The author aims to bridge the gap between audience studies and the linguistic analysis of computer-mediated interaction accomplished by the use of a toolset from linguistic and discourse analytic methodologies to analyse the "vague and polysemous concept of identity" in online discussions. More specifically, this innovative approach consists of the application of computer-supported, quantitative empirical tools derived from corpus linguistics, embedded in a multi-method design that aims to examine identity formation and development in online environments. The study aims to capture and process the dynamic nature of online exchanges, interconnectivity schemes and certain online activity values, such as number and type of the interactional exchanges between participants. Furthermore, the multi-method design also applies qualitative analysis of linguistic properties to complement the quantitative analysis results.

A second disciplinary boundary crossing is presented by Joke Beyl and Yuwei Lin in their chapter "Using Linguistic Ethnography to Study Techno Eliteness of Social Media Audiences". Focusing on the concept of 'techno elite' audiences, the chapter provides a methodological framework for in-depth studies on this concept by applying a combination of linguistic and ethnographic approaches. Its linguistic analytic approach complements traditional audience methods to focus on the analysis of the dynamics of power relationships in contemporary audiences in interactive social media environments. By using literary writers' weblogs, the authors elaborate why and how linguistic ethnography can enrich elite audience studies. They apply language analysis as a means to overcome for example the classic conception of static and categorical social hierarchies and to address elites as being dynamically negotiated through ideology and language in relation to social media.

The last chapter in this first method-oriented Part I of the book closes with a mixed-method study that served as a revitalising approach for a comparative study on news consumption. Cédric Courtois, Kim Christian Schrøder and Christian Kobbernagel present a methodological discussion as well as results from a study that uses Q methodology in their chapter "Exploring Landscapes of News Consumption Cross-Nationally". This chapter addresses two salient but under-researched dimensions of contemporary audiencehood: firstly, the inherent cross-mediality of audience practices and, secondly, the comparative dimension of audience practices in different national cultures. The chapter elaborates a framework that addresses these audience phenomena through the innovative approach to mixed-methods research, exemplified by a comparison of news consumption in two European countries (Denmark and Flanders, a region in Belgium), in a way which transcends the qualitative–quantitative divide and which challenges its epistemological, paradigmatic ramifications. Through the resulting news-media user typologies generated in each national context, the study invites renewed reflection about the interface of behavioural and interpretive paradigms, digging deeper into cultural orientations towards news consumption.

PART II: NEW FIELDS OF RESEARCH, NEW CHALLENGES

The chapter that opens Part II of the book offers a comparative framework for the study of two ends of the audience spectrum: children and older adults. The idea behind the chapter "From the Womb to the Tomb" was shaped through a lively discussion during a "Transforming Audiences, Transforming Societies" (TATS) Action workshop in Milano, in 2012. Coming from different backgrounds and fields of research, Dafna Lemish and Galit Nimrod, from the US and Israel, draw on wide research experience on each of these age groups in their relation to the media but so far had not considered the ground between them. Based on their own experience and on a review of literature from childhood studies as well as studies on ageing, the authors identify not only various forms of patronage but also common expressions of active involvement with media. This relational approach allows the authors to argue that these two populations share substantial commonalities, the recognition of which may inform the development of theory as well as empirical research.

The two following chapters focus on the complexity of social experiences lived by children and youth on the internet. In "Grey Zones" moral judgements that children (nine to sixteen years old) make in relation to what is risky online or not were collected through focus groups and individual essays in Norway and Portugal. These two countries represent not only different levels of internet penetration, educational level of parents, patterns of children's internet use and risk exposure but also different cultures in terms of children's rights and expected level of autonomy. Adopting a constructivist perspective on the analysis of the collected material from both countries, Ingunn Hagen and Ana Jorge note that children's norms and moral evaluations are related to the way children position themselves in a particular situation, thus going against generic and abstract evaluations on what is right or wrong. The comparison between the two countries lead the authors to conclude that cultural background seems to matter more than other demographic factors such as gender and age for children's risk perceptions related to internet use.

Similarly, going against the general trend in studies of youth media practices, the next chapter—"Using and *Not* Using Social Media"—addresses the reasons why some young people actively use certain social web tools and why others do not. Christine Trültzsch-Wijnen and Sascha Trültzsch-Wijnen, from Austria, and Andra Siibak, from Estonia, note the lack of research on non-users within this age group. Besides differences in access and economic background, factors such as differing levels of media literacy or the *habitus* of young people also, they argue, need to be taken into account. For an interdisciplinary perspective that focuses on the individual child, the authors articulate contributions from psychology, sociology and media and communication studies, each of which has explored media use by young people. The challenge from the perspective of audience research is to question these theories from the perspective of the non-user. As the authors conclude, the notion of active audience means people who make active and conscious decisions about their use and non-use of media.

A similar issue with a focus on adults is explored by Piermaco Aroldi and Nicoletta Vittadini, both from Italy, addressing the complexity of networked audiences, groups and publics in the connected environment provided by the social media. In "Audiences as Socio-Technical Actors", the perspective of audiences as 'socio-technical actors' exploring different *styles* of interaction transcends the mere differentiation by socio-demographic patterns. Considering the 'power of agency' of audiences, the perspective aims to explore and understand audience's behaviours in these multilayered environments. The discussion is based on a qualitative study on Italian Facebook users that revealed different styles of acting. The authors provide examples that describe how style appears as a form of self-reflexivity, thus highlighting how styles emerge in relation to the imagined self, the individual's online and offline self-reputation and his or her group affinity and affiliation. The authors conclude that style can cross different social positions and note the interest of a cross-country research on the topic.

Moving to the north, the next chapter analyses and discusses audience orientations in a cross-media environment. The introduction of digital television in Finland, in 2007, provides the context for a study of audience practices and identities in the wake of new changes in the television environment. The authors, Taisto Hujanen and Seppo Kangaspunta, analyse and discuss in "The Intermediality of Cross-Media Audiences" the relevance and nature of specific media identities and the consequent audience orientations through the concept of *intermediality*. Intermediality is defined as a social and cultural relationship in which different media are articulated in relation to and exercise power over one another. The research concludes that digitalisation of television encouraged an intermedial user practice which required audience members to reconsider their medium relationships. Although cross-media audiences can increasingly be characterised in terms of content and modalities such as genre, media use is not only about individual choice. That is why, the authors conclude, the institutional dimensions of audiences remain relevant in future research on media use.

The penultimate chapter refocuses attention on the urgent need for theory to adequately explore the challenges that audience research faces in pervasively software-supported and media-saturated cities. Seija Ridell, from Finland, notes in "Exploring Audience Activities and Their Power-Relatedness in the Digitalised City" that not only do these spaces multiply instances of urban mass media audiencehood but that mobile technologies have also diversified people's activities as urban audiences of others while allowing their own performances. Thus, the urban context constitutes a topic for theoretical and empirical attention. Based on an extensive and interdisciplinary review of literature, the author expands on analytical frameworks and key concepts such as domestication, developed by Silverstone. The perspective of exploring an 'urban triple articulation' (presentation, representation, non-representation) in the links between people and technologies is central to the proposal of understanding the mediated audience activities in urban space. Mapping topics of research for urban audience studies, the author also suggests an agenda for further research in "one of the most demanding theoretical and empirical challenges for future media audience studies".

The last chapter in this section also incorporates concluding remarks on currently debated questions regarding audience research. Frauke Zeller takes on one of the most heated and broadly discussed current concepts—big data—and asks critically what this means for audience research. In her chapter on "Big Data in Audience Research" she provides first of all a concise overview of the concept, serving as a boundary-crossing discussion topic on all societal dimensions (academic, political, economic) which can range from critical, controversial to promising and optimistic. The main focus of the chapter is, however, on how big data changes—either positively or negatively—audience research. The author depicts a systematic analysis of big data in terms of its potentials, challenges and practical, methodological affordances when applied in social sciences and audience research. She concludes that while being aware of the potential pitfalls research with large datasets entails, big data approaches can enrich audience studies by providing a different (although not necessarily better or worse) insight into audiences, particularly online audiences, as well as providing a very useful stimulus for much needed discussions within audience studies of concepts of 'data' and audience definitions.

TRANSFORMING AUDIENCES, TRANSFORMING SOCIETIES

Revitalising Audience Research is the third and closing volume of the COST Action IS0906 "Transforming Audiences, Transforming Societies" (TATS), which ran from 2010 to 2014. The funding body of TATS—COST—is an intergovernmental framework with a focus on bootstrapping and facilitating collaboration and networking among European academics (COST—European Cooperation in Science and Technology). Its rationale is that "fostering the networking of researchers at and international level [...] enables break-through scientific developments leading to new concepts and products [...]" (Patriarche, et al., 2014).

TATS was amongst the largest of recent COST Actions by bringing together more than 300 researchers from thirty-three countries. It was initiated with the notion of a changing media and communications landscape, and the need to identify those changes and their interrelationships with the social, political and cultural areas of European societies (COST, 2009). Hence, the overall aim was and is to "advance state-of-the-art knowledge of the key transformations of European audiences" (COST, 2009, p. 2). Further objectives of TATS were the following:

1. Revitalising the audience research agenda
2. Developing innovative approaches to audiences
3. Transcending established boundaries in the field
4. Promoting new empirical research on audiences
5. Scoping the new media and communication environment
6. Networking audience researchers and building capacity (TATS website)

Revitalising Audience Research concludes the Action's activities and publications, however it represents more an intermedial standpoint of cutting-edge audience research than the final and closing words. Indeed TATS stimulated its members to form and engage in new research collaborations which last beyond the formal COST Action grant period. These 'spin-offs' range from multinational, comparative research projects to newly initiated Temporary Working Groups within the ECREA (European Communication Research and Education Association) network as well as nurturing the development of a consortium (CEDAR—Consortium on Emerging Directions in Audience Research) that aims to foster collaboration between audience researchers in their early career years.

This edited volume therefore offers a concluding afterthought (given that it will be published after the Action has finally ended) in terms of its book publication activities. It thus follows the first edited volume of the Action—*Audience Research Methodologies: Between Innovation and Consolidation*—which represents the results of the Action's first international networking conference in Zagreb, Croatia, 2011. Taking up societal and audience transformations, the first book focuses on the issues and approaches related to the methodological discourses and practices that come with these transformations. Hence, it discusses in fourteen chapters from different perspectives the "diversification, integration and triangulation of methods for audience research", ranging from "the gap between the researched and the researchers, to the study of online social networks, and to the opportunities brought about by Web 2.0 technologies as research tools" (Patriarche, et al., 2014).

The second Action book—*Audience Transformations: Shifting Audience Positions in Late Modernity*—promotes the principal research themes of the Action. After a more methodological and instrumental-oriented perspective on the transformations of the first book, the second Action book discusses in fourteen chapters written by TATS Action members "these transformations in a societal, cultural, technological, ideological, economic and historical context" and by doing this it offers "a nuanced and careful analysis of the main changes" (Carpentier, Schrøder and Hallett, 2014).

This third volume covers fourteen chapters, of which nine chapters were written by teams from different research fields and institutions. Altogether twenty-seven authors (including the editors) in fifteen countries, including Europe, Israel, Canada, the US and New Zealand, developed this collection as a collaborative and boundary-crossing activity from the start. By focusing on the first two objectives of the Action—revitalising the audience research agenda and developing innovative approaches—it explicitly asked in its original contributions call for work that is based on one or more of these boundary-crossing perspectives: academic boundaries (i.e. disciplinary fields), methodological or theoretical boundaries (within one or across different audience research areas) or geographical boundaries (i.e. national or international collaborations). Hence, the editors aimed to both capture the revitalising processes by presenting already ongoing boundary-crossing collaborations as well as initiate new endeavours in this direction. This, in turn, was also meant to provide a platform to discuss innovative approaches in audience research.

There is a clear need for innovative research methods which will not only give access to the 'what' of media use but also to the 'where', the 'how' and the 'why'—the tensions, the conflicts and the motivations of everyday audience practices. In this sense, an audience-oriented perspective is intended to firmly anchor media engagement in relation to the diversity of contexts and purposes to which people put media in their daily lives, contexts and purposes often unanticipated by industries and professionals.

From the point of view of new fields of research, audience studies has often failed to fully understand how new technologies integrate into a rich and convergent media and communications environment. This volume acknowledges that audiences rarely use just one medium—use is always contextualised in a larger media repertoire in which different media interact with each other. Cross-media and hybridized content also question single-media approaches to reception and use, asking for new comprehensive approaches that fully recognise the many types of media with which people engage every day and help better our understanding of how single medium content (e.g. programmes) have now become pan-media brands (e.g. *Doctor Who*).

REFERENCES

Carpentier, N., Schrøder, K.C. and Hallett, L. eds., 2014. *Audience transformations. Shifting audience positions in late modernity*. Routledge Studies in European Communication Research and Education. New York and Abingdon: Routledge.
COST (European Cooperation in the field of Scientific and Technical Research), 2009. *Memorandum of Understanding*. [pdf]. Available at: <http://www.cost-transforming-audiences.eu/system/files/MoU_IS0906-e.pdf>

Kuhn, T.S., 1996. *The structure of scientific revolutions*. 3rd ed. Chicago and London: University of Chicago Press
OED Online, 2013. *Oxford English Dictionary*. Oxford: Oxford University Press. Available through: <http://www.oed.com/view/Entry/164905>.
Patriarche, G., Bilandzic, H., Linaa Jensen, J. and Jurišić, J. eds., 2014. *Audience research methodologies. Between innovation and consolidation*. Routledge Studies in European Communication Research and Education. New York and Abingdon: Routledge.

Part I
Methodological Revitalisation and Innovation

1 Lost in Transition?
Conducting a Hybrid Ethnography 'In' and 'Out' of Second Life

Katleen Gabriels and Joke Bauwens

INTRODUCTION

As argued at the outset of the age of Internet-mediated communication with its intensified social interaction and new audiences that interchange and share meanings, questions about culture, subjectivity and reflexivity would only gain importance within media and audience studies (see Poster, 1995; Förnas, 1998). Although we are now past the novelty of online communication platforms, a significant part of audience studies is still working on this agenda by questioning how the multiple communicative spaces we are involved in shape our sense of self, other and the world (see, for example, the many studies on Facebook and identity). We believe that studying contemporary audiences boils down to studying formations of people that increasingly transit multiple, intersecting as well as parallel communicative spaces, which inevitably brings about a pluralisation of social relationships (Moores, 2005) in a quantitative (more people to communicate with) and qualitative (other ways to communicate) way. Hence, if we want to understand if, when and how subjectivity is reconfigured, research should consider the particularity of different realms where people build and perform their identity.

One particular subfield of audience studies in which this issue is often addressed is what we could name 'avatar studies.' Often, although not exclusively analysed from an ethnographic perspective, these studies show that becoming and being an avatar (i.e. transiting corporeal and virtual realms) triggers reflexivity about one's basic conceptions of identity (see Heider, 2009; Hongladarom, 2011). With the everydayness of virtual sociality in many people's lives, dichotomous ideas about the 'online' and 'offline' as two separate realms have made way for a more holistic approach that aims to understand the interaction between the virtual and the actual in today's Internet-saturated cultures (e.g. Ess, 2013). This conceptual shift has brought about a methodological debate about studying Internet-mediated cultures in close connection to bodily experiences (e.g. Bakardjieva and Smith, 2001; Haythornthwaite and Kendall, 2010). Drawing on contemporary ethnographies of the Internet, it can be argued that research designs that entail a split between online and offline data gathering, with little or no attention devoted to the interplay between virtual and actual experiences, are far away from how people integrate the Internet in their everyday reality (Slater, 2002; Orgad, 2009; Beneito-Montagut, 2011).[1]

At the same time, the so-called hybridisation (Jordan, 2009, p. 182), in which virtual spaces "are fundamentally embedded within specific social, cultural and material contexts" (Orgad, 2006, p. 877), raises fundamental methodological questions about how to study the online and offline as part of the same reality without ignoring the distinct features and impact of the Internet on our lives and actions. Such an approach, as argued by others, needs to consider the particularity of online interactions, observations and settings and how these differ from their face-to-face variants in so-called conventional ethnography (Hine, 1998; Schaap, 2002; Davies, 2008).

From an anthropological and ethnographic point of view, social virtual worlds have often been conceptualised in terms of liminality (Turkle, 1995; Shields, 2000; 2003; Ramiller, 2007), not only for the participants involved but also for the ethnographers aiming to capture the "lived culture, worldly experiences and practical sense making" (Willis and Trondman, 2000 [2002], p. 5). If one steps into the virtual, one has to leave the familiar behind to cross the border to a world in which everyday lives are spaced off (Tella, et al., 1998, p. 241). Participants are disembedded from the rules of society, their identity and status, and re-embedded "out of the other side to be reintegrated into society with their new status and identity in place" (Bell, 2007, p. 36). This liminal experience matches to a certain extent with the attitude which ethnographers are expected to adopt, that is the stranger position (Hammersley and Atkinson, 2006; Agar, 2008; Gobo, 2008). Typically, studying cultures different from their own and allowing that all that is taken for granted is defamiliarised and estranged, the ethnographer is at the beginning somewhat lost. Even when he or she studies groups and settings that are close to him or her, the ethnographer needs to treat them as "anthropologically strange" (Hammersley and Atkinson, 2006, p. 9).

Precisely these experiences of virtuality in which everything is unsettled albeit not necessarily in the pejorative sense of the word (see e.g. Shields, 2000; 2003) have been the point of departure in our ethnographic study within Second Life (Linden Lab, 2003).[2] Starting from a moral-philosophical and media-theoretical framework, we studied the meanings of everyday morals, values and practices in this social virtual world. The foreshadowed research problem was if and to what extent virtuality influences our dealing with the other and, related to this, to what extent and with what ethical consequences there is dis/continuity between moral practices in virtual and actual worlds.

We have been involved in the lives of twenty Second Life residents (born between 1943 and 1985) over a period of one year in order to understand how they understand and articulate actual and virtual morality. We aimed to disentangle how residents construct and reflect not only on the in-world daily moral order and the existing in-world moral practices but also on the moral consequences of virtual experiences in their actual lives. Although the turn towards a combined actual–virtual ethnographic approach of internet-mediated cultures is strongly advocated (e.g. Miller and Slater, 2000; Leander and McKim, 2003; Orgad, 2005; Beneito-Montagut, 2011), relatively few studies have researched the meaning and experience of social virtual worlds in that way (not counting a few notable exceptions in game studies; see, for example, Celia Pearce, Bonnie Nardi and T.L. Taylor as discussed in Boellstorff, et al., 2012, pp. 124–126).

From a methodological point of view, the alternating movement between virtual and actual ethnographic participation raises significant issues. Linking up with ethnography's pursuit of reflexivity, this chapter deals with two particular questions. First, how do, in the words of Gergen (2001), the multiple self-positionings or discursive formations in multiple dialogue sites affect the relationship between researcher and residents? Second, how can we manage the interplay between virtuality and actuality as research sites of one lived and continuous reality? As our ethnographic encounters occurred both in embodied (through face-to-face meetings with actual selves) and disembodied ways (by means of avatar conversations and in-world observations), there are some particularities in integrating these two modes of ethnographic encounter, that is two types of social interaction and data.

The chapter starts with a concise contextualisation of our empirical investigation in the development of research on social virtual worlds. Next, we discuss the specificity of morality in virtual worlds which, as empirically substantiated by others (see below), is to a certain extent a prolongation of the meanings people attach to moral values and practices in their actual social lives. However, in virtual sociality, as Schaap (2002) has argued, "things work just a bit differently" (p. 112). Precisely that somewhat unsettling or at least "strange lapse of reality that cyberspace presents with us" (Schaap, 2002, p. 112) or that particular phenomenological experience of virtual worlds that is enabled by digital technologies as cultural forms (see e.g. Garza, 2002) has been our point of departure.

THE ACTUAL AND THE VIRTUAL: FROM DICHOTOMY TO HYBRIDISATION

The first-generation theorists of the 1990s mapped the virtual–actual relation in terms of an ontological dualism, also with regard to a Cartesian mind–body split, thereby emphasising how the virtual is radically divorced from the actual (see e.g. Benedikt, 1992; Turkle, 1995). At the end of the 1990s, however, this dualism was gradually disproved by empirical research and phenomenological approaches (see e.g. Markham, 1998; Baym, 1998; 2010; Wellman and Gulia, 1999; Slater, 2002; Kendall, 2002; Leander and McKim, 2003; Bakardjieva, 2003; Tuszynski, 2006; Jordan, 2009).

Nowadays scholars in general address "the intersection, crossovers, and synergies" between virtuality and actuality (Haythornthwaite and Kendall, 2010, p. 1083) and openly dissociate themselves from the dichotomous approach that set the tone in the 1990s. Rather than envisioning social virtual interaction as a separate realm, they conceptualise the relationship between online and offline in terms of hybridisation (see Jordan, 2009, p. 181).

This turn in thought has severely weakened the belief in virtuality's transformational powers, assuming that the virtual is a realm where existing forms of identity and community significantly alter. However, the mutual influence between online and offline forms of social life remains an important field of interest and raises questions about how hybridisation is affecting the way people make sense of their lives (see e.g. Bakardjieva and Smith, 2001; Jordan, 2009, p. 182). Consequently, recognition of the virtual–actual interrelation on a conceptual level needs to be addressed on a methodological level too (Orgad, 2009). Hybridisation forces researchers to rethink conventional ethnographic method leading to "a new type of ethnography" (Jordan, 2009, p. 181, p. 183). Subsequently, compelling questions are, Which methodological issues the combination of virtual and actual modes of data gathering bring about? and How we can capture and comprehend this complex hybrid social reality adequately?

In line with the theoretical development in the body of thought on the virtual–actual dialectic, most 1990s ethnographic research studied virtual space as an autonomous field site and subsequently generated 'online' data this way.[3] Although they received a lot of criticism (Slater, 2002), the so-called virtual ethnography approach (Hine, 1998) is still believed valuable if the enquiry takes place in virtual worlds (Beneito-Montagut, 2011, p. 719). For example Boellstorff (2008, p. 63) contends that virtual spaces are meaningful on their own and that it becomes problematic if one takes actual-world sociality as an explanation for virtual-world sociality, because the latter is not a simple derivation of the first. He strongly opposes the view that the ultimate objective of a virtual ethnography must be the addressing of the actual world, "which is taken to be the only 'real' social world" (2008, p. 62), because this view oversimplifies the interrelation between actuality and virtuality. If a researcher insists on meeting face-to-face this might point at a belief that the virtual is somehow inferior to the actual.

Researchers departing from notions of authenticity (Turkle, 1995) and attaching great importance to social contexts have often turned to actual ethnography approaches to study online user experiences (Bakardjieva and Smith, 2001). In particular social-determinist criticisms against the postmodernist ideas about 'free-floating' identities have pushed researchers into offline modes of data gathering that acknowledge the social and material roots of people's everyday practices. In fact, many hybrid ethnographies, combining online and offline methods of data collection, depart from this assumption. The position of Miller and Slater (2000/2001, p. 5), who conducted a hybrid ethnography on the everyday use and integration of the internet in Trinidad, is built on the idea that virtual spaces are "continuous with and embedded in other social spaces". To this aim, they combined both virtual and actual methods to meet and address the "diversity of relationships that people may pursue through the communicative media that they embed in their ongoing social lives" (Miller and Slater, 2000/2001, p. 55). Others also included online and offline encounters with informants in their ethnography. Orgad (2005; 2006; 2009) conducted a four-year hybrid study including actual and virtual interviews with breast cancer patients. In the first stage, Orgad conducted online interviews with patients who were active on breast cancer–related online spaces; in the next stage, she shifted to a face-to-face relationship with her informants (2006, p. 882). This transition from virtual to actual meetings was important to gain knowledge regarding why these women engaged on breast cancer forums and to attain understanding in the relation between their actual and virtual experiences (Orgad, 2009). Whereas Orgad (2005; 2006; 2009) moved out of the virtual into the actual, Bakardjieva and Smith (2001) followed the opposite direction by first meeting their informants at their home settings where they subsequently looked into their computers to study their virtual practices. Still, although many scholars have called for a combination of both approaches, that is from the virtual to the actual and from the actual to the virtual (see e.g. Leander and McKim, 2003; Beneito-Montagut, 2011), few hybrid ethnographies have systematically included both transitions so far. Drawing on the methodological literature and seeking to bridge this gap, we included both transitions in our study (see below).

HYBRID MORALITIES

Numerous people nowadays have avatars in virtual multi-user surroundings such as Second Life and World of Warcraft (Blizzard Entertainment, 2004). Many of the moral issues related to virtuality are not new but have taken on a new meaning because of technological specificities. For instance, it is argued that communication in virtual surroundings makes people less humane as the physical face, a precondition for moral responsibility, is missing (Lanier, 2011, p. 36, p. 69; Turkle, 2011, p. 11, p. 18). In addition, graphical representation makes the re-creation of unethical and illegal practices possible, such as the portrayal of virtual paedophilia in three-dimensional user-created virtual spaces, raising questions about the moral status of virtual practices (Søraker, 2011, p. 61; Strikwerda, 2011). Also, one can always log out or start over by creating an alternative avatar (alt), or one can take an alt for experimentation, exploration or even exploitation of others. These examples have provoked different theoretical considerations about the relation between virtuality and morality. First, we find authors who express critical concerns about the degeneration of morality because of virtual technologies (e.g. Introna, 2002). Second, there are scholars who look on virtuality as a positive equaliser to overcome distance, hierarchies, physical appearance and so on (e.g. McGonigal, 2012). These authors consider virtuality as a chance to improve humankind, for instance, by means of ethical game design to improve moral awareness (e.g. Castronova, 2007). Third, we come across authors who state that virtuality is an extension or a continuum of actuality. In virtual space, human behaviour and practices subsequently follow the same patterns as in actual contexts (e.g. Tuszynski, 2006; Heider, 2009).

In particular the last approach has been substantiated in empirical research. Findings from different fields (e.g. psychology, phenomenology, ethnography, media studies, game studies) show that norms of actual life interactions also regulate interactions in virtual environments. This continuation is also the case for Internet-mediated moral responses to virtual others (Miller, 2007). Two interesting online experiments demonstrate that if people are ordered to cause physical pain to other avatars (see Slater, et al., 2006) or to prevent the death of other avatars (see Navarrete, et al., 2011), they treat these others as if they were bodily people.[4] Ethnographic research also shows that people prolong basic ethical principles into virtual surroundings (Boellstorff, 2008, p. 186). People also tend to identify with their avatars, because they are "the embodied conception of the participant's self through which she communicates with others in the community" (Wolfendale, 2007, p. 114). However, notwithstanding that there is prolongation, one cannot ignore discontinuities between virtual and actual settings. Within virtual space, there is a lack of physical closeness and one often acts pseudonymously or anonymously. Also, virtual activities and interactions do not physically occur in the actual world, which raises questions about accountability. Consequently, although the virtual and the actual are part of one experienced reality, they share similarities and dissimilarities that cannot be overlooked in hybrid data gathering. In line with the hybrid view on virtuality and actuality, we support a hybrid view on virtual and actual morality, that is virtual morality as embedded in actual morality, although distinctiveness is possible (see also Baym, 2010).

A HYBRID ETHNOGRAPHY 'IN' AND 'OUT' SECOND LIFE

To meet our foreshadowed research objective, that is to what extent virtuality influences our dealing with the other and to what extent there is dis/continuity between virtual and actual moral practices, we conducted long-term research in which we alternated explorative and observational work with participation and interviews. Our interest in Second Life stemmed from a mixture of fascination for a world we knew from TV documentaries, on one hand, and our difficulties to grasp people's engagement in this kind of world, on the other. As argued by Agar (2008, p. 13), media representations are important to politically contextualise the field and people under study in order to understand how the other is dealt with in society. In the first stage of our research (2009–2010) we gained access to the field; dwelled in clubs, shops and cities; learned how to become an avatar; and made our first contacts. Although we were registered in Second Life, we first only had short and goal-oriented visits there with no significant personal investment. Our encounters with insiders took place in a formal way through four in-depth interviews (two offline/face-to-face and two mediated through Skype) and two offline focus groups with ten avid Dutch-speaking residents.

It was only in the second stage of our research that the ethnographic "paradox of professional distance and personal involvement" (Agar, 2008, p. 7) came to the fore. In particular, the above-discussed insights concerning the virtual–actual interrelation were essential for this stage of our empirical study (2012–2013), in which we brought together our two 'sites,' that is the face-to-face meetings and the Second Life encounters. The majority of the research participants of 2009–2010 ($N = 13$) were also involved in this stage, in which we conducted a hybrid ethnography with extensive recurrent virtual and actual meetings with twenty Dutch-speaking Second Life residents (eleven men and nine women). These insiders logged in for the first time in Second Life between 2005 and 2008. More than half of them were also part of the 2009–2010 sample, and we thus knew them first face-to-face before meeting their avatars. This way, a set of rich data of our informants and their everyday morals in Second Life was attained. Literally moving with them added the required context and in-depth understanding of the relationship between their virtual experiences and their actual lives and of how both configured each other. Moreover, because of the longer time frame, we were able to follow transitions in the lives of informants, which strengthened our study. In this stage, the Second Life observations, including many field notes and diary writings, were far more driven by our personal curiosity in this world and by our informants' practices and experiences in Second Life. Apart from this, there were also recurrent, diffuse encounters with residents who we did not meet face-to-face.

MULTIPLE SELF-POSITIONINGS AND TRUST

In our ethnographic study, there were physical and mediated transitions or "moves" (Wittel, 2000) at play: from virtual, anonymous and written encounters to actual and oral encounters and from actual and oral encounters to virtual, anonymous and written encounters. In these transitions, the researcher and the informants had multiple self-positionings (Gergen, 2001), not only in literal terms such as a physically embodied self and a virtual avatar representation but also concerning the conception that in the flux of polyvocal and transient dialogue of the Internet, the self can have multiple discursive formations. In line with the principles of ethnography (O'Reilly, 2009; Boellstorff, et al., 2012), it is important to note that we have always been open about our researcher's position in Second Life for which one (female) avatar was operated. However, many of the informants had multiple alts; although we met several alts, most conversations were held with so-called main avatars. Relevant information in terms of informants' multiple self-presentations thus remained hidden for us and our search for a holistic understanding of people's moral practices resulted in a situated ethnographic account, which others have described as the only task ethnographers can accomplish (Agar, 2008, p. 91; Boellstorff, et al., 2012, p. 30).

More interestingly, however, and in line with Orgad (2005, p. 62), the previously mentioned transitions forced us to reflect on the ways we came to know the informants both in actual and virtual spaces. In addition, also following Orgad (2005, p. 62), this forced us to recognise the complexity of the relationship between the informants' actual and virtual lives. This way, we gained insight in how one configures the other (Orgad, 2005, p. 64), and, additionally, we attained a long-term privileged relation with the informants. This relationship undoubtedly added context that we would have missed if we focused merely on the virtual or purely on the actual. This, however, demanded a serious investment (in terms of time and energy) from the researcher and the informants. This investment made our sample rather limited in size (twenty informants in the hybrid ethnography; see above), which nonetheless reflects our methodological aim to capture the interpretative processes in their integrity.

Because of the study's intensity, the building of a reciprocal trust relationship was essential. Obviously, establishing a trust relation with informants is always at the heart of ethnographic work, virtually or actually (Sanders, 2005, p. 77). This trust is especially essential if one wants to shift from the virtual to the actual, both from the researcher's and the informant's viewpoint, because both remain unseen until the point of meeting face-to-face (Eichhorn, 2001, p. 575). However, once a trust relation was established in our study, it turned out difficult to keep the balance between being close and empathetic to the informants while staying at the proper distance. In line with Orgad (2005, p. 56), our informants often disclosed sensitive issues, which is unquestionably related to the fact that we had recurrent talks, that we knew each other virtual and actual and that our research topic, that is morals, recalled sensitive experiences. The fact that we also were an active and experienced resident and that we subsequently were aware of the specific features of Second Life was extremely important to gain and build trust. Several informants referred to this during the face-to-face interviews; one of them explicitly stated that it would be impossible to talk about Second Life to someone who has not experienced it him- or herself. In addition, most research participants revealed more details from the moment we met them face-to-face. Of course, it became impossible to gain trust from everyone in Second Life; many inhabitants were suspicious of the presence of an academic researcher, and only the ones who were motivated wanted to participate.

The integration of both transitions and learning to meet our informants in both contexts undeniably added thickness to our data, which is crucial in ethnographic research (Brewer, 2000; Hammersley and Atkinson, 2006). This way, the aforementioned stranger position of the ethnographer (see e.g. Hammersley and Atkinson, 2006; Agar, 2008) had two interesting forms in our study, because we either knew their avatar first and then the person operating the avatar or the other way around. Although we already knew a part of our informants face-to-face before meeting them in Second Life, the first virtual encounter led to an experience of strangeness, because every new meeting goes together with expectations. In the same way, meeting informants in person for the first time after having met in Second Life also was strange, although there was a sense of familiarity. These stranger positions also added thoroughness to the importance of corporeal or embodied knowledge (Willis and Trondman, 2000 [2002]). By having two forms of embodiment, a physical body and a virtual avatar body, we learned to comprehend our informants' experiences and reflections from different perspectives.

MANAGING THE VIRTUAL–ACTUAL INTERPLAY

One important epistemological issue that deserves more attention in the methodological literature is the fact that researchers and possible informants can have deviating ontological underpinnings in light of the virtual–actual dialectic. Some informants who had no problem with being interviewed in Second Life refused to shift the relation to an actual setting because they believed, in line with Boellstorff (2008), that Second Life is meaningful on its own and that it is best to be studied in its own right. In doing so, they kept their virtual experiences strictly separate. Another informant, whom we interviewed two times face-to-face and who thus had no problem with meeting, also questioned why there were actual interviews included. The position of informants is thus crucial too, as they also conceive the relation between virtual and actual space differently.

We must acknowledge that there are many similarities between conducting a virtual, actual and hybrid ethnography in terms of the amount of time the ethnographer spends in the field to become fully integrated in the community, the extent to which the chosen field site is marked by difference, the building of a trust relationship, the importance of generating high quality data and, related to that, a strong research design that covers the objectives (see also Eichhorn, 2001, p. 568; Orgad, 2009). Undeniably, the research context and its specific objectives must always be the essential rationale in the decision for a specific methodology (Orgad, 2005, pp. 52–53). However, there are significant differences, such as the combination of two field sites in hybrid ethnographies. If one conducts a virtual ethnography, the field site is entered from the home or the office of the ethnographer (for a discussion on how this shift destabilised the boundaries between 'homework' and 'fieldwork' in ethnographic research, see Hine, 1998; Eichhorn, 2001). Because we conducted a hybrid ethnography, there was the field entered from the home or the office (in our case, Second Life) and the field where we met our informants face-to-face, mostly their home setting, and where we equally spent several hours. These two field sites have a distinct character, for instance with regard to the type of conversations: written versus oral. Written interviews demand a different sort of setting and are 'easier' to attain, because one does not have to transcribe any audio recording. Also, during virtual fieldwork, the researcher can leave the computer or look up information on the computer (see also Kendall, 2002, p. 7). Although face-to-face interviews can be interrupted as well, as someone can enter the room or the telephone can ring, the virtual encounter can also frequently be interrupted, either intentionally or unintentionally, by technical events such as a crash or the experience of 'lag' in Second Life. In her ethnography on MUDs (Multi-User Dungeons), Kendall (2002, p. 8) draws attention to the phenomenological consequences of these events as they "can abruptly destroy the conceptual space of the mud" and drop researchers "back full into experience of the physical world" (see also Hine, 1998). In addition, it is very easy to break off contact intentionally, by de-friending, banning or muting the virtual other or by simply not replying. During the fieldwork in Second Life, about ten virtual contacts de-friended the researcher. Another important difference is that friends pop up spontaneously as soon as they log in, whereas face-to-face meetings are planned. Unavoidably, there were more conversations in Second Life with some informants than with others, because this was dependent on the moments we appeared online at the same time.

Referring to this chapter's title, there were also times that we almost became lost in the transition from the virtual to the actual and the other way around. The time invested in the actual interviews was time unavailable for spending in the virtual field site and, subsequently, the expectations of the informants were not always met. In 2012 one informant, whom the researcher had known in Second Life and in actual life since 2009, de-friended her because he believed not enough time was devoted in Second Life to have extensive chats with him. Managing the literal transitions thus turned out to be very difficult sometimes. When the researcher did not log in for a while, some informants also asked where she had been all that time.

Apart from these struggles, we are convinced that a hybrid ethnography was the best way to meet our research objectives. By recurrently talking to our informants we gained context and in-depth understanding in their virtual experiences and how these intersected with their actual lives. In addition, we could follow informants' transitions over the years. For instance, the seventy-year-old Anne[5] logged into Second Life in 2007 after losing her husband. Becoming a widow made her feel lonely and isolated, and Second Life offered an opportunity to meet new people without leaving the house. When we first met her in 2009, she was still a heavy user. Nowadays, she is still an active resident albeit less frequent. She met her new partner in Second Life, and slowly but surely she started to literally move away from Second Life, as her relationship shifted to an actual one. Anne repeatedly told us how much she had needed Second Life to start living again in actual life.

Although it is true that actual lives cannot always explain virtual behaviour and the other way around, there are instances in which this, however, turned out to be factual. In 2007, the fifty-three-year-old Catherine logged in after she was diagnosed with cancer. One of her motives to join Second Life was a feeling of loneliness. After a few years she did not log in anymore; she was also cured from cancer. However, when she was diagnosed again in 2012 she became a very active resident all over again. She shaped her avatar like the person she was when she was still young, healthy and slim, as she gained several kilos because of medication. Second Life thus made it possible for her to behave like the person she used to be in actual life. At her actual home setting she showed many photos; the similarity with her avatar was indeed striking. We would have missed this significant context if we had not shifted from meeting her in her virtual home to her actual home.

During virtual meetings, as opposed to actual ones, one has to wait for the typed answer. As people talk faster than they type, more data were attained in an oral conversation within a similar amount of time than in a typed conversation. However, actual and virtual methods complemented each other in our ethnography; in Second Life we observed how informants encountered and dealt with (virtual) others and we extended these insights with virtual and actual conversations. We found that Second Life has separate in-world norms, for instance, with regard to jargon, looks and behaviour. For example one acceptable action, amongst others, for getting rid of someone is to fake a computer crash. However, if someone crosses a moral boundary, this person will be sanctioned, either by an individual or by the group. Symbolic (virtual) transgression invokes strong moral condemnation, such as having sex with a child avatar. Our informants subsequently did not treat their virtual experiences as a separate reality; on the contrary, we found an intertwining of virtual and actual identity, sociality and morality. Second Life is both a space with separate conventions and a space into which actual principles overflow and, in line with other studies (e.g. Sicart, 2009), the self remains an ethical subject with ethical capacities in virtual space. Subsequently, we argue that a study on the meaning of virtual morals preferably has to integrate actual meetings to fully attain a 'thick description' (Geertz, 1973) with regard to moral identity and its complexity.

CONCLUDING THOUGHTS

Starting from the idea that the constitution of subjectivity, of which morality is a crucial part, transpires in multiple communicative realms, we have argued that only in the combination of virtual and actual encounters and observations we can understand how and when corporeal life and Second

Life coincide and where they differ. In particular for the field of avatar studies, we believe that a hybrid ethnographic approach is much more helpful to understand the reciprocity between actual and virtual selves. By meeting informants in Second Life, we could observe their in-world behaviour in various settings. For instance, one of our informants worked as a deejay in her virtual club, so we went dancing there to observe and participate. These participant observations added context during the planned virtual and actual interviews. Although sensitive moral issues were mostly touched on during face-to-face interviews, the trust relation that existed both in virtual and actual contexts shaped the informants' openness. We were also often surprised by their kindness, for instance, by guiding us through the virtual world while we were a newbie.

Ethnographic research on virtuality should be more attentive not only to the interrelation of actuality and virtuality but also to the recursive transitions that people make between both realms. Hence, hybrid ethnographies are preferably not a matter of meeting participants in a one-off actual and one-off virtual situation but of hearing and seeing people recurrently in both realms. Because few hybrid ethnographies have systematically included both transitions so far, we tried to immerse ourselves in the phenomenological experience of moving among different contexts to feel how these transitions configure particular interactions and thoughts. The reflexive accounts of this experience were instructive as they made us aware of our assumptions about corporeal life and Second Life in terms of authenticity, trust, distance and intimacy. However, doing research simultaneously in two lifeworlds asks for an attentive management of the social contacts and, consequently, of the time you invest in them.

We found that residents often shift their closest virtual contacts to other mediated and non-mediated spaces (see also Boellstorff, 2008, p. 242) beyond our scope. Our informants maintained contact on blogs, forums, Skype and Facebook. Four informants shifted virtual friends to other virtual worlds and/or games. Only one of our twenty informants never met virtual friends face-to-face because they all lived abroad. All other informants shifted virtual friendship to actual contexts, and eight of them had an actual love relationship with someone they met (and fell in love with) in Second Life.

Due to time constraints we could not follow our informants through all these mediated and non-mediated spaces. Methodological literature and future research endeavours should be more attentive to the formation of new frameworks and methodologies that address the following and meeting of informants throughout these different contexts, exactly to deepen and expand research contexts (Beneito-Montagut, 2011). In doing so, it is important not to map the virtual–actual relation radically onto the online–offline pair, because the virtual–actual continuum also exists within the online setting. That is, participants value some of their online practices as real and some as virtual (see also Slater, 2002, p. 542).

NOTES

1. In our conception, the phenomenological distinction between 'virtual' and 'actual' does not necessarily coincide with the difference between 'online' and 'offline.' We hereby follow, among others,. Slater's (2002, p. 542) elaboration on the difference between both pairs of twin concepts because users treat parts of their online activities as virtual and some as actual: "[I]n one window one may be telling someone about what is happening in another window; the former is accorded a reality status from which the participant can comment on the 'virtual' action going on in the latter."
2. Katleen Gabriels conducted the empirical fieldwork within the light of her doctoral thesis, under the methodological supervision of Joke Bauwens. We use the 'we' form in discussing our methodological experiences, as they are built on two different perspectives. First is the perspective of Katleen Gabriels, who did the fieldwork and who was actually involved in talking with Second Life residents and observing their practices. Second is the perspective of Joke Bauwens, who advised and coached the fieldwork from the position of detached observer.

    We characterize Second Life as a three-dimensional, persistent, multi-user, computer-generated social, cultural and moral space inhabited by humans and their representational avatars. Other features are a first-person perspective, real-time interaction between actual people, a shared virtual reality and an open-end purpose. Linden Lab confines itself to the production of software and infrastructure and allows residents to create and sell virtual objects. Residents are free to choose how they spend their time in-world and how they assign meaning and purpose to their in-world activities.
3. The shift from an actual physical field site to a virtual one led to the destabilization of traditional ethnographic methods such as participant observation and to a re-conceptualization of the term *field site*. For discussion, see for example Ruhleder (2000), Wittel (2000), Eichhorn (2001), Leander and McKim (2003), Hine (2005), Sanders (2005) and Jordan (2009).
4. In the 1960s, Stanley Milgram conducted a series of experiments on human obedience to authority. Informants were asked by an authority figure to sanction a stranger by giving electric shocks every time he gave a wrong answer to a question. The informant did not know that the electric shocks were not real and that the stranger was in fact an actor. Slater, et al. (2006) extrapolated the Milgram experiments to a virtual setting, in which the stranger was only virtually depicted on a screen. Although the research participants thus knew that neither the stranger nor the electric shocks were genuine, they reacted to them as if they were factual (Slater, et al., 2006). Navarrete, et al. (2011) simulated the classic 'trolley problem' in an immersive virtual-reality environment to study the relationship between moral judgments and moral actions. The trolley problem refers to a famous philosophical thought experiment: "A runaway trolley is headed toward five people. In order to prevent their deaths, the trolley must be switched onto another track where it will kill one person" (Navarrete, et al., 2011, p. 365). Their findings indicate that the majority of informants either acted to cause one individual's death to save the others or to abstain from action if the action would kill five people instead of one (Navarrete, et al., 2011, p. 365).
5. All names are pseudonyms.

REFERENCES

Agar, M.H., 2008. *The professional stranger: an informal introduction to ethnography*. Bingley: Emerald Group Publishing Limited.
Bakardjieva, M. and Smith, R., 2001. The internet in everyday life: computer networking from the standpoint of the domestic user. *New Media & Society* 3(1), pp. 67–83.
Bakardjieva, M., 2003. Virtual togetherness: an everyday-life perspective. *Media, Culture & Society* 25(3), pp. 291–312.
Baym, N.K., 1998. The emergence of on-line community. In: S.G. Jones, ed. 1998. *Cybersociety 2.0: revisiting computer-mediated communication and community*. Thousand Oaks, CA: Sage. pp. 35–68.
Baym, N.K., 2010. *Personal connections in the digital age*. Cambridge: Polity Press.
Benedikt, M., ed. 1992. *Cyberspace. First steps*. Boston, MA: The MIT Press.
Beneito-Montagut, R., 2011. Ethnography goes online: towards a user-centred methodology to research interpersonal communication on the internet. *Qualitative Research* 11(6), pp. 716–735.
Bell, D., 2007. *Cyberculture theorists: Manuel Castells and Donna Haraway*. London/New York: Routledge.
Boellstorff, T., 2008. *Coming of age in Second Life. An anthropologist explores the virtually human*. Princeton, NJ: Princeton University Press.
Boellstorff, T., Nardi, B., Pearce, C. and Taylor, T.L., 2012. *Ethnography and virtual worlds. A handbook of method*. Princeton, NJ/Oxford: Princeton University Press.
Brewer, J.D., 2000. *Ethnography*. Buckingham: Open University Press.
Castronova, E., 2007. *Exodus to the virtual world: how online fun is changing reality*. New York: Palgrave MacMillan.
Davies, C.A., 2008. *Reflexive ethnography: a guide to researching selves and others*. Abington/New York: Routledge.
Eichhorn, K., 2001. Sites unseen: ethnographic research in a textual community. *Qualitative Studies in Education* 14(4), pp. 565–578.
Ess, C., 2013. Introduction to Part I. In: M. Consalvo and C. Ess, eds. 2013. *The handbook of internet studies*. West Sussex: Wiley-Blackwell. pp. 11–15.
Fornäs, J., 1998. Digital borderlands: identity and interactivity in culture, media and communications. *Nordicom Review* 19(1), pp. 27–38.
Garza, G., 2002. The Internet, narrative and subjectivity. *Journal of Constructivist Psychology* 15(3), pp. 185–203.
Geertz, C., 1973. *The interpretation of cultures: selected essays*. New York: Basic Books.
Gergen, K.J., 2001. *Social construction in context*. London: Sage.
Gobo, G., 2008. *Doing ethnography*. London: Sage.
Hammersley M. and Atkinson, P., 2006. *Ethnography: principles in practice*. Abingdon/New York: Routledge.
Haythornthwaite, C. and Kendall, L., 2010. Internet and community. *American Behavioral Scientist* 53(8), pp. 1083–1094.
Heider, D. ed., 2009. *Living virtually. Researching new worlds*. New York: Peter Lang.
Hine, C., 1998. Virtual ethnography. In: Internet Research and Information for Social Scientists, *IRISS '98*. Bristol, UK, March 25–27. Available at: <http://www.cirst.uqam.ca/pcst3/PDF/communications/HINE.PDF>
Hine, C., ed., 2005. *Virtual methods. Issues in social research on the internet*. Oxford/New York: Berg.
Hongladarom, S., 2011. Personal identity and the self in the online and offline world. *Minds and Machines* 21(4), pp. 533–548.

Introna, L. D., 2002. The (im)possibility of ethics in the information age. *Information and Organisation* 12(2), pp. 71–84.
Jordan, B., 2009. Blurring boundaries: the "real" and the "virtual" in hybrid spaces. *Human Organization* 68(2), pp. 181–193.
Kendall, L., 2002. *Hanging out in the virtual pub. Masculinities and relationships online*. Berkeley: University of California Press.
Lanier, J., 2011. *You are not a gadget: a manifesto*. London: Penguin Group.
Leander, K. M. and McKim, K. K., 2003. Tracing the everyday 'sitings' of adolescents on the Internet: a strategic adaptation of ethnography across online and offline spaces. *Education, Communication & Information* 3(2), pp. 211–240.
Markham, A., 1998. *Life online. Researching real experience in virtual space*. Walnut Creek, CA: AltaMira Press.
McGonigal, J., 2012. *Reality is broken. Why games make us better and how they can change the world*. London: Vintage Books.
Miller, D. and Slater, D., 2000/2001. *The Internet: an ethnographic approach*. Oxford/New York: Berg.
Miller, G., 2007. The promise of parallel universes. *Science* 317(5842), pp. 1341–1343.
Moores, S., 2005. *media/theory—thinking about media & communications*. London/New York: Routledge.
Navarrete, C. D., McDonald, M. M., Mott, M. L. and Asher, B., 2011. Virtual morality: emotion and action in a simulated three-dimensional "Trolley problem." *Emotion* 12(2), pp. 365–370.
O'Reilly, K., 2009. *Key concepts in ethnography*. London: Sage.
Orgad, S., 2005. From online to offline and back: moving from online to offline relationships with research informants. In: C. Hine, ed. 2005. *Virtual methods. Issues in social research on the Internet*. Oxford/New York: Berg. pp. 51–65.
Orgad, S., 2006. The cultural dimensions of online communication: a study of breast cancer patients' internet spaces. *New Media & Society* 8(6), pp. 877–899.
Orgad, S., 2009. How can researchers make sense of the issues involved in collecting and interpreting online and offline data? In: A. Markham and N. Baym, eds. 2009. *Internet inquiry: conversations about method*. Thousand Oaks, CA: Sage. pp. 33–53.
Poster, M., 1995. Postmodern virtualities. In: M. Featherstone and R. Burrows, eds. 1995. *Cyberspace/cyberbodies/cyberpunk*. Thousand Oaks, CA: Sage. pp. 79–95.
Ramiller, N. C., 2007. Virtualizing the virtual. In: K. Crowston, S. Sieber and E. Wynn eds. 2007. *IFIP International federation for information processing, Volume 236, Virtuality and virtualization*. Boston: Springer. pp. 353–365.
Ruhleder, K., 2000. The virtual ethnographer: fieldwork in distributed electronic environments. *Field Methods* 12(1), pp. 3–17.
Sanders, T., 2005. Researching the online sex work community. In: C. Hine, ed. 2005. *Virtual methods. Issues in social research on the Internet*. Oxford/New York: Berg. pp. 67–80.
Schaap, F., 2002. *The words that took us there: ethnography in virtual reality*. Amsterdam: Aksant Academic Publisher.
Shields, R., 2000. Performing virtualities: Liminality on and off the 'Net.' In: ORGANIZATION, *Performing Virtualities Workshop*. Brunel University, UK, May 2–3. Available at: <http://virtualsociety.sbs.ox.ac.uk/events/pvshields.htm>
Shields, R., 2003. *The virtual*. London: Routledge.
Sicart, M., 2009. *The ethics of computer games*. Cambridge, MA: The MIT Press.
Slater, D., 2002. Social relationships and identity online and offline. In: L.A. Lievrouw and S. Livingstone, eds. 2002. *Handbook of new media. Social shaping and consequences of ICTs*. London: Sage. pp. 533–546.
Slater, M., Antley, A., Davison, A., Swapp, D., Guger, C., Barker, C., Pistrang, N., Sanchez-Vives, M., 2006. A virtual reprise of the Stanley Milgram obedience experiments. *PLoS ONE* 1(1), e39.

Søraker, J., 2011. Virtual entities, environments, worlds and reality: suggested definitions and taxonomy. In: M. Thorseth, and C. Ess, eds. 2011. *Trust and virtual worlds. Contemporary perspectives.* New York: Peter Lang Publishing Group. pp. 44–72.
Strikwerda, L., 2011. Virtual child pornography: why images do harm from a moral perspective. In: M. Thorseth and C. Ess, eds. 2011. *Trust and virtual worlds. Contemporary perspectives.* New York: Peter Lang Publishing Group. pp. 139–161.
Tella, S., Kynäslahti, H. and Husu, J., 1998. Towards the recontext of the virtual school. In: S. Tella, ed. 1998. *Aspects of media education: strategic imperatives in the information age.* Helsingin yliopiston opettajankoulutuslaitos (Media education publications 8). Helsinki: University of Helsinki, Department of Teacher Education. pp. 233–258.
Turkle, S., 1995. *Life on the screen: identity in the age of the Internet.* New York: Touchstone.
Turkle, S., 2011. *Alone together—Why we expect more from technology and less from each other.* New York: Basic Books.
Tuszynski, S., 2006. *IRL (in real life): breaking down the binary of online versus offline social interaction.* Bowling Green: Bowling Green State University.
Wellman, B. and Gulia, M., 1999. Net surfers don't ride alone: virtual communities as communities. In: B. Wellman, ed. 1999. *Networks in the global village.* Boulder, CO: Westview. pp. 331–366.
Willis, P. and Trondman, M., 2000 [2002]. Manifesto for ethnography. *Cultural Studies <=> Critical Methodologies* 2(3), pp. 394–402. (Original article published in 2000 in *Ethnography,* 1[1], pp. 5–16.)
Wittel, A., 2000. Ethnography on the move: from field to net to internet. *Forum Qualitative Sozialforschung/Forum: Qualitative Social Research* 1(1), Art. 21. Available at: <http://nbn-resolving.de/urn:nbn:de:0114-fqs0001213>
Wolfendale, J., 2007. My avatar, my self: virtual harm and attachment. *Ethics and Information Technology* 9(2), pp. 111–119.

2 'If You Asked Me...'
Exploring Autoethnography as a Means to Critically Assess and Advance Audience Research

Alexander Dhoest

INTRODUCTION

As audience researchers, we all ask our respondents some sort of questions, be it in surveys or in interviews or in any other mode of research, except when we register or observe actual behaviour in a non-reactive way. Of course we think hard about our questions and if possible we base them on validated pre-existing questions, and/or we test them in pilot studies. In quantitative research, once this is done we tend to consider the responses as firm data, measuring audience behaviour of all kinds, and we tend to only return to the questions when the findings do not make sense. In qualitative research, we not only more systematically reencounter our questions when analysing the findings, but we also tend to focus primarily on the responses they provoked. In short, questions are a means to an end, which is understanding media uses and meanings.

However, it is worth remembering just how artificial audience research tends to be, that is how constructed the data are, created in the research context as a response to a particular stimulus. Although this point of view is widely accepted in contemporary (mostly qualitative) methodological literature (e.g. Denzin and Lincoln, 2003), in practice it is hard to ascertain to what degree our data manage to grasp actual media uses. Therefore, it may be a good practice to occasionally try to answer our own questions and to remember this experience when analysing and assessing our findings. More fundamentally, I argue that media autoethnography, writing about our own media histories and experiences, may be a good way to reflect on our own and by extension other people's media uses. As will be developed later, autoethnography is quite recent as such, and within media studies it has hardly been used to date, so this approach is highly innovative.

For these reasons, in this chapter, the potential of autoethnography as a way to complement and inform more classical methods of audience research is explored. It argues that reflection on one's own media use, as a researcher, may be useful as such, as a method to better understand the complexity and contextual nature of media uses and to indicate possible avenues for future research. It may also be useful, in particular, as a tool to critically assess some of the assumptions and questions underlying audience research and to provide explanations for certain responses. Of course, an individual account cannot be representative and media researchers are not typical media users (but who is?). Still, if the aim is not to generalise but to explore and question media uses and the ways in which they are studied, I contend that there is a lot to learn. In this chapter, I therefore reflect on my own media use and its meanings, in particular relating it to the kind of questions audience researchers could ask me.

From the start, I wish to stress that the approach I propose is not to be considered as an alternative but as a complement to other methods and instruments in audience research, providing the richest possible (if very individual) assessment of one person's media use. As will be illustrated, compared to other approaches to (audience) research, autoethnography is rather a-theoretical and inductive, but it may be useful for this very reason, as it is relatively uncluttered by preconceptions and frameworks, observation protocols and questionnaires. Although my own observations are, of course, informed by theory and research (which I refer to), my primary aim is to (try to) take an unbiased look at my own media use. Similarly, this chapter is unusually informal for an academic text, particularly when illustrating and reflecting on my own media uses, but this is a deliberate attempt to complement as well as reflect on the usual academic style of writing. Although this chapter primarily provides a methodological discussion rather than an illustration of autoethnography, some short examples of autoethnographic writing are included.

AUTOETHNOGRAPHY AND SELF-REFLECTION

Over the past decades, self-reflection has become a core characteristic of qualitative media and cultural studies research (e.g. Gripsrud, 1995, pp. 120–124; Hermes, 2004). Criticising former notions of distance and objectivity, qualitative research admits the unavoidable role of researchers in the construction of the reality they study, as well as their own position in that socially and culturally specific reality (Denzin and Lincoln, 2003). For instance, one of the key methods in qualitative research, the in-depth interview, is no longer conceived as a method to 'dig up' information but rather as an active, interactive event in which interviewer and interviewee co-construct knowledge and meanings (e.g. Holstein and Gubrium, 1995; Legard, Keegan and Ward, 2003). Mutual differences (in terms of gender, class, etc.) and perceptions are part and parcel of the interviewing process, often leading to tensions which in turn are increasingly reflected on (e.g. Seiter, 1990).

Although reflection on one's position as a media researcher has become quite usual, reflection on one's own media use is still rare. Short references to one's own stake in a topic or a field of research can be frequently found, but more extensive accounts are rare. Within the field of ethnography, however, such self-reflexive writing has recently developed into a subfield of 'autoethnography', building on a longer tradition of autobiographical storytelling and responding to the increasing focus on self-reflexivity in ethnographic research (Chang, 2008). Based on the growing awareness of the constructive and interpretive nature of ethnographic data (Hammersley and Atkinson, 2007) and the need for 'thick', detailed descriptions of reality (Geertz, 1975), reflexivity has become a core but contested characteristic of contemporary ethnography: "We are storied selves entangled with others' stories [. . .], our understandings of their stories, and their understanding of ours" (Berry and Clair, 2011, p. 95). In the context of the ensuing crisis of representation and legitimation, autoethnography is part of a turn towards interpretive, qualitative, narrative, critical inquiry (Holman Jones, 2005).

As defined by Chang (2008, p. 48), autoethnography is ethnographic in its methodological orientation, cultural in its interpretive orientation and autobiographical in its content orientation. However, in this chapter I define the interpretive orientation more broadly, because my focus is not on cultural differences and intercultural communication, as in Chang's research, but on media uses. While the term *autoethnography* can be used to refer to self-reflection on the part of the ethnographer, the 'native' or both (Reed-Danahay, 2001), in this context I restrict its use to self-disclosure on behalf of the researcher only. Often, however, autoethnographical reflections can also be found in ethnographic accounts of groups the researcher identifies with and/or is part of (e.g. Ryan, 2006).

By its very nature, any autoethnographical account is very personal so the researcher in this case is not only, as usual, powerful in being able to present, frame and interpret media uses. He or she is also vulnerable, in exposing his or her own, very private media uses: "It is vulnerable because the process exposes that which is always being concealed in scholarly research and particularly in ethnographic research—that being the positionality of the writer, and the biases that structure ethnographic perceptions, revealed and analyzed as a component part of reporting and full disclosure" (Alexander, 2011, pp. 105). As is becoming more and more usual in ethnographic research and, in particular, variants of media and cultural studies, this mode of writing entails elaborate reflection on one's own position as a researcher. This kind of self-disclosure may seem inappropriate and even narcissistic, but it is not that unusual in late modern times of self-disclosure and the erasure of public–private divides. Moreover, it is exactly this kind of disclosure of private worlds we expect from our respondents, so it seems only fair to also put oneself in this vulnerable and exposed position. As Judith Okely points out, "since almost nothing about the people studied is dismissed as private, taboo or improper for investigation, the same should apply to the investigator" (Okely, 1996, cited in Reed-Danahay, 2001, p. 413).

Listing some benefits of the method, Chang (2008, pp. 51–52) points to its friendly nature both for researchers, who have easy access to holistic, intimate data, and for readers who are (or, at least, could be) appealed to by the personal, engaging writing style. It can also lead to enhanced understanding of self and others. Mizzi (2010, p. 2) further adds multivocality to the advantages of autoethnography, that is providing representational space for the plural and possibly contradictory narrative voices located within the researcher, while provoking deeper understanding of the often silent tensions underlying observable behaviours. Multivocality illustrates that there is no single voice telling the story, past and present voices interacting in the researcher's story; it deconstructs competing tensions within the autoethnographer as he or she connects the personal self to social context; and it unfixes identity, exposing its fluid nature as it moves through particular contexts (Mizzi, 2010, p. 6). In short, autoethnography can help to translate the complexity of human experience to readers and it can help the self-discovery by the researcher of what lies underneath.

Beside these strengths, there are some weaknesses and points of critique. According to Chang (2008, pp. 54–55), pitfalls to avoid in doing autoethnographical research are an excessive focus on self in isolation from others and cultural context; overemphasis on narration rather than analysis and cultural interpretation; and exclusive reliance on personal memory, which can be misleading. Autoethnography should not limit itself to self-reflection and -disclosure, but it should also make a connection to broader theoretical and social contexts to transcend the purely individual. As stressed by both Chang (2008) and Mizzi (2010), autoethnographical writing can be intensely emotional, which explains the critique of narcissism often directed at autoethnographic writing. Another point of critique is the tension between the personal and 'objective' accounts of reality. As pointed out by Reed-Danahay (2001, p. 411), autobiographical and reflexive methods have long been viewed as unscientific and biased, as opposed to objective, more standardized forms of research. However, if—as mentioned earlier—all accounts of reality are constructed and mediated, many argue that there should also be a place for autobiographical, first-person accounts by subjects and researchers themselves (Reed-Danahay, 2001).

As already mentioned, autoethnography can be considered as a subfield of ethnography, with which it shares the close observation on everyday life and experiences. However, contrary to the broader field of ethnography, which has a long history and which has been theoretically and methodologically developed over the years, very little has been written about autoethnography as a method. Paralleling the object of this kind of research, the uses of autoethnography are highly personal and intuitive, most accounts lacking an extensive explanation of the process of research itself. Although this can be considered as a weakness, to a certain degree it matches the self-oriented and more implicit research process. Although traditional ethnographers need time to immerse themselves in a group or (sub)culture, which ideally involves a longer period of participant observation and gradual familiarisation, autoethnographers start from a deep and intimate knowledge of their own life. Therefore, such research can take place within a shorter period, although of course it is possible to 'observe' oneself over a longer period. Rather than gradually becoming familiar with a group as time unfolds, the autoethnographer typically looks back, so potentially the time frame under consideration can actually be longer than in other ethnographic research and it may involve reflection on historical, social as well as biographical changes and stages. In this process, rather than using the ethnographic tool of field notes (Hammersley, 2007, pp. 141–142), the self-reflective diary or essay is most commonly used. As a consequence, whereas the processes of data gathering and analysis are closely intertwined in ethnographical research as a whole, in autoethnography these processes virtually coincide, every 'observation' also includes reflection.

AUTOETHNOGRAPHIC MEDIA RESEARCH?

As mentioned earlier, self-reflection can be frequently found in qualitative media and audience research, but autoethnography is rarely and seldom explicitly used in this field. One early example is John Fiske's (1990) reflection on his and other people's reading of a TV programme (*The Newlywed Game*). However, rather than describing his reading, under the title of 'autoethnography' he reflects, in retrospect, on the different discursive practices by which he produced sense and pleasure: a professional discourse (considering cultural and political forces at work in TV), a popular discourse (as a fan with self-admittedly 'vulgar' tastes) and a set of intersecting discourses of gender, age, class and race (as a middle-aged, middle-class white male). He reflects on himself as a site and as an instance of reading, "not because the reading I produced was in any way socially representative of, or extrapolable to, others, but because the process by which I produced it was a structured instance of culture in practice" (Fiske, 1990, p. 86).

Another self-disclosing account can be found in Terhi Rantanen's *The Media and Globalization* (2005), in which she proposes the method of 'global mediagraphy' to study mediated globalisation. Attempting to connect micro accounts of migration and media use to macro accounts of globalisation, she uses a kind of multi-sited ethnography to study how four generations of three families use media and communication, drawing on life histories (Rantanen, 2005, pp. 12–14). Interestingly, one of the families she studies is her own (Rantanen, 2005, pp. 29–34), but rather than autobiographically reflecting on this, she describes this family as if she were an outsider, so the account is not really autoethnographic. Still, she explicitly brings her own experience into her research, something which is often implicitly the case as our research tends to reflect aspects of our personal lives and interests.

Mittell (2011) adopts a more self-reflexive mode, as he reflects on the intersection of two major changes in his life, having kids and getting TiVo. He admits that his account is quite 'self-absorbed', which is fairly uncommon

34   *Alexander Dhoest*

in media studies, but he does not consider himself to be typical or normative. Still, "by looking in the autoethnographic familial mirror, I can mine a depth of knowledge about the practices of everyday life and the way children experience media over a long period of time that are otherwise inaccessible in other families" (Mittell, 2011, p. 46). In the process, he hopes to draw connections and gain insights in the experience of media (in this case, convergent television) in everyday life, which resonate with other people's experiences.

Whereas the autobiographical elements in Mittell's account are quite limited, Boylorn (2008) interweaves autoethnographic reflections in the form of autobiographical 'vignettes' with a discussion on the representation of race in reality television, a rare example of actual autoethnographic writing in media studies (see also Wayner, 2009). Overall, it is fair to say that autoethnography is very rare in the field of media and audience studies, and therefore its introduction is potentially a strong innovation. At the same time, as mentioned previously, it is connected to a more general move towards reflexivity and the acknowledgement of the active role of the researcher, so it is not radically different but rather a logical step forward in media research.

DOING AUTOETHNOGRAPHY: AN ILLUSTRATED EXAMPLE

My Media Use

As mentioned earlier, in this chapter I do not intend to write a full-blown (media) autoethnography but primarily to reflect on my own experiences to comment on some of the questions asked and issues addressed in audience research. While the process of writing this chapter was accompanied by a parallel exercise in autoethnographic writing, in which I reflected on the connection between my media use and identity by going through a typical day, this essay is not fully included here because of space restrictions and because the focus of this chapter is more on the potential usefulness of the method for audience research than on its actual findings. However, I include some vignettes, as illustrations of how I wrote about my media use.
This is how I start:

> I wake up (too early), to the bathroom (half awake), turn on the radio to listen to Studio Brussel. It's a public service broadcasting 'young channel', trying to be 'cutting edge'. Unlike Radio 1 (lots of serious discussions about actual affairs), Radio 2 (more popular in style and music, the biggest channel), Klara (classical music) and MNM (the 'commercial style' public channel playing mostly contemporary pop & R&B), Studio Brussel typically covers 'alternative' music, rock and dance genres. Why do I listen to Studio Brussel? Partly it's a habit: I'm used to it, grew

> attached to some presenters, and dislike the talking (Radio 1), corny atmosphere (Radio 2), occasionally dusty classical music (Klara) and commercial pop (MNM and the commercial channels) on other channels. Perhaps you could say it's a lifestyle choice: wanting to appear hip and young, to be 'in' on new trends – but to be honest that's not how I would describe or perceive it. (I guess most people would not – like to – perceive their media choices as just 'trying to get the right image'.) I just like it most, in the mornings, to wake up, because they mostly have an upbeat, fun morning programme.

Between such rather descriptive passages, I also include more reflective parts:

> What strikes me most is how omnipresent media and ICTs are in my daily life, yet how inconspicuous they tend to become: they are integrated in everyday rhythms, I grew attached to them without noticing, and I use them with such ease that it often does not feel like a deliberate choice. Which, I guess, is their greatest power, for I believe media do influence us but not in the rather simplistic way often implied in media criticism: they mostly don't instil new ideas in my head, but they are involved in a continuous process of selection (on my behalf) leading to selective exposure to reality (on behalf of the media), not radically changing my views and tastes but slowly moulding them, building on what's there, reinforcing it and adding bits and pieces. So if I like 'Mad Men', I may expose myself to similar shows which, in turn, will confirm my tastes. I listen to Studio Brussel because I like some of their music, then get to hear similar music and expand my taste. I watch television that both forms and confirms my left-leaning sympathies. I watch shows that build upon and expand my intertextual reading skills.

I Don't Use Media All That Much . . .

After writing about my media uses throughout a typical day, I subsequently started to think about the questions a researcher could ask me and about the answers I could give. In the remainder of this chapter, I discuss a few of these issues in the personal—first-person—style I also used in my autoethnographic essay.

A first observation concerns the fact that many of the questions audience researchers ask are not that easy to answer. Starting at the most basic level, assessing actual media uses is supposedly the most straightforward thing to do, but it is known that respondents tend to underestimate their media use (Otten, Littenberg and Harvey-Berino, 2010). For instance, responding to the question, "How often do you watch television?" I would say I don't watch television very much, but in fact I watch it almost daily. As a media scholar, in an interview I would probably add that I watch a lot of television professionally, but although I try to keep up with new programmes professionally, most of the shows I regularly watch are 'for fun'. I would also say I don't watch that long, but depending on the day that could vary from one to three hours. As the previous statement indicates, my television use greatly varies: some days I don't watch, other days I watch all evening, so my estimation of the average duration is probably as misguided as any respondent's, be it in qualitative or quantitative research. Alternative methods such as diaries are useful and even necessary to more accurately estimate the duration and frequency of media uses. However, and even if I have never filled in a media diary myself—I would probably be a non-respondent, saying I'm too busy—I know for a fact that I would become sloppy and lose interest after quite a short while. Completely automatic registration of media use, for instance, through Portable People Meters, may well be the best way to grasp (traditional) media uses, but I'm not sure I would understand my own patterns of media use generated in this way, without at least some qualitative contextualisation. Sticking to the example of television, my patterns of viewing are strongly related to my partner's and are relatively regular because of that. When he's not around I watch the shows he dislikes (including, in the spirit of self-disclosure, *True Blood, Glee, Ugly Betty* and *The Walking Dead*); when he's around we watch the shows which are acceptable to both (such as *Homeland, The Killing* and *The Tudors*). My times and patterns of viewing, therefore, are not a purely personal matter, something which is hard to grasp in any kind of research.

Turning to the internet, a very long and complicated questionnaire or a refined set of open questions would be necessary to accurately describe how often and how I use it. I could say I use it all the time at work (particularly if you count e-mail, which is web based), but I could not assess how much time I actually spend on the net in a working day, as I do it intermittently. Moreover, I also use the internet at work for private matters (checking Facebook, answering private e-mails, checking out hotels which are not necessarily conference related). At home, I would say I don't use the internet much in the evening, as I want to avoid checking my (mostly work-related) e-mail too often, but I work a lot from home where on a working day my professional and private internet uses are even more intertwined. Moreover, I access the internet through my laptop, smartphone and tablet, and I could not possibly estimate the duration and nature of those uses, because it varies so greatly.

Media Meanings

Turning from patterns of media use to its meanings and interpretations, the plot thickens further. If questions on the former are hard to answer because the facts are not readily available, questions on the latter typically deal with issues one has rarely thought about before. Answers, both in quantitative and in qualitative research, are therefore 'constructions' or 'inventions', which does not imply they are necessarily and completely untrue, but they have at the very least been created at the time of research, not before. Based on my experiences as a respondent, I have to say I have a hard time filling in surveys with closed questions: on one hand, they are easy to deal with, because the possible answers are there; on the other hand, however, I rarely recognise myself (entirely) in the options provided. My most regular reflex is to think: "Yes, but . . .", "No, but . . .", "Somewhere in between option x and y" or "Both x and y". Because of this, I mostly go for the more neutral answers, hardly ever taking an extreme position. My answers to survey questions often hide mixed feelings or more complex stances, which disappear from view when people giving similar answers for different reasons are compiled for quantitative analysis. You may say I am recalcitrant, which is probably true, but I'm not sure the experience of not recognising oneself in the answers is that exceptional. I rather think most people just don't care enough to protest—leaving aside the fact that a survey generally does not give room for protest, apart from not responding.

In qualitative research, the constructive nature of the response is clearer and it is more readily recognised. The respondent creates certain answers as a response to particular questions, asked in a particular context. Again, based on my limited experience, I would say that this is not easy, particularly as you have generally not thought about, or at least not talked about, the issues that are addressed. Answering those questions is a struggle, stumbling and inventing as you go along. Having a way with words and being able to tell a coherent story is an advantage in this context, but it does not necessarily mean those answers are more 'true' or trustworthy. Rather, they are the expression of the ability to create and control a narrative and therefore, possibly, to hide or at least not to mention contradictory thoughts and feelings. This ability obviously correlates with one's level of education which implies the formal training people got in giving coherent and linguistically adequate answers to questions. This should make us wonder about the strong reliance on higher-educated (often university-level) respondents across the social (and other) sciences. Often, interviews with higher-educated respondents are more appealing and quotable, but they are not representative and even possibly misleading, because they suggest a coherence in thinking and talking about issues which is specific not only to higher-educated respondents but also to the interview context, not everyday life. In other words, both the external and the ecological validity of such answers can at the very least be questioned.

All these issues have been discussed in methodological literature (e.g. Bryman, 2004), and I am not saying we should not be doing surveys or in-depth interviews. Rather, what I would like to point at here, are the limited means we have at our disposal to control any of this. For instance, the interview context is hard to assess, be it the environment or the person(ality) of the interviewer. Although methodological literature would recommend conducting interviews in a quiet setting, some respondents may feel more at ease in a busy public place, whereas at home the presence of an interviewer may feel like an intrusion. Similarly, the interviewer may think that his or her presence and appearance (gender, age, clothes, looks) makes a certain impression on the interviewee (theoretically designated as 'reactivity'), but this may be misguided. Assessing the appearance one makes is very hard in research as it is in daily life, so in both cases the best we can do is to second-guess. For the sake of 'objectivity', we may also try to control the impression we make, but even if we present ourselves in the same way the effect is most probably variable because it also depends on the personality and mood of both the researcher and the respondent. For instance, being busy I may at times be irritated by questions asked by journalists and answer quite shortly and abruptly, but at other times I may embrace the timely break from other, more tedious work. So the same questions, asked by the same person to the same respondent, may result in very different answers. Being aware of this is one thing, controlling it is another thing altogether.

My (Not So) Active and Critical Media Use

Turning to some of the more concrete topics that are addressed in audience research, I limit myself to the research field I know best, broadly defined as 'cultural media studies'. Quite a lot of early cultural studies-inspired audience research dealt with the degree of participation, active involvement and critical reflection on, or resistance to, media content (e.g. Ang, 1985). This lead to a summary version of 'audience ethnographies' and the active audience paradigm, which has been subsequently questioned: audiences are not active let alone resistant all the time. Although I think the way this research is often summarised does not do justice to its complexity, often treating it as a naive celebration of audience power (for a discussion, see Morley, 1993), I do think it is flawed in a way that is indicative of a broader but generally implicit tendency in audience research, that is to take oneself as a touchstone of audience behaviour. Of course, I see the seeming irony of this statement in a chapter which does nothing but taking the author as a point of reference, but I think the main difference is that I do this explicitly, not implicitly, and that I do not aim to generalise from my own position.

As mentioned before, some questions asked in qualitative audience research address issues the average media user has never thought let alone spoken about: why you use or like a particular media product, whether you recognise yourself in or identify with film or television characters. As media use is not something very abstract nor something one tends to be (excessively) ashamed about, it is generally possible to answer those questions but it is worth remembering that these answers do not merely express previously held assessments or opinions. Expecting audiences to consciously and explicitly reflect on their media uses in the interview context is one thing, assuming that this represents how they usually deal with media is another thing altogether. I, for one, and despite the fact that I am highly educated and specialised in media studies, would not describe my own 'normal' media use as particularly critical or resistant. Of course, I do recognise the codes and conventions of mass media, and I do see through some of its constructions, but for instance when I watch television my main preoccupation is to be entertained. If you would interview me about my media use, I would be happy to display my media-savviness bordering on cynicism, but this 'critical' attitude does not preclude my almost shallow revelling in the distractions television provides on a daily basis. As research has shown, I am not alone in displaying such contradictory feelings of immersion and distancing,[1] and I would argue that television is mostly the former: a medium of entertainment and escape, not of reflection and criticism.

This confession may seem to confirm the worst fears of cultural and media pessimists: media such as television render the audience into passive and vulnerable 'dupes', who are blind to its hegemonic force. Of course, like most audience members I don't feel particularly influenced by television, and probably I actually am influenced just as much as the next person. But what I do know is that I very consciously choose what I watch and read and that I am not very often confronted with views or representations of reality I am fundamentally opposed to—so, in short, I don't see all that much reason to resist. Rather, what does frequently happen is that I get bored and therefore switch channels. I am not sure how typical this limited patience and attention span is, but if my behaviour is in any way indicative I would say that traditional television is in trouble, because most of the time I just watch documentaries, movies or TV drama I have digitally recorded or bought on DVD. This, of course, bespeaks my socio-economic (I can afford the DVD boxes) and educational (I feel too clever to watch mainstream TV) position, but again, I do not think I am alone in this case.

How Media Did (and Did Not) Help Create My Identity

Another issue I research myself but am simultaneously critical of is identity. In late modernity, media use is supposed to be of great importance for the creation of our identities, which are not ascribed anymore but are self-created, negotiated and fluid. One of the themes in my research is national and cultural identity, but to be honest, this is not an issue I regularly think about in my own life, with the exception of some, very particular contexts. For instance, I only feel very Flemish when I am forced to speak French in Brussels, the supposedly bilingual capital of Belgium—but then again I enjoy the opportunity to practice my French, which is not a language I often need or use. In media terms, I mostly consume Dutch-language Flemish media (newspapers, magazines, radio and television), although through those channels I do consume a lot of international (mostly English-language) content such as TV shows, movies and music. I am very predictable in consuming 'quality', slightly left-wing brands (*De Morgen*, *Humo*, *Studio Brussel* and *Canvas*, respectively, for the four media mentioned earlier), which probably colours my worldview more than I can be aware of. This media use reconfirms my cultural identity on an everyday basis and in a taken for granted way, so my cultural identity is not 'salient' most of the time in media use. Probably my most revealing experience, in terms of cultural identity awareness, was the one year I studied and lived in Britain, where despite understanding the language I was not familiar with the media and for the first time in my life felt very 'Belgian' and, by extension, continental European.

Minority identities are more easily salient so it should come as no surprise that my sexual identity (as a white, middle-class, male, Western but gay person) is most salient to me. That is it's the aspect of my identity that I can imagine to be important and related to my media use and vice versa. Particularly before and during my coming out process, reading about and finding representations of homosexuality was an issue for me. My sexual orientation inspired my media use and in turn was strongly influenced by the representations available to me. And although this period was, undoubtedly, defining for who I am now, I do not feel like I have consciously constructed my identity using media or other cultural sources. It was a struggle, indeed, but not a very conscious one or at least: media did not function as the 'building blocks' we often assume others (mostly adolescents) to use in crafting their own selves. At present, my sexual identity is but one of my sources of identification, and I would argue that this is not as fluid as contemporary literature on identity would have it. I do not feel like I continuously reshape who I am, but rather I have different sources of identification (such as gender, class, ethnicity, sexuality) which intersect and become salient at different times. In an interview about sexuality, it would probably sound as if sexuality was an issue to me all the time, but ethnicity could just as well come to the fore in an interview on that topic. Similarly, in my media use, my sexual orientation could come the fore in certain contexts (for instance, in watching a movie or documentary dealing with homosexuality) but in others it may not that clearly be an issue.

This being said, media have played an important role in shaping who I am. As a kid, I remember watching a lot of Dutch television, like many Flemish people of my generation or older, who grew up without commercial Flemish television and therefore turned to the more popular Dutch channels. I remember, in particular, watching a lot of music programs, probably wanting to be a star which, as you can note, sadly enough didn't work out for me. My parents consumed quality media such as *De Standaard* and *Knack*, a newspaper and news magazine I seem to have turned away from in my youthful rebellion and haven't returned to ever since (just to illustrate how socialisation does not always work in direct ways). Probably the most formative media experience is the period when, as a student, I discovered film through the student cultural centre, becoming an avid cinephile and switching from law to communication studies. Today, I would indeed position this in my search for an individual identity, but this 'conscious search' only became clear to me afterwards, retrospectively. Moreover, this identity is probably more 'socially determined' than I would like to admit, my twenty-year-old self wanting to distinguish himself (*la distinction*) by sitting through unintelligible and frankly boring art movies. Not to dismiss all of this as adolescent folly, but we should be careful in assuming that people go through this kind of formative experience all through their lives. The most fluid and therefore more exciting years—both to live and to research—are late adolescence and early adulthood, but we should avoid generalising the processes we witness at that time to the 'usual' dealings with media and identity.

CONCLUSION

Where does all of this leave us? First, I want to indicate that more extensive experimentation with autoethnographical writing is necessary to better understand its potential usefulness for audience and media studies, a field in which it has hardly been used to date. While individual autoethnographic accounts by media researchers could provide interesting in-depth insights in media uses and interpretations, more collective and/or systematic autoethnographical reflections could also be useful. For instance, a collection of autoethnographical essays by researchers would be helpful to establish broader patterns in (self-understandings of) contemporary media uses. Encouraging young researchers or even students to reflect on their own media uses may also be a pedagogical tool to stimulate critical (self-)awareness. Similarly, encouraging respondents to write about their own media uses or to recount them in life-history interviews may be a good way to get more spontaneous and personal accounts of everyday media use.

Second, although in this chapter I am quite critical of audience research, I do not mean to imply that we have to distrust our methods or our findings altogether; rather, I think we should remain conscious of their limitations, something that is easier said than accomplished in the everyday context of doing and writing about research. Taking some distance, through writing about or at least reflecting on our own media uses, may be helpful to avoid simplistic assumptions and questions. Based on my own media uses, I would claim that we should not assume that other people are like us, but neither should we assume that we are necessarily 'special' or 'exceptional'. Reading through interview transcripts, I recognise some of the contradictory or even crude responses as very similar to my own; I detect the wish to please the interviewer by coming up with a seemingly coherent and truthful answer; I even recognise the lack of rational arguments to support very strong beliefs I have of certain media outputs.

Finally, having briefly explored the field of autoethnography, I believe it truly has potential as a revitalisation of audience research, not only for the reader but also for the writer, who can indulge in a form of non-formalistic, personal writing, not forcing coherence upon the narrative but rather admitting its fragmented and contradictory nature and thus evoking the actual complexity of everyday media use. At the same time, I must admit this kind of writing is quite challenging as the subjectivity, self-disclosure and self-centeredness it implies go against one's training as an academic. Although the autoethnographic account in this chapter remains rather superficial, the essay it builds on is very personal and more emotional than any academic work I've ever done. On one hand, this is useful, as it discloses the deep personal involvement we—and most people—have with the media we use. On the other hand, it does feel awkward to share this with a broader readership, which is something we should bear in mind when we probe into other people's lives.

NOTE

1. See for instance the work of Ang (1985) and Liebes and Katz (1990) on *Dallas*.

REFERENCES

Alexander, B.K., 2011. Standing in the wake: a critical auto/ethnographic exercise on reflexivity in three movements. *Cultural Studies<=>Critical Methodologies* 11(2), pp. 98–107.
Ang, I., 1985. *Watching* Dallas: *soap opera and the melodramatic imagination*. London: Methuen.
Berry, K. and Clair, R.P., 2011. Contestation and opportunity in reflexivity: an introduction. *Cultural Studies<=>Critical Methodologies* 11(2), pp. 95–97.
Boylorn, R.M., 2008. As seen on TV: an autoethnographic reflection on race and reality television, *Critical Studies in Media Communication* 25(4), pp. 413–433.
Bryman, A., 2004. *Social research methods*. 2nd ed. Oxford: Oxford University Press.
Chang, H., 2008. *Autoethnography as method*. Walnut Creek: Left Coast Press.
Denzin, N.K. and Lincoln, Y.S., 2003. Introduction: the discipline and practice of qualitative research. In: N.K. Denzin and Y.S. Lincoln, eds. *The landscape of qualitative research: theories and issues*. London: Sage. pp. 1–45.
Fiske, J., 1990. Ethnosemiotics: some personal and theoretical reflections. *Cultural Studies* 4(1), pp. 85–98.
Geertz, C.L., 1975. Thick description: towards an interpretive theory of culture. In: C.L. Geertz, ed. 1975. *The interpretation of cultures: selected essays*. London: Hutchinson. pp. 3–30.
Gripsrud, J., 1995. *The dynasty years: Hollywood television and critical media studies*. London: Routledge.
Hammersley, M. and Atkinson, P., 2007. *Ethnography: principles in practice*. 3rd ed. London: Routledge.
Hermes, J., 2004. A concise history of media and cultural studies in three scripts: advocacy, autobiography, and the chronicle. In: J. Downing, Ed. 2004. *The SAGE handbook of media studies*. Thousand Oaks: Sage. pp. 251–270.
Holman Jones, S., 2005. Autoethnography: making the personal political. In: N.K. Denzin and Y.S. Lincoln, eds. 2005. *The SAGE handbook of qualitative research*. 3rd ed. Thousand Oaks: Sage. pp. 763–791.

Holstein, J. A. and Gubrium, J. F., 1995. *The Active Interview*. Thousand Oaks, CA: Sage.
Legard, R., Keegan, J. and Ward, K., 2013. In-depth interviews. In: J. Ritchie and J. Lewis, eds. 2013. *Qualitative research practice: a guide for social science students and researchers*. London: Sage. pp. 138–169.
Liebes, T. and Katz, E., 1990. *The export of meaning. cross-cultural readings of Dallas*. New York: Oxford University Press.
Mittell, J., 2011. TiVoing childhood: time-shifting a generation's concept of television. In: M. Kackman, M. Binfield, M. T Payne, A. Perlman and B. Sebok, eds. 2011. *Flow TV: television in the age of media convergence*. New York: Routledge. pp. 46–54.
Mizzi, R., 2010. Unraveling researcher subjectivity through multivocality in autoethnography. *Journal of Research Practice* 6(1), pp. 3–29.
Morley, D., 1993. Active audience theory: pendulums and pitfalls. *Journal of Communication* 43(4), 13–19.
Otten, J. J., Littenberg, B. and Harvey-Berino, J. R. 2010. Relationship between self-report and an objective measure of television-viewing time in adults. *Obesity* 18(6), 1273–1275.
Rantanen, T., 2005. *The media and globalization*. London: Sage.
Reed-Danahay, D., 2001. Autobiography, intimacy and ethnography. In: P. Atkinson, A. Coffey, S. Delamont, J. Lofland and L. Lofland, eds. 2001. *Handbook of ethnography*. London: Sage. pp. 407– 425.
Ryan, P., 2006. Researching Irish gay male lives: reflections on disclosure and intellectual autobiography in the production of personal narratives. *Qualitative Research* 6(2), pp. 151–168.
Seiter, E., 1990. Making distinctions in TV audience research: case study of a troubling interview, *Cultural Studies* 4(1), pp. 61–84.
Wayner, D., 2009. Walking in fear: an autoethnographic account of media framing of inner-city crime. *Journal of Communication Inquiry* 33(2), pp. 169–184.

3 Expanding the Reach of the Interview in Audience and Reception Research
The Performative and Participatory Models of Interview

David Mathieu and Maria José Brites

INTRODUCTION

The semi-structured interview remains the most common method in qualitative audience research. With a few exceptions (Lunt and Livingstone, 1996; Schrøder, et al., 2003), most discussions of the interview method remain general discussions of qualitative research (Alasuutari, 1995; Kvale, 1996; Silverman, 2005). In this chapter, the interview method is discussed in relation to context, a central notion in audience studies which in many ways defines our field and distinguishes it from other disciplines in which the interview is also used, such as sociology, psychology or pedagogy. Acknowledging the importance of these disciplines for the inception and development of the interview, it remains important however that the method meets the methodological challenges of audience research. In this regard, this paper argues for the fine-tuning of the interview method to the context or contexts of the audience.

Audience research can be defined as a contextual inquiry. As such, a crucial issue in audience studies is to properly capture the contexts of the audience. Indeed, context has been an important topic of discussion in the field, for example Radway's (1984) suggestion of "radical contextualism" or Corner's (1991) questioning in front of the task at hand. Corner asked, "What counts as context? Who decides what is context and with help of what criteria? Where does context begin and end?" While researchers make an honest attempt to lean on what they see as relevant contextual cues in the lifeworld of the audience, the operationalization of context is often left implicit in research.

Indeed, although the contextual nature of media reception and use is widely recognised (Jensen, 2002), the very notion of context is rarely discussed as a methodological principle of audience research, less so in interview research. This is even more surprising given that context is gaining recognition as a prime methodological issue in a variety of research areas: in relation to interaction and conversation analysis (Duranti and Goodwin, 1992; Verschueren, 1999), to discourse analysis (Widdowson, 2004; Stenvoll and Svensson, 2011), to the psychology of discourse (van Dijk, 2008; 2009). The issue that this chapter addresses concerns the ways the interview method can be conceived to take into consideration the important aspect of audience research that is context.

Much contextual inquiry works within what could be called a received view of context commonly found in humanistic research (Hammersley, 2008). Within this view, context has been understood as a 'sociological given', in terms of the socio-demographic characteristics of the audience, such as education and gender, or as an 'ethnological given', in terms of the viewing or reading situation (Corner, 1991). However, we want to argue that context is also dynamic, and dynamically generated, and that its study involves articulating the dynamics of audience's subjective meanings and everyday life at the centre of the contextual inquiry, and hence at the centre of the interview method.

This is not without difficulties, however. Not only is context a different reality for each member of the audience, but context is also constantly evolving and changing, as the process of semiosis sometimes precedes and motivates reading or is brought and integrated further in the lifeworld of the audience in a variety of circumstances that are hard to predict. How is the interview method to react in face of the variety and fluidity of context?

We propose to expand the reach of the interview method as a means of investigating context, with the aim of increasing its validity in capturing the diverse manifestations of context in media use and reception. Through a critique of the traditional conception of the interview method, which we present as a question–answer model,[1] in this chapter we suggest two articulations of the interview method in the framework of a contextual inquiry. The novelty of these approaches resides in the way they remodel the traditional interview to capture context in everyday life, whether this is the contexts of interpretation or the contexts of media uses. We first present a *performative model* of the interview, in which the context of reception is understood as a constructive, dynamic and emergent process of contextualisation performed by recipients. Second, we discuss a *participatory model* of interviewing, in which the interviewee is an active subject of the research who acts as a quasi-researcher, taking the role of interviewer.

It is important for any audience study that relies on the interview method to position itself vis-à-vis the methodological challenges that contextual enquiry poses. We hope to facilitate this discussion by (1) presenting the two articulations of the interview in their original theoretical, methodological and empirical contexts and (2) highlighting different methodological considerations that help distinguish the performative and participatory interviews from the traditional interview.

THE INTERVIEW AS QUESTIONS AND ANSWERS

Audience research has relied extensively on the semi-structured interview, both as in-depth individual interviews or as group interviews (Lunt and Livingstone, 1996; Schrøder, et al., 2003). Although there are some other types of interviews in use in audience research (such as the questionnaire, more connected with quantitative research), we focus our discussion on the semi-structured interview. The term *semi-structured interview* is commonly used to refer to an open-ended interview aimed to initiate conversation, reporting or storytelling (Kvale, 1996; Schrøder, et al., 2003), and spontaneous follow-up questions and probing (Ghiglione and Matalon, 1977 [2005]). The advantage of the semi-structured interview in audience research resides in its capacity to encourage the perspective of participants to emerge. As such, the reliance on the semi-structured interview came to define qualitative audience research in response to unchecked claims and implicit assumptions concerning the audience made in studies of the media text.

In its basic form, interviewing is a process of asking questions and receiving answers. Potter and Hepburn (2012, p. 156) call the question–answer pair the "central motor of interviews", in which the researcher assumes the role of the questioner, while the interviewee's role is to provide answers. Open questions are motivated by the research agenda and are asked to elicit knowledge from the interviewee, which provides the materials for analysis. Within this conception, the interview is regarded as a "friendly exchange between strangers" who discuss a topic of interest to both (Schrøder, et al., 2003, p. 149).

Despite the obvious reductionism implied by this schematisation, we find the question–answer model of interview a useful starting point for a discussion of innovative approaches that aim at taking the method out of its traditional mould. Clearly, the aim here is to be able to make visible, to discuss and to challenge the rationale of the interview method as it is conventionally presented, rather than to report on the variety of ways in which the semi-structured interview has been fruitfully used in audience research. Nevertheless, this simple schematisation helps to address the issues of validity of the interview method in the contextual enquiry and provides a position from which to consider our suggestions.

The conception of the semi-structured interview that is in question in qualitative audience research proceeds under a constructionist epistemology of research, in which knowledge is discursively produced through the exchange that takes place during the interview (Borer and Fontana, 2012; Ghiglione and Matalon, 1977 [2005]; Schrøder, et al., 2003). As such, audience studies have moved away from a modernist conception of the interview as a "straightforward result of asking questions and receiving answers" (Borer and Fontana, 2012, p. 57). Interview informants are not regarded as a "repository of answers" or as "treasure chests of knowledge that need to be cracked open but as co-constructers of the treasures themselves" (Borer and Fontana, 2012, p. 48). That is both the interviewer and the interviewee have an active role to play in the construction of relevant and valid knowledge (Kvale, 1996).

Yet, given the active role provided to both interviewer and interviewee, this collaboration is such that it potentially undermines the validity of the interview. This interaction means that the knowledge produced is as much the property of the interviewee as it is of the interviewer. The question of who is the author of the answers, rather than the principal or animator (Goffman, 1981) is crucial here. Therefore, a major challenge of interview research is to increase validity while acknowledging the constructive character of the interview inquiry.

In the traditional interview, questions are used to initiate, control and monitor the interviewee's contribution to the conversation, the interviewer playing the role of catalyst (Wang and Yan, 2012, p. 234). However, this needs to be done with tact, to secure the validity of the interview material. As Morse (2012, p. 194) puts it, "the researcher's goal is to obtain the participant's perspective without 'leading' the participant." This influence can however take place outside the awareness of all parts. Interviewees can orient themselves towards the researcher's authority and judgement, even before the interview has even started, and hence may produce data that bears the mark of the interviewer or the research agenda. To counteract this tendency, establishing a rapport with informants is recommended as a way of creating a more symmetrical relationship with the interviewee, hence increasing validity (Schrøder, et al., 2003).

However, this threat to validity is not simply dependent on the good will and openness of the interviewer towards the interviewee. Fundamentally, the problem rests on the very structure of the interview as question and answer. It is indeed important that the interviewer remains in its role as a questioner; the interview would be otherwise purposeless if the interviewee were to ask the questions. For Finlay (2012), the control authorised by the structure of the interview is such that the narratives told by the interviewee are always done within the constraints of the researcher's questions and reactions. According to Potter and Hepburn (2012), the traditional interview may lead to what they call 'flooding', that is when the agenda of the researcher sneaks itself into the interview situation, leading the analysis to be circular. To increase validity in the interpretation of interview material, it is therefore recommended that both answers and questions appear in the reporting of data so that answers can be properly interpreted in their interactional context (Potter and Hepburn, 2012).

The threats to the validity of the interview have implications for the way knowledge produced by this method relates to context. In the following, we suggest two approaches that are aligned along postmodern trends in interview research. Yet, we wish to relate these developments more directly to audience studies, and hence, our suggestions will consider specifically their implications for the study of context. Michael Ian Borer and Andrea Fontana (2012) summarise the shift from a modern interview towards new approaches that aim to rethink the existing rules of the game:

> One change from traditional to postmodern-informed interviewing is that the so-called detached researcher and interviewer are recast as

active agents in the interview process and attempts are made to de-privilege their agency. Another shift is that the interviewee's agency is privileged and in the name of the interviewee all manner of experimentation is undertaken to make evident his or her own sense of identity and representational practices.

(2012, p. 49)

The goal of our two approaches is to 'de-privilege' the agency of the researcher and privilege the agency of the participants with regard to context. That is we believe that context is not simply an objective category of analysis informing qualitative enquiry but is a reality of audiences that only they are in position to inform. Thus, access to context for participants in the interview situation needs to be given priority. In the traditional interview, this access has been approached as a discursive co-construction between the interviewer and the interviewee, in which language is the medium by which context comes into being as a reality for research. Agency is shared with the researcher and is constrained by the structure and interaction of the interview as question and answer.

THE PERFORMATIVE INTERVIEW

Looking at the interview as a performance is a rather recent perspective in the literature about the qualitative interview. Potter and Hepburn (2012) advise clarity about the tasks interviewees are asked to perform. In experimental research, *orienting tasks* often constitute an experimental condition, alongside the more classic variables vulnerable to manipulation such as the text or the subjects (Jenkins, 1979). Manipulation is, however, viewed with suspicion in qualitative research and the fact that the performance of interviewees is, explicitly or implicitly, oriented by the interviewer is not fully recognised, nor appreciated. In fact, a performance from the part of the interviewees would be understood negatively and therefore repressed, because it is often the goal of phenomenologically oriented interviews to obtain a natural or authentic situation to motivate the interviewees to reveal their private lifeworld. Thus, the performance of roles, identities or practices that do not reflect the reality outside the interview situation is seen as a threat to validity.

There remains, however, a *performative ambiguity* with regard to interview findings that is often not addressed. It is not always clear 'who' or 'what' is being performed, the performance can be oriented by the structure or the interaction of the interview, and failing to recognise these features of the research interview may indeed constitute the real threat to validity. For example it is not always clear what distinctions or implications have to be made when asking recipients to 'talk about', 'report', 'comprehend', 'memorise', 'interpret' or 'retell' media content, nor are the different identities endorsed by the recipients in an interview always made explicit. For instance, the seminal study of Liebes and Katz (1990), which compared the reception of the television programme *Dallas* in different cultural communities, cast recipients into national groups of friends, assuming the performance of social negotiation of meaning, without rendering explicit issues of memorisation in the retelling of the programme, nor gender identities in the formation of the focus groups.

In a study dedicated to investigating the processes of news comprehension, the performative aspect of the interview was not only acknowledged but also made a central element of enquiry. To explore comprehension, the interview method was adapted to follow closely the interviewees as they were reading whole news texts and probe them about different aspects of their process of comprehension. The project stressed the role of culture in the mind of individual recipients or "the ways in which we carry society and history in the mind, as we interact with media" (Jensen, 2002, p. 38). This objective posed unusual challenges for reception analysis, which were addressed by setting up a cross-cultural comparison of the comprehension processes of ten Danish and ten Canadian recipients, recruited among university students, who were reading news texts from both countries. In all, twenty recipients were asked to perform comprehension as a basis for an interview that aimed to explore the contribution of recipients to what is comprehended (and miscomprehended) in a news text, and especially the cultural dimension of comprehension.

The perfomative aspect of the interview was clarified with the interviewees, who were explicitly informed about the goal of the study as well as its method. A substantial part of the briefing of the interview served to explain and train the participants in the method, to clarify the task to be performed. That is, the performance was disambiguated both in relation to the method, its objectives, as well as through a rehearsal of the performance as a prelude to the interview, thus providing possibility for the interviewees to familiarise themselves with their expected performance.

The study articulated a specific methodology to the study of context, based on the idea that contexts are something that recipients articulate themselves in their reception of mediated discourse, rather than something that needs to be identified by the researcher. The *received view*, in which context is regarded as deterministic and given (van Dijk, 2008; 2009), gives the impression that context is objectively retrievable by the analyst. Rather, in considering context as reflexively formed by participants themselves in the course of their activity (Houde, et al., 1998, pp. 113–114), analysts do not need to involve their assumptions about what constitutes a relevant context (Silverman, 1993 [2011], pp. 10–11)—hence in effect making their own reading/analysis of the text (Schrøder, 2000). Instead, they need to attend to the 'analysis' that actual recipients make of the text, as a way to investigate the contexts used by these recipients.

Central to this discussion is the distinction between context as constructed by analysts and context as constructed by recipients. There is a tendency to blur the borders between these two categories of context in the traditional interview, given that accountability is shared and knowledge co-constructed. In this study, context was seen as a resource, an "ethnomethod" (Garfinkel, 1967) used by recipients to make sense of texts, and a main goal of the methodology was to avoid and counteract the influence of the analyst's contexts. In a critique of discourse analysis that is also relevant to media reception, Schegloff (1997, p. 167) urges to make space in analysis for the "endogenous orientations of the participants", to develop methods that can provide such a space and to interpret data in a way that is constrained by those orientations. For these reasons, the interview was turned into a performance as a way to create a commitment to attend to the orientations of recipients towards the text, and effort was invested to maintain a clear distinction between the two categories of context.

In this study, the interview was regarded as an online method (Findahl, 2001) in which it was important to follow closely the reading process in order to capture this dynamic feature of recipients' context. The interview, adapted from the think-aloud protocol (Schaap, 2001), consisted in generating reading protocols by following closely the reading of two news texts, paragraph by paragraph, and probing for comprehension. Both groups read a news text concerning politics from each country; that is each recipient was interviewed on their reading of two news texts, one from Canada and another from Denmark, thus allowing comparison across groups and across texts. Although the objective of the interview brought an artificial focus on comprehension, special attention was paid to let recipients report, from their own perspective, on their contextualisation in their attempt to make the text meaningful. By the interviewer's asking recipients to report on what they find relevant, as a starting point for probing comprehension, the interviewees are cast as active subjects of knowledge production in the interaction.

The interview method considered under the idea of a performance is the extension of the way the method is used within the methodology of reception analysis, in that its aim is to grasp the context of reception of a text (Mathieu, 2012), but it is also influenced by experimental psychology, with its focus on processes. As such, the approach expands considerably, reflecting on and providing insights on the performance involved in a situation of reception, hence pushing the boundaries of the interview as traditionally used within reception analysis. Similarly, the performative interview distinguishes itself from a classic experiment in that it still makes use of questions and answers to structure the interaction and of language in its mode of knowledge production. But contrary to the experiment, the performative interview retains one main advantage of the interview method, namely its openness towards the recipients' own point of view or "emic" perspective (Pike, 1967, cited in Schrøder, et al., 2003, p. 81). Yet, this emic perspective is supported and anchored in a performance, which can be said to provide an experimental character to its study.

An understanding and articulation of comprehension as performance brings a fresher approach to the study of cognition. Although experimental psychology has an interest in looking into the 'black box' of the mind, this does not need to be understood as the opening of peoples' heads or an exercise in mind reading, as has been suggested by criticisms of the cognitive paradigm. Rather, the black box of the mind is the analysis itself, and this analysis is constructed by setting the stage for a performance, in this case, the comprehension of news. The conceptualisation of the interview as a performance was indeed a useful way to rethink the study of cognition, and in particular, comprehension, within a constructionist epistemology of research.

This form of interviewing recognises the constructive character of the performance that is asked of the interviewee, and as such acknowledges the constructionist epistemology at the basis of reception research, as an application of the "observer's paradox" (Labov, 1972 cited in Schrøder, et al, 2003, p. 16). The study of comprehension is articulated precisely by setting the stage for its performance, which creates a specific methodological position for the data. As the performance becomes part of the conditions of enquiry, it is important to keep this aspect in mind during the interpretation of data. That is interview data need to be understood as a performance.

In this study on news comprehension, the think-aloud interview influenced the performance of comprehension and therefore, the knowledge produced could not be used to assess levels or depths of comprehension among the audience of news outside the interview situation. Rather than using the data to make inferences about the significance of the performance outside the interview, the data needed to be interpreted for what they revealed in the here and now, as a "specimen interview" (Alasuutari, 1995). As such, the performative interview is better suited to study the resources behind a performance, rather than to assess the performance itself.

A main objective of this study of news comprehension was to understand the contextual contribution of the recipients to textual meaning, and especially the cultural dimension of this contribution. The comparison of the performance of the two groups served as an interpretative procedure for an analysis of the implicit dimension of culture. That is the strategy aimed at making culture 'visible' in a way that resembles a "breaching experiment" (Garfinkel, 1967). The cross-cultural comparison aimed to systematically confront recipients with media discourse not intended for them as a way to investigate the elements of taken-for-grantedness in the comprehension of the group for which the discourse was intended. By comparing reading protocols to each other, the interpretation of data was properly anchored, and hence constrained, by the endogenous orientations of the recipients towards the text, as recommended by Schegloff (1997). In doing so, the performances were evaluated against each other, rather than for what they say about a reality outside the interview situation.

THE PARTICIPATORY INTERVIEW

Participatory interviews are those that offer participants an active role in the very process of the research, challenging and possibly changing the initial proposals and assumptions of the research. Participants can have such an active role in two ways. First, they contribute to the selection of issues. Their reflections and opinions on the research process (captured during interviews with the researcher) may change the course of the research. Second, they can reverse the roles in their interviews, becoming interviewers themselves and by doing so contribute to the research process and help capture context outside the primary research sample (see Table 3.1).

In both cases, the relationship of the researcher with the individual participants is critical. It is equally important to ensure the participants' understanding of the basis on which they take part in the research and to maintain their interest throughout (Kellett, 2009, p. 399). Interviewing becomes a collaborative and participatory task (Holstein and Gubrium, 1995, p. 4). In everyday life, we are always asking questions either in an informal way or in the media, in what Silverman (1993 [2011], p. 54) calls the "interview society". Even though research traditionally depends on using a formal question–answer model for its credibility, a more informal, although still critical and scientific, approach can be fruitful. The interview can escape from its normal boundaries and enter into other social dimensions.

The research for which the participatory interview was developed relied on a sample of ten youths selected from a larger group of thirty-five who participated in a Portuguese longitudinal research study from 2010 to 2011 on youth, journalism, and participation. The first group of thirty-five interviews was carried out between March and October 2010; the second group of interviews (with thirty of the initial interviewees) followed in January and February 2011, and small focus groups occurred between September and November 2011.

This part of the chapter focuses on ten young participants, aged from fourteen to eighteen, with varying experiences of participation from traditional to non-traditional forms. The intention was to address media culture "all in all", as proposed by Pertti Alasuutari (1999, p. 16), which means inside the context of social reality, freely considering the possibility of the multiple dimensions, impacts, uses and productions. The participatory actions of the youths were investigated along two task dimensions: (1) by asking them to reflect on the process of the research and media consumption and production, using these reflections as a dynamic process within the research, and (2) by asking them to conduct mini interviews and contribute actively to the research, turning interviewees into interviewers (see Table 3.1).

By expanding the boundaries of the interview process to reach a broader context for the interview method, the research was opened to participatory actions and reflections in the process of meaning making. Participants construct their own contexts for producing meaning about the research and

Table 3.1 Tasks and Roles in the Participatory Process

Task dimensions	Participatory role
1. Reflecting on the process of the research and associated connections to media consumption and production. The reflections contribute to the process of the research	• Suggest opportunities for the research • Future strategies • Relationship between researchers and participants
2. Conducting mini interviews with other youths outside the research sample–becoming interviewers	• Choose interviewees • Choose questions • Reflect on results

the media. Given this dynamic one of the challenges facing participatory interviews was to keep participants interested in the research (Bagnoli and Clark, 2010), not only by encouraging them to comment beyond the simple question–answer model but also by asking them to maintain their participation over time.

Incorporating the reflections of the participants into the research process can be seen as an opportunity for the research to move into directions that were not preordained and to capture the contexts of daily life of the audience in a mediated society. This was clear for the participants, because they knew the roles assigned to them from the beginning of the process. The relationship between the research and the participants was constructed from the beginning around the idea that participants were free to fill out ideas, ask questions, and interact well beyond the traditional model of question–interviewer/answer–interviewee. Here we must note that the promise of this relationship was fulfilled during the interview process by giving participants the chance to provide their opinion about the research and about how it influenced them.

Participants discussed media impact on their lives. They reported using the media extensively (not only for consumption) and spoke about their experience from the perspective of issues that go far beyond the media itself. For example participants were quite reflexive (far more so than the question–answer model would allow them to be) when discussing what they remembered, the settings (most recollections referred to the family environment) and the way some of them emphasised their critical views of news coverage. Among the more reflective and connected participants, there was no change in habits but, rather, a deeper understanding of their activity, because they always found reflection a relevant way to participate and express their views.

One of the major changes that occurred during the interviewing process and that benefitted from the active participation of the youths was the reconsideration of the relevance of family in the mediatised process of their lives. Although this theme was not brought up by the researcher as a starting point, the second interview focused extensively on the family settings of media appropriations. This happened because, during the first interview, participants attributed a significant relevance to the subject. This change in the research agenda was presented to them in the second round of interviews as being the direct outcome of their active contribution. In going further than the traditional question-and-answer model of interviewing, 'asking' becomes for the interviewer a way of 'listening', which provides opportunities of change in the research model that are to be attributed to the participants.

As part of the second dimension of investigation, interviewees became interviewers as they were invited to go into the field and implement their own small case studies. Participants were asked to conduct a small-scale research project by asking other young people questions about youth, journalism, and participation. Because this process was exploratory, they could opt to write down the interviews, to tape them or to simply take notes. Involving youth in researching the views of other youth can be an important element in participatory research undertakings (Higgins, Nairn and Sligo, 2007, p. 110). Wijnen and Trültzsch (2004, p. 77), who have been doing participatory action research with young people, refer to the role of youngsters as "assistant researchers". Compared to the traditional model controlled only by the researcher, an element of unpredictability situates participants within the research, challenging canonical research procedures and prompting informative discussions with researchers. Participants are asked to take the responsibility in assembling their own relevant sample and leading the discussion. After having completed the mini interviews (acting as quasi-researchers), participants took part in focus groups where they discussed the mini interviews and the issues that were discussed previously in individual interviews with the researcher concerning journalism and participation. Strong from their experience, participants could reflect about the results obtained in relation to the process of conducting interviews, a new activity for them. This participatory process allowed a more valid and reflexive assessment of the context of media use. The reference to the interview participants as quasi-researchers intends to identify processes in which young people make some of the scientific work that usually is conducted by the researcher (in this case, the participants made small scale interviews and actively contributed to the reflexivity of the research). The expression 'quasi' is used because the youngsters conducted an activity that is close to the research-making process while the researcher still played the relevant part in the integration of the analysis to the whole process, such that the youngsters are not really researchers.

The context of media use is closely related to processes of identity construction. Considering the impact of socialisation through research, it was noted that one of the participants—a girl—was very pleased to have an excuse to talk to her peers at school about participation in society, to hear their opinions and to try to politicise them. Another example is provided by a group of young boys who had reported to having a close relationship and identification with their mothers and grandparents. Although these boys were asked to only talk with other youths (mostly at school and with friends), they chose to talk with their families in addition to their peers. In some cases, they also talked with political party peers, thus intensifying their political identities. They used the research challenge to confront their family members with the notion of identity as it relates to the political environment, capturing what they called generational differences in media uses and in issues of interest (such as talking about censorship before the Carnation Revolution in Portugal, in 1974). With this approach, it was possible to understand the participants' use of the media in relation to contextual factors such as their grandparents' media practices or to relate the media coverage of the 2010–2011 protests to historical experiences of media and social change.

Their participation in the research was considered a very important moment for them, as they were able to report, reflect on and contextualise their choices and the results. The interviews gave them a sense of self-empowerment, allowing them to talk about different issues with their peers. This articulation of the interview model beyond the traditional question–answer format gave a better understanding of the research and gave insights into news media audience research that went far beyond the preconceived models of news and media consumption and production by young people.

In spite of the deep involvement of the researcher and participants in the participatory model, there was no intention of doing ethnographic research. Nevertheless, the close collaboration among all involved in the research is a model that can capture audiences in the context of daily life and identities in a way that the traditional model of interviewing cannot reach. Today media is an intensely integrated artefact in our lives which demands improvements in the models of research.

CONDENSATION OF INSIGHTS

In the following table (see Table 3.2), we attempt to schematise the lessons learned from the previous presentation of the two interview models. We hope that this schematisation provides additional methodological guidance to conducting interviews in audience research and equips researchers with concrete ways to position their own use of the interview as it relates to the study of context, be it the contexts of interpretation in media reception or the contexts of media use. These suggestions should be considered with reference to the study of context, and hence to the production of knowledge about context through the interview method, and not as comments on the interview method in general or as tailored in other disciplines.

This section presents insights that concern (1) the catalyst behind the production of interview statements, that is what these statements depend

Table 3.2 Types of Interview and Features of the Interview

Types/Features	Traditional	Performative	Participatory
Catalyst	Question	Orientation	Reflexivity
Knowledge production	Passive	Active	Active
Context	Discursive/socio-demographic	Resource/cognitive	Practice/everyday life
Validity	Rapport	Rendition	Motivation

on; (2) the interviewee as an active or passive subject of knowledge production about context through the structure and interaction of the interview method; (3) the way context is generated in different forms of interview; and (4) the type of validity concerned in each interview type.

The Dependency of Interview Statements

In the traditional semi-structured interview, it is evident that the answers provided by the interviewee are dependent on the questions asked by the interviewer. To increase validity, interview statements must be motivated by factors other than the research agenda and be aligned to the lifeworld of the interviewee. We believe that both performative and participatory interviews offer an alternative catalyst to the production of meaningful interview statements. In their own way, both these approaches argue that it is important for the 'participant-*cum*-audience' to be 'there' when and where context matters, rather than to instantiate audience context within a research discourse.

In the performative interview, interview statements are dependent on emic tasks performed by the interviewees themselves. In reporting about their comprehension, interviewees identify what becomes the object of questions, or more precisely the object of prompts that aim at exploring the sociocultural contexts that motivated these judgments of relevance on the text.

In the participatory interview, interview statements are the outcome of a process of enquiry by the interviewee, who plays the role of quasi-researcher. Interview statements are dependent on the reflexivity and practical contribution of participants to the development of the research, using their primary access to real-life contexts where they act as audiences. The reflexivity occurs when participants make comments about the research in light of their own life contexts and when they report on their mini interviews.

The Interviewee as an Active Subject of the Interview

The traditional interview tends to cast the participant as a passive subject of knowledge production and more specifically as the object of questions. The two suggestions that we make allow for recasting the research participant as an active subject of knowledge production with regard to context.

The traditional interview does not appreciate the role that interaction makes (or can make) in the production of knowledge (Holstein and Gubrium, 1995; Potter and Hepburn, 2012). In the performative interview, participants are given agency in the interaction, in assessing what is being comprehended and in which contexts. The participants are in charge of reporting what is of interest in the text and why. As such, they could be said to be taking interactional control of the topic of the interview, providing an essential dimension to the study, namely their own emic perspective on comprehension. Interactionally speaking, interviewees become the initiators of questions and are not simply cast in the role of respondent. Participants in the performative interview become the interactional subject of questions and hence active producers of knowledge about the contexts that are relied on in the reception situation.

The participatory model positions the participant as an active subject in relation to the structure of the interview. The interviewee is considered an active subject of the research and can contribute to decisions about the research. Participants also produce knowledge by bringing their social context into the research, for instance, by implementing their own small-scale interviews and by making suggestions and comments on the development of the research. The audience is, in this case, active in setting the agenda for the research.

The Generation of Context

In the traditional interview, knowledge about context is discursively generated through language and negotiation with the interviewer, and hence, the role of the research subject is often that of an informant. We want to argue that the production of knowledge about context may also depend on other 'realities' than language or discourse.

In the performative interview, the production of knowledge about context is attached to a task that the interviewee performs during the interview. Context is generated spontaneously through the performance of the interviewee and it is the orientation of the recipients towards the text that provides a point of entry for the study of context. Context is here conceptualised as a cognitive construct produced by recipients in their online reception of mediated texts. This conception sees context as a resource that incorporates and mobilises 'society' in its individual and cognitive encounter with mediated texts.

In the participatory interview, by contrast, the researcher sends the participants into the realm of everyday life and asks them to capture context in its widest expression regarding news and participation. The reliance on mini interviews behind the frontier of the traditional interview process (researcher–participant) provides insight from different settings and different audiences. The researcher can benefit from the questions and answers implemented in different and differentiated contexts of the audience (schools, home and work, among others) without having to go there as an outsider. Participants can act as quasi-researchers in their own communities and daily lives.

The Type of Validity Involved in the Interview

In the traditional interview, the validity of interview material depends on whether or not interviewees are honest or accurate in their reporting of their lived experience. Hence, the relationship or *rapport* between the interviewer and interviewees is seen as a remedy for validity threats in interview research (Alasuutari, 1995; Schrøder, et al., 2003). Rapport is also important in the performative and participatory interviews, but we want to argue that these types of interview rest crucially on a different form of validity.

In the performative interview, there is the possibility that the interviewee over- or underperforms. Just as in a theatre performance, interviewees may suffer stage fright, may feel uncomfortable with their role or miscomprehend aspects of their performance, and these are threats to the validity of the knowledge produced. Here, the researcher can exhibit skills at 'directing' as a way to address these validity threats. One remedy is indeed to be clear about the task that the interviewee needs to perform. Additionally, it is crucial to understand and acknowledge in analysis the position that the performance creates for the knowledge produced. This type of interview is especially suited to the study of the resources motivating a performance, such as the study of the contexts of reception of the audience, rather than using the performance as the sole source of inference. Indeed, performances are likely to be unique and therefore not equivalent. It is therefore difficult to compare or aggregate these performances into anonymous summaries, or to use these performances as indications of practices in the lifeworld of the interviewees.

The participatory interview model emphasises the need to capture audience attention toward the research issues so that the participants can feel more comfortable with the scientific model. This emerging approach to reception and media studies is useful because it provides tools to capture less biased reports and reflexivity in social context. Participants have a broader opportunity to contribute more actively to the research and this possibility keeps them interested and motivated.

CONCLUSION

Context is a difficult reality to grasp in any single study. What is certain is that more reflections and more explicit considerations have to be debated in audience research regarding the notion of context. No matter what approach to context is adopted, it is important to assess the methodological status of context with regard to the audience and to the researcher. We hope that the criteria provided earlier can help further researches in positioning their methodology towards this crucial notion of context that in many ways defines the essence of our field.

These proposals for interviewing are no substitute for ethnographic fieldwork, as the research remains confined to the interview situation and does not involve a close presence of the researcher in the field. Yet, these suggestions go far beyond the traditional interview process, without neglecting the benefits of the interview. The interview method remains an important tool to understand practices and behaviours through audience discourse, but our suggestions push the boundaries of the question–answer model further, creating more fluid and extensive research contexts for the interview to take place.

While the research interview traditionally provided a discursive space under the control of the questioning engine personified by the researcher, and needed to be analysed by discursive means, our suggestions open up new forms of analysis, new interpretations of the field and new uses of the interview method. Our recommendations render more explicit the linkage of the interview method with the field of audience research, whether this happens through a cognitive perspective or a focus on everyday life. Note here that the phenomena under analysis are not simply a topic of the interview but are an integral part of the interview process. Our suggestions not only provide a better anchoring of audience discourse in the realities of the field but also broaden our understanding of the ways audience discourse can and cannot inform research. Working towards situating audience discourse in the realities of the field appears necessary in an age in which media are increasingly an integrated part of our life.

In this chapter, the adaptation of the interview towards the needs of audience research has been conducted with the intention to capture the contexts of the audience. These suggestions also result in creating different 'research contexts' (participatory, performative), whose relationship with the contexts of the audience is more explicit. While we should not be naïve to believe in a fusion of research context with audience context—and this could be a prime epistemological difference between the interview approach and the ethnographic ambition—it is clear that the contexts of research made possible by the interview method gain in being embedded in the contexts of the audience in a multitude of ways. We have suggested two ways to achieve this, but these are two possibilities amongst many.

NOTE

1. A defining feature of the research interview remains the question-answer process. Even disguised as a conversation, the interview will always find its impulse in the questions of the researcher and the discourse of the interviewee will always find its value as an answer to these questions (Kvale, 1996, pp. 5–6). See the *SAGE Handbook of Interview Research* (Gubrium, et al., 2012) for further discussions concerning the connection of the interview with the activity of questioning, in particular the contributions of Wang and Yan as well as Potter and Hepburn.

REFERENCES

Alasuutari, P., 1995. *Researching culture. Qualitative method and cultural studies.* London: Sage.
Alasuutari, P., 1999. Introduction. In: P. Alasuutari, ed. 1999. *Rethinking the media audience. The new agenda.* London, Thousand Oaks, New Delhi: Sage. pp. 1–21.
Bagnoli, A. and Clark, A., 2010. Focus groups with young people: a participatory approach to research planning. *Journal of Youth Studies* 13(1), pp. 101–119.
Borer, M.I. and Fontana, A., 2012. Postmodern trends: Expanding the horizons of interviewing practices and epistemologies. In: J.F. Gubrium, J.A. Holstein, A.B. Marvasti and K.D. McKinney, eds. 2012. *The SAGE handbook of interview research: the complexity of the craft.* Thousand Oaks: Sage. pp. 45–61.
Corner, J., 1991. Meaning, genre, and context: the problematics of 'public knowledge' in the new audience studies. In: J. Curran and M. Gurevitch, eds. 1991. *Mass media and society.* London: Edward Arnold. pp. 267–284
Duranti, A. and Goodwin, C., 1992. *Rethinking context: language as an interactive phenomenon.* Cambridge: Cambridge University Press.
Findahl, O., 2001. News in our minds. In: K. Renckstorf, D. McQuail and N. Jankowski, eds. 2001. *Television news research: recent European approaches and findings.* London: Quintessence. pp. 111–127.
Finlay, L., 2012. Five lenses for the reflexive interviewer. In: J.F. Gubrium, J.A. Holstein, A.B. Marvasti and K.D. McKinney, eds. 2012. *The SAGE handbook of interview research: the complexity of the craft.* Thousand Oaks: Sage. pp. 317–333.
Garfinkel, H., 1967. *Studies in ethnomethodology.* Englewood Cliffs: Prentice Hall.
Ghiglione, R. and B. Matalon 1977 [2005]. *O inquérito.* Oeiras: Celta Editora.
Goffman, E., 1981. *Forms of talk.* Oxford: Basil Blackwell.
Gubrium, J.F., Holstein, J.A., Marvasti, A.B. and McKinney, K.D., eds., 2012. *The Sage Handbook of Interview Research.* London: Sage.
Hammersley, M., 2008. Context and contextuality. *The SAGE encyclopedia of qualitative research methods.* Los Angeles: Sage Publications [online]. Available at: <http://www.sage-ereference.com/view/research/n66.xml>.
Higgins, J., Nairn, K. and Sligo, J., 2007. Peer research with youth: negotiating (sub) cultural capital, place and participation in Aotearoa/New Zealand. In: S. Kindon, R. Pain and M. Kesby, eds. 2008. *Participatory action research, approaches and methods: connecting people, participation and place.* London and New York: Routledge. pp. 104–111.
Holstein, J.A. and Gubrium, J.F., 1995. *The active interview.* Thousand Oaks, London and New Delhi: Sage.
Houde, O., Kayser, D., Koenig, O., Proust, J. and Rastier, F., 1998. *Vocabulaire de sciences cognitives.* Paris: Presses Universitaires de France.
Jenkins, J.J., 1979. Four points to remember: a tetrahedral model of memory experiments. In: L.S. Cermak and F.I.M. Craik, eds. 1979. *Levels of processing in human memory.* Hillsdale: Lawrence Erlbaum Associates. pp. 429–446.
Jensen, K.B., 2002. *A handbook of media and communication research. Qualitative and quantitative methodologies.* London: Routledge.
Kellett, M., 2009. Children as researchers: what we can learn from them about the impact of poverty on literacy opportunities? *International Journal of Inclusive Education* 13(4), pp. 395–408.
Kvale, S., 1996. *Interviews. An introduction to qualitative research interviewing.* London: Sage.
Liebes, T. and Katz, E., 1990. *The Export of Meaning: Cross-Cultural Readings of Dallas.* Oxford: Oxford University Press.

Lunt, P. and Livingstone, S., 1996. Rethinking the focus group in media and communications research. *Journal of Communication* 46(2), pp. 79–98.
Mathieu, D., 2012. A contextual approach to the mediation of news discourse. A cross-cultural reception study of news comprehension situated in language, culture and cognition. Ph.D. Roskilde University.
Morse, J. M., 2012. The implications of interview type and structure in mixed-method designs. In: J. F. Gubrium, J. A. Holstein, A. B. Marvasti and K. D. McKinney, eds. 2012. *The SAGE handbook of interview research: the complexity of the craft*. Thousand Oaks: Sage. pp. 193–206.
Potter J. and Hepburn, A., 2012. Eight challenges for interview researchers. In: J.F. Gubrium, J.A. Holstein, A.B. Marvasti and K.D. McKinney, eds. 2012. *The Sage handbook of interview research: the complexity of the craft*. Thousand Oaks: Sage. pp. 555–571.
Radway, J., 1984. *Reading the romance: women, patriarchy, and popular literature*. Chapel Hill: University of North Carolina Press.
Schaap, G., 2001. Using protocol analysis in television news research: proposal and first tests. *Communications* 26(4), pp. 443–463.
Schegloff, E. A., 1997. Whose text? Whose context? *Discourse & Society* 8(2), pp. 165–187.
Schrøder, K. C., 2000. Making sense of audience discourses. Towards a multidimensional model of mass media reception. *European Journal of Cultural Studies* 3(2), pp. 233–258.
Schrøder, K. C., Drotner, K., Kline, S. and Murray, C., (2003). *Researching audiences*. London: Arnold.
Silverman, D., 1993 [2011]. *Interpreting qualitative data*. London, Thousand Oaks, New Delhi and Singapore: Sage.
Silverman, D., 2005. *Doing qualitative research*. London: Sage.
Stenvoll, D. and Svensson, P., 2011. Contestable contexts: the transparent anchoring of contextualization in text-as-data. *Qualitative Research* 11, pp. 570–586.
van Dijk, T. A., 2008. *Discourse and context: a sociocognitive approach*. Cambridge: Cambridge University Press.
van Dijk, T. A., 2009. *Society and discourse: how social contexts influence text and talk*. Cambridge: Cambridge University Press.
Verschueren, J., 1999. *Understanding pragmatics*. London: Arnold.
Wang J. and Yan, Y. 2012. The interview question. In: J. F. Gubrium, J. A. Holstein, A. B. Marvasti and K. D. McKinney, eds. 2012. *The SAGE handbook of interview research: the complexity of the craft*. Thousand Oaks: Sage, pp. 231–243.
Widdowson, H.G., 2004. *Text, context, pretext. Critical issues in discourse analysis*. Oxford: Blackwell Publishing.
Wijnen, C. and Trültzsch, S., 2014. Participatory design as an innovative approach to research on young audiences. In: G. Patriarche, H. Bilandezic, J. L. Jensen and J. Jurisic, eds. 2013. *Audience research methodologies. Between innovation and consolidation*. London, Routledge. pp. 73–86.

4 Software Studies and the New Audiencehood of the Digital Ecology

Craig Hight

INTRODUCTION

Software studies, a comparatively new field of enquiry that Lev Manovich and others have championed (Johnson, 1997; Fuller, 2003; 2008; Manovich, 2008; 2013; Hawk, et al, 2008; Kitchin and Dodge, 2011), claims to offer a new paradigm for thinking through the increasing significance of software within contemporary society. We are, insist its adherents, living in a software-based culture, one which fundamentally shapes the practices of our institutions and is inherent to any number of social, political and economic practices central to our everyday lives. Software studies, however, is currently preoccupied with software at the level of code and interface and has comparatively little to say about the entanglement of users with software at a variety of levels within the digital ecology.[1] My contention is that the encounter between software studies and audience research would engender a broader field of research strategies for both. In this chapter, in particular the premise that the nature of audiencehood itself has changed within the contemporary digital environment is explored, in ways that has both conceptual and methodological implications for audience research design. The following discussion looks at some general qualities of software culture, in particular how cultural logics embedded within computer programming, the ways in we increasingly rely on these for everyday communication and how creative practices potentially reshape notions of literacy and agency. The final section suggests the significance of software at the level of content generation by users, using digital video as the example to illustrate the need for software studies–informed audience research into a variety of aspects of user engagement within the contemporary media environment.

THE SOFTWARE STUDIES PARADIGM

> I think of software as *a layer that permeates all areas of contemporary societies*. Therefore, if we want to understand contemporary techniques of control, communication, representation, simulation, analysis,

decision-making, memory, vision, writing, and interaction, our analysis can't be complete until we consider this software layer. Which means that all disciplines which deal with contemporary society and culture—architecture, design, art criticism, sociology, political science, humanities, science and technology studies, and so on—need to account for the role of software and its effects in whatever subjects they investigate.
(Manovich, 2008, p. 8, emphasis in original)

Software studies insist that 'software', which encompasses many forms of computer programming, is the dominant cultural technology of our time. Software applications run in the background of many of our key institutions and systems, from the bureaucratic systems of a hospital, the organization of schools, the increasingly sophisticated communication and targeting capabilities of the military, to the automated information and financial exchanges that drive global share markets. All media are now also organized through and governed by various forms of software applications. At the macro level this is manifest most obviously in the platforms of social media such as Facebook, Twitter and YouTube, but software is a more pervasive and layered cultural technology than this. Almost all forms of media production involve engagement with software interfaces. At an infrastructural level, the internet itself is organized through software-based protocols (Galloway, 2004) that govern processes such as "routing email messages, delivering Web pages from a server, switching network traffic, assigning IP addresses, and rendering Web pages in a browser" (Manovich, 2011, p. 2). At this level, software operates in ways that are largely automated and rarely visible to ordinary users, unless they fail.

A core premise of software studies is the need to move away from seeing software platforms and applications as neutral tools, as simply things that you do something with (Fuller, 2003, p. 16):

> Software is written by programmers, individually and in teams, within diverse social, political, and economic contexts. The production of software unfolds—programming is performative and negotiated and code is mutable. Software possesses secondary agency that engenders it with high technicity. As such, software needs to be understood as an actant in the world—it augments, supplements, mediates, and regulates our lives and opens up new possibilities—but not in a deterministic way. Rather, software is afforded power by a network of contingencies that allows it to do work in the world.
> (Kitchin and Dodge, 2011, pp. 43–44)

The study of software, then, partly involves investigating the cultural discourses that are embedded in code, together with the broader implications for users of how these discourses operate through the application of that code. Software is also an evolving part of culture, 'an essentially unfinished product, a continually updated, edited and reconstructed piece of machinery' (Berry, 2011, p. 39), with components that may have their own life cycle, break down or be recombined towards new ends (Berry, 2011, p. 42). Crucially, many software applications also foster other creative acts; as Kitchin and Dodge outline, "software is itself a medium for intellectual work and invention" (2011, p. 112). If we return to Livingstone's definition for media literacy as "the ability of access, analyse, evaluate and create messages in a variety of forms" (2004, p. 3), for example we need to recognise that these are all types of social practice that are now *coded* in the sense that they are embedded within and shaped by programming code, and are evolving in tandem with specific sets of software tools (we will return to notions of literacy below).

AFFORDANCES

Software studies itself is currently still focused very much on the logics embedded within software applications themselves,[2] rather than building convincing models of user understandings of these applications derived from empirical research. The value of this paradigm for audience researchers partly lies in the ways it can serve to highlight the field of possible actions and practices that computer programs serve to establish and foster for users.

Manovich for example uses the term *cultural software* to refer to those programmes which are "used to create and access media objects and environments" (2008, p. 13), which includes everything from consumer-level applications such as Microsoft's Office Suite, stand-alone professional media design and management applications such as Adobe's Creative Suite, internet browsers such as Firefox and Internet Explorer, tools for sharing commenting and editing provided by social media sites such as Facebook and YouTube and the numerous media viewing, editing, and sharing apps available on mobile platforms (Manovich, 2008, p. 13).

He has offered a breakdown of cultural software into specific actions, involving sets of applications that users may use across a number of platforms and devices. Collectively, this breakdown includes key facets of contemporary digital media:

1. Creating, sharing and accessing cultural artefacts which contain representations, ideas, beliefs, and aesthetic values (for example, editing a music video).
2. Engaging in interactive cultural experiences (for instance, playing a computer game).
3. Creating and sharing information and knowledge (such as writing an article for Wikipedia).
4. Communicating with other people (email, instant message, voice over IP, online text and video chat, or through the variety of functions provided within social networking).

5. Participating in [the] online information ecology (for example, clicking "+1" button in Google+ or 'Like' button in Facebook).
6. Developing software tools and services which support all these activities (for instance, programming a library for Processing which enables sending and receiving data over [the] internet). (Manovich, 2011, pp. 10–11)

This is not a list that touches all current media (it covers computer-based and especially networked media), but it does highlight the extent to which many everyday acts of communication, work and creativity are now 'coded'. It is useful to remember that the forms of software outlined earlier have evolved according to the 'economics of proprietary software', which demand regular updates for reasons that are independent of user demand (Fuller, 2003, p. 150). And, as van Dijck (2013) has outlined, this code is generated and governed by a comparatively small number of global media corporations within a broader ecosystem. Her research into the major social media platforms provides a valuable political economy of key parts of contemporary software culture, demonstrating that at this level code operates to provide a broader infrastructure of engagement, a set of 'givens' for how users can engage, participate and interact (e.g. Facebook's 'like' button, or the comments sections of YouTube).

As any regular software user knows, these are not necessarily tools designed to operate seamlessly together. Specific software applications are engineered within their own social, cultural and economic contexts, building from earlier forms of proprietary intellectual property, and are designed to cater to particular sets of assumptions about users. This variety of possible actions establishes an often confusing and difficult terrain that new users must negotiate (everything from understanding the conceptual model underpinning an interface, what actions are available, through to how to adapt default settings and so on).

For the user, each software platform or individual application 'affords' particular actions. McGrenere and Ho provide a useful definition of affordance, derived from a detailed critique of earlier work by Gibson and Norman among others:

> An affordance is an action possibility or an offering. Possible actions on a computer systems include physical interaction with devices such as the screen, keyboard, and mouse [. . .] The application software also provides possible actions. A word processor affords writing and editing at a high level, but it also affords clicking, scrolling, dragging and dropping. The functions that are invokable by the user are the affordances in software. Functions may include text-editing, searching, or drawing. The information that specifies these functions may be graphical (buttons, menus) or it may not exist at all.
>
> (2000, p. 6)

This notion of affordance applies to the interfaces and activities embedded within social media platforms, e-mail programmes, or computer games—these all provide software experiences within carefully designed parameters. If we look at a software application as providing a set of possible actions, then it is vital to map how these affordances appear within a specific hierarchy, with some made easily available to users, and how they are more generally organised to support or constrain what users can use that application for. At a more fundamental level, if we extrapolate from the set of affordances of groups of commonly used applications and begin to consider the kinds of practices which are supported and encouraged, we can start to envisage the challenge which programming code provides for audience researchers engaging with these forms of the media. What, for example, are the implications for users who only use a particular application, who may start to equate particular practices themselves with the set of affordances that a specific application provides? (And in some cases to determine the language used to describe actions; at what point did the verb *to Google* become a substitute for 'to use a search engine'?) In these terms, how each of the forms of software listed earlier appear to users, how their configuration of affordances are understood by different groups of users, and used within specific social, cultural, economic and political contexts, becomes of vital interest to contemporary media research.

CUT, COPY AND PASTE

It is also important to recognise how forms of creative activity are open to being refashioned within software culture, and often in fundamental ways. Translating any creative practice into programming code involves simulating the affordances of that practice, possibly augmenting that practice in some fashion (such as allowing greater speed), automating those aspects that can be distilled to a programmable logic (such as spell-checking), and carries the potential for a transformation of the nature of the very practice which is being simulated (whether it be mechanical or social). Automation, in particular, is a fundamental facet of software culture which facilitates the transformative potential of coded practices, as it involves allowing aspects of a practice to be translated into algorithmic form, and hence scaled up to whatever size is desired, limited only by available processing power. By combining different automated processes, sequentially or in parallel, software culture can start to exhibit practices that take on their own distinctive quality, and in ways that eventually become 'naturalised' for software users (Mackenzie, 2006, p. 44).

The broader history of the translation of creative practices into software, combined with the emergence of the personal computer from the 1970s onwards, have created the conditions for an under-researched but arguably profound transformation of the nature of creative endeavour itself.

If we consider the practice of writing, to take one obvious example, the transition from long hand to a 'cut, copy and paste' form of writing practice is arguably a key cultural moment. Word processing software became widely available from the early to mid-1980s, with the Microsoft Office package (Word, Excel and PowerPoint) beginning to dominate from the early 1990s (Baldwin, 2002). Johnson argues that word processing applications allow for a quicker, more conversational writing style, as they favour a trial-and-error approach derived from the ability to easily cut, copy and paste sections of texts (Johnson, 1997, pp. 142–143). Heim insists that this increased speed, together with the ability to have multiple windows open at once, has changed the ways in which we approach the task of writing, how we read and what we ultimately value in our reading (Heim, 1987, p. 192). Manovich suggests that such cut, copy and paste tools emerged as the perfect tools for a postmodern approach toward culture, as the sampling and remixing of online material became the default online creative practice (Manovich, 2001, pp. 130–131). Although intriguing, these are all conclusions that are still largely untested by empirical research.

The software studies paradigm argues that as particular affordances become familiar to users, and become naturalised to some extent within specific forms of practice, they can become associated with new ways of thinking. The repetition of cut, copy and paste as tools across a variety of pieces of software applications for example may have broader implications for how users conceive of the possibilities of creating media content, and even conceptualise what 'media' are (Manovich, 2013). Software studies as a field currently offers a provocative series of arguments for a shift not just in the specifics of social, economic, political and cultural practices, but for a series of possible conceptual shifts in these realms. To date, however, these are speculative conclusions generated from an analysis of the code, affordances and interfaces of software itself. The task of mapping how specific tools have been used within particular contexts, by specific groups of users, is something that has been largely neglected by researchers from the humanities and social sciences.

I argue here not only that software studies provides a convincing case for redefining 'audiencehood' in relation to software culture, but also that audience research in turn is necessary as an informant and corrective to the current preoccupations of software studies. Any attempt to derive user interpretations purely from a 'textual analysis' of software interfaces and affordances is of limited value. If we return to cut-copy-and-paste software, we can argue that the dominance of Microsoft Office as a suite of everyday media editors has obviously played out differently across a variety of institutional settings. For example there are debates over the significance of PowerPoint as a ubiquitous software tool across business and educational practices, although again these are currently informed more by rhetorical stance than detailed empirical research (Tufte, 2003; Doumont, 2005; Adams, 2006; Frommer, 2012). PowerPoint is a good example of software which has apparently 'captured' a large user base because it affords a variety of levels of practice; it is accessible to new users yet has the functionality to satisfy more frequent and proficient users (Tidwell, 2011, p. 8). Central to the 'seductive' power of software more broadly lies in the apparent ease with which it affords particular kinds of creative and communicative practice. But how do such affordances play out for users in different social, political economic and cultural contexts?

THE 'PERFORMANCE' OF SOFTWARE

We can characterise an individual user's encounters with individual software applications using a particular understanding of the notion of 'performance'. Drawing in particular from Brenda Laurel's (1992) work, Manovich (2008, p. 17) uses the term more generally to describe all of the ways in which we interact with cultural software. When using the most basic operations of a word processor, the application obviously informs and shapes how we perform options for navigating, editing and sharing of that content. And at the level of the operating system, opening programmes, opening files, selecting and opening files, resizing and moving windows, are all also actions waiting to be performed by the user. At this level of software (e.g. an individual user operating a PC), we can see that nothing happens without the active intervention of the user.[3] In this sense, a complex interplay between affordance and performance, which plays out each time a user engages with any application, is assumed.

The situation becomes more complicated at the 'macro' level of software culture. There are further aspects of the digital ecology that we need to recognise, and these complicate this initial definition of performance—just as they complicate notions of agency associated with the participation of users within contemporary media (van Dijck, 2009). Programming code needs to be understood as engendering 'both forces of empowerment and discipline', increasing efficiencies and productivity, generating entirely new markets and providing new forms of play but also providing "a broad range of technologies that more efficiently and successfully represent, collate, sort, categorize, match, profiles, and regulate people, processes, and places" (Kitchin and Dodge, 2011, pp. 10–11). This tension between 'empowerment' and 'discipline' offers a broad frame for understanding the layered and complex role which software plays at a variety of levels especially within networked media. In particular, we need to recognise the scale and implications of the automated systems that govern networked media:

> (1) in a way that is completely new, software allows the delegation of mental processes of high sophistication into computational systems. This instils a greater degree of agency into technical devices than could have been possible within mechanical systems; (2) networked software, in

particular, encourages a communicative environment of rapidly changing feedback mechanisms that tie humans and non-humans together into new aggregates. These then perform tasks, undertake incredible calculative feats, and mobilise and develop ideas at a much higher intensity than in a non-networked environment; (3) there is a greater use of embedded and quasi-visible technologies, leading to a rapid growth in the quantification that is taking place in society.

(Berry, 2011, p. 2)

User activity takes on multiple, complicated and unexpected dimensions within this kind of context. The software actants at this level may be considerably more autonomous and insistent than a single application on your machine waiting for commands. For example Bucher (2012) has usefully detailed the role which software design has in fundamentally shaping Facebook's notions of friendship and relationships, particularly with the key algorithms that serve as actors in encouraging, prompting and shaping specific forms of behaviour from the site's users. An integral aspect of Facebook, YouTube and other social media sites (as well as product-centred sites such as Amazon, iTunes and Netflix) are recommendation systems that rely on elaborate filtering mechanisms[4] to predict user preferences for products, content and even, in the case of Facebook, potential social relationships. Users play an integral (if often unintended) role here, as each online action is automatically collated and aggregated into data that is mined to generate relatively sophisticated patterns of collective behaviour (in this sense, we can see that the performance of software is a social activity which is fundamental to the operations of the online economy).

Manovich insists that there is a further distinction to be made here between the types of audience activities that are integral to the digital ecology, and those which more clearly characterised the mass media of the last century. He highlights the increasing kinds of media activity in which users' performance of software is integral to the ways in which content is generated in real time:

So whether we are exploring a dynamic web site, play a video game, or use an app on a mobile phone to locate particular places or friends nearby, we are engaging not with pre-defined static documents but with the dynamic outputs of a real-time computation happening on our device and/or the server. Computer programs can use a variety of components to create these performances: design templates, files stored on a local machine, media from the databases on the network server, the real-time input from a mouse, touch screen, joystick, our moving bodies, or another interface, etc.

(Manovich, 2012)

At the level of users' engagement with a screen, a number of core assumptions are of particular interest here. On desktop and laptop computers, mobile devices such as smartphones, and gaming platforms, we are assumed to increasingly engage less with content that can still be classified as media 'texts' and more with 'streams' of digitised content. Although in this particular quote Manovich is using a conception of performance that appears to give greater agency to the software itself than to users, this reflects some of the difficulties of talking about the agency of users in situations where we are responding to prompts from highly sophisticated, algorithmically based systems. The key claim of interest here is that user performance of software lies not just at the centre of how content is accessed but is crucial to understanding how that content itself is generated and effectively customised for each user. In a sense, each user's performance in this context serves to 'attract' particular data streams, tailored in their scale, intensity and specific content to that user.

These media processes obviously do not apply to all contemporary media, but they are nevertheless aspects of contemporary media technology which need to be accounted for in conceptual models of audience activity associated with software culture. And they immediately problematise those efforts to theorise whether engagement with digital media is inherently more 'active' or 'passive' than twentieth-century mass media, to revisit a familiar debate within audience research. In Berry's terms "the change represents a move from a notion of *information retrieval*, where a user would attend to a particular machine to extract data as and when it was required, to an *ecology of data streams* that forms an intensive information-rich computational environment" (Berry, 2011, p. 143, emphasis in original). Users within these networked environments are continually watching data flows, engaging with these directly to initiate the display of information on screens or delegating the collating and highlighting of particular data forms to algorithms or devices. In fact in many cases we are effectively serving as 'managers' of that content using the affordances of specific software applications, including assigning our own preferences or amending software defaults.

And, as suggested earlier, our actions in generating, engaging and participating with such content produces data streams ready, in turn, to be collated, analysed, aggregated and partially fed to other users. Berry argues that these real-time streams can be viewed as fragmentary, interrupted 'distributed narratives' that run across media and platforms (Berry, 2011, p. 145) but which are made coherent through our attention and interpretation. This involves a broader a model of user cognition, activity and agency which obviously moves beyond earlier conceptions of 'information literacy', or its expansion into notions of 'digital literacy' (Livingstone, et al., 2014).

SOFTWARE LITERACIES

To summarise the argument so far, we can derive from the core assumptions of the software studies paradigm the beginnings of a model of audiencehood which is of interest to audience researchers investigating the distinctive nature of how we participate with things digital and especially with networked media. At the centre of this model is the understanding that any implications of these forms of (digital) participation are inseparable from the manner and ways in which specific pieces of software, from platforms to individual applications, are actually performed through specific practices, in specific contexts, and by specific users.[5] Furthermore, we should recognise that software is always performed by users who bring their own media experiences, motivations and literacies into their encounters with specific software tools, in the pursuit of their own creative and communicative practices (this last point is a given for audience researchers but does not appear to be discussed widely within software studies literature). Ultimately this also implies investigating questions of agency (and its cultural and political implications) through exploring the empowering and disciplining possibilities of various forms of software across the diversity of social, cultural, economic and political contexts in which that software is performed by users.

To add more useful detail to the model of audiencehood outlined earlier, I would like to offer here a tentative schema for distinguishing between different forms of software literacy,[6] which can be added to and extend existing conceptions of digital and information literacies. This is a skills-based schema, but one which also anticipates that users can scaffold from a basic learning of skills to appreciate the configuration and especially limitations of specific tools, and potentially a broader awareness of software as a cultural artefact and how it might operate to support and constrain their own practices. This schema includes three levels:

1. A basic skill level, where a learner gains the ability to use a particular software for a specific purpose, to complete specific tasks (whether this is creating and editing a word processing document, editing and sharing a video or viewing and commenting on a YouTube video)
2. An ability to independently troubleshoot and problem solve issues faced when using a software application or engaging with a platform (which implies not only an autonomy and competence in using the software but also the ability to draw upon various resources to help solve difficulties)
3. And ultimately the ability to critique different forms of software, including being able to apply a similar analysis to a range of software designed for similar purposes and to incorporate these understandings toward new software learning (and potentially here, this might include an ability to source alternatives, such as pirated software, or open source variations of popular media editors, or alternative social media platforms)

In these terms, the most 'critically literate' users both develop the ability to identify the affordances of particular software tools and interfaces and are able to apply and extend their understandings to a range of purposes and contexts. In common with some conceptions of media literacy, there is also the assumption that users may become more 'empowered' through developing some understanding of how agency is coded in a broader sense. In other words, the more literate users are assumed to build towards an awareness of the role of software generally in creating a context and arena for their actions through hierarchies of affordances generated by applications, platforms and infrastructures.[7]

Users may acquire software literacies through a combination of any number of means; through trial and error, learning informally from peers and family, consulting online resources (such as YouTube video tutorials, to note a common method used by my students) or training in a more formal or structured way using manuals and technical support. Software literacy, then, is couched within a variety of social, technological, institutional and other contexts that have long been recognised in media literacy debates (Livingstone, et al., 2014). My own experience of teaching software in a tertiary environment suggests that most software learning occurs informally, with users developing skills in ad hoc and unstructured ways, prompted by immediate tasks and challenges and always shaped by a complex set of social factors. As with other forms of media literacy, there are complexities here that demand greater attention from researchers (e.g. I am constantly surprised by how often sophisticated software skills acquired by my students in one context are not necessarily easily and immediately transferable to other contexts involving different forms of software).

A broad assumption underlying this approach is that the nature of the software literacies which each user draws on for specific practices effectively serve to contextualize their agency. I see the dialectic between empowerment and discipline (outlined previously) playing out through these different levels of literacy: software literacies intimately inform whether, and to what extent, a particular piece of software serves to 'empower' or 'discipline' a user within a specific context. This can suffice as a broad hypothesis; however, there are nuances to the power relations between human and nonhuman actants that can only be teased out through detailed empirical research. To give an everyday classroom example, if a teacher using PowerPoint never moves beyond choosing the same built-in template and filling in its preselected bullet points, what does this suggest about her teaching practice? Is this teacher 'empowered' by this application, or has he or she been 'captured' by a subset of its affordances? How is the teacher's performance of this software in this instance shaped by his or her literacies and a variety of contextual factors?

To study the complexities of audiencehood within digital media, then, we need to acknowledge and include an investigation of the variety of factors which shapes users' contingent performances of specific pieces of software, as they are applied in pursuit of specific practices. There are obviously discursive, physical, affective, historical, and broader dimensions to the encounters between users and software which I have not mentioned.

For example users typically interface with this content through any number of input devices, but increasingly using those that mimic real life gestures, which appears to enhance and broaden the seductive appeal of engaging with software culture.[8]

SOFTWARE TOOLS AND DIGITAL VIDEO PRACTICES

To provide a more detailed and compelling illustration of the need for software-informed audience research, this final section discusses ongoing research exploring the explosive growth of online video, a key area of what is often termed 'user-generated' culture. The broader context for this growth is a digital video ecology fostered and facilitated by an array of technologies that include everything from search engines, RSS feeds, mobile devices for capturing and accessing media "and the technologies which enable transfer of media between devices, people, and the web" (Manovich, 2008, p. 33). This assemblage (DeLanda, 2006) of technologies has helped to create the conditions for a considerable increase in the actual volume of video footage which is being distributed, through platforms such as YouTube. The introduction of YouTube in 2005 is a key milestone in terms of online distribution, and an accelerant in the exchange of video by everyday users as the site in some sense has served as a giant community teaching itself how to upload and share content (Burgess and Green, 2009; Snickars and Vonderau, 2009; Strangelove, 2010).

Participatory culture more generally is currently characterised by expanding social practices of self-documentation, arising especially from the intersection of mobile devices, social networks and the variety of technologies which support, augment and exploit their capabilities. One prominent result is a proliferation of photographic and video 'documents' of the everyday; streams of visual and audio-visual material from a broad range of practitioners. In terms of video, the most common uploaded forms are reported to be within categories such as home videos, travel videos, and recordings of live performances or sporting events (Purcell, 2010). This wealth of user-generated material is designed to be shareable and inserted into the networked communities of users and is variously celebrated as a return to an imagined ideal of folk culture, condemned as evidence of a broader dilution of professional practices or viewed as symptomatic of conflicted labour relations within the digital economy.

I am interested in whether a broad range of users engaged in what Burgess (2006) terms "vernacular creativity" are sufficiently empowered by hardware and software tools to move beyond practices that simply produce documents of their immediate social experiences. In particular, under what conditions, and to what extent, are users able and encouraged to explore more deliberately motivated, diverse, layered and nuanced audio-visual constructions or those assumed to explore the language of moving images in coherent, purposeful and politically charged ways? The movement from simplistic documents to more 'edited' sequences is a crucial one here, as it suggests a transition to practices that are focused on creating content with an assumed audience broader than immediate personal networks, and designed toward wider social, cultural and political purposes (of the kind assumed in many media literacy debates over the nature of empowerment). Software has emerged as an actor of vital interest in this transition, and one whose role thus has obvious social, cultural and political significance.

Despite major changes in the technologies of moving image capturing, storage and distribution, a key technical constraint for budding videographers has long been the creative but laborious practice of editing. For example, Buckingham's 2005–2008 study into the use of camcorder technology in United Kingdom households offers some pointers to how time and motivation continue to serve as important constraints on the editing of video footage. Few of these projects' participants were motivated to either learn editing skills or apply them once they had acquired them (Buckingham, Willett and Pini, 2011). A feature of contemporary software culture, however, are large amounts of investment (including from software giants such as Google, Facebook and Apple) in entry-level editing tools that aim to lower the threshold for users wanting to move from rudimentary practices of capturing and uploading video documents to the building of more complex and deliberately designed moving image sequences. A key question driving this research, then is, 'What are the implications of emerging software tools, applications and infrastructures for digital videography?'

The field of video-editing applications is now considerable, numbering now hundreds of possibilities from professional editing software through to open-source variations of these, down through a variety of forms of consumer-directed software such as iMovie and Windows Moviemaker, to a plethora of smartphone apps operating at a more granular level and catering to low levels of skill and motivation. There is a proliferation of entry-level editing tools in particular, designed for novice video practitioners and ranging from low-budget, freeware and open-source applications available across various platforms (downloadable to desktop/laptop machines, bundled with camcorders, available as apps for smartphones or as cloud-based applications). Collectively, these have potentially profound implications for the development of online culture, in terms of the practices that are extended, reinforced or generated anew using these tools. A critical analysis of these tools offers some insights into broader patterns within software culture as a whole.

A key objective for the designers of entry-level editing software (aimed at consumers and 'prosumers') is how to provide an experience that is apparently effortless and capable of generating a completed video for sharing within short periods. The overall agenda here has consistently been on fostering the production of short videos typically constructed as a highlights package, perhaps set to music but always intended to be shared to friends through social networks. There are other more recent and overlapping experiments in software-based editing, including social editing (which distributes the labour of editing through social networks),[9] experiments with forms of fully automated editing (which cede the building of video sequences completely to algorithms)[10] and a variety of cloud-based online editing systems that overlap with the apps industry (which open possibilities for more collaborative networked practices).[11] These new assemblages suggest the variety of emerging practices that are *distinctive to software culture* (i.e. which do not have clear precedents in pre-software-based practices). There is not the space here to detail all of the changes which are occurring—and no doubt many of these would be out-dated by the time this is published—but a key point to emphasise is that these all feature a much reduced and streamlined conception of 'editing', and (most crucially) are facilitated by higher levels of automation than is typical of professional digital non-linear editing systems. Users' creative activity is channelled toward algorithmically driven practices that involve ceding creative control and agency to software at a variety of levels. Agency is currently being eroded not just at the level of software tools which the user can directly manipulate (e.g. the controls of specific smartphone apps) but occurs at deeper levels, through the coded logics governing everything from conversion to favoured codecs during upload, to constraints on image size and resolution, to the control of recommendation systems interlinked with platform-specific search engines.

Embedded within the affordances and interface design of individual consumer-level video tools is a relatively stable and insistent set of criteria for generating video material, one which meshes with those of common distribution platforms such as YouTube. Videos must be short in duration, immediately accessible (that is lacking in narrative complexity and peaking early) and essentially disposable. This overall ethos favours compressed forms of communication (video postcards) and, as with other forms of everyday documentation such as photographs, assumes that each individual item forms part of broader streams of online material competing for users' attention and is intended to be organised, tagged and commented on in online groupings (Reading, 2008).

This emerging digital video culture is only in its initial stages; despite the celebratory rhetoric associated with participatory culture (Jenkins, 2006; Johnson, 2001; Tapscott and Williams, 2006), there is still only a comparatively small percentage of online users that are actively engaged in creative production, that is who could be termed 'practitioners' in any sense. The choice of entry for video users appears to depend very much on levels of software literacy: competence and confidence in using software, knowledge of the possibilities of software generally and the ability to learn specific applications (formally or informally). Within this ecology, there is a vital need to understand the ways in which interaction with software at a variety of levels operates to inform, shape, empower and constrain emerging video practices. For example while it is now feasible for newly 'empowered' users to begin with rudimentary applications that generate moving image sequences, then 'graduate' to more sophisticated software packages, limited only by their ambitions and the more persistent constraints of cost and time, it is simply unknown whether this is in fact happening. It is also feasible that large groups of users will be seduced and captured by entry-level software tools, and effectively cede creative agency to various forms of algorithmic-based editing systems. At stake is the very nature and quality of the development of this part of 'cut, copy and paste' culture. What is the future for a user-generated (video) culture that is generated by these aggregates of human and non-human, entangled in structures of engagement provided by commercially driven software platforms? Obviously, any number of related questions here demand empirical research, because these broader currents will be determined partly by how users individually and collectively make sense of this environment and learn how to navigate the possibility spaces of software culture.

The objective of this chapter has been to outline a conceptual framework for a reconsideration of contemporary audiencehood, in the light of changes to the nature of (digital) media ecologies themselves. I have barely touched on the methodological implications of researching this new model of audiencehood, but for audience researchers this framework still generates a broad range of possibilities for quantitative and qualitative research projects which overlap with existing methodologies. Manovich (2012) has outlined methods for the automated 'tracking' of users' performances of software, an approach that holds the potential for scalability to a user population of dozens, or thousands or hundreds of thousands. This is an approach which is obviously conversant with the technology-centred data-gathering mechanisms that serve at the core of the business models of Google and Facebook themselves (Kirkpatrick, 2010; Levy, 2011). In contrast, van Dijck (2013) has collated and analysed online commentaries as evidence of user resistance to changes in the technologies used by Facebook and other key social media platforms, (or what she terms the "ecosystem of connective media").

For qualitative researchers more focused on the micro contexts of media practice, another approach might be software-centred ethnographic methodologies that involve engaging with individual users, or groups of users, to explore their perceptions of their own agency within software culture, including the manner in which they learn pieces of software, the factors which shape their performance of specific applications, and the extent to which they can appreciate and are able to critique their affordances. These examples, and the model of audiencehood outlined earlier, are obviously only broadly suggestive of a larger field of possible inquiry. My intention here is to encourage more explorative and innovative audience research design in recognition of new (expanded and reoriented) models of audiencehood which more accurately map changes in the nature of engagement and participation in the contemporary digital ecology.

NOTES

1. Adapting Fuller's (2005) outline of the term *media ecology*, I use the term *digital ecology* to refer to the broader ecosystem of media forms, platforms and infrastructures of digital media. In practice this encompasses almost all media forms, but I use this term to highlight the fact that the discussion in this chapter focuses specifically on media which are computer based.
2. For example Manovich (2013) has assigned himself the task of detailing key media editors in the professional field.
3. Our performances are also inevitably shaped by the *hardware* on which the software operates, and in fact many software ecosystems are designed to automatically reconfigure the interface and how it presents affordances to us based on the device we are using.
4. http://en.wikipedia.org/wiki/Recommender_system.
5. Kitchin and Dodge suggest the term *code/space* (2011, p. 16), insisting that engaging with code also has a spatial dimension, as software inevitably operates within time and space and has implications for people within time and space. I prefer the term *coded practice* because it is more centred on social, cultural and political actions.
6. This is a schema developed from my own experiences in teaching software, the findings from a number of eLearning research projects and a project funded by the Royal Society of New Zealand (which provides the case study outlined later in this chapter) that investigated online video through a combination of software analysis, textual analysis and audience research.
7. This draws on a notion of 'programmed agency', inspired by Bucher's (2012) notion of 'programmed sociality', in her analysis of Facebook.
8. Jacob, et al use the term *post-WIMP interfaces* as an umbrella to cover a range of new forms of interface which includes the gesture set for engaging with touch screens, or the physical movements that Wii gaming consoles demand (WIMP refers to Windows, Icons, Menus, Pointers and has served as the standard schema for operating systems and applications that employ a mouse and keyboard; Jacob, et al., 2008)
9. See WeVideo.com.
10. Such as Magisto.com.
11. See systems such as Vyclone.com.

REFERENCES

Adams, C., 2006. PowerPoint, habits of mind, and classroom culture. *Journal of Curriculum Studies* 38(4), pp. 389–411.

Baldwin, S., 2002. Purple dotted underlines: Microsoft word and the end of writing. *Afterimage* 3(1), pp. 6–7.

Berry, D., M., 2011. *The philosophy of software: code and mediation in the digital age*. Houndmills: Palgrave Macmillan.

Bucher, T., 2012. The friendship assemblage: investigating programmed sociality on Facebook, *Television & New Media* 14(1), pp. 479–493.

Buckingham, D., Willett, R. and Pini, M., 2011. *Home truths? Video production and domestic life*. Ann Arbor: University of Michigan Press.

Burgess, J., 2006. Hearing ordinary voices: cultural studies, vernacular creativity and digital storytelling. *Continuum: Journal of Media & Cultural Studies* 20(2), pp. 201–214.

Burgess, J. and Green, J., 2009. *YouTube: online video and participatory culture.* Cambridge, Polity Press.

DeLanda, M., 2006. *A new philosophy of society: assemblage theory and social complexity.* London: Continuum.

Doumont, J.-L., 2005. The cognitive style of PowerPoint: slides are not all evil. *Technical Communication* 52(1), pp. 64–70.

Frommer, F., 2012. *How PowerPoint makes you stupid: the faulty causality, sloppy logic, decontextualized data, and seductive showmanship that have taken over our thinking.* New York: The New Press.

Fuller, M., 2003. *Behind the blip: essays on the culture of software.* New York: Autonomedia.

Fuller, M., 2005. *Media ecologies: materialist energies in art and architecture.* Cambridge: MIT Press.

Fuller, M., ed., 2008. *Software studies: a lexicon.* Cambridge: The MIT Press.

Galloway, A.R., 2004. *Protocol: how control exists after decentralisation.* Cambridge: The MIT Press.

Hawk, B., Rieder, D.M. and Oviedo, O., eds. 2008. *Small tech: the culture of digital tools.* Minneapolis: University of Minnesota Press.

Heim, M., 1987. *Electric language: a philosophical study of word processing.* 2nd ed. New Haven: Yale University Press.

Jacob, R.J.K., Girouard, A., Hirshfield, L.M., Hom, M.S., Shaer, O., Solovey, E.T. and Zigelbaum, J., 2008. Reality-based interaction: a framework for post-WIMP interfaces. In: *CHI 2008 proceedings: Post-WIMP*, Florence, Italy, 5–10 April, 2008, p. 201.

Jenkins, H., 2006. *Convergence culture: where old and new media collide.* New York: New York University Press.

Johnson, S., 1997. *Interface culture: how new technology transforms the way we create and communicate.* New York: HarperCollins Publishers.

Johnson, S., 2001. *Emergence: the connected lives of ants, brains, cities and software.* London: Penguin Books.

Kitchin, R. and Dodge, M., 2011. *Code/space: software and everyday life.* Cambridge: The MIT Press.

Kirkpatrick, D., 2010. *The Facebook effect: the inside story of the company that is connecting the world.* London: Simon & Schuster.

Laurel, B., 1992. *Computers as theatre.* Boston: Addison Wesley Longman Inc.

Levy, S., 2011. *In the plex: how Google thinks, works, and shapes our lives.* New York: Simon & Shuster.

Livingstone, S., 2004. Media literacy and the challenge of new information and communication technologies. *Communication Review* 1(7), pp. 3–14.

Livingstone, S., Wijnen, C.W., Papaioannou, T., Costa, C. and Grandío, MdM., 2014. Situating media literacy in the changing media environment: critical insights from European research on audiences. In: N. Carpentier, K.C. Schrøder and L. Hallet eds. 2014. *Audience transformations: shifting audience positions in late modernity.* New York: Routledge. pp. 210–227.

Mackenzie, A., 2006. *Cutting code: software and sociality.* New York: Peter Lang.

Manovich, L., 2001. *The language of new media.* Cambridge: The MIT Press.

Manovich, L., 2008. *Software takes command* [online]. Draft available at: <http://lab.softwarestudies.com/2008/11/softbook.html>

Manovich, L., 2011. Inside Photoshop. *Computational Culture: A Journal of Software Studies* [e-journal] (1). Available at: <http://computationalculture.net/article/inside-photoshop>

Manovich, L., 2012. *How to follow software users* [online]. Available at: <http://lab.softwarestudies.com/p/publications.html>

Manovich, L., 2013. *Software takes command*. International Texts in Critical Media Aesthetics, Vol. 5. New York: Bloomsbury Press.
McGrenere, J. and Ho, W., 2000. Affordances: clarifying and evolving a concept. *Proceedings of Graphics Interface 2000*. 15–17 May, Montreal, Quebec, Canada. pp. 179–186.
Purcell, K., 2010. *The state of online video* [online]. Pew Internet and American Life Project & Nielsen. Washington, DC: Pew Research Center. Available at: <http://pewinternet.org/Reports/2010/State-of-Online-Video.aspx>
Reading, A., (2008). The mobile family gallery? Gender, memory and the cameraphone. *Trames: A Journal of the Humanities and Social Sciences* 12(2), pp. 355–365.
Snickars, P. and Vonderau, P., eds., 2009. *The YouTube reader*. Stockholm: National Library of Sweden.
Strangelove, M., 2010. *Watching YouTube: Extraordinary videos by ordinary people*. Toronto: University of Toronto Press.
Tapscott, D. and Williams, A.D., 2006. *Wikinomics: how mass collaboration changes everything*. London: Penguin Books.
Tidwell, J., 2011. *Designing interfaces*. 2nd ed. Sebastopol: O'Reilly.
Tufte, E.R., 2003. *The cognitive style of PowerPoint: pitching out corrupts within*. Cheshire: Graphics Press.
van Dijck, J., 2009. Users like you? Theorizing agency in user-generated content. *Media, Culture & Society* 31(1), pp. 41–58.
van Dijck, J., 2013. *The culture of connectivity: a critical history of social media*. Oxford: Oxford University Press.

5 Emergent Group Identity Construal in Online Discussions
A Linguistic Perspective

Barbara Lewandowska-Tomaszczyk

INTRODUCTION

An area of innovation in the field of computer-mediated communication (CMC) and online audience studies concerns online users' emotion dynamics, online interaction types and emergent group identity profiles. The main focus of the chapter is on the application of linguistic methodology to audience research. Language usage provides the most immediate and authentic source of computer-mediated interaction, constituting both direct and indirect evidence of what users are doing in such communication acts. Linguistic and discourse analytic methodologies offer a well-researched and developed toolset that allows the study of the types of audiences' communicative interaction patterns in online communication. The present chapter seeks to bridge the apparent gap between audience research and the linguistic analysis of computer-mediated interaction by illustrating how qualitative and quantitative language analytic methods can be applied in audience research. Practical examples are enhanced by a critical discussion as to how the challenges of online communication research can be met by the usage/application of tools from other disciplines.

In particular, the chapter deals with how online identities are constructed and developed by researching three different corpora and which refer to distinct subject matters. The innovative nature of this chapter lies in approaching this notoriously vague and polysemous concept of identity by means of the analysis of online discussions as loci of emergent group identity construal. With the application of computer-supported, quantitative empirical tools derived from corpus linguistics, this chapter presents a new way to examine identity formation/development in online environments. The concept of individual identity, approached through qualitative and quantitative investigation of an individual's network of discourse strategies, is likely to uncover stronger or weaker inner bonds in the ongoing interaction, most likely pointing to the emergence of more or less cohesive particular group identity.

RATIONALE

The study of identity, originally introduced by Cooley (1962) and Mead (1932), has become a central theme within current sociological thinking. The traditional interpretation of social identity, denoting the way an individual perceives him- or herself as a member of a social group, first introduced by Henri Tajfel and John Turner (1979), aims at describing intergroup behaviour and the self-perceived position of the individual in this group. This is referred to as the individual's self-categorisation as labelled by Turner (1978). The most immediate data manifesting details of the emergent group category building is computer-mediated interaction. Karen Cerulo's (1997) observation, made twenty-five years ago, is relevant in this regard:

> New communication technologies have freed interaction from the requirements of physical co-presence; these technologies have expanded the array of generalized others contributing to the construction of the self. Several research foci emerge from this development: the substance of "I," "me," and the generalized other in a milieu void of place, the establishment of "communities of the mind," and the negotiation of copresent and cyberspace identities.
>
> (p. 375)

The observation captures essential changes both in identity studies, which have shifted towards a discussion of collective identities, and in the evolution of new types of media identities, which is even more relevant at present. The outcomes of the present study are also likely to be relevant to a discussion of the similarities and differences between offline and online communication patterns. Both bear a striking resemblance to some of the major behavioural properties of users while the massive scale of online communication can facilitate detection of differences (Lewandowska-Tomaszczyk, 2012).

The process of identification of individuals in online interaction is a dynamic, contingent process, and because of the relatively lower incidence of visual clues in the online comments of the investigated type, the issue of linguistic performance starts to play a major role. It is primarily through their verbal action and discourse engagement that users both develop their own personal identification marking and, at the same time, observe similarities in other online discussants. In this way, users build a mini group of individuals acting and thinking alike. The perception of other online participants as individuals not sharing either their knowledge of the outside world or judgements, is one of the causal elements leading to the development of occasional interpersonal coalitions with like-minded users in contrast to their opponents. This consolidates shared judgements even more, even at the risk of the simultaneous downplaying of the differences (see Buckingham

2008), and is conducive to the development of emerging in-group stability and inter-group pressure.

The primary data providing information on these processes and the participants of online discussions are the language and linguistic structures commentators use, as well as the reference to knowledge of the outside reality alluded to during the interaction. Language data constitute direct evidence of what users are verbally doing in such communication acts. This fact alone is a sufficiently strong reason to apply linguistic and discourse analytic perspectives to study the types of authors'/audiences' communicative interaction patterns in online communication. Audience research and the linguistic analysis of Internet comments is bridged in the present chapter by the application of a battery of qualitative and quantitative language analytic methods to uncover the dynamics of the identity profile in such encounters.

Essentialist versus Dynamic Ego

An ongoing debate in social psychology in terms of a dispute between essentialist and non-essentialist interpretations involves the issue of how the concept of identity should be understood. The essentialist, normative conception of identity (Butler, 1990; Goffman, 1959) assumes a stable universal cognitive and social basis of this concept whereas the latter considers identity as a dynamic and fluid notion (Giddens, 1991). Although CMC data might generally favour the non-essentialist view, in which identity is considered as a dynamic, provisional or hybrid notion, the materials analysed here uncover a more complex picture. There is some part of a person's identity, not necessarily explicitly declared but clearly inferred, particularly in the context of political and social debates, which is more stable, related to the personal 'ego' and linked to the person's identity preference structure. This core part, a 'real self', more entrenched in the context of language and culture acquisition, often surfaces in discourse. It is complemented by the other part or facet of identity, more local and occasional, which is dynamic, changing, negotiable, subject to change or modification in a communication act. Both facets are a carrier of a virtual, constructed portrayal of the self and serve the purpose of positive self-identification in the virtual world. The faceted identity then is only one of those many faces users can present to the mass online public. On the other hand, certain parts of what they say and how they say it, who and what they like and dislike are more stable, more independent parameters construing their essentialist 'real self' core. Typical Because they are not able to, in fact, in view of the preceding discussion, Internet users do not present their complete real selves in online encounters. Instead, as argued by danah boyd (2001), the user presents to audiences a "faceted" identity, "a fragmented, broken up digital self", portraying a narrow view of a person. People manage these fragmented facets of their identity and use them to carry out successful communication. The communicative patterns as used in the social media are symbolic of a new type of media identity,

Emergent Group Identity Construal Online 83

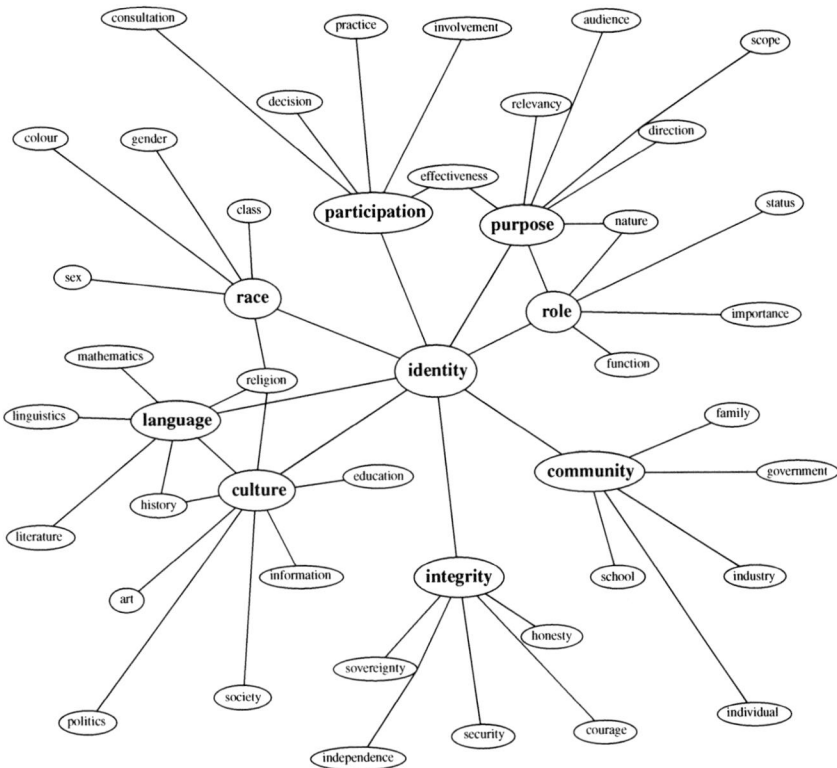

Figure 5.1 Infomap 'Identity'

'cohort identity', and involve patterns of negotiations over one's own signs of belonging and non-belonging, clearly visible in some samples analysed in the present study. Out of the many ingredients of the concept of identity, the notion of participation and its manifestation in 'participatory media culture' (Jenkins, 2006) is a symbolic characterisation of this type of identity 1 (see Figure 5.1 to identify a fuller list of identity ingredients).

The Infomap (Information Mapping Project) software was created at Stanford University's Center for the Study of Language and Information. It performs automatic indexing of words and enables concept-based information retrieval from language corpora. In the case of the concept of *identity* presented in the present chapter, the corpus used was the British National Corpus (BNC; www-csli.stanford.edu) and was generated online by the author from the BNC resources.

According to classical interpretations of social psychology and social science in general (Tajfel and Turner, 1979), in-group community members are likely to maximise social effects of their activity. In other words, their activity is addressed mostly to benefit in-group members, sometimes at the expense of out-group members. In each of the selected samples, maximisation of group activities is likely to bring effects of varying benefits to members of a particular group. The analysis presents that the maximisation of efforts in the group with the strongest foreseeable effects is likely to contribute to a stronger activity profile in this group of CMC users than in the two others. Needless to say, a participant, typically associated with a number of distinct social roles, can enter a number of coalitions depending on the context of situation, thus manifesting their dynamic self (Chen and Li, 2006).

LANGUAGE AND IDENTITY

Clustering of Identity Concepts: Linguistic Form-Meaning Iconicity

Identity is a polysemous notion. It is understood in this study as a composite cluster of related concepts, each of which presents some of its facets. A number of researchers of cognitive linguistic provenance (e.g. Haiman, 1980) point to the phenomenon of 'form-meaning iconicity' observable in authentic interactions. Speakers tend to use concepts with similar meanings in physically adjacent positions in their utterances. In other words, the similarity of semantic senses is portrayed in the physical neighbourhood of their forms in an utterance; that is the form-meaning iconicity can be observed in what is referred to in linguistics as the relevant distribution of linguistic forms. For example in the Euronews data presented in Lewandowska-Tomaszczyk (2012, p. 28), the negatively marked evaluative words (italicised) are used in adjacent positions to reinforce the overall effect: "Why then has the electoral campaign at times resembled *a life and death struggle,* with *the adversary* perceived as if it *threatened* the country's *survival?*"

Decisive to the applied methodology is the amount of language data accessible. The more language data are available, the more reliable are the results that can be obtained concerning the meanings conveyed in discourse. Large databases of authentic spoken and written utterances (language corpora) are built to make it possible to uncover regular form-meaning dependencies conveyed in language. Data acquisition from language corpora can be performed by means of especially dedicated computerised corpus tools.

To generate a composite semantically related cluster of the identity concepts as presented in Figure 5.1, which, by means of distributional criteria concerning the position of the lexical item identity in syntactic patterns, calculates a distance of the word with respect to other, semantically related, lexical forms in the 100-million-word BNC, a corpus-analytic tool developed at Stanford University was used.

Similar to most concepts of this kind, the concept of identity is language and culture specific. Thus, identity in English, as defined by the linguistic distributional criteria, is understood in terms of its degree of similarity to a number of closer or more distant forms (concepts), which are used in the closer or more distant syntactic neighbourhood in utterances produced by English users. The multidimensional concept of identity comprises a radial cluster of related notions, presenting more granular, partly overlapping, areas of interacting nodes. These areas cover the properties of participation (surfacing in language also as the form involvement), community (in terms of family, school, industry, government, etc.), language (linguistics, mathematics, literature, etc.), role (identifiable in utterances as the forms function, status, effectiveness, audience, importance, etc.), integrity (honesty, courage, independence, security, sovereignty, independence, etc.), culture (art, history, politics, society, information, education, etc.), ethnicity (race and colour), religion, class, sex and gender.

The concept of identity is polysemous in a number of different, although related, senses, all pertaining to the sense of self-categorisation, either in terms of an individual or in the context of a group. In the present research, identity is treated as an emerging construct, manifested in terms of discourse and linguistic properties as used by the online discussion commentators. Some of the identity properties in the materials examined here overlap with those generated from the BNC; some others are downplayed or absent. Similar to any other categorisation task, identity relies on the recognition and sharing of similarities and differences between individuals and groups. The identity claims need to be recognised by others, that is other individuals in the case of personal identity and other in-group and out-group members for cases of social identity. From a functional viewpoint, identity is a partly dynamic concept, shaped by a number of more essential, core properties and the contingent properties, forming together new configurations and emerging in a new shape in the course of ongoing interaction.

In the context of online discussions, identity is constructed via the language used by an individual in the interaction. The clustering of identity lexical senses is user and group specific. Different individuals and different groups show preference for distinct interpretations of the concept by resorting to different configurations of the identity conceptual clustering, for example emphasising stronger links, expressed in terms of more frequent discourse reference, to race, religion, role and so on, as can be seen in Figure 5.1. Significant also is the preference towards engaging (participation) in the discussion on particular outside world events. The role and the visibility of some of these attributes as expressed in CMC are a matter of present-day intensive online communication research (see Herring, 1993; Kapidzic and Herring, 2011).

Language Indicators of Identity

The language corpora are studied by means of quantitative and qualitative tools, generating both authentic discourse samples (concordances) and their frequencies, as well as the frequencies of words, keywords, collocations (i.e. phraseology) and clusters of words in the collected materials. They are generated in the present study by WordSmith corpus tools (Scott, 2012). These clearly targeted text analytic findings are part and parcel of what I call participants' 'Online Discourse Activity', whose main component is another parameter: the 'Online Interconnectivity Value' (Lewandowska-Tomaszczyk, 2012), which shows the *type* and the *number* of interconnecting interactive links among discussion participants, visually modelled by means of the publicly available online Gephi tool. The Interconnectivity Values constitute one of the major manifestations of the emerging group building in the present study. It can be associated with the ongoing interaction dynamics as expressed in the use of particular discourse strategies and their linguistic realisation analysed by means of the following criteria: type/token ratio (see Table 5.1), forms of address (e.g. addressing an interlocutor with a title or the first/family name), metaphor and other figurative uses (similes, metonymy, etc.), utterance positive or negative polarity (positive or negative sentences), axiology status expressed as valence associated with particular judgments and opinions (i.e., considering a fact, event, etc., as positive or negative) and verbal manifestations of emotional arousal (i.e., neutral or emotional language). Those parameters constitute language-related qualitative discourse measures of the applied methodology. Further qualitative linguistic properties of identity discourse manifestation are style (formal, informal, colloquial, vulgar, intimate, etc.), visible in word and phrase selection, syntactic constructions and preferred lexical patterning (idioms, collocations, clusters).

MATERIALS

The following three online discussion corpora are used in the study:

a) Corpus 1: Noam Chomsky's social and political views (from 14 February till 23 August 2012) as presented in eight lectures by Noam Chomsky, followed by the users' comments available from *The Huffington Post* (corpus 1):

Corpus 1 is supplemented by Peter Schweizer (corpus 1a): 'Noam Chomsky, Closet Capitalist—Chomsky Talks an Anti-Capitalist Game, but What Does He Practice? Market Economics at their Most Profitable' (Hoover Institution, Stanford, 2006).

b) Corpus 2: Text and comments on *The Guardian* article 'Airport-Style Screening to be Considered for Train and Tube Stations' (19 August 2012)—a proposal issued by the British Home Office of a regulation introducing airport-style mass security screening at mainline rail stations and across London's tube network.

c) Corpus 3: Text and comments on a *FamilyGP news* article (21 February 2012) 'Five-Year-Old Boy Opts to Become a Girl' at http://uk.lifestyle.yahoo.com/five-year-old-boy-opts-to-become-a-girl.htm—a report on a 5-year-old boy who was three when he started questioning his gender and has now been living as a girl.

Internet comments, posted in response to the online texts, are examined. Texts and comments, collected over more than three months are subdivided into separate subcorpora by means of the corpus criteria listed above, and referenced to the BNC and other English-language corpora (Longman and Microconcord) to generate lists of keywords characteristic uniquely for the examined interactions. These criteria jointly considered underlie the dynamics of the examined online exchanges.

The analysed exchanges involve CMC participants commenting on three different types of events which instigate their initial and growing emotional reactions and contribute to the development of three different types of online group identities with varying degrees of cohesiveness. Group cohesiveness can be uncovered by means of the linguistic discourse analysis of particular Interconnectivity Values (IV) as well as the polarity of particular exchange turns (supporting interactional moves vs. disconfirming moves) as well as the positive or negative marking and the valence of the linguistic expressions used in the discussions.

LINGUISTIC IDENTITY CONSTRUCTION AND RECONSTRUCTION

Negotiating Background Knowledge: Linguistic Construal of Events

Identity development and maintenance is a contextual matter to a large degree, depending on the type of event the individual acts in or refers to. To identify the most salient events discussed in the three samples, the subject of the present analysis, first full-word lists, then sets of keywords are generated, involving the lexical items of the highest and those of the lowest frequencies in a particular discourse, as compared with those in so-called reference corpus (BNC and Longman/Microconcord corpora). Based on the criterion of word frequency and keyness, the data presents a number of thematic areas as the most salient (i.e. the most frequently referred to) in the texts, in contrast to other texts. The salience of particular events is examined by means of keywords frequency measures, generated independently from the online versions of the English samples using the Wordsmith corpus tools.

Online Syntax

Essential for the analysis are different portrayals of the same event, conveyed by a user by means of a range of syntactic constructions and referred to in the cognitive linguistic literature as different construals of an event (cf. Langacker, 1987 [1991]). Language users may focus on a more sequential perspective of the event with foregrounded individual participants such as the agent of an action or an experiencer, cause or instrument or they may adopt a more general, reified perspective towards the same event. To shape the perspective and the point of view, language users have at their disposal a whole array of language-specific grammatical tools, which are used either spontaneously or more consciously as (metalinguistically) controlled devices. These grammatical tools include for example nominalisation (i.e. transforming a verb-based expression into a more noun-like one) as contrasted with a fully elaborated sentence structure. The nominalisation indicates an action as in the phrase *the introduction of airport-style mass security screening at mainline rail stations* (corpus 2), which makes it possible to express an activity downplaying its agency, as contrasted with the sentence *Clearly G4S need to be employed to screen everyone wanting to get on their bike!* which profiles G4S agentive accountability, although indirectly expressed again in terms of the agentless passive this time. The active-/passive-voice distinction is a powerful rhetorical instrument as in the two sentences: *a state that spends a sum equivalent to half of national income is either 'just right' or not big enough* versus *Thus vast sums of money (taxes) must be spent to buy the latest electronic gadgets*. Each of these constructions expresses a different conceptualization of the event and points to distinct causality and agency attribution by the users in the description of the event, revealing an important part of their knowledge, beliefs and convictions.

Figurative Language and Emotions

Identity is linguistically constructed and reconstructed by resorting to further numerous linguistic and discursive devices such as forms of address, distancing strategies, metaphoricity and other figurative tools, and often by the use of emotionally charged lexis, not infrequently combined with irony and sarcasm. Metaphors and other figurative language add to the event construction an evaluative or emotional charge such as irony, sarcasm or aggression, anger or hate as in marked offensive or vulgar vocabulary.

The simile *Like a nasty tumor, the security industry in this country is huge and growing larger by the year* (corpus 2) is based on a source domain, that is a domain which provides a comparative, material, a concrete and physical object or event to be mapped to a more abstract and illusive target domain (Lakoff and Johnson, 1980). In the preceding sentence, the simile includes the base concept of a medical condition with a dangerous and life-threatening tumour which is getting larger, and serves as the source of a comparison with the security industry. The figurative layer of meaning which substantiates the sense involves the metaphoric *animation* of the tumour as expressed via the form *growing*.

Another group of linguistic identification is emotion terms, frequently structured as complex figurative clusters. The term *fear*—represented as the metaphorical entity *instil a fear* as in *Some con artist who likes to instil a fear of terrorists then prey on that fear once it's been firmly fixed* (corpus 3)—expresses a higher degree of the speaker's involvement than the corresponding basic sense of *the artist exploits a fear of terrorists*. The concept of *preying* introduces a double metaphor/metonymy structure of the *con artist*, metaphorically conceptualised as a predator whereas *prey on fear* is metonymically interpreted in terms of the part-for-the whole construction as 'prey on the audience's fears'. The scenario of 'the fear firmly fixed' portrays fear metaphorically as a thing in its reified conceptualisation. The figurative language on a whole is a powerful tool. On one hand, it is less concrete and conveys certain indeterminacy of meaning, whereas on the other, it encourages stronger associations in its inferential part.

One type of emotional arousal marking of the metaphoric type involves comparisons referred to as a Godwin's Law (Godwin, 1995), which states that when a discussion is progressing the probability of a comparison involving fascism, the usage of the term *Nazi* and related expressions increases. Other domains of a similar function identified in example 2 from corpus 1, as follows, are also part of Godwin's discourse effect[1]:

(1)
- a) If only we all had your razor-like insight, and weren't too stupid to throw off the shackles of the evil, *baby-killing fascist state* we live in
- b) Well *bin-Laden, Al-whatsit and all the other groupings* have obviously won in one sense
- c) *More Big Brother* is watching YOU!

Distancing and Forms of Address

An important role of pointing to the speaker's attitude towards the object of discussion and other interactants is played by distancing elements like *so-called* or *as is referred to* as well as forms of address. The latter show interpersonal relations among the interaction participants, whereas the former are markers of self-presentation and responsibility disclaimers (see example 10c). Both function as powerful identity markers in discourse.

An example from comments to Chomsky's text ((2) from corpus 1) involves characteristic forms of address, which uncover the academic background and positive emotional attitude of commentator 2 towards Noam Chomsky's political views by resorting to academic linguistic conventions of respect by addressing a person with a degree or title.

(2)
Commentator 1: (785 Fans); Additionally, Mr. Chomsky asserts that Iran accepts the plan. It does not.
Commentator 2: (1557 Fans); Where's your *respect*? He's *not* 'Mr. Chomsky;' he's *Dr. Chomsky*.

The last comment, supported by a large group of users, situates commentator 2 at the opposing side of the argument with reference to commentator 1 and his 785 supporters. Both are influential representatives of the two respective emerging groups as identified in the sample.

CORPUS ANALYSIS

Statistics

The three corpora of comments focusing on three different themes are statistically analysed from the point of view of the quantitative Interconnectivity Value and their *Type/Token Ratio* (TTR).[2] Although the TTR can partly uncover users' linguistic sophistication, it is also sensitive to the length of the sample. In longer texts more lexical repetitions are used; that is the number of unrepeated words decreases.

Some of the investigated platforms and sites keep all records of the commentators and (optionally) their profiles, so it is possible to get some more clues with regard to the identity profile of particular users (*Huffington Post—Social News—Friends—Friends' Activity*, Activity, Comments, Fans, although some of them are restricted to Friends only). The family, gender, corporate and other types of self-identifying properties are partly inferable from the content of the posted discussions and the linguistic forms framing them, which reveal some of the users' linguistic and interactional preferences and related identity parameters.

Corpus 1

Corpus 1 includes comments to Chomsky's texts. The users[3] are in vast majority members of *HuffPost Social News*, active for many years, publish online and post extensively. The comments are grouped into eight sub-corpora and the visualisation of the IVs is presented in terms of undirected graphs (Figures 5.2–5.5). A graph is a structure interpreted as a collection of *vertices/nodes*, which signify individual users, and a collection of *edges* that connect pairs of vertices, which represent the interconnectivity relations among them. The number of edges and the length of the lines represent the number of (inter)connective comments of a given user. Some commentators (the largest number of interconnecting links) are more active, and they either directly or via intermediate links refer to the author of the main text (the central node in the graph) or engage in subgroup interaction.

Qualitative Analysis: Linguistic and Discourse Markers.
The posts commenting on Chomsky's views (corpus 1) identify two distinct groups of users: their political preferences and personal traits. The use of language is presented by the statistics—for sub-corpus 1 in the sample—with its high IV and the type/token ratio:

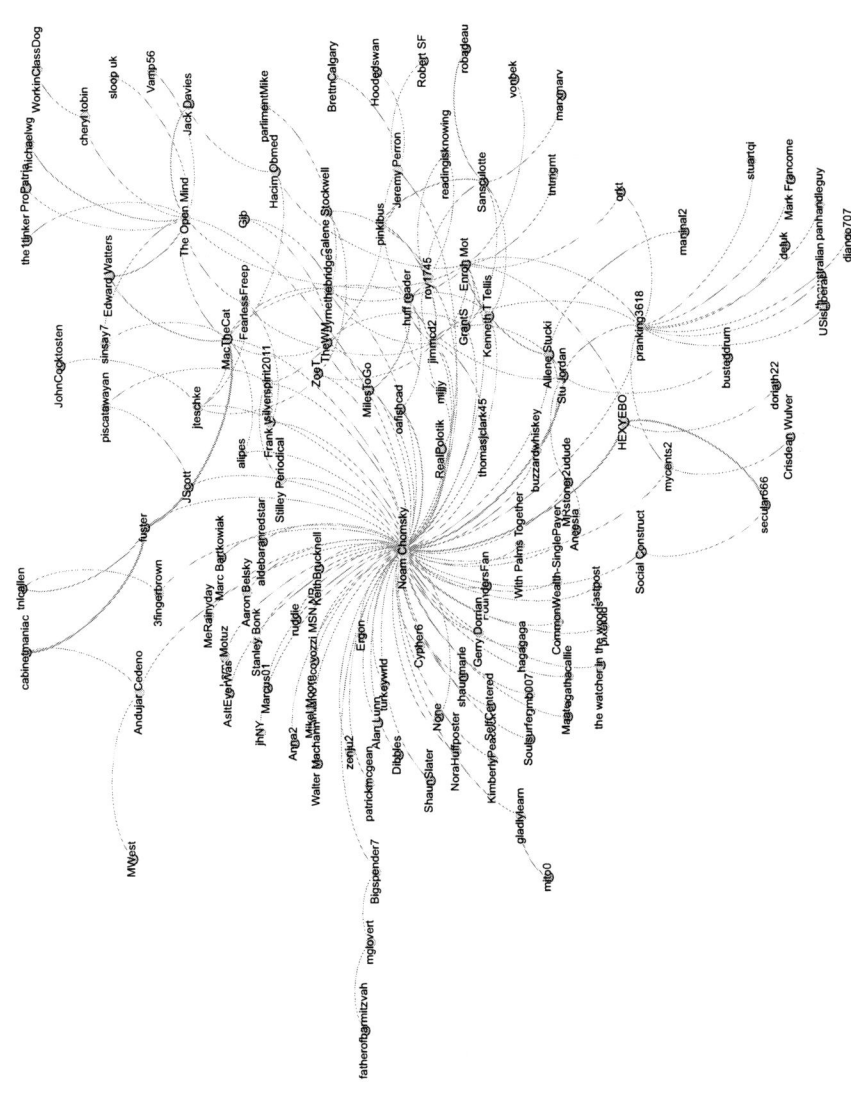

Figure 5.2 Interconnectivity Values for Sample 1

Table 5.1 Type/Token Ratio

Interconnectivity Value	Words	TTR
4,360	18,099Tp 71,000Tk	6,68

The cultural and historic references (example 3) serve a positive self-projection of individual users, whereas the use of positive (4) and negative (5) modification patterns structures their group membership.

Corpus 1 (Magna Carta)

(3) Historical references. The Magna Carta placed a limit on the Kings power and made the King answerable to the people.

(4) Supporters. Professor Chomsky's vision is *clear* and *accurate*, perhaps as *close to truth* as our human perception, *intelligence* and *wisdom* can take us under historical and present constraints.

(5) Opponents. Chomsky has an interesting habit of writing long and interesting historical reviews followed with a whole *bunch* of *unrelated* contentions and other *crap* that are *neither well-connected* to the introduction *nor even logically presented or supported.*

The interaction structure (6) reveals what I dub *a ping-pong pattern* with the discussants confronting one another around the main issue, using first witticisms and humour (with occasional graphic symbols, icons or, more frequently, fonts and spelling as in example 9), marked modifiers, metalinguistic and eventually ad personam comments.

(6)

Commentator 1

The old guy is well past his sell-by date as philosopher or logician. . . . . . and no longer can reasonable connect his knowledge and theories to the real world.

Commentator 2

I also sensed the disconnect between his review of history, and the assertions he made.

Commentator 3

"A whole bunch of unrelated contentions and other crap that are neither well-connected to the introduction nor even logically presented or supported."

Yet you failed to refute a single one.

Reasonably is the adverb you are seeking. :-]

(...)

Commentator 1

In other words you prefer rhetoric to reason. :-]

Commentator 3

You are arguing first by ad hominem and then by dismissal.

Invert that. :-]

(...)

Perhaps, I am of the intellectual elite, but I cannot think that the majority can fall for such dubious arguments, when presented with argument and evidence.

Commentator 4

Pronouncing yourself an intellectual elite is sure proof of your absence from their numbers.

(...)

You are not a leader or part of the intellectual elite. You are a sucker.

Face threats and face-saving strategies are present and interactionally marked. The (double) *ping pong* discourse game in (6) shows increasing dynamics of personal and aggressive attacks (*maybe the truth hurts you . . . You are not a leader or part of the intellectual elite. You are a sucker.*) Commentators 1, 2 and 4 share views and oppose commenter 3. The comment by commenter 2 directly endorses that of commenter 1, whereas the post by commenter 4 structures the identification pattern to be perceived as homogenous with those of both commenters 1 and 2. The three are fighting at the same front as emerging allies. Commenter 3, a well-read, linguistically trained participant, has already found his allies in the previous exchanges. The two camps are developing their group identification marking.

Quantitative Analysis: Linguistic and Discourse Markers

Apart from the qualitative analysis of language, quantitative linguistic data reveal additional semantic layers. The keywords generated from corpus 1 Chomsky texts (7) and corpus 1a, the Hoover report, (8), uncover the outside world political and cultural context for the references made in the discussion.

94 Barbara Lewandowska-Tomaszczyk

(7) Corpus 1

Table 5.2 Selected Keywords[5]

N[1]	Key word	Freq.	%	RC. Freq.[2]	RC. %[2]	Keyness[3]
10	IRAN	317	0,10	115	2	060,69
12	AMERICA	435	0,14	1,236	1	637,15
14	YOU	2,935	0,97	76,377	1	301,22
15	US	971	0,32	12,860	1	262,89
18	OBAMA	143	0,05	0	1	153,49
19	IRAQ	163	0,05	37	1	124,60

[1] N stands for the ranking in the corpus results.
[2] RC stands for reference corpus.
[3] The keyness of a term is calculated by using a reference corpus that must be bigger than the actual corpus.

(8) Corpus 1a

Table 5.3 Keywords

N[1]	Key word	Freq.	%	RC. Freq.[2]	Keyness[3]
1	CHOMSKY	37	2,22	16	617,89
2	NOAM	6	0,36	2	101,62
5	HOOVER	4	0,24	23	51,09
6	SPEECHES	5	0,30	246	43,16
7	TAX	6	0,36	663	42,23
8	RIGHTS	7	0,42	1,470	40,45
9	FEE	4	0,24	148	36,77
10	CAPITALIST	5	0,30	561	35,04
12	PROPERTY	6	0,36	1,572	32,08
15	FUND	4	0,24	380	29,34
16	RADICALS	3	0,18	95	28,49
17	CORPORATIONS	3	0,18	96	28,43

[1] N stands for the ranking in the corpus results.
[2] RC stands for reference corpus.
[3] The keyness of a term is calculated by using a reference corpus that must be bigger than the actual corpus.

Emergent Group Identity Construal Online 95

The controversial issue concerning Chomsky's actions meets with two conflicting stands I and II in corpus 1a (I: *the Hoover Institutes bogus essay on Chomsky*, II: *It's very profitable to be an anti-capitalist millionaire with a trust fund*), and yet the interaction, although emotional and explicitly evaluative, does not resort to either arguments or language beyond the accepted conventional limits. Such a scenario does not characterise a single event; rather, it involves *a more coherent community of users* (Dewey 1927 [1954]), who share certain interactional rules, notwithstanding the differences in their worldviews.

chomsky_one_2 introduces a contrastive visualisation of (*Chomsky* text IV) users' activities with the top user's seventy-two replies; the most active interaction involves thirteen users only, with four particularly salient and active.

Figure 5.4 (file "chomsky_one_7") introduces IV visualisation of the comments to Chomsky's article "Is the World Too Big to Fail? The Contours of Global Order" one of the users ("natureman44"); sixty-seven replies are distributed among twenty-seven commentators; the interaction is of a ping-pong style; intensive exchanges are observed in terms of the number of emotionally charged words and phrases, types of argument.

Figure 5.5 (file "chomsky_one_5") represents a contribution of another thread instigator ("Syllogizer"), commenting on Chomsky's "American Decline in Perspective", corpus 1, subcorpus 2. There are thirty-four replies there, distributed among twenty-seven users; as the graph structure represents, the discussion is carried out primarily between 'Syllogizer' and his respondents. The varying structure of the interactions can be also followed in the source.

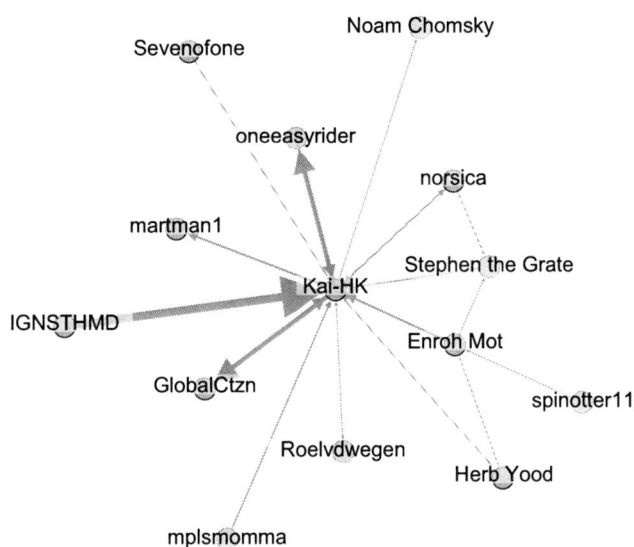

Figure 5.3 Visualisation of the Top User's Interconnectivity

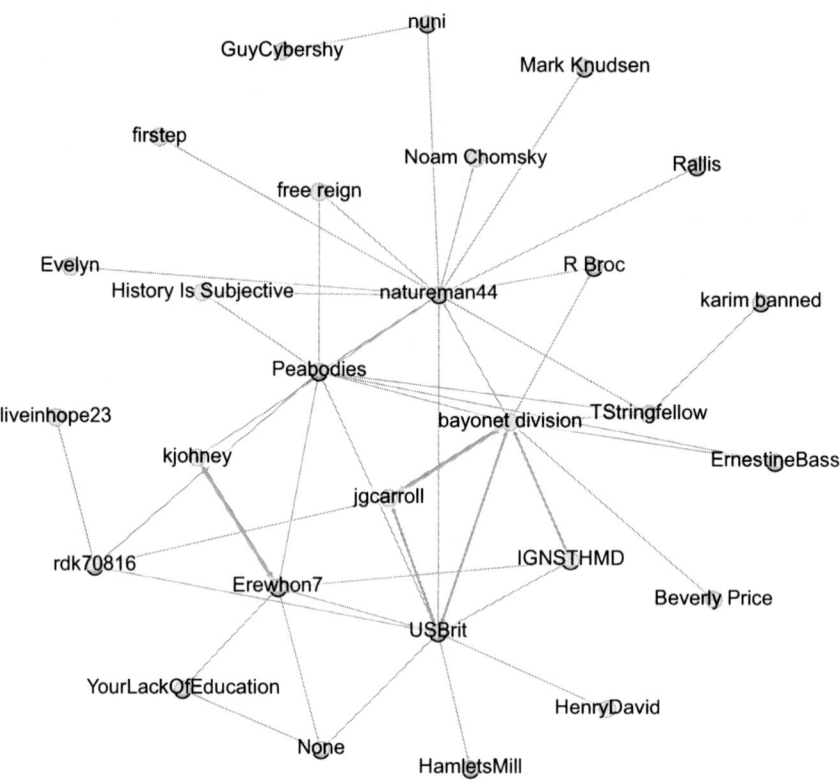

Figure 5.4 Visualisation of a Ping-Pong Interaction

Although Figures 5.4 and 5.5 visualise two differently structured subthreads of corpus 1, they can be considered *model visualisation schemas* for the interaction dynamics and the IV identified further in corpus 2 (graph 5) and sample 3 (Figure 5.4).

Corpus 2

Corpus 2—qualitative analysis: linguistic and discourse markers. The users commenting the main text "Airport-Style Screening" in corpus 2 identify themselves as mainly Londoners, males and females, all of whom, except for one moderating opinion, oppose the regulation. Such unanimity makes the communication mono-targeted. It is also progressively cumulative due to a growing number of the commentators in the course of the interaction and to the number and emotionality of the comments. And yet, the discussion shows a relatively low level of interconnectivity among the commentators. This type of online communication can be perceived as a *snowball* type, similar to the proportionally larger movements of the OCCUPY or ACTA

Emergent Group Identity Construal Online 97

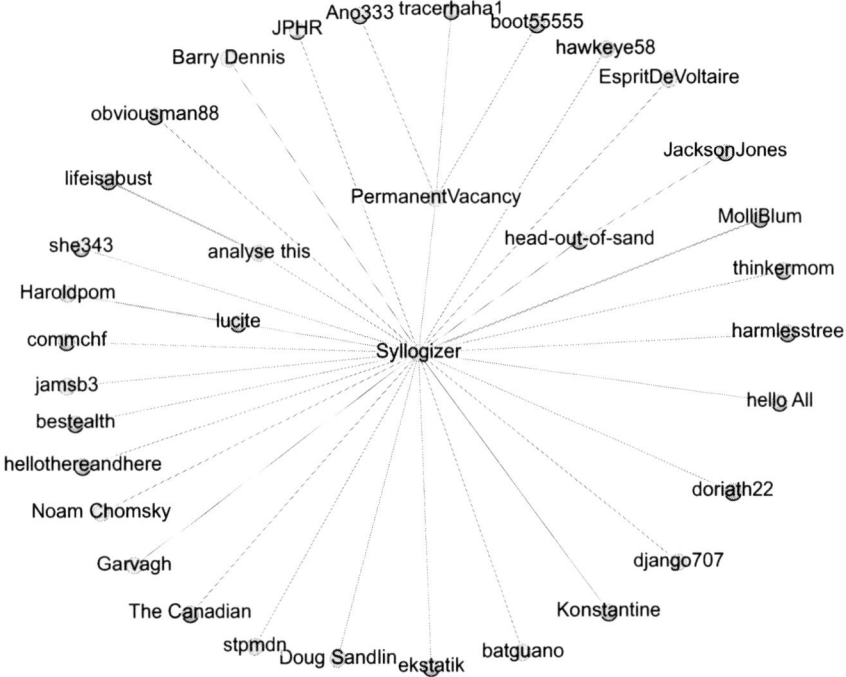

Figure 5.5 Visualisation of a Subordinate Thread Interconnectivity

networks, with its climaxes, followed by a relative decrease in intensity when the movement succeeds to attain their goals. The relevant discourse markers involve familiar strategies of sarcasm and irony, rhetorical questions, and figurative language. There is a higher incidence (example 10) than in the other corpora, of setting false opposition, ironic rhetorical questions and distancing strategies, besides meaningful spelling changes such as in (9):

(9)
>Blunkett may at last be able to rake in **mi££ions** via his ID card making company

(10)
> a) False opposition
>   Another move to scare us into following orders, meekly submitting to observation and scrutiny, losing our privacy etc *rather than manning up and tackling islamic terrorism at source.*
> b) Rhetorical qs
>   What next, stopping us carrying drinks on to a train for fear that they might be liquid explosives?

c) Distancing (quotes) and emphasizing (capitalization)
And next they ll want to body search you every time you walk down the road. NO NONO . They are already FAR TOO MANY assorted "security" checks

Quantitative analysis: linguistic and discourse markers. Corpus 2 contains 221 comments, fifty-five-word long on average, that were evaluated based on a sample of fifty randomly selected comments.

(11)
Table 5.4 Word Frequency List (Selection)

N[1]	Word	Freq.	%
39	SECURITY	40	0,37
40	ALL	39	0,37
41	WE	39	0,37
45	PEOPLE	32	0,30
59	STATIONS	24	0,22
60	TRAIN	24	0,22
75	RAIL	18	0,17
76	TERRORIST	18	0,17
78	GOVERNMENT	17	0,16
93	PASSENGERS	14	0,13
94	SCREENING	14	0,13
95	STATE	14	0,13
103	THREAT	13	0,12

[1] N stands for the ranking in the corpus results.

The commentators pursue the common goal, opposing the new regulation proposal. Hence, the polarity of the discourse is unambiguously negative, with a high level of emotionality. The identification of the group is narrowly constructed by the users' cumulative conversational contribution to the extent that no pressure is observed among the commenters to engage in or specify it in more intensive interactional terms. The identity affiliation of the emergent group is unambiguous in this case, which contributes to its strong cohesion characterised by enactment of a uniform communicative action for this particular goal.

Corpus 3

Qualitative analysis: linguistic and discourse markers. The commenters in corpus 3 are international and include gender minorities members and supporters of various parenthood styles, who in the sex change in a five-year-old, take either supporting, rejecting or neutral positions with regard to the issue, with the opponents in the majority.

A characteristic feature of corpus 3 is the allusions to and reflections on the commenters' own life experiences, which are much more frequent with the gender minorities members. This process of self-projection is constructed by digressive sub-threads in the interaction. The utterances are of a highly personal (intimate) character and often left uncommented on by the others. The communication is loosely structured, along individually determined unpredictable trajectories (*loose balloons* types).

The interactional turns are initially of a short length (up to forty words) but increase in size and emotionality in the course of the discussion to finally become sarcastic and aggressive as in example 12 that follows. The incidence of wrong spelling, misuse of words and grammatical inadequacies is higher here than in the two other samples. This is possibly due to the higher number of international users (posting location is identified with the majority), some of them supposedly non-native or less educated. The opinions are divided; the incidence of supporting (12), rejecting (14), and undecided (13) voices is skewed towards the opponents' distance; and the reasoning used reveals deeper parameters of the users' respective identities, such as with respect to religion, parenthood and so on (see particularly [14]). The commenters' personal identities with their strongly reflexive component (15) map onto the structure of the discourse. The structure forms a multi-tiered construction, elucidating the participants' experiential background and the present selves and the negotiating processes of the current online identities. Considering the number and style of emotional utterances, emotionality marking is stronger in the opponents' opinions (14).

(12)
> *supporters.* You know, in this day and age, you all have access to the internet, so how can you WILLFULLY remain so ignorant about gender identity issues. Just google it. Google transgender. Read. LEARN SOMETHING BEFORE YOU GIVE US YOUR BRILLIANT UNEDUCATED OPINION! sorry for shouting but honestly, you people . . .

(13)
> *undecided, neutral.*
> a) Only dressed as a girl—not a gender change—poor little chap
> b) Its a matter of choice..

(14)
> *opponents (highest frequency).*
> a) Give psychological test to the sick parents . . . They controlled this, and they made this happen!!!..
> b) The child needs to be disciplined.
> c) God does not commit mistakes in assigning genders to a person

(15)

digressive, reflexive.

a) I am transgender 25 years old ,,, well i understand her.. cause me since when i was born since i start develop my mine i was 3 or 4. . i really feel that i am woman,, i was only drop in man bod, but my mine, heart and soul is completely a woman . . . and i m lucky i have family who support me. .

Corpus 3

Quantitative analysis: linguistic and discourse markers. Corpus 3 contains 2,264 comments of an average length equal to 75 words, evaluated on the basis of a sample 300 randomly selected comments.

(16)

Table 5.5   Frequencies of Selected Content Words

N[1]	Word	Freq.	%
30	BOY	12	0,48
37	GIRL	10	0,40
43	GENDER	8	0,32
49	HAIR	7	0,28
52	SEX	7	0,28

[1] N stands for the ranking in the corpus results.

Corpus 3 presents a case different from corpus 1 and corpus 2 in some respect, as the issue discussed involves a more universal topic and engages a cross-cultural section of commentators (the US, the UK, Europe, Asia). These aspects make it considerably different from corpus 1 and corpus 2, which are focused on political issues as perceived by two fairly cohesive groups in the former and a regulation addressed to UK (particularly London) residents, emerging as the most cohesive group in the latter. The multinational character of the comments in corpus 3 introduces new or modified dimensions, similar to those observed in Lilach Nir (2012), who, in the analysis of cross-national differences in political discussions, shows how multinationality represented in this type of discourse contributes to the increase of number and size of discussion turns and moderates the contribution of individual differences. The consequence of this is the least cohesive structure of corpus 3 group identity, which lies at the interface between a more public and homogenous identity on the one hand and an individual, private, one on the other.

DISCUSSION AND CONCLUSION: GROUP IDENTITY EMERGENCE

This chapter identified three types of online discourse practices which shed new light on the conditions under which communicative interaction and language usage uncover patterns of group identification.

The structure of the online participation and its linguistic expression are subsumed in terms of three basic types of online communicative practice which structure emerging group identity in varying degrees.

1. *Ping-pong* communication (corpus 1) represents an autonomous and confrontational profile, targeted towards two polar judgements. It includes a relatively high number of feedback loops (replies, *likes*). It is framed in an argumentative, aggressive, debate discussion type, digressive and crossing a single domain boundary at some points. It presents mini climaxes at the interactional turns in which particular communities in conflict determine or negotiate their identities and are instrumental in identifying exclusive identities of their opponents.
2. *Snowball* communication (corpus 2) has a fully determined communicative profile and a fairly uniform community type with a clearly defined ultimate objective and an external opponent. The moves and turns are equally or more strongly confrontational than in the ping-pong type. The structure has an observable magnifying axis—stimulated by an increasing flow of energy present and rising, which leads to a climax, and not infrequently success, in real life.
3. *String balloons* communication (corpus 3) presents a looser interactional structure often around issues of social and moral values, with a gradual development of more and more clearly identifiable group identities. This is weakly polarised between that representing traditional and more conservative values, fearing the collapse of traditional social norms, culture and values (God, family, gender roles), and engaging also what it considered to be "common sense" and that generally considered more progressive and "modern." This communication practice contains no one climax. It represents rather sets of interactional moves back and forth along a controversial theme, with frequent reminiscence of the individual's personal life experiences, in which users often digress from the main topic of the exchange.

The interaction types from the perspective of the IV represent also three kinds. The first is a one-to many-to one type (graph 3) with few salient interactional partners. The second type has a complex centred structure (graph 5) and the third one represents a complex multilayered interactional type (graph 4). Some of the types (particularly those represented in corpus 1 and corpus 3) may correspond to the interactional dynamics of face-to-face discourses whereas some others (corpus 2) are shown to be more constrained and predominantly occurring in online many-to-many mass-communication exchanges. It is also characteristic of this type of online exchange that the emergent group identity observed in corpus 2 manifests the most cohesive type of identification towards a common goal.

The complex dynamics of online communication proposed by boyd (2001) can also be identified in the analysed corpora. Although the problem of validating the true identity of online users cannot be unambiguously handled in all contexts, the 'invisible audience' is most clearly seen in corpus 2, which is also most characteristic for the second of boyd's dynamics, namely 'collapsed contexts'. Corpus 1, on the other hand, presents collapsed context to a weaker extent, whereas in corpus 3 more individualised contexts are created, determined by the users' own beliefs and experiences. In the same corpus, the dynamics of blurring the public and private is also most strongly foregrounded.

The analysis of the identity of online communities identifies the factors conditioning the shifts in the interaction dynamics indicated, both with respect to the expression of individual opinions as well as with regard to wider segmentation of online communities. The qualitative and quantitative discourse properties in the study of the dynamics of online exchanges presented in the present chapter corroborate some of the assumptions of a more extensive research project. This involves an interaction of a number of sub-tasks such as the identification of types of online communication dynamics (Lewandowska-Tomaszczyk, 2012; Lewandowska-Tomaszczyk and Zeller, 2012), the place and function of emotion expression in such interactions (Lewandowska-Tomaszczyk and Wilson, 2010) and the concept of emergent faceted identity of groups of Internet users. The CMC users' emergent groups, correlated with the postulated communication types, exhibit varying degrees of group cohesiveness, manifested in their online content preferences expressed verbally.

The types of group identities described represent different degrees of cohesiveness. One group (corpus 2) represents the strongest cohesiveness ('snowball' effect), with a homogenous, clearly targeted objective, and less frequently substantiated intra-group connectivity, expressed by a lower number of multiparty interactional turns (inclusive identity emergence). Corpus 3 presents the lowest cohesiveness in the examined types, with stronger in-group connectivity (more smaller subgroup turns) and weaker interconnectivity subcomponents (weakly inclusive/exclusive identity), and corpus 1 represents a schema involving two strongly identifiable intra-connectivity subschema, characterised by the opposite polarity feature of interactional turns (a number of disconfirming moves) and a high interconnectivity value (two polarised groups of commentators), thus revealing a ping-pong discourse dynamics with strongly cohesive identities of each of the two groups. This strongly polarised inclusive/exclusive pattern thus represents two opposing groups and is found to be similar to that emerging in corpus 3, the difference being the degree of involvement and arousal as well as the absence of personal digressive moves, which are much more frequent in corpus 3 than in corpus 1.

The results of the analysis reveal a novel picture of three basic types of online dynamics in CMC interactions, which contribute to and structure group identity emergence. A question may arise as to whether it is technology and the digital medium that contribute to the group cohesiveness. Some of such contingencies seem overstated, in that they are very much alike traditional non-digital communication practices (particularly evident in sample 1). On the other hand, the digital medium transforms precisely our experiences and shapes both the character of the interaction into massive encounters as well as the temporal dynamics with which users develop into a group, of varying degrees of cohesiveness. Social context and identity formation in digital media then are not a mono-directed phenomenon. Rather, as pointed out by Raymond Williams (1978) and endorsed further by Buckingham (2008), "technology is both socially shaped and socially shaping," and identity formation also displays a dialectic character. This chapter has presented the advantages of applying linguistic methodology to audience research and in showing how language used in computer-mediated interaction constitutes direct evidence of what users are doing in such communication acts by the application of the well-researched and developed methodological tools of a qualitative and quantitative character. In this way, the present chapter contributes to overcoming the gap between audience studies and linguistic methodology. The exploration of the processes discussed is supported by the computer-aided linguistic research methodology presented, which helps to enrich traditional instruments in social sciences for media effects studies.

ACKNOWLEDGEMENTS

Research was carried out within COST Action IS0906 "Transforming Audiences, Transforming Societies", supported by The Polish National Science Centre (Narodowe Centrum Nauki) grant "Przemiany w postrzeganiu rzeczywistości a język nowych mediów" (Transformations in the Perception of the World and the Language of New Media) no. 740/N-COST/2010/0.

I wish to acknowledge the assistance of Lukasz Drozdz, M.A., member of the project, in the graph generation and formatting.

NOTES

1. The spelling, punctuation and typographic devices are retained in all examples as in the original texts.
2. The Type-Token Ratio is calculated as a number of lexical types (Tp) divided into the number of their actual occurrences in the texts (tokens Tk) and multiplied by 100.
3. The information on the commentators is available in terms of the number and content of their comments in relation to the texts posted by accessing their nicks in the comments in the hypertext format.

4. The sets of data which are the basis for the graph construction (Figure 5.2–5.5) are available from the author in separate files.
5. The units of the structural and technical types such as articles and editorial data are omitted from the lists.

REFERENCES

boyd, d., 2001. *FACETED ID/ENTITY: Managing representation in a digital world*. A.B. Computer Science. Brown University, Providence, Rhode Island.

Butler, J., 1990. *Gender trouble*. London: Routledge.

Buckingham, D., 2008. Introducing identity. In: D. Buckingham, ed. *Youth, identity, and digital media*. The John D. and Catherine T. MacArthur Foundation Series on Digital Media and Learning. Cambridge: The MIT Press. pp. 1–24.

Chen, Y. and Xin, S.L., 2006. *Group identity and social preferences* [online]. Available at: <http://people.exeter.ac.uk/maf206/chen_li_2006.pdf>

Cerulo, K.A., 1997. Identity construction. New issues, new directions. *Annual Review of Sociology* 23, pp. 385–409.

Cooley, C. H., 1962. *Social organization: a study of the larger mind*. New York: Schocken Books.

Dewey, J., 1927 [1954].*The public and its problems*. New York: Henry Holt.

Giddens, A., 1991. *Modernity and self-identity*. Cambridge: Polity.

Godwin, M., 1995. Godwin's law of Nazi analogies (and corollaries). *EFF.org*. Electronic Frontier Foundation. Net Culture—Humor" archive section. <http://w2.eff.org/Net_culture/Folklore/Humor/godwins.law>.

Goffman, E., 1959. *The presentation of self in everyday life*. New York: Anchor Books.

Haiman, J., 1980. The iconicity of grammar: isomorphism and motivation. *Language* 56(3), pp. 515–540.

Herring, S.C., 1993. Gender and democracy in computer-mediated communication. *Electronic Journal of Communication* 3(2). [online] Available at: <http://ella.slis.indiana.edu/˜herring/ejc.doc>.

Herring, S.C., 2003. Gender and power in online communication [online]. In: J. Holmes and M. Meyerhoff, eds. 2003. *The handbook of language and gender*. Oxford: Blackwell Publishers. pp. 202–228. Available at: <http://ella.slis.indiana.edu/˜herring/gender.power.pdf>.

Jenkins, H., 2006. *Convergence culture: where old and new media collide*. New York University Press.

Kapidzic, S. and Herring, S.C., 2011. Gender, communication, and self-presentation in teen chatrooms revisited: have patterns changed? *Journal of Computer-Mediated Communication* 17(1), pp. 39–59.

Lakoff, G. and Johnson, M., 1980. *Metaphors we live by*. Chicago: University of Chicago Press.

Langacker, R.W., 1987 [1991]. *Foundations of cognitive grammar*, vols.1 and 2. Stanford: Stanford University Press.

Lewandowska-Tomaszczyk, B., 2012. Blurring the boundaries: a model of online computer-mediated communication activities (OCA). In: A. Bednarek, ed. 2012. *Interdisciplinary perspectives in cross-cultural communication*. München: Lincom Publishers. pp. 8–35.

Lewandowska-Tomaszczyk, B. and Wilson, P., 2010. A contrastive perspective on emotions: surprise. *Review of Cognitive Linguistics* 8(2), pp. 321–350.

Lewandowska-Tomaszczyk, B. and Zeller, F., 2012. The media in transforming audiences and societies. In: P. Pezik, ed. 2012. *Corpus data across languages and disciplines*. Frankfurt a. Main: Peter Lang. pp. 127–148.

Nir, L., 2012. Cross-national differences in political discussion: can political systems narrow deliberation gaps? *Journal of Communication*, 62(3), pp. 553–570.

Scott, M., 2012. WordSmith Tools. [computer software]. Liverpool: Lexical Analysis Software.

Tajfel, H. and Turner, J., 1979. An integrative theory of intergroup conflict. In: S. Worchel and W. Austin, eds. 1979. *The social psychology of intergroup relations*. Monterey: Brooks/Cole. pp. 7–24

Turner, J.C., 1978. Social categorization and social discrimination in the minimal group paradigm. In: H. Tajfel, ed. 1978. *Differentiation between social groups: studies in the social psychology of intergroup relations*. London: Academic Press. pp. 235–250.

Williams, R., 1974. *Television: technology and cultural form*. Glasgow: Fontana.

6 Using Linguistic Ethnography to Study Techno Eliteness of Social Media Audiences

Joke Beyl and Yuwei Lin

INTRODUCTION

In this chapter, we offer a methodological framework for an in-depth study on 'techno elite' audiences. Elite research usually looks into the relationships between those who rule and those who are ruled, the social characteristics of those who exercise power, the relations between elites and society, elite recruitment and elite circulation (Aron, 1950a; 1950b; Putnam, 1976). A social analysis of elites in an era profoundly shaped by digital technologies is timely and vital to update existing understanding of power relationships and societal structures in relation to media content production and consumption. Traditionally, research methodology for elite studies is based on static social categories fixated in sectors, organisations and positions. As argued by many scholars in elite, intellectual and class studies, it is difficult to define who the elites are given the fuzziness and overloaded meanings of the term and the increasingly convergent media industries. The notion of "elites", argued Kidd and Nicholls (1998), just like those of "middle class" or "intellectuals", needs to evolve from a "primitive sense of classification, that is of an attempt to position individuals within a static social hierarchy, to one in which it signifies complex social characteristics and dynamic social relationships" (p. xvii). That said, elite cannot be understood (solely) "as an objective phenomenon, measurable in terms of income or occupation or some other clearly definable index"; instead, and perhaps more practically, it should be understood as "one with a subjective component—with consciousness, ideology and language" (Kidd and Nicholls, 1998, p. xvii). It is precisely in this latter realm that we want to investigate 'techno elite audiences' from a linguistic ethnographic perspective, because a combination of linguistic and ethnographic approaches helps understand how 'eliteness' of both cultural producers and their audiences is demonstrated, expressed, constructed and situated.

We explain in this chapter why and how the use of linguistic ethnography can renew existing methodologies for understanding the dynamics of the power relationships between cultural producers and contemporary audiences in an environment saturated with interactive social media. Bourdieu, who considered literary writers as cultural producers, argued that literary writers should be comprehended as "producers of symbolic goods" (1985, p. 14). Their audiences are, traditionally speaking, the consumers of these symbolic goods. This perspective on literary writers as cultural producers positions writers as professionals who have to find a balance between a creative notion of artistic freedom (they no longer need to be dependent on patronage) and an economic notion of a market of symbolic goods on which they sell their "products" (Bourdieu, 1985, p. 15). We address how the participation of audiences online, through communicating their opinions, co-construct, strengthen or challenge established authoritative identity and, in the meantime, build or shape their own identities and accumulate some social, cultural, technical and economic capital that Bourdieu (1986) proposes. We elaborate on how to study the comments that readers post on literary writers' personal weblogs, and we reflect on the meanings of these comments in relation to construction of eliteness embedded in the traditional relationship between literary writers as cultural producers and their audiences as cultural consumers.

The importance of this chapter lies in showing the need for and the implementation of a multi-method research framework to grasp the extent to which audiences in a digital environment question or reinforce the eliteness of cultural producers such as literary writers.

ELITE IDENTITY AND SOCIAL MEDIA

Technological development and technical practices (e.g. adoption of new technologies) mutually shape sociocultural practices. Practices of cultural production and consumption have changed due to the proliferation of digital technologies and social media. But often people take for granted that technologies empower audiences, provide egalitarian and collaborative opportunities and have the capabilities to democratise access to production and consumption of media. These claims are made without recognizing the huge amount of efforts invested to engineer sociality (Bucher, 2012; van Dijck, 2012; 2013). Besides, there exists some fundamental inequality in social media user participation when a microscope is applied to scrutinise what actually happens on the ground (e.g. 'the 1% rule' or 'the 90–9–1 principle' which says that the demography of an Internet community usually consists of 90% of the participants of viewing content, 9% of the participants editing content, and 1% of the participants actively creating new content; see Arthur, 2006; Nielsen, 2006). Given existing inequalities, it is sensible to ask who are the elite audiences these days and what are the processes of constructing elite identities and behaviours in a social media context.

Take literary writing, for example. The authoritative elite identity of literary writers stems from a long tradition (Bennett, 2005), and as such can be related to Max Weber's notions of traditional and charismatic authority

(Weber, cited in Parsons, 1964). Weber sees traditional authority as a system in which legitimacy is ascribed to a specific person whose status is "believed in on the basis of the sanctity of the order and the attendant powers of control as they have been handed down from the past" (Weber, cited in Parsons, 1964, p. 341). In line with this conceptualization of traditional authority, one can find resemblance with the image of writing as a highly regarded occupation in which writers have always been very much aware of their predecessors (Bennett, 2005) and in which this tradition of literary ancestors functions as "symbolic resources" to the writer (Meizoz, 2007, p. 189, own translation). Moreover, one can find further echoes of literary authority in Weber's understanding of charismatic authority as "a certain quality of an individual personality by which he is set apart from ordinary men" (Weber, cited in Parsons, 1964, pp. 358–359). In a similar vein, Bourdieu (1986 [1993]) referred to the writer's charisma as the foundation of the literary field in the nineteenth century. What is more, Weber's notion of the "followers" (Weber, cited in Parsons, 1964, pp. 359, 362) of the person who has charismatic authority is similar to the way Bourdieu (1992 [1994]) several decades later characterised the celebrants and the believers of acknowledged artists. Such charismatic authority is accompanied by the belief in a particular person's "call" or "spiritual duty" that, as a result, is "foreign to economic considerations" (Weber, cited in Parsons, 1964, p. 362). In this regard, various scholars theorise the anti-economic logic as a distinct characteristic of the literary writer (e.g. Bourdieu, 1986 [1993]; Franssen, 2010).

Whereas literary writers today are still widely considered in romantic terms, that is as a unique, talented individual (Bennett, 2005; Donovan, Fjellestad and Lundén, 2008), their established elite identity might be challenged on social media where readers' voices coexist. Bourdieu, whose work is crucial for theorizing the structure of society as a result of class conflicts and status competition, sees "the literary field" as a social field, which, like other social systems, is highly stratified and has its own hierarchy (Gerhards and Anheier, 1989; Bourdieu, 1992 [1996]). With the prevalence of social media, such a hierarchy could potentially be broken down in the train of the circulation of user-generated and user-distributed content, as observed elsewhere.[1] If literature is a social product shaped by both authors and readers (Eagleton, 1988), its co-constructed nature is even more evident in modern times where writers and readers meet and interact seamlessly in a closely networked online environment. For example Skains states that online novel communities expand the dynamic between writers, texts and readers because they allow readers to "influence and shape the texts the author is creating, through feedback and reader-contributed material" (2010, p. 96). According to Skains, blogs can be used to build a reciprocal conversation between a writer and the readers who can use the blog to ask questions, to share ideas or to give feedback. However, Skains underlines that it is the author's choice to change this author–reader relation and to engage in a dialogue online (2010, pp. 100–103). This begs for the following questions: Who wields power on social media? Are the elites on social media the same as those in real life? and What factors contribute to their elite identities?

TECHNO ELITENESS

Ongoing theoretical development around elitism and the elitist paradigm has critiqued a "normative dimension" and some conventional and widely shared assumptions (or "myths") of modern societies, because it produces in consequence "a polarizing, polemical style of discourse" (Marcus, 1983, p. 23). It is methodologically and theoretically challenging to study elites and difficult to generalise findings because of the problem of identifying whom the elites are and what they do (Moyser and Wagstaffe, 1987). A common agreement in existing elite studies emerging from frequent arguments over definitions and selection procedures is that classes and identities are neither fixed nor durable categories (e.g. Kidd and Nicholls, 1998). To overcome problems with definitions, some scholars have used Bourdieu's (1992 [1996]) theory of the interconnection between art and the structures of social relations within which art is produced and received to renew methods for elite and social class studies (Heemskerk, 2007; Savage, et al., 2013). Here, techno elite audiences refer to those who have the capabilities of manipulating digital technologies to acquire, maintain, manage and mobilise resources effectively (a range of rich intellectual, economic, social, cultural and technical capital in Bourdieu's [1986] terms) and thereby possess power to become (economical, political, cultural) elites. The possession of such capital gives them power (be it social power [Kidd and Nicholls, 1998, p. xxviii] or economic power[2] [Swedberg, 2011]) to challenge existing authoritative elite opinions, (re-)creating or (re)claiming elite identities. That said, techno elites can (1) render new elite norms and practices; (2) challenge, subvert or sabotage the existing elite norms or practices; and/or (3) reinforce existing eliteness of cultural producers. In a digital world that is highly connected and networked, techno-elite audiences are often seen to exercise their collective power, a collective form of 'techno eliteness'.

By creating and maintaining a set of resources that can be converted into different forms of capital, traditional author–reader relationships start to shift, especially in online environments where cultural producers (e.g. literary writers) become more approachable and cultural consumers more vocal. Knowledge, expertise, experiences (tacit and local knowledge) or any other cultural assets can now be inscribed and negotiated and exchanged through online communicative encounters between authors and readers. Compared to the kind of "active audience" discussed in reader-response literary criticism in the 1970s or in cultural studies and reception studies in the late twentieth century (Harrison and Barthel, 2009), the interactive nature of the web today further blurs the division between reader/viewer and author. Authors and readers co-construct sometimes collective, sometimes conflicting, but always temporary and constantly changing identities. This co-production phenomenon is reminiscent of Jenkins's (1992; 2004; 2007) fandom research, in which audiences, on one hand, strengthen authors' authority as originators of a story and a set of characters but, on the other hand, produce new content. In this sense, the emergence of techno elites challenges the traditional boundaries between professionals and amateurs. This notion parallels but simultaneously questions some other theories treating audiences in terms of "produsage" (Bruns, 2012) as "co-producers" (Loosen and Schmidt, 2012) who demonstrate greater interests in (pro-)active and meaningful "participation" (Carpentier, 2011) rather than simply being a product or a recipient who is informed, entertained, educated or engaged.

If we define the techno-elite audiences as those who have the power to influence, enact, enable and accumulate social, economic and technical capital in a particular online environment, they can now be found almost everywhere owing to the popularisation of Web 2.0 social media. For example the "You" chosen as the *Time* magazine's Person of the Year 2006; more recently, the Media Guardian's annual ranking of "You" as one of the UK's 100 most powerful industry figures 2013;[3] and other instances on the usage of alternative media for shaping politics in scholarly publications (e.g. the work included in Couldry and Curran, 2003), all reflect the extent to which society and industry (traditionally dominated by moguls, editors and celebrities) are being shaped and transformed by the development and adoption of digital technologies. This omnipresence, which subsequently creates vagueness of meanings and a problem of defining 'elite', requires a robust methodological framework to approach the subject. It is worth noting that we do not consider the public as falling into the category of techno elites. In theory, in a democratic and ideal world, everyone has the potential to become part of the techno elite. However, often the inequalities observed in the real society are often replicated in virtual worlds. Our proposal to move away from generalising the elite category allows a practice-based perspective that sees eliteness as 'situated'. To us, eliteness is contextualised, demonstrated and performed through narratives and interactions. In this regard, linguistic ethnography serves as a useful methodological framework for grounding 'techno eliteness' in different contexts and local storytelling.

In contrast to Livingstone's (1998) and Davis's (2005) more narrowly-defined notion of elite,[4] Lin's investigation (2012) into how the BBC engaged with techno elites with their Backstage project, how contemporary media corporations render and recruit elites, and the ease or difficulty of entering the system focuses on practices rather than on socio-economic positions. Lin draws on internal corporate documents, web content and ethnographic fieldwork data to focus on a techno elite group who can analyse data and code. This focus allowed Lin to find out how the BBC envisioned the roles of techno elites in participatory media and finally how the BBC built a techno-elite community around the BBC's resources (data, content, facilities and human social networks). Although the rich ethnographic data she collected documents many impromptu, spontaneous interactions through which novel ideas were conceived and exchanged, the study embodies many of the common challenges facing ethnography such as standardisation of observation processes, data gathering, comparison and data analysis. This is where linguistic ethnography comes into its own.

LINGUISTIC ETHNOGRAPHY: ORIGINS AND SCOPE

Linguistic ethnography can be associated with several research traditions, such as sociolinguistics, the ethnography of communication, and linguistic anthropology, all of which bear an interdisciplinary character. Yet, several scholars (see infra) point out distinct differences between linguistic ethnography and its antecedents. In general, linguistic ethnography can be distinguished based on its focus on local, personal and relational uses of language to construct identities.

Tusting and Maybin mention that a reconfiguration of approaches as well as "increasing attention to social and cultural dimensions of language" (2007, p. 576) marks sociolinguistics. Nevertheless, in recent years these scholars have seen "a growing interest among some British sociolinguists in the potential of combining linguistic analysis with ethnography, in order to probe the relationship between language and social life in more depth" (Tusting and Maybin, 2007, p. 576). Linguistic ethnography, thus, differs from sociolinguistics in its focus on individual practices in a particular context. Moreover, the focus of linguistic ethnography on the "relational" and "interactional" aspects (the first being a broader process, the latter referring to particular moments that build on these relations) of "the building of social worlds" differentiates linguistic ethnography from a sociolinguistic approach (Tsitsipis, 2007, p. 631). In this regard, it is essential, according to Jan Blommaert, to understand ethnography (including linguistic ethnography) as a "theoretical outlook" and a methodology rather than as a method (2007, p. 684).

Creese (2008) also underlines some characteristics of linguistic ethnography which make it distinct from other linguistic anthropological traditions: (1) its place within "the new intellectual climate of late modernity and post-structuralism" (p. 229); (2) its drawing on methodological approaches other than "those typically associated with earlier work in linguistic anthropology" (p. 233); (3) its combination of "fields of study not typical in earlier linguistic anthropology, such as media studies, feminist post-structuralism and sociology" (p. 234); and (4) its focus on "language rather than culture as its principal point of analytical entry" (p. 234). In other words, linguistic ethnography is more "disciplinary-eclectic" and less centred on "genealogy" as is cultural anthropology (Creese, 2008, p. 236), and it "aligns itself with a particular epistemological view of language in social context" (Creese, 2008, p. 229).

This particular epistemological view marries the analytical frameworks provided by linguistics and ethnographic processes of reflexive sensitivity to obtain a close, in-depth analysis of "local action and interaction as embedded in a wider social world" (Creese, 2008, pp. 232–233).

To Rampton (2007), linguistic ethnography is characteristic of (1) an ethnographic focus on the "context for communication" and on the way "meaning takes shape within specific social relations, interactional histories and institutional regimes" and (2) a linguistic analysis of "the internal organisation of verbal (and other semiotic) data" (p. 3). As a result, linguistic ethnography is fit for studying "communication within the temporal unfolding of social processes" (Rampton, 2007, p. 3). It enables the researcher to consider simultaneously (1) persons; (2) situated encounters, which means "the events, genres and types of activity in which people, texts and objects interact together" as well as actions and "the use of semiotic materials (signs, language, texts, media)"; and (3) institutions, networks and communities of practice, implying the shaping and possible reproduction of institutions through texts, objects, media, genres and practices (Rampton, 2007, p. 3).

Finally, Georgakopoulou (2007) sees linguistic ethnography as a subdivision of a broader tradition of ethnography of communication, which is "a way of tapping into ecologies of meaning-making and the participants' own sense-making and structuring features, their tacit and articulated understandings" (2007, p. 20). In her opinion, linguistic ethnography serves as a way out of reductionist approaches to context as it "allows us to tap into processes of recontextualization and dialogicality thus providing valuable insights into natural histories of discourse" (Georgakopoulou, 2007, pp. 20–21). This is the reason why linguistic ethnography focuses on the personal and localised construction of narratives in interactions instead of on the use of discourses in conversations or publications. De Fina and Georgakopoulou (2008) suggest that insights can be generated through linking micro occurrences with macro social processes to understand societal structures, dynamics of exclusion and inclusion, institutional routines and the performance of social roles. They consider a linguistic ethnographic approach appropriate as this social interactional approach takes into account the contextualised construction in time and place of identity narratives (De Fina and Georgakopoulou, 2008, p. 383).

LINGUISTIC ETHNOGRAPHY AND SOCIAL MEDIA AUDIENCES

Social media can be defined in terms of the stories that users tell and share about personal experiences and that express distinct identities (Page, 2012, pp. 1–3). Page situates her work on social media within the sociolinguistic and discourse-analytic research traditions of computer-mediated communication studies as well as in literary-critical narrative theory. Her aim is to understand "the ways in which narrative genres, and in particular narratives of personal experience, are being reworked in online contexts at the outset of the twenty-first century" (2012, p. 5). She believes that this understanding of the "reworking" of personal experience can be obtained by studying, for instance, weblogs. Moreover, she defines social media as Internet-based applications that promote social interaction among participants. As such, social media helps construct networks of participants in which everyone can distribute content, yet in which everyone at the same time becomes part of a collective, large-scale audience for this content. Although interaction was inscribed in the Internet's core, it was not until the mid-1990s that interaction became possible and determinant: "Social media emphasizes the social aspects of the web genres in question, particularly the communicative interaction between participants and the implications this might have for macro-social issues such as personal or group identity" (Page, 2012, p. 7).

According to Rettberg (2008a), blogs in particular can be understood as evolving "narratives" of one's identity. These narratives may be fragments taken from a larger story, but still embody one's perspectives. Other scholars share this view that blogs can be understood in a narrative way: Dennen, for instance, says that "bloggers weave the narratives of their lives into posts" (2009, p. 23). Hevern argues that "weblogs enable their authors to share ongoing personal narratives of daily and seasonal life in ways that no other cyberspatial form allows" (2004, p. 332). Hookway refers to blogs as "self-narratives" (2008, p. 39), and Serfaty conceptualises blogs as "personal narratives" and "self-representational writing" (2004, p. 1). Despite this established understanding of the weblog in terms of constructed narratives, there is a lack of empirical studies on "the narrative potential of blogs" (Page, 2011, p. 220). Page argues that, given the interactive potential of the blog, the study of blogging as an activity and blogs as personal accounts can help to understand the construction, use and "refashioning" of narratives in today's digital society (2011, p. 223). She states that "the comments seem to have a co-constructive influence on the narrative development" of the blog content (Page, 2011, p. 225), because comments influence the narrators' linguistic choices, which results in the emergence of a "heterogeneous and polyvocal mixture of [. . .] narratives" (Page, 2012, pp. 58–59). Serfaty also argues that this narrative of the self cannot be constructed in isolation and is characterised by a collaborative process whereby others constantly intrude in the blogger's private space. Rather than talking about a private space, she delineates a weblog as a "micro-society created by a weblog and its audience" (Serfaty, 2004, p. 65) in which either one-to-one or one-to-many conversations between bloggers and distinct readers take place, or readers engage in many-to-many communication (Tapscott, 1985; Aigrain, 2006) among themselves.

Most of the methods used for audience studies in today's convergent digital media environment are still divided into quantitative methods (e.g., social network analysis and content analysis) and qualitative research methods (e.g., interviews, observation, discourse analysis of historic or policy documents; see e.g. Patriarche, et al., 2014). What is more, often in new media studies one may find a focus on the actions of users and participants dominating over a focus on the construction and the meaning of the actual texts. For instance, an overview of weblog research by Schmidt (2007, p. 1410) suggests that narrative studies of identity- and authority-building are largely missing or are marginal. Often researchers "give the social actors analytical precedence over the textual manifestation of blogging routines", Schmidt concluded (2007, p. 1414). By contrast, we argue that to truly comprehend how and to what extent the online communicative encounter between a blogging literary writer and the commenting audiences is challenging the traditional identity and authority of literary writers, attention should go to the construction of elite identity in the text. This calls for a methodology that is directed at understanding textual interactions and that concentrates on the communicative actions, both in a narrative and in a relational dimension, where techno-elite audiences are gaining a voice in the construction of identities in the online space of a writer's personal weblog. As a result, linguistic ethnography adds to the practice-based perspective by enabling a deeper analysis of the comments that techno elite audiences publish in response to cultural producers' weblog posts and of how this might undermine, nuance or strengthen the traditional cultural producer's authoritative identity and eliteness.

STUDYING ELITENESS OF BLOGGING WRITERS AND COMMENTING READERS

Common methodological issues arising from using qualitative methods for elite studies include managing access to fields, securing interviews with elite respondents (it is often reported that elite respondents were reluctant to be interviewed; e.g. Galaskiewicz, 1987), limitation of generalising findings from observational research based on selective perception and partial recording (e.g. Brannen, 1987; Winkler, 1987) and ethical issues regarding data protection, privacy and confidentiality. To overcome these issues and to account for the relation between the narrative content and the communicational form of (online) representations of elite identity, linguistic ethnography is a valuable methodology for elite studies.

To grasp how exactly a linguistic ethnographic research approach can help to study and understand techno eliteness of social media audiences, we refer to the analytical framework developed in light of the linguistic ethnographic analysis of literary writers' personal weblogs that was conducted to understand how literary eliteness is constructed in a digital culture (Beyl, 2011; 2013). In this study of literary writers' personal weblogs a linguistic ethnographic approach instigates an analysis of the interdependence of a particular blog's narrative content, relational form and personal context.

First, a thematic narrative analysis (Riessman, 2008) is conducted of a selection of a specific literary writer's blog posts and related reader comments. A thematic narrative analysis of the reader comments aims to unveil the narratives that the commenting readers use to represent and construct the blogging writer's literary identity. As such, it can be understood how these readers, by making use of an elite position by having their voices heard, co-construct the literary writer's elite identity in a narrative way. This means that to study the narrative content of a particular literary writer's personal weblog in relation to the construction of elite identity of the literary writer, "narrative" should be understood in a thematic and expressive manner. Riessman's (2008) work, which connects narrative with the way meaning is communicated and relates narrative to personal lives in terms of self-construction, offers a good guideline. Riessman considers narrative as a biographical statement that "encompasses long sections of talk-extended accounts of lives in context" (2008, p. 7). Moreover, Tamboukou emphasises the fluidity and openness of this type of narratives (2008, p. 290). This perspective results from a sociological understanding of narrative as a practice, a sense-making process, and as conversation that takes place within the context of social relations (Hyvärinen, 2008, pp. 452–453), whereas at the same time attention is paid to narrative as an individual's use of symbolic representations (Bornat, 2008, pp. 347–352).

Coding narrative themes that found the 'text' of the blog posts and comments allows the researcher to consider the literary writer's personal weblog as a space in which both the writer and the readers construct a symbolically meaningful representation of literary identity. Specifically, according to Riessman (2008, p. 64), this means circling and highlighting words in the (blog) texts. During this process of reading and rereading the texts, themes emerge. The researcher then connects concepts, discursive constructs, and categories from prior related research, theory and analysis to this "nominal" thematic analysis (Riessman, 2008, p. 64) to understand to what extent research subjects make use of and construct both narratives and counter-narratives in their texts. Narrative analysis, thus, considers "the active constructing processes through which individual subjects attempt to account for their lives" (Emerson and Frosh, 2004, p. 7), which implies thorough knowledge of the specificity of the case as well as of prior theory and concepts to inform coding and interpretation of narrative segments in the text under study.

Concretely, this means that in literary writers' blog posts and their readers' blog comments, it is of interest to look for the way prior narratives on literary identity, namely traditional and charismatic narratives such as 'the writer as genius', are called on or are nuanced in the comments that are published in a particular writer's personal blog. Codes, which the researcher attaches to the readers' comments, are thus a combination of prior theory development and in vivo constructions, for example 'reinforcing mystique', 'personal life of the reader', 'identification with the writer', and so on (Beyl, unpublished doctoral research). It follows from this that the readers' comments in which, for instance, readers express similar personality traits or comparable personal experiences indicate that the readers identify with the writer and consider themselves as equal conversation partners to the writer. This devalues the charismatic narrative of the writer as genius who is considered as superhuman. Hence, the narrative analysis of a particular writer's blog shows that the commenting readers nuance, omit or complement the narratives, as present in the theory on literary identity, with other and newer narratives, such as a narrative wherein the encounter and similarity between writers and readers is stressed. By contrast, reader comments that highlight the impact that the literary work of the writer in question has on them in terms of "magic", "a spell", "a gift" or even "a medicine" reinforce the traditional and charismatic identity of the literary writer (Beyl, unpublished doctoral research).

Second, a linguistic ethnographic approach calls for a thematic analysis of the relationality of the writer's and the readers' blog comments. The aim here is to explore the communicational form, apart from the narrative content, of the interactions between the blogging writer and the commenting readers. This implies a recoding of the words and phrases in the blog comments put forward by both the readers and the literary writer, this time in relation to notions of dialogue and dissemination that may be simultaneously present in these particular online encounters (Rettberg, 2008b, pp. 5–6). This part of the analysis of literary writers' personal blogs results in codes such as "agreeing with the writer" and "defending the writer" (dissemination), or "disagreeing with the writer" and "referring to personal memories" (dialogue; Beyl, unpublished doctoral research). This shows the extent to which interactions reach their fullest potential, that is as communication in which the literary writer and the reader regard one another as equal conversation partners (dialogue), or to what extent there remains a predominance of the writer's voice (dissemination).

Third, a linguistic ethnographic account requires an analysis of the personal context of the weblog in question. This part of the study serves as a way to frame and to understand the distinctiveness of the online (self-) representations and interactions. This contextual analysis can involve in-depth interviews with the blogging writers and the commenting readers in an attempt to understand their motives for blogging and commenting as well as their perception of their relationships both online and offline. Furthermore, it accounts for a detailed interpretation of the extra-situational representation of the blogging writer, for instance, of the self-representation on the writer's personal website, the publisher's promotional representation of the writer, the interface and the layout of the comments on the writer's weblog as well as the writer's offline (literary) performances and occupations. This allows one to get a better idea of the type of writer whom one stands for and of the extent to which this extra-situational representation returns in the blog.

In sum, considering the analysis of the narrative content, of the relational form as well as of the context of a particular writer's personal weblog allows the researcher to understand how social media audiences make use of their capital to co-construct (strengthening, nuancing or undermining) the literary writer's eliteness as cultural producer. As such, a linguistic ethnographic analysis makes it possible to overcome the limitations of earlier studies of literary self-representation that do not account for the narrative and interactional "affordances" (Chemero, 2003) of a particular genre (such as the personal weblog) that is used for self-representation (e.g. Meizoz, 2007), or that do not relate literary self-representation, by means of particular genres, to the construction of eliteness in a multiple and fluid way through interactions between cultural producers and their audiences (e.g. Franssen, 2010).

CONCLUSION

The concept of 'techno elites' interrogates, politicises, conceptualises and provokes thoughts on the power relationships between cultural producers and their audiences in digital societies. The concept allows us to ponder this compound socio-technical process of negotiating power. Adopting a practice-based perspective, techno eliteness is seen as liquid, fluid and temporal. Linguistic ethnography advances elite and social media audience research by providing an interdisciplinary, mixed-analytical analysis of (online) texts to understand the practices, representations, interactions and communications that construct identities. Through the interactive construction of representations, in which traditional and charismatic eliteness is challenged and/or strengthened, audiences respond to traditional cultural producers via social media, and in turn build their own techno elite identities. The value of linguistic ethnography lies in its effectiveness for studying various linguistic usages and the construction of (self-)narratives, and in turn (self-selected, self-enrolled) elite identities in online interactive encounters, weblogs in particular. Instead of employing a range of static groups defined by their occupations or incomes (or properties) and presenting the techno elites as a fixed category, linguistic ethnography allows one to think more flexibly and realistically about the roles and practices of contemporary audiences in a digital era and to effectively address the fluidity of identities in liquid modernity (Bauman, 1991). In comparison to classic ethnographic studies, linguistic ethnography allows us to comprehend how identities are constructed through narratives in a personal context. Moreover, it seeks to unveil how participants adopt and adapt several narratives in their interactions and what kind of identities result from these narratives and interactions. In so doing, linguistic ethnography adds rigour by offering a contextualised, practice-based, narrative-focused perspective to elite studies.

We argue that the nature and characteristics of social media need to be studied in relation to the contexts in which they are used, the actual texts that are produced, as well as the interaction between users (including audiences, broadcasters, writers) who are involved in digital self-representation, in order to understand the changing practices in media industries. Fornäs, et al. (2002, pp. 5–8) state that computer-mediated communication (CMC) needs to be studied as a symbolic construction of identity. In a similar vein, we argue that the weblog text, in terms of both its narrative content and its relational form, should serve as the fulcrum of analysis. Analysing the narrative content allows one to treat a distinct cultural producer's weblog as both a public and personal space that instigates the construction of a symbolically meaningful representation of cultural identity through weblog posts and comments. Moreover, studying the relational form of the interactions (dialogue vs. dissemination) that take place on a weblog may lead to a rethink or redefinition of the asymmetrical–symmetrical form of the author–audience relationships on the cultural producer's weblog. Finally, contextualising weblog content and form allows one to examine to what extent the weblog is used in a congruous or disconnecting way in comparison to the way one is (self-)represented outside of one's blog. To touch on all three aspects, linguistic ethnography is viable and valuable because it instigates a multi-perspective analysis of how social media genres, such as weblogs, play a part in the construction of techno eliteness of social media audiences in view of cultural producers' traditional and charismatic eliteness.

Linguistic ethnography lends itself to a practice-based perspective, which is adequate for capturing the socio-technical dynamics in the formation process of a techno-elite group, taking into account the uncertainties and contingencies introduced by new, emergent technologies, on which techno elites so much depend. Because of its capability of capturing everyday narratives and practices, the linguistic ethnography methodology discussed in this chapter is intended to contribute to the ongoing search for robust methodologies for elite research. It innovates communication and audience studies by allowing researchers to study how exactly cultural producers and their audiences negotiate narrative, interactive and contextualised constructions of multiple elite identities in a social media context.

NOTES

1. For example the development of free/open source software used for the websites for civil and social actions (e.g. mySociety.org and Ushahidi.com, both of which use digital technologies to make people powerful by developing free and open source software for individual and organisations around the world who want to build copies of the sites they build) and the openly accessible Wikipedia, preceded the Arab Spring movement, a revolutionary wave of political demonstrations, protests, and civil wars occurring in the Arab world that began on 18 December 2010 and are still ongoing.

2. The latter can be exemplified by the kind of self-publishing practices or monetisation and commodification of readers' stories in modern times.
3. http://www.theguardian.com/media/2013/sep/01/mediaguardian-digital-consumer-most-powerful
4. The elite commentators Livingstone (1998) illustrates include those ruling political elites (politicians, policymakers) and broadcasters, a definition provided by Liebes and Katz (1990). Davis (2005) studies the elite use of media of stock market workers who seemed to fall into the category of "the new capitalist elite" (Freeland, 2012).

REFERENCES

Aigrain, P., 2006. Diversity, attention and symmetry in a many-to-many information society. *First Monday*, [online] 11(6). Available at: <http://firstmonday.org/htbin/cgiwrap/bin/ojs/index.php/fm/article/view/1337/1257>

Aron, R., 1950a. Social structure and the ruling class: part one. *The British Journal Sociology* 1(1), pp. 1–16.

Aron, R., 1950b. Social structure and the ruling class: part two. *The British Journal of Sociology,* 1(1), pp. 126–143.

Arthur, C., 2006. What is the 1% rule? *The Guardian* [online] 20 July. Available at: <http://www.guardian.co.uk/technology/2006/jul/20/guardianweeklytechnologysection2>

Bauman, Z., 1991. *Modernity and ambivalence.* Cambridge: Polity Press.

Bennett, A., 2005. *The author.* London and New York: Routledge.

Beyl, J., 2011. A narrative approach to studying writers' weblogs as interactive processes of identity performance. In: S. Fragoso, et al., eds. 2011. *AOIR-Selected Papers of Internet Research, IR 12.0 Performance and Participation* [online]. Available at: <http://spir.aoir.org/index.php/spir/issue/view/1>

Beyl, J., 2013. Blogging writers: (de)mystification of authority? In: P. Runnel, P. Pruulmann-Vengerfeldt, P. Viires and M. Laak, eds. 2013. *The digital turn: user's practices and cultural transformations.* Frankfurt am Main, Berlin, Bern, Bruxelles, New York, Oxford, Wien: Peter Lang International Academic Publishers, pp. 128–140.

Beyl, J., 2014. *Finding authority in a digital culture. A linguistic ethnography of literary writers' personal weblogs.* Ph.D. Vrije Universiteit Brussel, Brussels, Belgium.

Blommaert, J., 2007. Commentaries. On scope and depth in linguistic ethnography. *Journal of Sociolinguistics* 11(5), pp. 682–688.

Bornat, J., 2008. Biographical methods. In: P. Alasuutari, L. Bickman and J. Bramen, eds. 2008. *The SAGE handbook of social research methods.* Los Angeles: Sage. pp. 344–356.

Bourdieu, P., 1985. The market of symbolic goods. *Poetics* 14(1–2), pp. 13–44.

Bourdieu, P., 1986. The forms of capital. In: J. Richardson, ed. 1986. *Handbook of theory and research for the sociology of education.* New York: Greenwood. pp. 241–258.

Bourdieu, P., 1986 [1993]. The production of belief: contribution to an economy of symbolic goods. In: R. Johnson, ed. 1993. *The field of cultural production. Essays on art and literature. Pierre Bourdieu.* Cambridge: Polity Press. pp. 74–111.

Bourdieu, P., 1992 [1994]. *De regels van de kunst. Wording en struktuur van het literaire veld.* Amsterdam: Van Gennep.

Bourdieu, P., 1992 [1996]. *The rules of art: genesis and structure of the literary field.* Translated from French by S. Emanuel. Cambridge: Polity Press.

Brannen, P., 1987. Working on directors: some methodological issues. In: G. Moyser and M. Wagstaffe, eds. 1987. *Research methods for elite studies*. London: Allen & Unwin, pp. 166–180.

Bruns, A., 2008. *Blogs, Wikipedia, Second Life, and beyond. From production to produsage*, New York: Peter Lang Publishing.

Bucher, T., 2012. Want to be on the top? Algorithmic power and the threat of invisibility on Facebook. *New Media & Society* [online first: 8 April 2012]. Available at <http://nms.sagepub.com/content/early/2012/04/04/1461444812440159>

Carpentier, N., 2011. The concept of participation. If they have access and interact, do they really participate? *Communication Management Quarterly* 21(6), pp. 7–12.

Chemero, A., 2003. An outline of a theory of affordances. *Ecological Psychology* 15(2), pp. 181–195.

Couldry, N. and Curran, J., eds., 2003. *Contesting media power: alternative media in a networked world*. Oxford: Rowman & Littlefield Publishers, Inc.

Creese, A., 2008. Linguistic ethnography. In: K. A. King and N. H. Hornberger, eds. 2008. *Encyclopedia of language and education, 2nd edition, volume 10: research methods in language and education*. New York, NY: Springer Science+Business Media LLC, pp. 229–241.

Davis, A., 2005. Media effects and the active elite audience: a study of communications in the London stock exchange. *European Journal of Communication* 20(3), pp. 303–326.

De Fina, A. and Georgakopoulou, A., 2008. Analysing narratives as practices. *Qualitative Research* 8(3), pp. 379–387.

Dennen, V.P., 2009. Constructing academic alter-egos: identity issues in a blog-based community. *Identity in the Information Society* 2(1), pp. 23–38.

Donovan, S., Fjellestad, D. and Lundén, R., 2008. Introduction: author, authorship, authority, and other matters. In: S. Donovan, D. Fjellestad and R. Lundén, eds. 2008. *Authority matters. Rethinking the theory and practice of authorship*. New York: Editions Rodopi. pp. 1–19.

Eagleton, T., 1988. Two approaches in the sociology of literature. *Critical Inquiry* 14(3), pp. 469–476.

Emerson, P. and Frosh, S., 2004. *Critical narrative analysis in psychology. A guide to practice*. Hampshire and New York: Palgrave Macmillan.

Fornäs, J., Klein, K., Ladendorf, M., Sundén, J. and Sveningsson, M., 2002. Into digital borderlands. In: J. Fornäs, K. Klein, M. Ladendorf, J. Sundén, and M. Sveningsson, eds. 2002. *Digital borderlands. Cultural studies of identity and interactivity on the Internet*. New York, NY: Peter Lang. pp. 1–47.

Franssen, G., 2010. Literary celebrity and the discourse on authorship in Dutch literature. *Journal of Dutch Literature* 1(1), pp. 91–113.

Freeland, C., 2012. *Plutocrats: the rise of the new global super-rich and the fall of everyone else*. London: Penguin Books.

Galaskiewicz, J., 1987. The study of a business elite and corporate philanthropy in a United States metropolitan area. In: G. Moyser and M. Wagstaffe, eds. 1987. *Research methods for elite studies*. London: Allen & Unwin. pp. 147–165.

Georgakopoulou, A., 2007. *Small stories, interaction and identities*. Amsterdam and Philadelphia: John Benjamins Publishing Company.

Gerhards, J. and Anheier, H.K., 1989. The literary field: an empirical investigation of Bourdieu's sociology of art. *International Sociology* 4(2), pp. 131–146.

Harrison, T.M. and Barthel, B., 2009. Wielding new media in Web 2.0: exploring the history of engagement with the collaborative construction of media products. *New Media & Society* 11(1–2), pp. 155–178.

Heemskerk, E.M., 2007. *Blurring line of the relations of elites and citizens – decline of the corporate community: network dynamics of the Dutch business elite*. Amsterdam: Amsterdam University Press.

Hevern, V.W., 2004. Threaded identity in cyberspace: weblogs & positioning in the dialogical self. *Identity: An International Journal of Theory and Research* 4(4), pp. 321–335.
Hookway, N., 2008. 'Entering the blogosphere': some strategies for using blogs in social research. *Qualitative Research* 8(1), pp. 91–113.
Hyvärinen, M., 2008. Analyzing narratives and story-telling. In: P. Alasuutari, L. Bickman and J. Brannen, eds. 2008. *The SAGE handbook of social research methods*. Los Angeles, CA: Sage. pp. 447–460.
Jenkins, H., 1992. *Textual poachers: television fans and participatory culture*. New York: Routledge.
Jenkins, H., 2004. The cultural logic of media convergence. *International Journal of Cultural Studies* 7(1), pp. 33–43.
Jenkins, H., 2007. Reconsidering digital immigrants . . . [blog], 5 December 2007. Available at: <http://henryjenkins.org/2007/12/reconsidering_digital_immigran.html>
Kidd, A. and Nicholls, D., 1998. Introduction: the making of the British middle class? In: A. Kidd and D. Nicholls, eds. 1998. *The making of the British middle class? Studies of regional and cultural diversity since the eighteenth century*. Stroud, Gloucestershire: Sutton Publishing Ltd. pp. xv–xl.
Liebes, T., and Katz, E., 1990. *The export of meaning*. Oxford: Oxford University Press.
Lin, Y.-W., 2012. The emergence of techno-elite audience and free/open source content: a case study on BBC backstage. *Participations: Journal of Audience & Reception Studies* 9(2), pp. 597–613.
Livingstone, S., 1998. Audience research at the crossroads: the 'implied audience' in media and cultural theory. [pdf]. London: LSE Research Online. Available at: <http://eprints.lse.ac.uk/archive/00000392>
Loosen, W. and Schmidt, J.-H., 2012. (Re-)discovering the audience. The relationship between journalism and audience in networked digital media. *Information, Communication & Society* 15(6), pp. 867–887.
Marcus, G.E. ed., 1983. *Elites: ethnographic issues*. Albuquerque: University of New Mexico Press.
Meizoz, J., 2007. *Postures littéraires. Mises en scène modernes de l'auteur*. Genève: Editions Slatkine.
Moyser, G. and Wagstaffe, M., 1987. Studying elites: theoretical and methodological issues. In: G. Moyser and M. Wagstaffe, eds. 1987. *Research methods for elite studies*. London: Allen & Unwin. pp. 1–24.
Nielsen, J., 2006. *Participation inequality: encouraging more users to contribute*. [online] Available at: <http://www.nngroup.com/articles/participation-inequality/>
Page, R., 2011. Blogging on the body. Gender and narrative. In: R. Page and B. Thomas, eds. 2011. *New narratives. Stories and storytelling in the digital age*. Lincoln and London: University of Nebraska Press. pp. 220–238.
Page, R., 2012. *Stories and social media. Identities and interaction*. New York and London: Routledge.
Parsons, T., ed., 1964. *Max Weber: the theory of social and economic organization*. London: Collier-Macmillan.
Patriarche, G., Bilandzic, H., Jensen, J.L., and Jurisic J., eds. 2014. *Audience research methodologies: between innovation and consolidation*. London: Routledge.
Putnam, R.D. 1976. *The comparative study of political elites*. Englewood Cliffs: Prentice Hall.
Rampton, B., 2007. Linguistic ethnography, interactional sociolinguistics and the study of identities. *Working papers in urban language & literacies*. London: King's College London.
Rettberg, J.W., 2008a. *Blogging*. Cambridge: Polity Press.
Rettberg, J.W., 2008b. Blogs, literacies and the collapse of private and public. *Leonardo Electronic Almanac* 16(2–3), pp. 1–10.

Riessman, C.K., 2008. *Narrative methods for the human sciences.* Los Angeles, New York, London, New Delhi, and Singapore: Sage.

Savage, M., Devine, F., Cunningham, N., Taylor, M., Li, Y., Hjellbrekke, J., Le Roux, B., Friedman, S., and Miles A., 2013. A new model of social class: findings from the BBC's great British class survey experiment. *Sociology* 47(2), pp. 219–250.

Schmidt, J., 2007. Blogging practices: an analytical framework. *Journal of Computer-Mediated Communication* 12, pp. 1409–1427.

Serfaty, V., 2004. *The mirror and the veil: an overview of American online diaries and blogs.* Amsterdam: Rodopi.

Skains, R.L., 2010. The shifting author-reader dynamic. *Convergence: The International Journal of Research into New Media Technologies* 16(1), pp. 95–111.

Swedberg, R., 2011. The economic sociologies of Pierre Bourdieu. *Cultural Sociology* 5(1), pp. 167–182.

Tamboukou, M., 2008. Re-imagining the narratable subject. *Qualitative Research*, 8(3), pp. 283–292.

Tapscott, D., 1985. *The digital economy: promise and peril in the age of networked intelligence.* New York: McGraw-Hill.

Tsitsipis, L.D., 2007. Relationality in sociolinguistics: A dialogue with linguistic ethnography. *Journal of Sociolinguistics* 11(5), pp. 626–640.

Tusting, K. and Maybin, J., 2007. Linguistic ethnography and interdisciplinarity: opening the discussion. *Journal of Sociolinguistics* 11(5), pp. 575–583.

van Dijck, J., 2012. Facebook as a tool for producing sociality and connectivity. *Television & New Media* 13(2), pp. 160–176.

van Dijck, J., 2013. *The culture of connectivity. A critical history of social media.* Oxford and New York: Oxford University Press.

Winkler, J.T., 1987. The fly on the wall of the inner sanctum: observing company directors at work. In: G. Moyser and M. Wagstaffe, eds. 1987. *Research methods for elite studies.* London: Allen & Unwin. pp. 129–146.

7 Exploring Landscapes of News Consumption Cross-Nationally
The Use of Q Methodology to Fuse Quantitative and Qualitative Approaches for Increased Explanatory Power in Comparative Research

Cédric Courtois, Kim Christian Schrøder and Christian Kobbernagel

INTRODUCTION

Although there is no dearth in contemporary media and communication research of many varieties of audience research as such (to which this book bears witness, as well as, for instance, Bilandzic, Patriarche and Traudt [2012]; Carpentier, Schrøder and Hallett [2013]; and Parameswaran [2013]), there is as yet little empirical audience research which inscribes itself explicitly into the much-discussed processes of mediatisation (Hjarvard, 2008; Strömbäck, 2008; Hepp, 2013).

There appears to be widespread agreement among scholars that we live in an age of mediatisation, which, in spite of some definitional disagreements, is generally conceptualised as an epochal metaprocess on a par with the metaprocesses of individualisation, commercialisation and globalisation. But so far there has been little sustained effort within media and communication research to situate the role of audiences within the mediatisation phenomenon, let alone to explore this role empirically.

The need to do so springs from the fact that mediatisation in most conceptualisations is seen as a trans-local phenomenon. Therefore its local manifestation in specific cultures (be they national, regional, ethnic or otherwise) is highly dependent on the concrete ways in which its technological, institutional and symbolic affordances are domesticated by local audiences in addition to important institutionalised actors in political, legislative and commercial systems and actors anchored in communitised contexts of civil society.

In this chapter we present the findings of a cross-national comparative research project in which we have explored, with an innovative methodology, the ways in which recent trans-local developments in the mediatised cultures of news (such as the emergence of twenty-four-hour TV news channels and free dailies, the rise of online platforms for the dissemination of news, the growth in ubiquitous mobile news acquisition, and the opportunities for user-generated content) have become 'territorialised' by audiences in two national regions in Europe: Denmark and Flanders (Belgium).

The study's analytical apparatus is innovative in its contribution to audience research by showing how our combination of qualitative and quantitative analysis integrates coherently and non-sequentially, generating valuable insight into the complex multifaceted field of news consumption. Although the emphasis is on the qualitative properties, we blend a quantitative translation procedure into the qualitative process, in order to fortify the qualitative findings, for more reliable comparative analysis than previously seen in qualitative audience research.

As an additional, related objective, our comparison also serves to dispel the tempting taken-for-grantedness of the findings from any one country in itself. The findings from the Danish study may seem, at least when presented to Danes, not very surprising, even predictable. However, the comparison with findings from a culturally neighbouring country enables the insight that other realities in audience navigations in the landscape of news are possible, maybe desirable. Thus, insights about an 'Other' news culture can be offered as incentives for policymakers and other stakeholders to adopt a reflective stance towards the seeming naturalness of the home culture.[1]

THE RECIPROCITY OF MEDIA LOGICS AND AUDIENCE LOGICS

The distinctive differences between the various positions within the current debates about mediatisation primarily have to do with the allocation of formative cultural power over the way societies and civilisations function and change. Our research has been conducted in accordance with the theoretical framework most recently propounded by Andreas Hepp (2013), but which has also, in more embryonic form, permeated some earlier studies which sought to complexify our notions of media power (Gamson, 1992; Schrøder and Phillips, 2007).

Whereas we do not deny that 'media logics' may play a key role in some transformative processes, perhaps particularly in the realm of politics (Hjarvard, 2008; Strömbäck, 2008), we adhere more to the view that we need to examine the mutual interweaving of media logics and audience logics if we wish to properly grasp the transformations of mediatised cultures. This is what Hepp (2013) analyses as what he terms—more cautiously—the "moulding forces" of the media, that is the way in which media as technologies and institutions "exercise a certain 'pressure' upon the way in which we communicate" (Hepp, 2013, p. 54), without having direct and immediate 'effects'. Instead the shaping properties of the media are seen to work through the co-creative powers of audiences as users, who build and make sense of their media repertoires in everyday life (Hasebrink and Popp, 2006), and who inhabit the various communities of civil society.

In the age of mediatisation it is "an analysis of people's communicative action which forms the core of the study of media and communications" (Hepp, 2013, p. 138), because they selectively encounter, make sense of and appropriate the technological and discursive affordances which the culture of mediatisation so richly offers.

One of us has argued elsewhere that citizen-consumers are guided in their selective sense-making encounters with the multitude of (news) media by a principle, or 'logic', of *worthwhileness* (Schrøder and Larsen, 2010): for a news medium to be adopted into the individual's news repertoire, it must be subjectively experienced by this individual as worthwhile. Worthwhileness is a multidimensional phenomenon encompassing at least seven different dimensions, so that in order to become part of an individual's news diet, a news medium must

1. be worth the *time* spent: some news media, perceived to be important, will be used regularly, whereas others will be relegated to time pockets of free time.
2. be acceptable to peer networks, which operate by tacit or explicit *normative pressures*.
3. maintain *public connection*, that is provide discursive links, through relevant news *content*, to networks and the wider society. A subdivision is possible into 'democratic worthwhileness' and 'everyday worthwhileness'.
4. have *participatory potential*, through the medium's technological affordances, making it possible to respond, vote, offer user-generated content and so on.
5. be affordable in terms of *price*.
6. have *technological appeal*, as especially offered by the more recent media gadgets.
7. have *situational fit*, in terms of the location of use (at home, during transport, etc.)

As people are doing their daily shopping in the 'supermarket of news', these worthwhileness dimensions enter into the 'worthwhileness equation' as constituents of the personal aggregate 'logic' of news media consumption. These audience logics ultimately decide the success or failure of the news formats offered by news media organisations and may pressure them to innovate the affordances they offer in the areas of technology, aesthetics and meaningful discursive content, in their specific territorial and cultural anchorage.

NEWS CONSUMPTION: THE CROSS-MEDIA RESEARCH IMPERATIVE

In a mediatised society, we are constantly confronted with an abundance of alternative forms of mediation. It is perhaps a truism to say that audiences are now, more than ever, confronted with an ever-broader palette of choices when it comes to composing a media diet, or media repertoires (Hasebrink and Popp, 2006; Schrøder, 2011). Audiences have always been confronted with multiple options, but today these options have grown significantly in number. Media are all around, and in this media-drenched environment, people are audiences all the time without devoting much attention to it. It is a constitutive of the everyday, aiding in forming and regulating the mundane. According to Abercrombie and Longhurst (1998) we have evolved into diffused audiences, characterised by dispersion and fragmentation, by routine, omnipresence and casual inattention. This form of audience succeeds yet also incorporates simple audiences involved in direct, ritualised and publication communication as well as mass audiences, which are highly mediated and typically dispersed across private and public settings.

This ubiquity of media consumption, crystallised in media repertoires, causes reflection. For instance, rather provocatively, Deuze (2011; Deuze, Blank, and Speers, 2012) writes about a *media life*, which refers to the symbiotic intertwining of media consumption and the everyday. Insofar as media "form our constant remix of the categories of everyday life (the public and the private, the local and the global, the individual and the collective), they have become invisible" (Deuze, 2011, p. 137). In this respect, people are seen as part of, and constituting media: they live *in* rather than *with* media. They take an active part in constructing reality and a sense of belonging, through scattered and constantly occurring consumption and production. Deuze further argues, in an argument that carries resonances of the "media repertoires" phenomenon, that "people increasingly move through the world (more or less deliberately) assembling a deeply individualized media system—in other words: Living in their own personal information space—such a viewpoint can form the basis of investigation and understanding of everyday life" (2011, p. 139).

Nevertheless, this very claim of invisibility was criticised by Kubitschko and Knapp (2012), arguing that the central feature of invisibility does not comply with the prominent idea that media are also utilised in explicit strategic and deliberate manners and that there is no absolute internalisation of the interface with media. Still, routines are of undeniable importance in understanding media consumption (Courtois, 2012). As Couldry (2012) argued, they are an indispensable feature of 'media practices', next to (a) the social dimension because action is predominantly oriented to others, rendering media practices social constructions; (b) the broad link with human needs as dependent of the requirements of social life; and (c) normative thinking on how we should live with media. The main question, Couldry (2012, p. 37) continued, is "[W]*hat are people doing in relation to media across a whole range of situations and contexts? How is people's media-related practice related, in turn, to their wider agency?*"

Building further on Couldry's central question, in this chapter, we deliberately focus on cross-media news consumption repertoires both in Denmark and in Flanders. As important frames of references, news media constitute an indispensable element of our perception and making sense of reality. They offer ample opportunities to access and to fuel various domains of associational interaction (i.e. public spheres), which are considered a precondition to actively develop the necessary literacies to exercise civic agency (Dahlgren, 2006). When media audiences embrace the possibility to interact with each other and with power holders of various kinds, their role even transforms from being part of audiences into being part of publics, the latter of which is related to active engagement and the development of citizenship (Livingstone, 2005).

CROSS-NATIONAL COMPARATIVE RESEARCH: WHAT AND HOW TO COMPARE

The 'What' of Cross-National Comparison: Living with Informed Territorial Essentialism

As Livingstone (2003) observes, the extent of contemporary globalisation processes in the area of culture and media makes it natural—and "impossible yet necessary" (p. 482)—to adopt a comparative perspective on the similar and different properties of media cultures, poised between the local/national and the trans-local/transnational contexts. Although Livingstone readily defines comparative research as "a study that compares two or more nations with respect to some common activity" (2003, p. 478), she also discusses the potentially problematic taken-for-grantedness of equating the comparative with the comparison of nations, which Hepp and Couldry (2009, p. 36) label "territorial essentialism". In some ways, she argued, "the nation itself is not a proper unit of comparison. Nations are far from self-contained, closed or homogeneous, but rather comprise multiple cultures with diasporic and global trends making for a poor mapping of culture onto nation" (Livingstone, 2003, p. 479). Along similar lines, Hepp and Couldry (2009) argued that the cross-nation perspective "obscures our view of what media cultures might be in an era of media flows that consistently overlap national borders" (2009, p. 32).

However, we take the view that the nation state continues to be relevant in comparative media research, because "communication systems are still in significant respects national [. . .] the nation is still a very important marker of difference" (Curran and Park, 2000, p. 11). We also rest this position on the powerful argument of Billig (1995) that most people are willy-nilly in the grip of a banal nationalism, a self-evident national 'we' which is discursively reproduced by the media day in and day out.

The strength of national belonging is also acknowledged by Hepp and Couldry, when the comparison takes place in the area of politics and news media, because democratic citizenship is by and large exercised within the borders of the nation state: "There are aspects of media communication related to the state that must be discussed in a territorialized state frame" (Hepp and Couldry, 2009, p. 36).

At the same time, as argued above, we are very much aware that many of the phenomena we observe and map in the two countries are actualisation of technological, discursive and aesthetic affordances deriving from translocal processes of mediatisation. We follow Hepp and Couldry (who in turn are following Löfgren [2001]) in conceptualising these territorialisation as cultural "thickenings", or domestications, effected by the national media political culture. Under this perspective the national media cultures of Denmark and Flanders become precisely cultures "whose translocal communicative thickening has been territorialized in such a way that national frontiers are the main borders of many communicative networks and flows" (Hepp and Couldry, 2009, p. 38). The typologies of news consumption which we present in the following can therefore be seen as the specific "cultural "thickenings generated by the two historically anchored national media cultures.

The 'How' of Cross-National Comparison: Q Methodology as the Best of Both Worlds

The studies presented in this chapter are qualitative, but used the techniques and procedures of Q methodology to collect and analyse a combination of quantitative and qualitative data (Davis and Michelle, 2011). The focal point of attention is the structure of news consumption repertoires, and these repertoires' subjective, differential bases in people's everyday lives. As such, participants are treated as variables, variably incorporating news media outlets into their personal repertoires. This approach renders Q method, until now hardly used in audience research, especially valuable. The idea of a qualitatively founded Q-sort task is to invite participants to (verbally) reflect on a fixed number of attributes presented on cards. In this case, these attributes consisted of twenty-five news media that are deemed to be representative for the wealth of possible news outlets (i.e. the concourse). During the task, participants dynamically sort the attributes one by one, along a predefined normal distribution that covers a single dimension (i.e. does [not] play a role in my life). In this particular case, nine positions were presented, each representing a distinct score (see Table 7.1).

Table 7.1 Fixed Q Grid with Nine Positions, Presented to the Participants

⇐ Does not play a role in my life								Plays a role ⇒ in my life
				0				
			−1	0	1			
		−2	−1	0	1	2		
	−3	−2	−1	0	1	2	3	
−4	−3	−2	−1	0	1	2	3	4
1 item	2 items	3 items	4 items	5 items	4 items	3 items	2 items	1 item

The data from all participants are then combined in a single two-dimensional matrix. In this matrix, the columns represented participants, whereas the rows were made up by the twenty-five news media. The cells consist of the predefined scores per position. Next, based on participant correlations, principal component analysis is used to find similarities and dissimilarities among Q sorts and then group these according to the extraction of a set of factors. This factor structure reflects a distinct pattern of similar participants in the initial data set. Hence, groups of highly correlated Q sorts reflect shared ways participants consume news.

The final step is to figure out what the shared pattern within the groups of news consumers reveal. To grasp what news media a group consider worthwhile, factor scores are computed per factor. A relatively high factor score for a news medium in a specific factor means that the typical consumer in the group especially values that news outlet in his or her repertoire. As such, each pattern's news media preferences are uncovered.

In essence, Q methodology is a qualitative method which profits from utilising the quantitative technique of Q factor analysis to help uncover patterns in small samples. Thus, in our study the Q sort task was embedded in a much richer qualitative interview, functioning as a probing technique. The Q factor analysis served to illuminate nuanced latent patterns that are difficult to infer through qualitative analysis alone, thus allowing us to combine the best of 'both worlds'. Still, questions remained regarding how we can understand these patterns, why they take a certain shape and in what circumstances they were built.

Because of its hybrid character that integrates qualitative and quantitative methods, Q methodology is able to overcome some of the epistemological barriers that traditionally beset both quantitative and qualitative comparisons of media audiences in different cultures (Schrøder, 2004). On one hand, Livingstone argued that "quantitative data can be straightforwardly collected, coded and analysed in accordance with universal conventions of sampling representativeness, reliability and statistical testing" (2003, p. 448), yet this comes at a price: the validity of quantitative comparison is dubious, because the data are meagre in contextual anchorage and cultural specificity. On the other hand, qualitative data "are context dependent, reliant on the local knowledge of the researcher", but their meanings as shared through translated verbal accounts are difficult to compare rigorously (Livingstone, 2003, p. 488). In other words, quantitative findings operate at a level of abstraction that is weakly related to real life, whereas qualitative findings deliver case studies that are difficult to generalise reliably (Livingstone, 2003, p. 489).

When using Q methodology, this dichotomy is avoided altogether, because each country is analysed on its own terms, even if this is done through the standardised research vehicle of the card sortings on the grid: the relational configuration of the sorted cards, which follows the individual subjectivities of the informants, guarantees cultural specificity and context dependence, because it derives meaningfully from the integrated qualitative and quantitative data, which is from the think-aloud dialogue about news media taking place while the informants are building the relational maps on the grid in front of them.

The integrated qualitative–quantitative method we used in our comparative study thus offers an innovative approach to cross-cultural comparative research, by preserving the contextual, qualitative anchorage of the news experience in each country, in a form that lends itself to more rigorous comparison than traditional qualitative research.

The Danish study took place in 2009 and was replicated by the Flemish study in 2011. This means that we had to approach the results with a certain caution, to attribute differences not only to national differences but also to evolving (global) media systems. Also, as is inevitable in comparative research designs, in the course of devising the Flemish concourse, we noticed how certain types of news media did not perfectly translate and required a different interpretation (e.g. tabloid newspaper is not the exact same thing in the two cultures; cf. infra).

DENMARK: HOW CITIZEN-CONSUMERS NAVIGATE IN THE DANISH NEWS LANDSCAPE

The original Danish study was carried out in the fall of 2009 with thirty informants demographically divided so as to include substantial numbers of men and women, people with high and low educational profiles, different adult age groups between twenty and seventy and different geographical locations (including urban and semi-urban areas). The Q elicitation cards numbered twenty-five, which represented all significant publicly available news media, formats and genres (see the Table 7.2 for the complete lists).

Based on the data produced through Q sorting, the Q factor analysis revealed seven types of news consumers, each distinctively differentiated from the other six types by the way they rank the twenty-five news media in order of what role each plays in everyday news consumption.[2] Table 7.2 presents the rank orders of news media per factor, based on the factor loadings of each news medium. The lower the number, the more indispensable a typical member of the factor would consider that specific news medium. Thus, a 1 means that the user type ranked this news medium as the most indispensable, whereas a 25 designates the least indispensable news medium. For clarity of presentation, the top five news media per group type are highlighted. The table should be read in conjunction with the following more descriptive account of the seven user types, in which we account in prose for the news media which they perceive as worthwhile, and the news media to which they attribute less importance in their lives.

Type 1. The Traditional, Versatile News Consumer

Those in type 1 (nine participants) relied on a number of fairly heavy news media, including national newspapers and serious current affairs TV programs. Among the top five, we also found prime-time TV news, radio morning news and Net-based news services, altogether a news media repertoire that includes both overview and background news media oriented towards democratic citizen roles. Radio current affairs programmes, specialised newspapers and cultural news on the net also figured prominently in their news diet. Of low importance were mobile phone news, blogs with news and tabloid newspapers. In our sample these people tended to be college educated and older than thirty-five to forty years.

Type 2. The Popular Culture–Oriented Digital News Consumer

The primary news sources for these participants (four participants) were web-based media, with social media in first place closely followed by the websites of established news institutions. Their chief kind of public connection thus appeared to be that generated by their own digital networks. This does not mean that they were not also attuned to mainstream traditional news media, such as prime-time TV news and radio morning news. They received their overview from free dailies and text-TV, whereas their background news diet consisted of more entertaining, chat-based TV current affairs programs. Of low importance were serious current affairs TV programmes, international TV news and current affairs, and international online news. In our sample these people tended to be in their twenties, not (yet) with college degrees.

Table 7.2 Danish and Flemish Q Results

	Denmark 2009							Flanders (Belgium) 2011							
	Traditional, versatile news consumer	Popular culture-oriented digital news consumer	Background-oriented digital consumer	The light newspaper reader	Heavy newspaper reader	News update addict	Regional omnivorous news consumer	Traditional mainstream news consumer	Hybrid light news consumer	Traditional background news consumer	Mobile, light news consumer	Online, social background news consumer	Mobile background news consumer	Hybrid background news consumer	Online, social light news consumer
	F1	F2	F3	F4	F5	F6	F7	F1	F2	F3	F4	F5	F6	F7	F8
Prime time news on national TV	1	3	3	1	2	2	1	3	11	3	14	8	3	4	11
24-h news channels	20	16	14	12	10	1	12	23	21	15	21	6	20	18	14
Serious current affairs on national TV	4	23	8	7	8	13	3	11	18	7	17	9	5	3	13
Entertaining current affairs on national TV	11	4	11	5	16	8	7	4	13	6	12	5	8	8	20
Current affairs on international TV	15	24	7	8	14	17	22	16	20	8	22	23	10	16	9
Radio news (before 9 a.m.)	3	8	24	16	24	7	17	1	3	2	5	19	18	20	16
Radio news (after 9 a.m.)	7	17	9	10	15	10	8	6	5	11	9	3	15	22	18
Radio current affairs	6	21	17	19	19	24	20	19	12	10	23	4	16	19	24
National mainstream (quality) papers	2	13	10	20	1	22	15	12	19	1	18	18	11	13	6

Medium	1	2	3	4	5	6	7	8	9	10	11	12	13	14	15
National specialised newspapers	9	12	19	25	**5**	18	19	13	24	17	11	12	25	**1**	17
Free dailies	13	**5**	**5**	**3**	9	11	14	10	14	**5**	**2**	24	24	15	**4**
Tabloid newspapers	25	18	25	**2**	21	21	18	**2**	17	25	6	11	12	**5**	10
Local/regional dailies	21	22	23	22	12	20	**2**	22	10	22	8	10	19	7	15
Local free weeklies	17	20	21	14	7	15	10	**5**	6	23	10	13	23	10	22
Professional/news magazines	10	10	16	23	17	16	6	14	**4**	14	20	7	22	12	12
Family and women's magazines	22	9	22	11	18	19	**4**	7	9	24	24	17	**4**	9	**2**
Magazines about lifestyle, health, culture	12	14	6	18	11	9	9	24	**2**	19	**3**	25	**2**	6	19
News on national newspaper/TV websites	**5**	**2**	**1**	**4**	**4**	**4**	**5**	25	**1**	**4**	**4**	**2**	7	**2**	**5**
News on other websites	8	6	**4**	17	6	6	13	9	22	9	19	15	13	11	**3**
Newsblogs	24	11	12	15	23	23	24	20	7	18	15	16	17	23	7
Social media	16	**1**	**2**	9	13	**5**	11	15	16	21	7	**1**	9	25	**1**
News on international websites (by media corp)	14	25	15	13	20	14	25	17	15	12	13	20	21	24	21
News on international websites (not by media corp)	18	15	20	24	22	25	23	21	23	13	16	21	14	14	8
Text-TV news	19	7	18	6	**3**	**3**	16	8	8	20	25	22	6	17	23
News through mobile appliances	23	19	13	21	25	12	21	18	25	16	**1**	14	**1**	21	25

Note: The numbers reflect the factor scores' rank orders: the lower, the more worthwhile a news medium is perceived in the repertoire. The top five news media are marked in grey.

Type 3. The Background-Oriented Digital News Consumer

The top five profile of this group (three participants) was almost identical with that of type 2, pointing towards fairly similar worthwhileness profiles. However, entertaining TV current affairs programs were ranked considerable lower. Conversely, serious current affairs programs and international TV news were fairly high on the list. Of low importance are local daily newspapers, morning radio news and tabloid newspapers. In our sample these people tended to be in their twenties and to live in Copenhagen.

Type 4. The Light Newspaper Reader

Whereas these five participants, like everyone else, looked to prime-time TV news and online news for substantial parts of their news diet, they were clearly distinguished by their allegiance to tabloid newspapers and free newspapers. They sought a mixture of entertaining and serious current affairs programs. Of low importance were professional magazines, international non-media news sites and national niche newspapers. In our sample these people tended to be male, with no college degree and live in the greater Copenhagen area.

Type 5. The Heavy Newspaper Reader

These three participants relied heavily on print news media: national newspapers and specialised newspapers in the top five, with local weeklies and free newspapers in the top ten. But these print media were strongly supplemented with prime-time TV news and net-based news. Overviews came from net news, text-TV and twenty-four-hour TV news. Of low importance were news blogs, morning radio news and mobile phone news. In our sample these people tended to be college educated and older than sixty.

Type 6. The News-Update Addict

This group (four participants) owed its label to their having twenty-four-hour TV news in first place, whereas other groups placed this news medium between tenth and fourteenth or lower. The craving for news updates was supported by text-TV, also in the top five, and the highest place of mobile phone news of any group. But the mainstream source of prime-time TV news was also salient. Of low importance were news blogs, radio current affairs and international non-media news sites. In our sample these people tended to be male, younger than forty and with no or a limited college education.

Type 7. The Regional Omnivorous News Consumer

The distinguishing feature of this group (three participants) was the prominent worthwhileness of regional dailies. Another feature of this group was its high and close ranking of news media that were either ranked lower or with greater rank differences by other groups: serious and entertaining TV current affairs programs, weekly magazines and professional magazines (e.g. trade union members' magazines). But the similarity with other groups in terms of the high worthwhileness of prime-time TV news and online news was evident. Compared with type 1, the regional daily had taken over the role of the national daily, and type 7 were more open to social media and twenty-four-hour TV news. Of low importance were international non-media news sites, news blogs and international news media websites. In our sample these people tended to live in a provincial town and to have fewer years of college education.

Our Q methodological approach made it possible to afterwards insert the hybrid qualitative/quantitative relational findings based on the Q factor analysis into a purely qualitative framework, which was provided by the record of the qualitative think-aloud feature of the informant interview sessions. Here we could harvest, in the form of the informants' own words, the subjective sense-making about news media which underlies the aggregate card sorts of the members of a type. For reasons of space, we provide such a glimpse of the complementary 'thick description' of the user types only in connection with the Flemish study.

Concluding Remarks about the Danish Scene

It is striking that in spite of the complex configurations of news media consumption among the Danish informants, they relied almost equally on the 'old' news medium of television and the 'new' medium of internet news sites maintained by the major Danish newspaper publishers. This situation is unlike what was found in the contemporary Pew Research Center (2008) study in the United States, in which there was a clear division between the 'traditionalists', who used almost no online news media, and the 'net-newsers', who rarely resorted to print and TV news. Another pattern showed that all groups relied on a mixture of 'overview' and 'depth/background' news media, with some groups leaning more towards the former (types 2, 4 and 6) and others giving a high rank to news media with a 'serious' content profile (types 1, 3 and 5), with one group falling between these categories (type 7). Because the data were collected in 2008, few yet found it worthwhile to use mobile media as a regular and important news source, but social media figured prominently in the news diet of three of the groups (types 2, 3 and 6).

FLANDERS: HOW CITIZEN-CONSUMERS NAVIGATE IN THE FLEMISH NEWS LANDSCAPE

The Flemish part of the study involved thirty-two face-to-face interviews lasting about an hour and half, administered in the spring of 2011. The interview's topic list largely mirrored its Danish predecessor by starting with an overview of a day in the life with the news media, then centring on the Q task, followed by further probing into the day-to-day relevance of news media. The analysis of the Q data, which happened independently of the Danish analysis and interpretation of the results, led to eight factors with an eigenvalue over one, jointly explaining 83 per cent of the initial variance in the pool of participants. Again, we refer to Table 7.2 for a full enumeration of the rank orders of news media per factor. The lower the rank, the more indispensable a specific news medium is.

Type 1. The Traditional Mainstream Consumer

A first group in the Flemish Q solution consisted of seven participants. They started the day with radio news, and further depended on tabloid newspapers and prime time news on national television. Entertaining current affairs, radio news after 9 a.m. and local free weeklies were less valued. Hence, this kind or repertoire was oriented to a general news oversight, obtained by classic media outlets.

Type 2. The Hybrid Light News Consumer

The second group, comprising five participants, was pinpointed as the *hybrid light news consumer*. The primary sources of news were national newspaper or television websites, followed by lifestyle magazines and prime-time television news. These consumers, attracted by lighter types of news, were marked as hybrid because they mix traditional and online media. Although the majority of worthwhile news media were traditional (radio, paper, television), online media such as news websites and blogs took on a relatively prominent role.

Type 3. The Traditional Background News Consumer

Third, we encountered four *traditional background news consumers*. Similar to the first group, traditional forms of media, such as newspapers, radio and television were generally favoured. Still, they primarily bought quality newspapers, and current affairs news was secondary to these newspapers. Interestingly, news websites came in fourth place. Labelling this type of repertoire as hybrid, albeit to a much smaller extent, therefore could be argued.

Type 4. The Mobile, Light News Consumer

Those with this repertoire primarily were dominated by the perceived worthwhileness of mobile appliances, which clearly distinguished them from the previous patterns in which this type of news outlet were considered all but significant. The mobile aspect was further extended with free dailies and lifestyle magazines. Consequently, we further labelled these participants as light news consumers.

Type 5. The Online, Social Background News Consumer

Next, the fifth type consisted of four participants who were clearly tied to social media as news sources. This was further extended by news websites, prime-time television news, current affairs on radio and entertaining current affairs on television. As such, the online component clearly stood out, next to the search for deepening information through current affairs programmes.

Type 6. The Mobile Mainstream News Consumer

Like the fourth type, mobile appliances were perceived most worthwhile in those in this type, which included three participants. This repertoire was also driven by lighter news, although in contrast with the fourth type, we did notice traces of consulting deepening information through serious current affairs on television and keeping up-to-date through text news and news websites.

Type 7. The Hybrid Background News Consumer

The seventh type was made up by two participants and was dominated by national specialised newspapers as the primary source of news, followed by news in national newspapers and television websites, as well as serious current affairs programmes on television, prime-time news on television and tabloid newspapers. Generally, we noticed a tendency towards background information, which is gratified by traditional as well as online media.

Type 8. The Online, Social Light News Consumer

Finally, the eighth type again involved two participants with a primary focus on social media as news sources. This was further complemented by family and women's magazines, as well as by news on websites other than those of newspapers or television channels. It was therefore a repertoire dominated by online media, directed to lighter news genres.

Complementing Factor-Analytical Profiles with Qualitative Thick Description

Here we demonstrate the potential of qualitative enrichment of the bare Q factorial structure, which demonstrates the merit of thickening patterns with participants' own voices. In the following excerpts, we want to hint to the factors that underlie the apparent differences between traditional news media consumers (type 1) and their mobile counterparts (type 6).

The traditional media, so prominent in the first user type, seemed to serve as structuring elements in daily practices. Each type of news outlet was, routine-wise, tied to a timeslot. Carine explained:

> I got up at seven, just before seven, and I listened to the news about the government, then the weather forecast. Around noon I went sporting and at night I watched the news, and I saw we now finally have a government. Then I watched the weather forecast again, that's about all . . . in the evening, I also read my newspaper, superficially, to read about all kinds of things, just browse through it. That's about fifteen to twenty minutes. No sports, just, what happened, in general.

Didier, a participant with a similar repertoire, added:

> I get up at 6:30, have a shower and shave, go off to work, start at 7:30, and then my day begins until 16:00. I'm a forklift driver. I listen to the radio a lot. My radio is always on in my forklift. So I'm up to date about the news all the time . . . After work I get home, do groceries, prepare dinner, do the dishes. Then I watch a little TV. Again the news. You heard it on the radio, but you haven't seen it on the television.

In contrast, our mobile participants exploited the permanent availability of news, regardless of context, which allows for much broader degrees of freedom in their news engagement. They consulted news at the pace of their lives, not the pace of media. Guy elaborated:

> Even if I don't have the time to use a computer, I have my tablet I take everywhere: the kitchen, the bathroom. And if I'm somewhere, mobile, at work or so, I use my smartphone. So I'm basically always on, watching stuff, everything . . . I use Nieuwsblad.be and deredactie.be. Everything's on it, very short, you can choose articles, click them, read what you want.

Concluding Remarks about the Flemish Scene

The Flemish news consumers divided into more than a handful of patterns, clearly marking a rich diversity in assembling news consumption repertoires. Still, we were able to identify several basic building blocks, seemingly distributed along several dimensions. A first dimension concerning media choice contrasts *traditional* and *online media*. On one hand, we noticed consumers who stick to classic outlets such as television, radio and newspapers, but on the other hand, we noticed how a considerable proportion of participants are oriented to social media and online news products. Nevertheless, hybrid patterns appeared to combine both types. A second dimension concerns the *depth or richness of valued news source*. Whereas light news consumers were drawn to magazines and swift general news coverage, background consumers sought deepening commentary in dedicated current affairs programmes. Next to these two dimensions, we discovered two potentially additional nuances. The first, as already touched on, considers the social aspect of news consumption, as reflected by social media users. The second nuance involves the relatively popularity of mobile appliances, centring on 'always on' consumers.

COMPARISON: EXPLAINING THE SIMILARITIES AND THE DIFFERENCES

The comparative Q exercise has indicated a considerable number of similarities and differences between the two sets of informants. The elements used in the labels already hint at some substantial overlap. In both studies, we found nuances in terms of traditional media versus online media. Interestingly, the Danish participants all highly valued television news, much more than their Flemish counterparts did, in spite of a considerable offer in Flanders, both by the public service broadcasters and by commercial players. It is unclear why this is so, but possible explanations might be the time difference and the uptake of other channels in Flanders, which render television news less 'up-to-date', repeating what one already knows. Also, (elements of) television broadcasts are remediated online, available on multiple other devices.

Furthermore, in the Flemish case, mobile media clearly stood out in two patterns. This was less apparent in the Danish case, although this is again most likely because of the time lapse. This also applies to the rise of social media as gates to socially filtered news items. Still, the role of social media in this respect is ambiguous: they are not news sources themselves, albeit allowing redirections to actual news sources.

Regarding the use of news content, we found similarities in dispersion over lighter forms of use, mainstream general updates and the consultation of background sources. An interesting difference, however, was the value addressed to regional media in Denmark. This was less apparent in the Flemish case. We see two reasons: first, 'national' newspapers in Flanders come with a regional agenda, and second, local television was not included because it was not included in the original Danish concourse. Also, for instance, the concept of 'tabloid' differs between Denmark and Flanders. In Denmark, it refers to popular newspapers bought separately through the day, whereas in Flanders, it is possible to get a subscription and have them delivered in the morning.

A methodological lesson therefore has to do with a structural difficulty in setting up comparative research: how far to go in standardising probing materials. In this case, we handled the same concourse, and performed separate analyses. Still, arguments could be made in favour of media-system-specific concourses, whereas in contrast, researchers could opt for simultaneous analysis or indeed for imposing similar factor structures on all involved samples. There is no clear roadmap for Q methodology in cross-national research. Crucial decisions need to be made at every stage: devising the concourse, performing the analysis, interpreting the items, labelling the patterns and drawing conclusions. A clear communication between researchers and towards readers is therefore an absolute prerequisite.

CONCLUSION: BEYOND TERRITORIAL COMPARISON?

While our analysis has been predicated on what Hepp and Couldry (2009) term 'territorial essentialism', we have argued above that such a process of inquiry is justified given the national anchorage and orientation of news media as vehicles of democratic citizenship. But we are not impervious to the argument that there are now transnational trends in our media culture which make it challenging to map and analyse such trends empirically: "Without the data first being aggregated on a national-territorial basis, the cases from various cultural contexts are compared the one with the other. In this way one can obtain a system of categories that describes not simply national differences, but more general common factors and differences in cultural patterns" (Hepp, 2013, p. 140).

Concretely, it would be possible to do a factor analysis of all the informants' Q sorts across territorial boundaries, in a way that would allow direct similarities and differences between the Danes and the Flemings to emerge in alternative, interesting patterns. This typology would presumably display types which encompassed individuals from both territorial cultures, in interesting configurations, showing that some Flemings may have more in common, in terms of news media consumption, with some Danes (and vice versa) than with their own countrymen and -women.

However, the feasibility conditions of such an analysis require further discussion. One could argue that a valid comparison will have to be based on more strictly equi-temporal data, which are data collected at approximately the same stage of technological development. If we brought the Danish 2009 data together with the Flemish 2011 data, the difference in media-technological affordances available to the two groups (and, hence, their different configurations of worthwhileness dimensions) might make their mediatised worlds too different to warrant a direct trans-local comparison. Survey research conducted in Denmark in 2011 shows that the breakthrough of mobile and social media as news acquisition devices happened precisely in this two-year period. Thus, had we had Danish Q data from 2011, we could claim that the temporal and situational vocabularies and grammars of mediated everyday life would be sufficiently similar in order to warrant a direct comparison.

Presumably we would also have to scrutinise the stimulus statements even more closely, reflecting on the historical and media systemic differences mentioned above, in light of which we had to analyse the nation-specific data, in order to build a genuinely bi-territorial set of stimuli statements. Finally, in addition to the 'same time' requirement, such a trans-territorial comparison, encompassing more countries than just our two, will make more sense, the more the individuals and groups researched belong to territorial environments that are not too divergent in terms of key technological, demographic and cultural indicators. The precise nature and degree of such required commonalities pose a challenge in whose solution we invite our readers to join us.

NOTES

1. See also the nine-country comparative survey in Reuters Institute (2013)
2. The methodological procedures of the Danish study have been reported elsewhere (Schrøder and Kobbernagel, 2010)

REFERENCES

Abercrombie, N. and Longhurst, B., 1998. *Audiences.* London: Sage.
Bilandzic, H., Patriarche, G. and Traudt, P. eds. 2012. *The social use of media. Cultural and social scientific perspectives on audience research.* Bristol: Intellect. BFI.
Billig, M., 1995. *Banal nationalism.* London: Sage.
Carpentier, N., Schrøder, K.C. and Hallett, L. eds. 2013. *Transformations. Shifting audience positions in late modernity.* New York: Routledge.
Couldry, N., 2012. *Media, society, world. Social theory and digital media practice.* Malden: Polity Press.
Courtois, C., 2012. *The triple articulation of audiovisual media technologies in the age of convergence.* Ph.D. University of Ghent, Belgium.
Curran, J. and Park, M.-J., 2000. Beyond globalization theory. In: J. Curran and M.-J. Park, eds. *De-Westernizing Media Studies.* London: Routledge.
Dahlgren, P., 2006. Doing citizenship: The cultural origins of civic agency in the public sphere. *European Journal of Cultural Studies* 9(3), pp. 267–286.
Davis, C. and Michelle, C., 2011. Q methodology in audience research: bridging the qualitative/quantitative 'divide'? *Participations* 8(2), pp. 559–593.
Deuze, M., 2011. Media life. *Media, Culture & Society* 33(1), pp. 137–148.
Deuze, M., Blank, P. and Speers, L., 2012. A life lived in media. *Digital Humanities Quarterly* [e-journal] 6(1). Available at: < http://www.digitalhumanities.org/dhq/vol/6/1/000110/000110.html>.
Gamson, W., 1992. *Talking politics.* Cambridge: Cambridge University Press.
Hasebrink, U. and Popp, J., 2006. Media repertoires as a result of selective media use. A conceptual approach to the analysis of patterns of exposure. *Communications* 31(3), pp. 369–387.
Hepp, A., 2013. *Cultures of mediatization.* Cambridge: Polity Press.
Hepp, A. and Couldry, N., 2009. What should comparative media research be comparing? Towards a transcultural approach to 'media cultures'. In: D.K. Thussu, ed. 2009. *Internationalizing media studies.* Abingdon: Routledge.

Hjarvard, S., 2008. The mediatization of religion: a theory of the media as agents of religious change. *Northern Lights 2008. Yearbook of film and media studies.* Bristol: Intellect Press. pp. 9–26.

Kubitschko, S. and Knapp, D., 2012. An invisible life? A response to Mark Deuze's 'media life'. *Media, Culture & Society* 34(3), pp. 359–364.

Livingstone, S., 2003. On the challenges of cross-national comparative media research, *European Journal of Communication* 18(4), p. 477–500.

Livingstone, S., 2005. On the relation between audiences and publics. In: S. Livingstone, ed. 2005. *Audiences and publics: when cultural engagement matters for the public sphere*. Bristol: Intellect.

Löfgren, O., 2001. The nation as home or motel? Metaphors of media and belonging. *Sociologisk Årbok* 14(1), pp. 1–34.

Parameswaran, R. ed. 2013. *Blackwell's international companion to media studies: audience research*. Malden: Wiley-Blackwell.

Pew Research Center, 2008. *Audience segments in a changing news environment: key news audiences now bland online and traditional sources*. Washington, DC: Pew Research Center for the People and the Press.

Reuters Institute, 2013. *Digital news report 2013* [online]. Oxford: University of Oxford. Available at: <https://reutersinstitute.politics.ox.ac.uk/fileadmin/documents/Publications/Working_Papers/Digital_News_Report_2013.pdf>.

Schrøder, K.C., 2004. Mapping European identities: a quantitative approach to the qualitative study of national and supranational identities. In: I. Bondebjerg and P. Golding eds. 2004, *European culture and the media*. Bristol: Intellect Books.

Schrøder, K.C. (2011). Audiences are inherently cross-media: audience studies and the cross-media challenge. *Communication Management Quarterly* 18(6), pp. 5–27.

Schrøder, K.C. and Kobbernagel, C., 2010. Towards a typology of cross-media news consumption: a qualitative-quantitative synthesis. *Northern Lights. Yearbook of Film and Media Studies*, 11, pp. 115–137.

Schrøder, K.C. and Larsen, B.S., 2010. The shifting cross-media news landscape. *Journalism Studies* 11(4), pp. 524–534.

Schrøder, K.C. and Phillips, L., 2007. Complexifying media power: A study of the interplay between media and audience discourses on politics. *Media, Culture & Society* 29(6), pp. 890–915.

Strömbäck, J., 2008. Four phases of mediatization: an analysis of the mediatization of politics. *The International Journal of Press/Politics* 13(3), pp. 228–246.

Part II
New Fields of Research, New Challenges

8 From the Womb to the Tomb

Conceptual Similarities in Studying the Youngest and the Oldest of Audiences[1]

Dafna Lemish and Galit Nimrod

INTRODUCTION

Media audiences are comprised of people at various ages and life stages. As the field evolved, it became widely accepted that age is an important factor explaining audiences' preferences and behaviours. As a result, the study of media audiences expanded to a variety of populations, including the young and the old age groups, and the body of knowledge regarding these two audiences became considerably developed. The goal of this chapter is to offer a comparative framework for the study of two ends of the audience studies spectrum: the study of media and children and the study of media and older adults.

There are two main rationales for comparing these two fields of studies, the first being theoretical. Current older individuals were born in a period of limited media alternatives, both technologies and genres, and witnessed gradual development to which they slowly adjusted (or not). In contrast, today's children were born into an era of accelerated technological change and information explosion that they perceive as normal and even take for granted. Therefore, comparing the study of these two cohorts offers a promising springboard for the study of generations in a changing media environment (Loos, Haddon and Mante-Meijer, 2012). The second rationale is more practical and results from the fact that both children and older adults are the heaviest consumers of various types of media. Thus, understanding these audiences and the complex role media play in their lives may promote the production of media services and contents that might benefit these age groups.

Dafna Lemish has been studying the role of media in children's lives for three decades and Galit Nimrod has been studying independently those related to older adults for fifteen years. Our recent interactions have surprisingly led us to discover how much in common the two areas of scholarship have. We make the case for the substantial commonalities, as well as differences, between the two populations and their fields of study, the recognition of which may inform the development of theory as well as empirical research in the field of media and audiences. For this purpose, we have delineated five major conceptual themes that we develop in this chapter. The innovation in this chapter is reflected in the attempt to link the two seemingly unrelated ends of the audience research continuum, and the importance of this attempt rests in the various lessons that this linkage yields for scholarship in this area.

THEME I—SOCIAL CONSTRUCTIONS

Models of individuals' development across the life course have emerged in the last fifty years, arising out of various disciplines such as psychology, sociology, economics and marketing. Two of the most prevalent models are life-span developmental theory (Baltes, 1979) and life course theory (Elder, 1974). Both of these theories suggest that human development is a multidirectional and continuous process—that is that development across the life span is characterised by gains and losses from birth to death. The life-span models also address the notion that the context of an individual's development is extremely important (Bronfenbrenner, 1979). Contextual factors such as historical events, the age and timing of events in an individual's life, and socio-economic and cultural factors shape how an individual develops and adapts across the life span. These contextual factors allow for a great degree of difference in the development of individuals while providing some rationale for the similarities in the development among persons across similar ages, birth cohorts (groups of individuals born during a particular period) or backgrounds.

Accordingly, sociology of childhood recognises that the biological variable of age itself does not explain differences among children in all aspects of life (cognitive, social, emotional, physical, behavioural). Rather, it is agreed that the definition of childhood is fluid, ever changing and contextualised within cultural and temporal circumstances (James, Jenks and Prout, 1998). Furthermore, the construct of childhood is constantly reimagined by political, religious, technological and market forces. "Only through such an understanding does 'childhood' have meaning and significance, and only within these differing contexts can childhood be studied and interpreted" (Lemish, 2013a, p. 71).

The relatively new category of 'tweens,' can serve as an illustration. This preadolescent age group has been targeted by marketers as a profit-driven strategy, capitalizing on cultural tastes and consumption of goods, such as clothing, accessories and media in the process of identity formation. Similarly, the media industry has captivated the desire of parents to offer their babies and toddlers a developmental head start and has redefined the characteristics and needs of this early period of life through the offerings of media products and contents designed especially for this age group (Lemish, 2013a).

Gerontologists, too, recognise that the definition of later life is fluid, ever changing and greatly dependent on various circumstances. As far back as 1875, old age in the UK was defined as "any age after 50" (Roebuck,

1979). Thanks to various advances in modern medicine and individuals' quality of life, the life expectancy in most parts of the world has dramatically increased, and people in their fifties are currently considered relatively young. Nowadays, the definition of older person in most developed-world countries is the chronological age at which a person becomes eligible for statutory and occupational retirement pensions (typically sixty or sixty-five years). Still, this age-based definition does not adapt well to the situation in low-resources countries such as many in Africa, on one hand, and fails to accurately describe millions of healthy and active older adults in their seventies and even eighties in Western countries, on the other hand (World Health Organization, 2013).

More accurate means of defining old age take into account changes in social roles (e.g. work and parental roles) and physical and cognitive capabilities (Glascock and Feinman, 1980). Still, transitions that occur throughout later life may change the trajectory or path of a person's development, and their impact may significantly differ among individuals. Some influential transitions in later life include becoming a grandparent, the onset of disease or disability, retiring from the workforce and the loss of a spouse. All of these experiences have the ability to affect adults' physical, mental and social well-being as well as their leisure behaviour and media use.

THEME II—SOCIETY'S 'OTHERS'

Both children and older adults have been 'othered' by many societies, and as a result, their communication rights and needs have been neglected. This type of marginalization is often manifested as different forms of 'ageism' (i.e. stereotyping and discriminating against individuals or groups because of their age), resulting in limited research attention and funding, as well as in scholars' attitudes regarding their research subjects. Having sincere intentions to contribute to the social and psychological well-being of children and older adults, scholars often unconsciously regard them in patronizing manners.

Generally, childhood is perceived to be a period of vulnerability, innocence, dependability and one that lacks productivity. At the same time, children have also been framed as unruly, out of control and posing a danger to the orderly adult world. News coverage representations of children in particular have perpetuated these two extremes of the innocent "angel" and the dangerous "savage" in a variety of forms (Olson and Rampaul, 2013), contributing to "a growth in imagery that deliberately sets out to shock" (Holland, 2004, p. xiii). As a result, children's movement has been restricted, as have the spaces they are allowed to occupy, whether because they may be endangering themselves or are disturbing the social and/or physical environment. They are thus constructed in a dichotomous manner: either as a threat or as threatened by others (Ribak, 2013). They are disfranchised, not deemed as citizens, do not vote and are not held accountable as adults for their actions by the law (Carter, 2013). Furthermore, children lack space and a voice and hence have been regularly positioned as not having agency and not able to define and act on what is in their best interest. This approach has been evident in both the theorizing of childhood as well as in its representations, in many cultural forms (James, Jenks and Prout, 1998; Lesko, 2001).

The various forms of patronage and ageism experienced by children have resulted in the need to protect them. Thus, the area of children and media has been dominated by a concern for harmful media effects (e.g. sex, violence, substance abuse, obesity, consumerism and the like—see e.g. Calvert and Wilson, 2008; Singer and Singer, 2011). With the growing dominance of digital and mobile media in the lives of children, this focus on vulnerability, on the one hand, and malice, on the other, is experiencing a strong revival (Livingstone, et al., 2011). Pornography, bullying, sexting and meeting online contacts offline have all been raised as issues of great concern for children, both as victims of antisocial behaviours as well as perpetrators of it. Other risks, more culturally unique, have also been suggested, such as being a victim of terrorist plots in Israel (Lemish, Ribak and Aloni, 2009) or of financial scams in the US (Ribak and Turow, 2003).

Later life, too, is perceived as a period of vulnerability and dependability. Older adults face continual increase in the number and degree of constraints to social involvement, including cultural-environmental constraints (e.g. as social isolation), psychological constraints (e.g. lower motivation and self-efficacy), technical constraints (e.g. income) and health-related constraints (Nimrod, 2003). In addition, even though many older adults are formally and informally involved in various volunteer activities (Kleiber and Nimrod, 2008), retirement is typically associated with decreased productivity and even with being a burden on society.

Nevertheless, it should be noted that ageism towards children and older adults does not take the same form. The literature on ageism distinguishes between 'hostile prejudice', which includes hatred, fear, aversion or threat which involves older or younger people, and 'benevolent prejudice', when they are being pitied, marginalised or patronised (Bugental and Hehman, 2007). The tendency to pity is linked to seeing older or younger people as 'friendly' but 'incompetent'. However, far more negative stereotypes are linked to old age rather than to childhood. This is probably because "these stereotypes help younger persons deny the self-threatening aspects of old age (e.g. that one will become frail and die eventually)" (Nelson, 2005, p. 214). In addition, children have the potential—and expectation—of becoming fully productive adults and are often framed as 'the citizens of tomorrow', while the elderly will never be that anymore. It is interesting to note that the two populations are also being pitted against each other, for example in the case of employing conceptions of childhood dependency in a verbal discourse and the visual imagery of infantilisation of older age (Hockey and James, 1993). As a result, the various forms of patronage and ageism experienced by older adults have mainly been studied with regard to representations of old age in media contents and their effects on the elderly (e.g. Mares and Cantor, 1992). Expressions of ageism towards children in media contents and their impacts have not been sufficiently recognised.

The marginalization of children and older adults, and the study of these audiences, is also evident in the fact that there seems to be little flow between these sub-areas and other sub-areas in media studies. This seems quite surprising given that many of the areas of investigation in these fields are quite similar, focusing on questions related to audiences, contents and institutions. A contributing explanation for this state of affairs can be found in the feminist interpretation for the devaluation of questions pertaining to the private sphere of family and care traditionally associated with femininity. This, in comparison to the study of the public sphere of politics, economy and news; which was typically dominated by men. Not surprisingly, we find that the majority of researchers in the area of children and media are women. This division of interests continues to perpetuate the traditional gender roles and responsibilities (Lemish, 2013b). The implications of this state of affairs are evident in the marginalisation of these areas of studies in funding and policy priorities, the hardship involved in developing educational interventions for media literacy and the lack of resources for quality media productions for children (Wartella, 2004; Buckingham, 2013).

THEME III—FALSELY PERCEIVED AS HOMOGENEOUS

Historically, children and older adults have been construed as homogeneous categories. 'Children', usually up to the age of 18, the end of high school and/or legal age, were squeezed into one lump of 'non-adults'. Gradually research agendas that recognise the various developmental stages and the diversity of characteristics and needs within this population have evolved. The underlying premise of various approaches that focus on the interaction of the individual child with a medium is that children's cognitive, emotional and social skills develop overtime. This is based on the assumption adopted from developmental psychological theories: Children's media experiences and the effects media have on them are related to the skills and tools children acquire with age and experience (Calvert and Wilson, 2008).

Studies of children and media have gradually become more sensitive to the existence of the diverse dimensions that childhood encompasses: difference of human characteristics, such as gender, ethnicity and class, are gaining more and more prominence in addition to those related to children's age. Greater emphasis is now put on ecological approaches that consider the micro context of the homes in which children grow and develop, as well as to the macro environments of the society, culture and nation around them. Those approaches revisit and even challenge some of the basic premises of stage theories, echoing the established nature/nurture debate. They contend that child development might be more influenced by environmental circumstances and cultural differences than we previously understood and accounted for (Kolucki and Lemish, 2011). All of these add new dimensions of understanding to the already complex nature of the relationships between children and their media.

Like children, older adults were typically grasped as one group, and parallel to the study of children gerontologists recognised the various stages and diversity of characteristics and needs within this population. Gerontology literature provides solid evidence demonstrating increases in physical, sociological and psychological variability with age (Dannefer, 1998; Wolfe and Snyder, 2003; Yang and Lee, 2010). Therefore, older adults are currently considered a rather heterogeneous audience if not the most heterogeneous audience of all.

Segmentation analysis involves dividing a broad audience into subsets of audiences with common characteristics, needs, perceptions, attitudes and/or behaviours. Thus, segmenting the current substantial group of older adults may enhance our understanding of older audiences. Over the past few decades, approaches to segmentation of mature audiences have emerged out of various disciplines, such as psychology, sociology, economics and marketing, of which three are considered dominant: *socio-demographic* segmentation, based on characteristics such as age, gender, health, retirement and family status (e.g. Garfein and Herzog, 1995); *behavioural* segmentation, based on seniors' activities and lifestyles (e.g. Gollub and Javitz, 1989) and *psychographic* segmentation, based on measures such as values, attitudes and well-being (e.g. Moschis, 1996; Wolfe and Snyder, 2003).

In spite of these advances, and unlike most of the current research in the sub-area of children and media, many studies of older adults and media still consider seniors as homogenous groups. These studies do not use any segmentation method and simply relate to a population that has passed a certain age. Even the most recent literature on older adults' use of Information and Communication Technologies (ICT) lacks differentiation between users. Most studies on this topic have tended to examine seniors who are relatively young, healthy, wealthy and educated (Wagner, Hassanein and Head, 2010; Xie, Huang and Watkins, 2012). Older adults with chronic health conditions, people with dementia, minorities and immigrants have typically not been included in the examined populations. This approach may lead to potentially misleading generalisations, which limit our understanding of older audiences.

THEME IV—'BECOMING'/'DECLINING' VERSUS 'BEING'

Both areas have traditionally focused on processes towards an end—that is in the case of childhood, the process of 'becoming' adult, with a hypothetical 'end product' of a grown-up and in the case of the older adults, the process of 'decline' toward the 'end product' of death. To an extent, these two processes mirrored each other (Hazan, 1994). For example children were perceived as gaining knowledge and various cognitive abilities, whereas older adults were perceived as experiencing cognitive decline. Children were perceived as gradually gaining independence and control, whereas older adults were perceived as individuals who gradually lose autonomy. The latter process manifested itself in physical evidence (e.g. losing teeth or using diapers), bringing older adults to a physical and social status similar to that of babies.

The conceptual model of 'becoming' in the research on children and media resulted in a limited presentation of children's voices in research about them which mainly focuses on testing or comparing them to a yardstick of the imagined ideal adult. This focus on child-deficit theories in developmental psychology and media studies has dominated much of the research on children's uses of media originating mainly from the US media effects traditions (Lemish, 2015). For example recently theories of culture and the sociology of childhood have challenged the assumption that children needed to be viewed in relation to the process of becoming fully grown adults, as the ideal human prototype. In its place, they suggested that childhood be assumed to be a form of 'being' in its own right. The being conceptual model recognises the unique being of each stage of development, with its characteristics, needs and abilities—all of which have a significant impact on the various roles media play in children's lives.

Accordingly, this approach highlighted the need to allow children, in each stage of their development, to be fully recognised as having a unique personal voice that deserves to be listened to and understood with empathy. This theoretical and ideological turn has also led to adopting a wider range of methodologies for studying children: in addition to surveys and experiments, a need developed for finding ways that facilitate a more active role of children as participants with an independent voice, such as in-depth interviewing, participant observation of their media-related behaviours and play, as well as analysis of their artwork and written accounts (Lemish, 2015).

The idea of decline in modern gerontology was introduced in early theories such as Walter Cannon's (1942) theory of diminishing homeostatic capacity with aging, which focused on physical decline, and Cumming and Henry's (1961) disengagement theory, which focused on social decline. For example the latter is a sociological theory that claimed that the older a person becomes, the more he or she will withdraw from society and that this process is universal, inevitable and mutually accommodating for the individual and society. It argued that disengagement helps the aging individual to focus on life culmination, while enabling their families and friends to separate gradually.

Although theories of social decline are considered controversial if not offensive, recent evidence suggests that some level of disengagement might be positive. For example, the widely accepted model of Selective Optimisation with Compensation (SOC) advanced by Baltes and colleagues (e.g. Baltes and Baltes, 1990; Freund and Baltes, 2002) essentially argued that it is adaptive and healthy to respond to the limiting factors that accompany aging. This can be done by being selective about the activities one chooses, abandoning the activities that are less meaningful, and by compensating for losses of meaningful activities in ways that optimise the reduced range of activities that continue.

Nevertheless, it should be noted that current literature on later life does not focus on decline and/or adjustment solely. In fact, many theories of successful aging emphasise opportunities for development and growth in later life. For example the theory of beneficial constraints (Kleiber, et al., 2008) suggests that the various constraints seniors face may serve as catalysts for change and growth. Innovation theory (Nimrod and Kleiber, 2007; Nimrod and Hutchinson, 2010) suggests that adapting new activities in later life may lead to self-preservation or self-reinvention, which contribute to seniors' psychological well-being. An illustration of the positive impact of innovation in later life is provided by many studies, which demonstrate that learning computer and internet skills enhances a sense of independence (e.g., Henke, 1999), creates a process of empowerment (e.g. Shapira, Barak and Gal, 2007) and enables older adults to develop new friendships and interests both online and offline (e.g. Nimrod, 2014). Hence, just like childhood, later life may be a period of discovery and growth.

THEME V—LESS RESPONSIBILITIES, MORE LEISURE

One of the main problems of time use in current society and the work–leisure equation is not the one of working longer hours, as one may think, but rather the uneven distribution of leisure across the life cycle (Godbey, 1996). The large gains in free time, which have occurred in western society during the past century, accumulated during the first and last ten to twenty years of life. To a large degree, children and older adults enjoy more freedom and fewer responsibilities than any other age group. Even after doing homework, participating in various formal leisure activities and doing chores, children still may have plenty of free time at hand, particularly in industrialised societies. Similarly, older adults typically retire in their early sixties and can expect a decade and a half or more of free time.

The paradox of leisure, however, is that those who have the greatest amount of free time (i.e. children and older adults), are exactly those that face more constraints to beneficial use of leisure. Leisure may be a powerful factor contributing to individuals' health and well-being. Yet, it may become a burden in conditions of multiple constraints and absence of sufficient opportunities. Both populations may experience intense physical instability and need constant adjustments and changes that influence mobility and access to social resources. As a result, both age groups share a heightened dependency on others, and more conveniently on media, as major socialisers and as extensions to the social world outside their reach. In fact, they are considered the heaviest consumers of various forms of media, including the internet and mobile phones among children, radio and printed newspapers among older adults and television in both groups. This heavy use, while fulfilling a host of important functions and needs, does not always contribute to their well-being and, in some aspects, may even harm it.

Children's movement and accessibility to the social world are highly restricted for a variety of reasons, including, as stated earlier, the fact that they may be posing a danger to themselves and to others and that they are dependent on adults for transportation and financial support (Ribak, 2013). The separate spaces designated for children in their homes, educational institutions, or public places allow for higher levels of supervision and control of their whereabouts, social contacts and behaviours. As children grow older they tend to spend more time using media independent of family and in the privacy of their own bedrooms, participating in what has been coined "bedroom culture" (Bovill and Livingstone, 2001; Lincoln, 2013). For example the use of mobile communication devices illustrates how children in many ways are defined by the space they occupy and the relationship they develop with their family and peers. The mobile phone, serving as an 'umbilical cord', allows parents to let their children to get away while staying connected and supervised (Ribak, 2009; 2013).

Older adults' mobility may decrease with age as a result of various physical, psychological and technical constraints. Consequently, there is a transition from physical activities to those demanding less physical effort and a corresponding shift from outdoor to indoor activities (Van Der Meer, 2008). The outcome, as it comes into practice in the lives of the oldest old, is substantial time in discretionary activities done alone and at home, with television viewing being most prevalent (Robinson and Godbey, 1997; Horgas, Wilms and Baltes, 1998).

Communication scholars have suggested that older adults use traditional media as a substitute for interpersonal contact and participation and as information sources for social interaction (e.g. Graney and Graney, 1974). However, an accumulating body of knowledge demonstrates that excessive media use in later life is associated with lower morale and satisfaction with life and higher levels of depression and loneliness (Rahtz, Sirgy and Meadow, 1989; Chory-Assad and Yanen, 2005; Van Der Goot, Beentjes and Van Selm, 2012). Results are somewhat different with regard to new media, as they offer active participation rather than passive experience (Wagner, Hassanein and Head, 2010; Xie et al., 2012). Still, additional research is needed to explore the potential of media to support healthy and active aging.

CONCLUSION

The comparative framework offered in this chapter enabled the linking of two seemingly unrelated ends of audience studies: the study of media and children and the study of media and older adults. Apparently, these two areas of scholarship have much in common, and it seems that the study of both groups also experienced similar transitions. In both areas, scholars realised that (a) the social constructions of childhood and later life are fluid and greatly dependent on cultural and temporal contexts; (b) each of these life phases includes various developmental stages, and thus children and older adults are not homogenous groups; and (c) these life phases should not be studied as processes towards an end product (becoming or declining) but, rather, as a form of being in its own right. In addition, both areas of scholarship recognised that (d) whereas children and older adults have the greatest amount of free time, they also face more constraints to beneficial use of leisure. Last, it was acknowledged that (e) both children and the older adults have been 'othered' by many societies, and thus, both groups are exposed to various forms of ageism (reflected in daily life, in media content and by scholars' attitudes).

Both stages of childhood and later years, just like any other stage of the life course, pose various psychological challenges including life transitions and some painful losses. Both populations may use media to help individuals cope with such challenges and adapt to new life circumstances. Thus, studying the array of roles of media in the lives of young and old audiences is informative and enriching, particularly in relationship to information acquirements and social engagements, including processes such as para-social interaction, identification and attachment to media characters and narratives. Moreover, the growth of the concept of well-being seems to characterise both ends of the human audience spectrum as additional research enriches our understanding of how media are contributing to (and/or threatening) the well-being of both children and older adults. Generally, this concept considers the roles of media in all aspects of audiences' lives holistically: physical, mental, emotional and social. Given the intricate and complex matrix of media-related issues that are so crucial for the well-being of children and young people, this concept that has emerged out of the health professions and has been applied in the field of gerontology for many years, has been gaining momentum and been applied recently in several symposia and publications (e.g. Handsley and Rich, 2010; Lemish and Götz, 2013; Romer and Jordan, 2014).

In spite of the many similarities, this chapter revealed considerable differences between the two areas of research. These differences highlighted gaps in each body of knowledge and, thus, illustrated directions for future research. As mentioned before, models of individuals' development across the life course (Elder, 1974; Baltes, 1979) suggested that human development across the life span is characterised by gains and losses from birth to death. Whereas studies of older adults put great emphasis on losses and decline, they also recognised opportunities for development and growth in later life (Nimrod and Kleiber, 2007; Kleiber, et al., 2008). However, the study of children mainly focused on gains and development (emotional, intellectual, etc.). More attention to the losses associated with children's development may deepen our understanding of the way media are used in coping with the various challenges and life transitions in childhood. In addition, just as done in studies of older adults (e.g. Mares and Cantor, 1992), future studies should further explore the various forms and impacts of patronage and ageism towards children in media contents.

Similarly, there are some key lessons that the study of media and older adults may learn from the study of media and children. First and foremost, studies of older adults and media must avoid considering seniors as homogenous groups, and relate to sub-segments within the older segment. This may prevent misleading generalisations and expand our knowledge regarding older audiences. Second, greater attention should be given to harmful media effects. Contemporary research in both fields is exploring the active engagement with media in both groups and the potential for personal and social empowerment (e.g. Shapira, Barak and Gal, 2007; Fisherkeller, 2011). However, whereas the study of children's use of new media has led, among others, to increased interest in their vulnerability (Livingstone et al., 2011), very little attention has been given, so far, to negative effects of media use on older adults.

Last, the commonalities and differences between children and older adults portrayed here may inform the development of theory as well as empirical research in other sub-areas in media studies. Many of the questions asked in these fields are quite similar. Thus, researchers may use some of the key issues we highlighted to examine what issues are studied in their sub-areas and which topics need further exploration. For example the subject of ageism is relevant to all age groups. Yet, expressions of ageism were mainly studied regarding older adults. Studies of media content and its impacts may benefit from exploring other forms of ageism. Similarly, there are additional audiences that may experience the paradox of leisure suggested here. For example unemployed individuals, some people with disabilities and stay-at-home parents may have significant amount of free time, yet they may also experience considerable constraints to beneficial use of leisure. Exploring the extent to which they use media as a substitution for leisure activities and interpersonal contact, and how media are contributing to (and/or threatening) their well-being, may clarify the role media play in their lives.

The comparison between children and older adults presented in this chapter is inevitably limited. By using many concepts from the sociology of childhood, gerontology and media fields, we could not detail or relate to all the extensive literature that is relevant for this comparison. Still, it is precisely the more general approach which made this comparison possible and, hopefully, valuable. It demonstrated the various ways in which both areas of research can inform the other as well as studies of audiences more generally.

NOTE

1. This chapter is based on the early work of the authors.

REFERENCES

Baltes, P. B., 1979. Life-span developmental psychology: some converging observations on history and theory. In: P. B. Baltes and O. G. Brim, Jr., eds. 1979. *Life span development and behavior*. New York: Academic Press. pp. 255–279.

Baltes, P. B. and Baltes, M. M., 1990. Psychological perspectives on successful aging: the model of selective optimization with adaptation. In: P.B. Baltes and M.M. Baltes, eds. 1990. *Successful aging: perspectives from the behavioural sciences*. New York: Cambridge University Press. pp. 1–34.

Bronfenbrenner, U., 1979. *The ecology of human development: experiments by nature and design*. Cambridge, MA: Harvard University Press.

Bovill, M. and Livingstone, S., 2001. Bedroom culture and the privatization of media use. In: S. Livingstone and M. Bovill, eds. *Children and their changing media environment*. Mahwah: Lawrence Erlbaum Associates. pp. 179–200.

Buckingham, D., 2013. Representing audiences: Audience research, public knowledge and policy. *Communication Review* 16(1–2), pp. 51–60.

Bugental, D. B. and Hehman, J. A., 2007. Ageism: s review of research and policy implications. *Social Issues and Policy Review* 1(1), pp. 173–216.

Calvert, S. L. and Wilson, B. J., 2008. *The handbook of children, media and development*. New York: Wiley.

Cannon, W.B., 1942. Ageing of homeostatic mechanisms. In: E. Cowdry, *Problems of ageing*. 2nd ed. Baltimore: Williams & Wilkins. pp. 567–582.

Carter, C., 2013. Media news consumption and meaning. In: D. Lemish, ed. 2013. *The Routledge international handbook of children, adolescents and media*. New York and Abingdon: Routledge. pp. 255–262.

Chory-Assad R.M. and Yanen, A., 2005. Hopelessness and loneliness as predictors of older adults' involvement with favorite television performers. *Journal of Broadcasting & Electronic Media* 49(2), pp. 182–201.

Cumming, E. and Henry, W., 1961. *Growing old: the process of disengagement*. New York: Basic Books.

Dannefer, D., 1988. What's in a name? An account of the neglect of variability in the study of ageing. In: J. E. Birren, V. L. Bengtson, eds. 1988. *Emergent theories of ageing*. New York: Springer. pp. 356–384.

Elder, G.H., 1974. *Children of the great depression: social change in life experience*. Chicago: University of Chicago Press.

Fisherkeller, J., ed., 2011. *International perspectives on youth media: cultures of production and education*. New York: Peter Lang.

Freund, A. M. and Baltes, P. B., 2002. Life-management strategies of selection, optimization and compensation: measurement by self-report and construct validity. *Journal of Personality and Social Psychology* 82(4), pp. 642–662.

Garfein, A. J. and Herzog, R. A., 1995. Robust aging among the young-old, old-old, and oldest-old. *Journals of Gerontology Series B: Psychological Sciences and Social Sciences* 50B(1), pp. 77–87.

Glascock A.P. and Feinman S.L., 1980. A holocultural analysis of old age. *Comparative Social Research* 3, pp. 311–332.

Godbey, G., 1996. *The problem of free time: it's not what you think* [online]. Available at: <http://www.fritidsvetarna.com/1_Kultur_och_fritid/8_The_problem_of_free_time.pdf>.

Gollub, J. and Javitz, H., 1989. Six ways to age. *American Demographics* 11(6), pp. 28–34.

Graney, M. J. and Graney, E. E., 1974. Communications activity substitutions in aging. *Journal of Communication*, 24(4), pp. 88–96.

Handsley, E. and Rich, M., 2010. *Harvard-Australia symposium on media use and children's wellbeing*. Adelaide: Flinders University.

Hazan, H., 1994. *Old age: constructions and deconstructions*. Cambridge: Cambridge University Press.
Henke, M., 1999. Promoting independence in older persons through the internet. *CyberPsychology & Behavior* 2(6), pp. 521–527.
Hockey, J. and James, A., 1993. *Growing up and growing old: ageing and dependency in the life course*. London: Sage.
Holland, P., 2004. *Picturing childhood. The myth of the child in popular imagery*. London: I.B. Tauris.
Horgas, A.L., Wilms, H.U. and Baltes, M.M., 1998. Daily life in very old age: everyday activities as expression of successful living. *The Gerontologist* 38(5), pp. 556–568.
James, A., Jenks, C. and Prout, A., 1998. *Theorizing childhood*. Cambridge: Polity.
Kleiber, D., McGuire, F., Aybar-Damali, B. and Norman, W., 2008. Having more by doing less: the paradox of leisure constraints in later life. *Journal of Leisure Research* 40(3), pp. 343–359.
Kleiber, D.A. and Nimrod, G., 2008. Expressions of generativity and civic engagement in 'third age' adults. *Journal of Adult Development* 15, pp. 76–86.
Kolucki, B. and Lemish, D., 2011. *Communicating with children: principles and practices to nurture, inspire, excite, educate and heal*. New York: UNICEF.
Lemish, D., 2013a. Feminist theory approaches to the study of children and media. In: D. Lemish, ed. 2013. *The Routledge international handbook of children, adolescents and media*. New York and Abingdon: Routledge.pp. 68–74.
Lemish, D., 2013b. Introduction: children, adolescents and media—creating a shared scholarly arena. In: D. Lemish, ed. 2013. *The Routledge international handbook of children, adolescents and media*. New York and Abingdon: Routledge. pp. 1–14.
Lemish, D., 2015. *Children and media: a global perspective*. Malden, MA: Wiley.
Lemish, D. and Götz, M., 2013. Conflict, media and child well-being. In: A, Ben-Aieh, F. Casas, I. Fornes and J. Korbin, eds. *Handbook of child well-being volume 4*. Dordrecht: Springer. pp. 2013–2029.
Lemish, D., Ribak, R. and Alony, R., 2009. Israeli children go on line: a reason for a moral panic? [in Hebrew]. *Megamot* (Trends) 46(1–2), pp. 137–163.
Lesko, N., 2001. *Act your age! A cultural construction of adolescence*. London: Routledge.
Lincoln, S., 2013. Media and bedroom culture. In: D. Lemish, ed. 2013. *The Routledge international handbook of children, adolescents and media*. New York and Abingdon: Routledge. pp. 315–321.
Livingstone, S., Haddon, L., Görzig, A. and Ólafsson, K., 2011. *Risks and safety on the internet: the perspective of European children. Full findings*. London: EU Kids Online.
Loos, E.F., Haddon, L. and Mante-Meijer, E.A., 2012. *Generational use of new media*. Farnham: Ashgate.
Mares, M.L. and Cantor, J., 1992. Elderly viewers' responses to televised portrayals of old age empathy and mood management versus social comparison. *Communication Research* 19(4), pp. 459–478.
Moschis, G.P., 1996. *Gerontographics: life stage segmentation for marketing strategy development*. Westport, CT: Quorum
Nelson, T.D., 2005. Ageism: prejudice against our feared future self. *Journal of Social Issues* 61(2), pp. 207–221.
Nimrod, G., 2003. Leisure after retirement: research review and mapping. *Gerontology* 30(1–2), pp. 29–46.
Nimrod, G., 2014. The benefits of and constraints to participation in seniors' online communities. *Leisure Studies* 33(3), pp. 247–266.

Nimrod, G. and Hutchinson, S., 2010. Innovation among older adults with chronic health conditions. *Journal of Leisure Research* 41(1), pp. 1–23.

Nimrod, G. and Kleiber, D., 2007. Reconsidering change and continuity in later life: toward an innovation theory of successful aging. *International Journal of Aging and Human Development* 65(1), pp. 1–22.

Olson, D. and Rampaul, G., 2013. Representations of childhood in the media. In: D. Lemish, ed. *The Routledge international handbook of children, adolescents and media*. New York and Abingdon: Routledge, pp. 23–30.

Rahtz, D. R., Sirgy M. J. and Meadow, H. L., 1989. The elderly audience: correlates of television orientation. *Journal of Advertising* 18(3), pp. 9–20.

Ribak, R., 2009. Remote control, umbilical cord and beyond: the mobile phone as a transitional object. *British Journal of Developmental Psychology* 27(1), pp. 183–196.

Ribak, R., 2013. Media and physical spaces. In: D. Lemish, ed. 2013. *The Routledge international handbook of children, adolescents and media*. New York and Abingdon: Routledge. pp. 307–314.

Ribak, R. and Turow, J., 2003. Internet power and social context: a globalist approach to web privacy concerns. *Journal of Broadcasting and Electronic Media* 47(3), pp. 328–349.

Robinson, J.P. and Godbey, G., 1997. *Time for life: the surprising way Americans use their time*. University Park: Pennsylvania State University Press.

Roebuck J., 1979. When does old age begin?: the evolution of the English definition. *Journal of Social History* 12(3), pp. 416–28.

Romer, D., and Jordan, A., 2014. eds. *Media and the wellbeing of children and adolescents*. Oxford: Oxford University Press.

Shapira, N., Barak, A. and Gal, I., 2007. Promoting older adults' wellbeing through Internet training and use. *Aging and Mental Health* 11(5), pp. 477–484.

Singer, D. and Singer, J., eds., 2011. *Handbook of children and the media*. CA: Sage.

Van Der Goot, M., Beentjes, J.W.J. and Van Selm, M., 2012. Meanings of television in older adults' lives: an analysis of change and continuity in television viewing. *Ageing and Society* 32(1), pp. 147–168.

Van Der Meer, M.J., 2008. Sociospatial diversity in the leisure activities of older people in the Netherlands. *Journal of Aging Studies* 22(1), pp. 1–12.

Wagner, N., Hassanein, K. and Head, M., 2010. Computer use by older adults: a multi-disciplinary review. *Computers in Human Behavior* 26, pp. 870–882.

Wartella, E., 2004. *Respondent: children, media, and the public interest: assessing the role of research in the policy-making process*. In: the annual meeting of the International Communication Association, New Orleans, LA, May 27–31.

Wolfe, D. B. and Snyder, R. E., 2003. *Ageless marketing: strategies for reaching the hearts & minds of the new customer majority*. Chicago: Dearborn Trade Pub.

World Health Organization 2013. *Definition of an older or elderly person*. [online] Available at: <http://www.who.int/healthinfo/survey/ageingdefnolder/en/index.html>.

Xie, B., Huang, M. and Watkins, I., 2012. Technology and retirement life: A systematic review of the literature on older adults and social media [online]. In: M. Wang, ed., *The Oxford handbook of retirement*. Oxford: Oxford University Press. Available at: <http://terpconnect.umd.edu/~boxie/Technology_Retirement_Life_Xie_Huang_Watkins_Feb27_2011.pdf>.

Yang, Y. and Lee, L. C., 2010. Dynamics and heterogeneity in the process of human frailty and aging: evidence from the U.S. older adult population. *Journals of Gerontology Series B: Psychological Sciences and Social Sciences* 65B(2), pp. 246–255.

9 Grey Zones
Audience Research, Moral Evaluations and Online Risk Negotiation

Ingunn Hagen and Ana Jorge

INTRODUCTION

A major area of concern for parents, teachers and policy makers is the question of risks that children and young people face in the course of their everyday use of the internet. Consequently, much research has been devoted to the subject of internet-related risks (Livingstone and Haddon, 2009b; Livingstone, et al., 2012). To advance the audience research dimension, however, this chapter argues for a focus on young people's ethical perspectives on internet uses, practices and risk taking. Addressing the moral dimension of internet use is relatively new (Orgad, 2007; Flores and James, 2013); heretofore, it is a topic associated more with audience practices in relation to television viewing. We argue that attending to the point of view of ordinary audiences, rather than constructing a priori labels for practices as risks, is necessary. Accordingly, this chapter proposes the concept of *positioning* to capture how individuals, including young people, negotiate public discourses about what is worthy of attention, risky or considered acceptable both on the internet and in traditional media channels.

The chapter argues that in evaluating what is risky or ethically acceptable when using the internet, children and young people need to develop their own moral compass. Such a moral compass or inner moral sense is developed while young people position themselves, negotiate with their peers and draw on advice from parents and other discourses, ranging from general cultural values to discourses about internet use and abuse in a media and in a school setting. Such a moral compass then serves to guide what is appropriate behaviour in the online world. Bauwens suggests that "teenagers explore and construct a morality of their own, sometimes imagining themselves beyond parents' and teachers' scope, but more often negotiating with values they get from adults, *i.e.,* parents, but also media discourses" (2012, p. 32). Therefore, the focus of this chapter is on the moral judgements that children and young people (nine- to sixteen-year-olds) make in relation to what is risky online or not, based on qualitative data in which they define risk and discuss their internet-related experiences in their own terms.

The data and contextual background for this study derive from comparative research, conducted in Norway and Portugal, two countries not only with different levels of internet penetration, patterns of children's internet use and risk exposure but also with different cultures in terms of children's rights and expected levels of autonomy. We emphasise the importance of context in this study, examined here by exploring how children in two different cultures define what is risky or dangerous and what discourses and norms they draw on for this. The young people we studied had a number of concerns about the "risky business" of their daily online lives, from managing personal data to concern about viruses. However, some themes stood out, and so, in the following, we focus on our informants' discussion of bullying or teasing and the references to contact with strangers or meeting new friends as the two dominant themes in the research.

MEDIA, MORALITY AND POSITIONING

Media morality has been placed on the audience research agenda as a concern with the moral dimensions involved in everyday media use (Bengtsson, 2012). Audience researchers have observed that people often view their media use in moral terms, questioning whether it is something that is valuable to spend time on or not (Alasutaari, 1996; Hagen, 2000). Perhaps the most well-known concern with morality in media research is the recurring theme of 'moral panics', which is particularly topical in debates about young people's adoption of new media. For instance, Drotner (1992) demonstrated how different generations of media have historically generated 'media panics', waves of anxious reaction from adults in response to the pioneering adoption of new technologies by young people, expressing the fear of losing cultural and social control by the mere introduction of media into play, in itself an exaggeration of the power of the media. Concerns vary along a continuum from more moralist perceptions (related to Puritanism and guilty pleasures) to moral evaluation (regarding what is ethical, right or wrong; Bengtsson, 2012).

Whereas some view morality as the judgement of action towards others and constituting a general set of principles concerning life in society, others, for instance, Silverstone (2006, p. 4), have emphasised how the media has come to occupy an important role where "the formation of social, civic and moral space" takes place. Silverstone (2006, p. 6) states that the "world's media are an increasingly significant site for the construction of a moral order", by simultaneously connecting and keeping others at a distance. Following Silverstone's work, Orgad (2007) has further developed this theme in the field of internet research, focusing on the differences between the intimacy allowed by digital media and the responsibility and *proper distance* maintained in cyberspace. This can be seen in the case of bullying, which we focus on in this chapter to illustrate our perspective, where different aspects of morality are also examined as predictors of cyberbullying behaviour as well as traditional bullying (Perren and Gutzwiller-Helfenfinger, 2012). According to Horton (2001, p. 274), bullying is so "highly moralised" that people's discourses about it tend to be different from their actual behaviours. Online behaviour more generally can translate into different moral engagements by users because of the distance between perpetrators and victims.

People's behaviour also tends to be ambivalent, a side of morality that Bauman (1993) emphasised. Bauman adopts a postmodern perspective on morality, viewing it as socially specific and contextual. Because there are now less commonly agreed norms and values, as Bauman (1993) reminds us, individuals need to make their own choices and develop their own normative positions. As indicated, humans are seen as morally ambivalent, a trait which is central to human interaction, because most moral choices have to be made between frequently contradictory impulses. Thus, Bauman suggested that "[t]he moral self moves, feels and acts in the context of ambivalence and is shot through with uncertainty" (1993, p. 11). Moral impulses are therefore seen as the "raw material" in sociality and commitment to others.

Moreover, acting towards others through the media involves a negotiation of the morality that is passed on by other subjects, depending on the individual's relative standpoint. Thus, we believe the discourse analytical concept of *positioning* can help illuminate people's moral evaluations regarding the media (Hagen, 2007). Positioning refers to "the discursive process whereby selves are located in conversations as observably subjectively coherent participants in jointly produced story lines" (Davies and Harrè, 1990, p. 48). According to this perspective, human beings are seen both as products of specific discourses and as discourse producers/subjects who can not only reproduce but also contribute to change by creating and negotiating meaning. This perspective therefore entails a particular ability to exercise power over others, which is "dependent on how [individuals] are positioned and position themselves in relation to social and moral orders" (Horton, 2001, p. 270). In this chapter, we examine the topics of internet use and of how young internet users draw on available discourses on internet-related risk to position themselves strategically (Fairclough, 1989; Winter-Jørgensen and Phillips, 1999; Buckingham, 2000) vis-à-vis their peers and families.

EVERYDAY ONLINE RISK AND YOUTH CULTURE

Dominant discourses among youngsters on online risk are negotiated in their peer cultures, often closely connected to the consumption of popular and media culture, where the internet plays a dominant role. Pasquier (2005) argued that media and peer culture have facilitated the prevalence of a horizontal cultural transmission, as young people have gained autonomy, and both parents/families and teachers have lost their role as authorities over children's cultural socialisation. As such, there are less evident differences attributed to class; young people fall prey to a great normativity in relation to peer groups and are more likely to conform to the "tyranny of the majority", an expression Pasquier borrows from Hannah Arendt, especially when social ties between peers are weak.

This logic of autonomy regarding adults and conformism towards peers may translate into the institution of "peer-driven morality" (Bauwens, 2012, p. 44), in which the dominant morality transmitted by parents may be questioned and pushed to the limits and a context-specific set of rules arises. As Bauwens (2012, p. 31) reminded us, "vertical processes of adolescent socialization by adults, *i.e.*, parents and teachers are, it is claimed, increasingly juxtaposed to and undermined by horizontal or peer-to-peer processes of adolescent socialisation". Contributing to this is the fact that many teens, like our interviewees, are involved in participatory cultures, for example through their use of social media such as Facebook, MySpace and online games. In such interactions, youngsters may feel that their contributions matter; they may also care about the opinions of others regarding their contributions. Some of the challenges related to ethics include the breakdown of traditional socialisation that may prepare young people to become part of this participatory, online culture, while also being exposed to and having to negotiate alternative norms (Jenkins, et al., 2009).

As such, a constructionist perspective is adopted in this chapter, whereby young people's norms and moral evaluations are dynamics that can be explored in the way they position themselves in interviews, towards what they define as acceptable, problematic or even risky behaviour and what they regard as foreseeable consequences. Thus, we develop the constructionist perspective adopted in reception research whereby media audiences and internet users are understood as active meaning-making actors (Hagen, 1992). Further research, we argue, needs to understand not just how the internet is a stage for interaction, socialisation and culturalisation of young people but also how morality between peers contributes to a definition of what is acceptable and how to behave with others online, be they friends, acquaintances or strangers (Flores and James, 2013). Also, there is a need to move from a more philosophical level of discussion to an understanding of how real audiences relate to the sphere of morality in their everyday use of and discussions around media. This is why we believe a study focusing on moral judgements among young people may also reveal new and unexpected considerations regarding children's experiences and sense-making, including those related to risk taking (Ponte, Simões and Jorge, 2013), as well as the value of analysing relations of power among different children, and between children, parents and other adults.

Such a perspective is also aligned with constructionist theories of risk that emphasise the weight of contextual and subjective factors in the definition of what constitutes risk (Lupton, 1999). The definition of online risks is open to discussion, not only in academia but also among ordinary audiences. Whereas realistic perspectives on risk pose them as objective processes, constructionist theories have argued that the perception of what is risky varies according not only to different cultural and social scenarios but also to different people within the same settings and to diverse situations by the same person (Lupton, 1999). A constructionist view stresses that the social, cultural and historical contexts are essential to understanding risk, which amounts to the ambivalence Bauman attributed to morality. Based on Beck's notion of risk in the context of modernisation and its hazards and uncertainties, lay people respond by reflexively evaluating alternatives offered by expert knowledge systems that suppose rational counterparts. Lupton and Tulloch (2003) therefore argued for attention to the way ordinary people perceive risk in their everyday lives, including the dimension of pleasure that is often ambivalently involved in risks and that may help to explain voluntary risk taking. Lupton and Tulloch further emphasise the need to take account of the cultural dimensions of risk and risk taking to understand how risk is experienced as part of everyday life and to consider how the perceptions and experiences of risk are affected by factors such as gender, social class, sexual orientation or geographical location. The fact that people have different and contextualised perceptions of risk, and how it affects them, also has implications for audience research. If we take a constructionist view of risk and morality regarding media, these cannot be evaluated merely by actions and behaviours; research has to look instead into discourses in which audiences position themselves in relation to others and the world and negotiate general principles (Ponte, Simões and Jorge, 2013).

Recognising the ambivalence of risks is crucial to understanding the online experiences of children and young people. Different people may not perceive risky activities in the same way. Youngsters may even actively seek certain risky activities. The case of meeting strangers is one in which the image of the child in danger can also be read as that of an individual seeking to meet new people, be it to find people with similar interests, to make new friends, to maintain existing friendships or to revive old ones and sometimes to explore online dating in the hope of developing love relationships.

The EU Kids Online project distinguishes the level of risk and harm to illuminate the different factors that elevate risk exposure (Livingstone, Haddon and Görzig, 2012). Still, for many of the risks children and young people encounter online, a survey conducted in 2010 with 25,000 European internet users aged nine to sixteen revealed that the risks of actual harm are often low (Livingstone, et al., 2011). There are many different factors involved such as age, gender, socio-economic status or country probabilities of risk and harm, itself a factor of prevention and coping strategies, mediations and skills. Nevertheless, despite the important research performed by EU Kids Online, there are gaps in the knowledge about how children themselves understand and cope with what they find unpleasant online, and "little is known of how children evaluate websites, determine what is trustworthy, cope with what is problematic and respond to what is dangerous" (Livingstone and Haddon, 2009a, p. 5). Understanding what constitutes risk and the processes by which children and young people incorporate these in their everyday life and their interactions with peers remains an important topic of research.

COMPARING MORALITY AND RISK NEGOTIATION ACROSS CULTURES

Bauman's (1994) conception of morality is inherently social and therefore contingent and specific to the culture in which it is developed. Nevertheless, in moving from a more abstract discussion to the audience level, research focusing on morality should not result in compartmentalised accounts; instead, it should aim to find cultural specificities as well as commonalities across cultures. By comparing qualitative data from two countries, we hope to explore the weight of contextual factors, examining similarities and differences in children's risk assessments and evaluations in two rather different European contexts, Norway and Portugal. We argue that a meso or micro analysis of internet cultures in different countries may represent an important contribution to the study of audiences in their immediate contexts, while making sense of the contextual differences determined by the geographical situation and cultural setting.

Therefore, to capture children's own perceptions of risk, their norms and moral evaluations on internet use, we conducted focus group interviews with children and young people aged nine to sixteen (gathered in groups of similar ages), in Norway ($N = 51$) and Portugal ($N = 50$). The Norwegian fieldwork was performed towards the end of 2011 in two schools in the suburbs of Trondheim and a third one in a nearby village; fieldwork in Portugal took place in three schools in two suburban areas of Lisbon at the end of 2012 and early in 2013. In each country, there were two to four groups at each age level, with an overall gender balance. Participants were also invited to respond to open questions in the form of short essays about their daily use of the internet and what they regarded as *fun* and *not so OK*.[1] While we expected focus groups to reveal social negotiations between young people and, by rapport, their families (Schrøder, et al., 2003), the essays attempted to prompt more personal and reflexive moral positions.

The context of internet use is relevant to understanding differences in relation to risk in the two countries and how moral discourses come into play in relation not only to other agents, such as parents and teachers, but also to society at large. In 2010, as much as 80 per cent of Norwegian children used the internet every day or almost every day, compared to 55 per cent in Portugal; Norwegian children also start using the internet at an earlier age (Livingstone, et al., 2011; Staksrud, 2011). However, there are also similarities between the countries, such as gendered user patterns: girls use the internet more for social interaction, whereas boys play more games. Such differences in user patterns may also result in different exposures to risk.

On one hand, cross-cultural comparisons of children's and young people's use and understanding of the internet have been conducted. As mentioned, the EU Kids Online project (Livingstone and Haddon, 2009a; Livingstone, Haddon and Görzig, 2012) has offered a comprehensive view of uses, skills, risks and harms of children online in twenty-five countries. Lobe and Ólafsson (2012) have attempted a macro analysis of cross-cultural differences at the technological, educational, socioeconomic and regulatory levels; however, it has not been possible to test the cultural dimension. On the other hand, family cultures and styles of child rearing vary significantly in different countries, as do levels of internet diffusion and education, which are significant in terms of the probability of risk and harm to children in different countries (Kirwil, et al., 2009). Thus, even a two-country comparison may help to gain intelligibility over processes on the formation and negotiation of norms regarding internet use.

For the southern and northern European countries involved in this study, there are great differences in terms of internet usage patterns, education levels and culture. Generally, Norway has been characterised as a high-use/ high-risk country, whereas Portugal is a country of lower use/some risk (Haddon and Livingstone, 2012). Portugal is a moderately individualistic culture, whereas this feature is stronger in Norway and other Nordic countries (Kirwil, et al., 2009). This is reflected in parental mediation, as there is a greater likelihood for competent, communicative families in Norway than in Portugal, where a restrictive style is more present. Unskilled families, with an uneasiness to accompany children in their internet use, are also more likely to be found in Portugal (Paus-Hasebrink, et al., 2013, p. 15). Generally, Norwegian children are "supported risky explorers", with the support of families, in contrast to Portuguese children who are "protected by restriction" (Helsper, et al., 2013).

The EU Kids Online survey has shown different levels of perception and experience of risk among children. Staksrud (2011) pointed out that, although bullying is not the most commonly experienced risk, it is what Norwegian children fear the most. On the contrary, pornography and violent/aggressive content, which were the top concerns expressed in the EU Kids Online survey's open question (Livingstone, et al., 2013), were less present in our study as having resulted in harm by youngsters across Europe. In our group discussions, bullying was a more prevalent topic, which may be attributed to cultural taboos and the unease felt by children and young people in a group context to talk about pornography. In the 2010 survey of the same project, Portuguese parents were the most reluctant to admit their children had seen sexual images online (only 4 per cent of parents said that they had, whereas 13 per cent of children said they saw such images), which may be explained, in part, by the influence of Catholicism.

The essays in our study were a means to allow young people to position themselves regarding issues that they did not find space to do within mixed-gender focus groups. In Portugal, while younger children referred to pornographic videos as 'inappropriate videos', thirteen- and fourteen-year-olds mentioned "pornography/ic" and even "porn" or "porno" for some fifteen- and sixteen-year-olds, revealing a greater familiarity with the content, even though they say younger kids should not see those videos. Similarly, when Norwegian informants expressed concern about pornography, it was mainly that it was available to children younger than themselves and that it was too much "in your face".

BULLYING OR LEG-PULLING

As indicated, cyberbullying was the main concern among children and young people in our studies. However, the meaning of many of the experiences our informants had online depended very much on the relationship they had with the people involved and the context within which situations took place. The ambivalence in moral discussions about internet-related experiences was particularly evident with regard to online bullying, a focus of concern expressed mostly in essays, whereas in focus groups young people showed more negotiation. There was a reason behind our informants' concern about cyberbullying, as European children's experience of online bullying was most harmful and hurtful (Livingstone, et al., 2011). Lenhart and her colleagues (2011) write that 88 per cent of American teens using social media have witnessed other people being mean or cruel on social networking sites.

In fact, the main concern expressed by Norwegian youth in the essays was about bullying: they feared that people would write mean things to them or to others, but there was also a concern about 'Faceraping' and one's identity being hacked. In the interviews, all children expressed that they were aware of bullying, even though most of them had not experienced it themselves. One thirteen-year-old Norwegian girl talked a lot about being bullied and seemed very hurt by this. She was a great Justin Bieber fan and would take hateful comments about him personally as well. This girl also experienced bullying directed at her personally, for example nasty comments about her pictures, saying that she was "a whore, fat and ugly". Some of the informants in the other focus groups commented on this case: they felt that she acted mean towards others, too, and was lying, so no one wanted to be friends with her. There was some consensus among peers around the moral position that 'if you are bad to others, you deserve the same treatment'. On the other hand, there was a common understanding among Norwegian respondents that there was more 'pulling each other's leg' on the net and that many dared to say nastier things online than offline. However, in many cases it was ambiguous whether there was bullying or harassment going on or whether someone was just 'pulling your leg'.

This tendency to define something as teasing or bullying as dependent on who did it was also a widespread trend in focus group conversations conducted in Portugal. When a friend wrote something naughty, that was often interpreted as fun or harmless teasing, but if another person did the same thing, his or her intentions were seen as malicious and perceived as bullying. A sixteen-year-old boy explained that "when we know the person, we can tell when they're teasing and when they're not". Thus, there was no universal way to draw the difference between playing with friends and bullying. In Portugal, none of the respondents said they had been bullied, nor did they offer examples they knew, but several expressed the opinion that bullying was "one of the worst problems online" (fourteen-year-old boy's essay). Many participants, aged thirteen and fourteen, said that "it's ok, it's normal" to joke with friends. Another fourteen-year-old boy thought it was so relative that you could not tell everything to parents, "because they wouldn't understand", because they were out of context, pointing not only to the different moral spheres that Jenkins, et al. (2009) mention but also to their negotiation of autonomy.

One of the situations that could go from being a practical joke between friends to cyberbullying, depending on who did it, was 'Facerape' (when someone enters your profile on Facebook by gaining access to your password, or if someone leaves the profile open and that person can write things on your profile, which appears to others as if you wrote it). Reactions varied from fun to unpleasant, depending very much on the relationship with the Faceraper and on what was done, written or posted during the Facerape. For a group of Portuguese fourteen- and fifteen-year-old boys, Facerape was a joke they had done to each other, posting pictures that implied the other friend was gay; one did it first and then the other avenged himself before concluding that "we now laugh about the situation", because it was just for fun.

One Norwegian girl had experienced someone pretending to be her and her friends made her aware of this. She said she told those with the false profile to remove her picture, which they did, so she did not tell her parents about the incident. Teenagers seemed to leave parents out of such incidents and tried to deal with situations on their own. Another informant, a sixteen-year-old Norwegian boy, said he chose to contact the police about a similar case, and he felt the police took this case seriously and dealt with it efficiently: "they found out who had made it, so they asked them to remove it". Others mentioned someone had made false Facebook profiles of their friends, so they dealt with it by reporting to Facebook. Fake profiles were also used in connection with harassment and online bullying, something we did not find among Portuguese informants. A sixteen-year-old Norwegian girl interpreted irony and intent according to her relationship with the person interacting with her: "For example, they will make a fake profile of others and then they write nasty comments and they will make comments that can be hurtful. For example: You are damn pretty could mean that you are damn ugly".

Most of the participants defined bullying based on the intention of the person, according to the relationship they maintained, on the offensive nature of the comments and on the repetitiveness. However, a fifteen-year-old Portuguese boy considered bullying as "not when it's repetitive, but when the other person [victim] thinks it's too much". He put the onus of drawing the limits on others, which was an ethical or emphatic behaviour capable of putting oneself in other subject's situation, including unknown people (Flores and James, 2013, p. 837), pointing to the idea of *proper distance* that Silverstone (2006) talks about. A fifteen-year-old girl stated in her essay a principle and a prohibition regarding online behaviour: "respect other people's virtual space and don't do anything harmful to others", to which she abided. The opposite positioning was that of a thirteen-year-old girl, the only respondent who proudly admitted she bullied others: "bullying others? I've done that", showing that she partook in it without moral engagement (Perren and Gutzwiller-Helfenfinger, 2012).

Some of the thirteen- and sixteen-year-old participants from Norway mentioned posting pictures as a potentially problematic area which could also be perceived as bullying. Posting pictures of each other without permission seemed to happen often, but the extent to which this was considered a problem varied. Several of the informants said that they or their friends had experienced non-consensual publication of photos. They could then ask that the pictures be removed. A 13-year-old girl explained: "they do that, then you just tell them, do not publish my picture and they will remove it if they are good friends". Again, problems appeared to be solved if children were friends with each other and therefore the moral compass for evaluating what was acceptable or not appeared to be fluid and very much dependent on trust and authenticity of relationships. For example,

Girl, 13 A: You did not ask me about the picture where it was only me.

Girl, 13 B: I think that was very cute, so . . .

Girl, 13 A: It is OK if the pictures are very nice. It is fun [to display] when we were smaller.

Girl, 13 B: Yes, to show them pictures of us when we were small, then it is not . . . It is silly to get cross about that really, because it is only funny.

Girl, 13 A: It depends on the picture then. If they wrote: 'Oh, you were so cute in that picture . . .' And you were cute, then it did not matter.

Among sixteen-year-olds, there also seemed to exist fluid borders between what they experienced as playfully embarrassing and embarrassing or unpleasant. They also related flexibly to the rule that pictures should be removed if the person portrayed requested this. Everybody regarded removing pictures when asked as an "unwritten rule", as one girl called it, but they often broke this norm, even if it was a close friend asking. In Portugal, a fifteen-year-old boy took an individualistic stance (Flores and James, 2013,

p. 837) in relation to the same matter, stating in his essay that "we shouldn't do to others what we didn't want done to us", a moral position that placed personal interest as a guideline for abiding by norms. In fact, some fifteen- and sixteen-year-old boys from Portugal positioned themselves in a realm of moral relativism, leaving to individual responsibility and judgment the moral evaluation of online behaviours: "each person knows what they should and shouldn't do", wrote a sixteen-year-old in his essay, and his colleague of the same age stated that on the internet "we don't necessarily have to tell the truth". In fact, some of the older participants showed greater negotiation regarding rules about which younger participants still felt restraint. Among Portuguese respondents, whereas ten- to twelve-year-olds were more protective of their image; among older respondents, girls were more concerned about having their pictures posted without their authorisation.

CONTACT WITH STRANGERS OR MEETING NEW FRIENDS

Another main theme in our studies was contact with or by strangers. In their comparative study of Facebook use, Almansa and Castillo (2013) suggest that, although teenagers claim to know the risks, they tend to accept strangers as friends and share large amounts of private information with them. In our studies, there was also uneasiness and sometimes ambivalence expressed about being contacted by strangers. Even those who accepted strangers as 'friends' or who played online games with people they did not know, were bothered by the thought of potential paedophiles.

Among younger respondents, there was a greater fear of strangers and a greater awareness of prevention and coping strategies compared with the case of bullying, as boundaries were more defined. A ten-year-old Norwegian girl provided an example: "I noticed once that someone asked about my name, but I did not respond. Many [people] say that it is wise to respond with another name". The children in this age group had learnt not to give their real names and especially their phone numbers, because there were warnings in MovieStar Planet about this. Portuguese children also mentioned they that should not reveal their school in any case. A group of ten-year-old Norwegians discussed what was the "wise[st] thing" in terms of safety, because being contacted by strangers was a permanent concern and was fairly common. A ten-year-old girl explained: "There are many people you do not know. However, it is not necessarily a 40-year-old man trying to make contact with you. It is not for sure, but it could be. Because there are people trying to make contact with others".

Being contacted was not necessarily unpleasant; it was the idea of how this person had sought them out and uncertainty about their intentions: Were they friends of friends, peripheral acquaintances trying to get to know them, or something quite different? A Norwegian girl, aged thirteen, thought that "it is scary if someone adds you on Facebook, and then you ask your friends if they know who this is and they do not. Then: 'How did you find me on Facebook?'" When this happened to her, she chose not to accept the person's friend request and told her mother, who suggested contacting the police in case this person made contact again, which did not happen. Contacts by strangers are more consensually dealt with by youngsters and parents than bullying seems to be, as it is more difficult to define. Other youngsters chose to ignore strangers. A sixteen-year-old Norwegian girl explained: "I am not on Facebook that often. So, if I am there, I see many people who try to add me. I do not bother to do anything about it. I just let them be".

Both in Norway and in Portugal, the most common strategies among younger respondents when contacted by strangers were to find out who that person was, to ignore the person or to block the possibility of being contacted by him or her again. Other reactions were presented as part of positioning as cunning players, able to outsmart strangers who contacted them. A boy talked about his experience on a games site:

Boy, 13: A chap wanted to know where I lived. And then I gave him false information.
Interviewer: So you wanted to fool him?
Boy, 13: I said that it was the police.

Thus, contacts from strangers can be something unpleasant, but also something *fun* and an opportunity to meet new people, something which shows intersections with children and youth cultures. Some youngsters accepted strangers as friends. It was more common to talk to people that children did not know beforehand on games websites. A thirteen-year-old Norwegian girl said, "I add people from the whole world who add me and then I become friends with . . . when I do not know them in real life". A fourteen-year-old Portuguese boy showed a side of experimenting with identities when talking to other people, when he said he has talked to people he didn't know "on Chat roulette. Sometimes I create 'fake' [sic] accounts, which are accounts that are false, you know, to talk. . . it's fun to talk with people!". About being contacted by strangers, a sixteen-year-old Norwegian boy said, "I do not mind, [. . .] I have friends all over the world". Whereas these informants added or talked to people from all over positioned themselves as global players, a thirteen-year-old Norwegian shared her not so pleasant experiences and came across as feeling helpless, which helped demonstrate that the amusement of the experiences of contact with others presupposed control over relationships:

Girl, 13: For me, when I played online, I met a Norwegian chap who started writing nasty things about me. And he knew I was Norwegian, as I had a Norwegian flag in my background. And then he wrote: Who are you? And then he wrote many nasty things.

Interviewer: What did you do?
Girl, 13:   Nothing. I cannot do anything. I do not know who this is.

In fact, there seemed to be gender differences in both countries. In Portugal, only one fifteen-year-old girl said she had met people online and talked to them, but no girl confessed to having met boys face-to-face, which may reflect a cultural expectation regarding female roles. A group of one boy and three girls aged fifteen and sixteen agreed that it was easier and safer for boys than for girls to meet new people, which showed a dominant morality in peer culture. In Norway, sixteen-year-olds also said they had been contacted mostly by friends of friends on Facebook. Apparently, it was especially girls who experienced people approaching them, something which was both related to gender roles and to gendered user patterns. This can have implications for the level of privacy young people chose for their profiles on Facebook. In Norway, whereas a number of informants had their profiles only open to friends, others chose to have their profile fully open. One sixteen-year-old Norwegian girl explained: "I think I do not care that much anyway, because there are not so many embarrassing things on my profile, so it does not really matter". Both in Portugal and in Norway, informants positioned themselves as proficient about the privacy settings on Facebook, despite some challenges when Facebook suddenly changed its privacy settings. Moreover, this could mean that there were moral judgements, mostly depending on gender, among peers regarding the level of exposure teenagers chose.

On the other hand, Norwegian participants, aged thirteen, reported a joke concerning contact with strangers, as some friends would send each other's names to other friends, which the first person then did not know. A thirteen-year-old girl experienced this "a number of times" and said, "I find it unpleasant when some of my friends send my name to people they are friends with from other countries and such". Again, the unpleasantness seemed to relate to the girl's feeling that she was not in control and girls seemed to experience this more intensely. As one sixteen-year-old Norwegian girl expressed that "it is harder being a girl than a boy".

On one hand, being contacted by people they 'did not know', as Norwegian teenagers put it, was an experience of most respondents: this could be friends of friends, or someone they met in some setting, but did not really know, which was mentioned by teenagers from both countries. For a sixteen-year-old Portuguese boy, Facebook was a means to meet friends of friends or people who they just met once, like "people we've met in parties". This was an opportunity to meet young people of the opposite sex that many young people, especially boys aged fourteen or more, seized and some told us about having arranged meetings offline with girls from their school or nearby schools. This showed a youth cultural habit that was being negotiated and was becoming more acceptable, as it revolved around consent and was regarded as good relations. Still, they might hold back from meeting new people for safety reasons but felt it was not wrong. In discussing prevention and coping strategies that youngsters should take when meeting strangers, the police seemed to appear as a protective entity and similarly so among Norwegian respondents, whereas, regarding illegal downloading (of movies, games or music), Portuguese youths tended to view the police as prosecutors and some even felt they had to guarantee their anonymous participation in the study. In fact, when discussing whether *illegal downloading* was right or wrong, some felt it was an opportunity to have free access to popular culture, even if they knew they were breaking intellectual property rights, whereas others held back for fear of viruses. A fourteen-year-old wrote, "it's not right, but it's popular", which spoke to the appeal of having access to entertainment that was part of youth culture (Pasquier, 2005) and of a particular morality that negotiated general principles in the face of young people's interests.

CONCLUSION

By looking at children's and young people's negotiations of online risk, we hope to have demonstrated the advantage of studying online risk from the point of view of ordinary audiences, rather than constructing a priori labels for practices as risks. We also highlighted the importance of understanding audience's motivations and negotiations of norms in their use of the media and mediated relationships with others. Furthermore, we argue that it is useful to focus on the notion of *positioning*: how do children and youth position themselves in various types of interviews, vis-à-vis certain topics (e.g. values, norms and morality) and in relation to discourses promoted by parents, peers or other actors.

In the discussions with children and young people from two European countries as diverse as Portugal and Norway, we found fewer apparent differences between children in the two cultures than expected. Young people's preferences for platforms (e.g. Facebook) and the manner in which they negotiated what could be regarded as risky with their peers in both countries bore similarities. Clearer differences were mostly related to age; different perceptions of values could actually help to explain the different exposures to risky situations and how children would cope. Whereas younger children were more cautious, followed rules and relied more on their parents for help, teenagers were more likely to negotiate with peers on what was risky or could be part of their youth cultures. Autonomy and risk taking in the experience of the internet may be a sign of the negotiation of norms among peers in relation to families, although most risks were imposed, not voluntary (Hestvaag, 2013). We could also detect differences in terms of values and in approaches to authorities (e.g. regarding the police).

The definition of risks among children and young people appears in truly grey zones. Society is anxious about bullying and contacts by strangers, and children react to public agendas. Still, to children there are grey zones between teasing, leg pulling and bullying as much as between strangers as potential paedophiles or new friends through games or social networking sites (SNS).

Children's evaluations of what is acceptable or not when they are online can therefore nuance or even challenge more objective perceptions of risk. What is constructed as risky is rather subjective and is negotiated mainly among peers, but also with parents, whereas it also relates to factors such as age (cohort), gender and context. Likewise, the constitution of morality is bound to a specific context of peer relations where playing with boundaries of acceptable and non-acceptable behaviours is sometimes part of the fun. Examples of this are the perceptions of comments or actions as bullying or harassment as dependent on the relationship one has with the person who commits the act; and the posting of pictures without one's consent is acceptable if one looks good. Norms and riskiness are relative and subject to negotiation according to one's own perceptions, the other's perspective on what is acceptable and right and on the relationship between them. However, negotiations are not always peaceful and reveal power positions; issues of control and vulnerability come into play, because some children show efficient coping strategies to regain control whereas more vulnerable children are more upset.

Incorporating more countries in a longitudinal study or combining different age and gender participants in focus groups to test interactions, as well as conducting individual interviews can develop this comparative study further. We believe this investigation of ordinary audiences' perceptions of risk, of the intention of actors and negotiation of norms can contribute to audience research discussion of the internet as a moral space, beyond questions of netiquette, and rather, in Orgad's (2007) terms, as a sphere where the focus is on responsible behaviour in dealing with mediated others.

NOTE

1. In Norway, the younger group was not asked to write essays, only those in middle and secondary schools; therefore, only thirty-two essays were collected.

REFERENCES

Alasutaari, P., 1996. Television as a moral issue. In: I. Crawford and S. D. Hafsteinsson, eds. 1996. *The construction of the viewer: media ethnography and the anthropology of audiences*. Højberge, Denmark: Intervention Press. pp. 101–117.

Almansa, O. F. and Castillo, A., 2013. Social networks and young people: a comparative study of Facebook between Colombia and Spain. *Comunicar: Scientific Journal of Media Education* 40(1), pp. 127–134.

Bauman, Z., 1993. *Postmodern ethics*. Oxford: Blackwell.

Bauwens, J., 2012. Teenagers, the internet and morality. In: E. Loos, L. Haddon and E. Mante-Meijer, eds. 2012. *Generational use of new media*. Surrey: Ashgate. pp. 31–48.

Bengtsson, S., 2012. Imagined user modes: media morality in everyday life. *International Journal of Cultural Studies*, March 2012, 15(2), pp. 181–196.
Buckingham, D., 2000. *After the death of childhood: growing up in the age of electronic media.* Cambridge: Polity Press.
Davies, B. and Harré, R., 1990. Positioning: the discursive production of selves. *Journal for the Theory of Social Behaviour* 20(1), pp. 43–63.
Drotner, K., 1992. Modernity and media panics. In: M. Skovmand and K.C. Schrøder, eds. 1992. *Media cultures: reappraising transnational media.* London: Routledge. pp. 42–62.
Fairclough, N., 1989. *Language and power.* London and New York: Longman.
Flores, A. and James, C., 2013. Morality and ethics behind the screen: young people's perspectives on digital life. *New Media & Society* 15(6), pp. 834–852.
Haddon, L. and Livingstone, S., 2012. *EU Kids Online: national perspectives* [online]. London: EU Kids Online, LSE. Available at: <http://eprints.lse.ac.uk/46878>.
Hagen, I., 1992. *News viewing ideals and everyday practices: the ambivalences of watching Dagsrevyen.* Unpublished Ph.D. thesis. University of Bergen.
Hagen, I., 2000. Modern dilemmas: TV audiences, time use and moral evaluation. In: I. Hagen and J. Wasko, eds. 2000. *Consuming audiences?: production and reception in media research.* Cresskill: Hampton Press. pp. 231–249.
Hagen, I., 2007. 'We cannot just sit the whole day and watch TV': negotiations about media use among youngsters and their parents. *Young* 4(15), pp. 369–393.
Helsper, E.J., Kalmus, V., Hasebrink, U., Sagvari, B. and de Haan, J., 2013. *Country classification: opportunities, risks, harm and parental mediation* [online]. London: EU Kids. Available at: <http://eprints.lse.ac.uk/52023/>
Hestvaag, H., 2013. *'We know where to go and where not to go, what to do and what not to do online' a qualitative study of Norwegian children's activities, risk assessment, and coping strategies on the internet.* Unpublished thesis. Norwegian University of Science and Technology, Trondheim.
Horton, P., 2001. School bullying and social and moral orders. *Children and Society* 25(4), pp. 268–277.
Jenkins, H., Purushotma, R., Weigel, M., Clinton, K. and Robison, A.J., 2009. *Confronting the challenges of participatory culture: media education for the 21st century* [online]. Cambridge: The MIT Press. Available at: <http://mitpress.mit.edu/sites/default/files/titles/free_download/9780262513623_Confronting_the_Challenges.pdf>.
Kirwil, L., Garmendia, M., Garitaonandia, C. and Martinez-Fernández, G., 2009. Parental mediation. In: S. Livingstone and L. Haddon, eds. 2009. *Kids Online: opportunities and risks for children,* London: Policy Press. pp. 199–215.
Lenhart, A., Madden, M., Smith, A., Purcell, K., Zickuhr, K. and Rainie, L., 2011. *Teens, kindness and cruelty on social network sites. How American teens navigate the new world of "digital citizenship"* [online]. Pew Research Center's Internet and American Life Project. Washington, DC: Pew Research Center. Available at: <http://pewinternet.org/Reports/2011/Teens-and-social-media.aspx>.
Livingstone, S. and Haddon, L., 2009a. *EU Kids Online final report* [online]. London: EU Kids Online. Available online: <http://www.eukidsonline.net>
Livingstone, S. and Haddon, L., 2009b. *Kids online: opportunities and risks for children.* London: Policy Press.
Livingstone, S., Haddon, L., Görzig, A. and Ólafsson, K., 2011. *Risks and safety on the Internet. The perspective of European children* [online]. London: EU Kids Online. Available at: <http://www.eukidsonline.net>
Livingstone, S., Haddon, L., Görzig, A. and Ólafsson, K., eds. 2012. *Children, risk and safety on the internet: research and policy challenges in comparative perspective.* Bristol: Policy Press.

Livingstone, S., Kirwil, L., Ponte, C. and Staksrud, E., 2013. *In their own words: what bothers children online?* [online]. London: EU Kids Online. Available at: <http://www.eukidsonline.net>.
Lobe, B. and Ólafsson, K., 2012. Similarities and differences across Europe. In: S. Livingston, L. Haddon and A. Görzig, eds. 2012. *Children, risk and safety on the internet*. London: Policy Press. pp. 273–285.
Lupton, D., 1999. *Risk*. London: Routledge.
Lupton, D. and Tulloch, J., 2003. *Risk and everyday life*. London: Sage.
Orgad, S., 2007. The internet as a moral space: the legacy of Roger Silverstone. *New Media & Society* 9(1), pp. 33–41.
Pasquier, D., 2005. *Cultures lycéennes: la tyrannie de la majorité*. Paris: Éditions Autrement.
Paus-Hasebrink, I., Bauwens, J., Dürager, A. and Ponte, C., 2013. Exploring types of parent-child relationship and internet use across Europe. *Journal of Children and Media* 7(1), pp. 114–132.
Perren, S. and Gutzwiller-Helfenfinger, E., 2012. Cyberbullying and traditional bullying in adolescence: differential roles of moral disengagement, moral emotions and moral values. *European Journal of Developmental Psychology* 9(2), pp. 195–209.
Ponte, C., Simões, J.A. and Jorge, A., 2013. Do questions matter on children's answers about internet risk and safety. *Cyberpsychology: Journal of Psychosocial Research on Cyberspace* 7(1). Available at: <http://www.cyberpsychology.eu/view.php?cisloclanku=2013021801&article=2>.
Schrøder, K., Drotner, K., Kline, S. and Murray, C., 2003. *Researching audiences: a practical guide to methods in media audience analysis*. London: Arnold.
Silverstone, R., 2006. *Media and morality: on the rise of the mediapolis*. Cambridge: Polity Press.
Staksrud, E., 2011. Norske barn på internett. Høy risiko—lite skade? (Norwegian children on the Internet. High risk—little damage). *Nordicom-Information* 33(4), pp. 59–70.
Winter-Jørgensen, M. and Phillips, L., 1999. *Diskursanalyse som teori og metode* (Discourse analysis as theory and methodology). Copenhagen: Samfundslitteratur/ Roskilde Universitetsforlag.

10 Using and *Not* Using Social Media
What Triggers Young People's Practices on Social Network Sites?

Christine W. Trültzsch-Wijnen, Sascha Trültzsch-Wijnen and Andra Siibak

INTRODUCTION

Current media developments offer various possibilities for communication, participation, self-presentation and acquisition of knowledge. Information and Communication Technologies (ICTs) have become an integral part of the lives of young people in modern societies. More than 60 per cent of six- to sixteen-year-olds across Europe go online daily (and an extra 33 per cent are online once a week). In northern countries this rate is even higher (Livingstone, et al. 2011, p. 12). Because some 40 per cent of European youth use mobile devices to go online (ibid.), it is obvious that the Internet is omnipresent in the everyday lives of young people. In fact, findings from a recent Austrian study indicate that more and more younger people are starting to use the internet, compared to findings from earlier studies which identify age twelve and thirteen years as the age of first use (Trültzsch and Wijnen, 2012).

There is a large body of research on the ways young people use ICTs (boyd and Ellison, 2007; boyd, 2009; Peter, Valkenburg and Fluckiger, 2009; Baym, 2010; boyd and Marwick, 2011; Trültzsch and Wijnen, 2012), much of which focuses on the risks and opportunities related to ICTs and the well-being of young people (Livingstone, 2008; 2009; Kalmus, et al., 2009b; Livingstone, et al., 2011; Livingstone, Ólafsson and Staksrud, 2011; Kalmus, Siibak and Blinka, forthcoming). These studies suggest that differences in internet use practices among young people can be explained, to some extent, by socio-demographic factors, while others indicate that media literacy could have an important role to play in young people's new media usage practices and preferences (e.g. Schmidt, Paus-Hasebrink and Hasebrink, 2009; 2011).

Participating in social network sites (SNS) is one online activity that has become ubiquitous among millions of young people in Western societies encouraged by claims that if you are not on SNS then 'you don't exist', referring to the fact that usage of SNS has become the norm among modern youth. Research shows that these platforms are used mainly by young people to present themselves, to manage their relationships and to communicate with their peers (boyd, 2008; Ito, et al., 2008; Kalmus, et al., 2009a;

Peter, Valkenburg and Fluckiger, 2009; Schmidt, Paus-Hasebrink and Hasebrink, 2009; Siibak, 2009). Several scholars have claimed that social media, and SNS in particular, play an important part in the (media) socialisation and identity construction of contemporary youth (e.g. Siibak, 2009; 2011; Hernwall and Siibak, 2011; Krämer and Haferkamp, 2011). In this context, we would agree with Laura Portwood-Stacer's (2012, p. 7) argument that in today's "media-saturated consumer society, it is quite meaningful to be a person who says no to media consumption". However, very few researchers (Baker and White, 2011; Ryan and Xenos, 2011; Baumer, et al., 2013; Madden, et al., 2013; Rainie, Smith and Duggan, 2013) go beyond this and ask *why* some young people are *not* using social media and SNS in particular.

In this chapter, an overview is provided of some of the main reasons why millions of young people across the world decide to use SNS and analyses the reasons why some young people decide *not* to create SNS profiles. Because traditionally audience research focuses on exploring the use of different media, and recent research of online uses focuses mostly on different uses of the social web (in particular SNS usage), addressing the question of non-usage is a novelty in audience research.

We exploit several theoretical approaches to analyse the phenomenon of SNS usage by young people. Thereby, we consider approaches focussing on the individual and his or her motivations for using/not using SNS and leave out other theories such as systems theory and network theory. We begin by analysing several of the approaches used in media and communication studies that have been applied to explain the motives for young people's social media usage. We then provide a short overview of the various reasons given by young people for using and for not using social media especially SNS. Although the majority of the research so far focuses on young people's reasons and motivations for using SNS, we try to differentiate and discuss the reasons given for non-use or abandoning SNS by either deleting their profiles or just no longer visiting the sites. We discuss the state of the art in research on young people's SNS usage practices. We provide extracts from a recent qualitative study on Austria in order to support the findings (Trültzsch and Wijnen, 2012; Wijnen, 2013).

THEORETICAL APPROACHES TO THE USE OF SOCIAL MEDIA

Various theoretical approaches have been used to describe and explore the use of social media. Depending on the disciplinary background these approaches emphasise particular aspects of media usage such as motives, practices, outcomes and so on. We highlight four action theory approaches commonly used to study online communication. We acknowledge that this focus excludes other approaches, but the discussion that follows centres on the individual.

(1) Because self-representation is an integral part of social web usage it is closely linked to identity construction. For this reason, research in

the field of psychology, including impression management theories that go back to Goffman (see Krämer and Winter, 2008; Lewis, Kaufman and Christakis, 2008, pp. 82–83; Siibak, 2009) are especially relevant. These theories stress that by creating SNS profiles, users are able to reveal or conceal aspects of their personality in their online representations (Krämer and Winter, 2008, p. 106; see also system factors in this chapter). This strand of research is based on personality items, such as the 'Big Five' in modern psychology[1] proposed by Allport and Odbert (1936; see also Gerlitz and Schupp, 2005; Dehne and Schupp, 2007). Some items used to measure the influence of personal characteristics are openness, conscientiousness, extraversion, agreeableness and neuroticism regarding one's SNS profile (e.g. Tidwell-Collins and Walther, 2002; Back, et al., 2010; Correa, Hinsley and de Zuniga, 2010; for an overview see Weissensteiner and Leiner, 2011, pp. 529–530). The results in these studies show that almost all users tend to create profiles true to their 'real' identities, while the personality descriptions that are a result of the Big Five items have no influence on their behaviour regarding SNS-profiles. At the same time, extraversion (used more for relationship networking) and neuroticism (self-presentation in relation to social factors) correlate with the use of SNS (Weissensteiner and Leiner, 2011, p. 530). This implies that "extroverted persons with a broader offline network can accordingly communicate with a broader online network too" (ibid.)—which is the outcome we would expect. At the same time, the results of several studies that use these personality items are rather incoherent or even contradictory (ibid.).

(2) Research based on social capital in Bourdieu's (1979) sense, focuses on the positive effects of social capital for users. While the concept of social capital has different sources in sociology, (see Portes, 1998) and was developed further by Putnam (1995; 2000), Bourdieu's (1986) central point is to distinguish four kinds of capital, namely economic capital ("directly convertible into money [. . .] institutionalized in the form of property rights"; Bourdieu, 1986, p. 47), cultural capital (knowledge based, institutionalised via formal degrees and diplomas) symbolic capital (i.e. reputation of a person; Bourdieu, 1986, p. 56) and social capital ("made up of social obligations ('connections')"; Bourdieu, 1986, p. 47). More precisely, "[s]ocial capital is the aggregate of the actual or potential resources which are linked to possession of a durable network of more or less institutionalized relationships of mutual acquaintance and recognition" (Bourdieu, 1986, p. 51). With regard to SNS, Ellison, Steinfield and Lampe (2007, p. 1146) state that especially bridging (i.e. building up new connections) social capital "can take the form of useful information, personal relationships, or the capacity to organize groups" (see informational, recipient and relationship factors in this chapter). In addition to 'strong ties', such as relationships with family and friends (bonding social capital), connecting with so-called weak ties—such as neighbours, friends of friends and so on—can also be considered (bridging) social capital (Granovetter, 1982). SNS can increase the circle of 'weak ties' since it facilitates the maintenance

and tracking of such loose contacts (Putnam, 2000; Donath and boyd, 2004; Ellison, Steinfield and Lampe, 2007). Ellison, Steinfield and Lampe (2011, p. 5) argue that, in addition, SNS include "latent ties", which might become weak ties. For example the students in a class might see from Facebook that they live in the same town; they make friends on Facebook and chat in their subsequent classes about their common background (ibid.). Thus, although the majority of young SNS users do not use SNS to meet and connect with strangers (e.g. Ellison, Steinfield and Lampe, 2007; Subrahmanyam, et al. 2008), they have the potential to establish new weak ties and thereby gain (or increase) social capital. Accordingly, not using SNS means losing networking opportunities and accompanying resources and benefits.

(3) Another approach that is also related to Bourdieu's work is Silverstone's (2006) concept of the moral economy of the household, which developed as a result of his and his colleagues' work on domestication of the media (Silverstone, Hirsch and Morley, 1992; Silverstone and Haddon, 1996). According to this concept, technology serves as a tool to reproduce and distinguish one's social position in the realm of symbolic and cultural forms (Aroldi and Vittadini, 2010; Trültzsch, Kõuts-Klemm and Aroldi, 2014, p. 204). The integration of technologies into everyday lives (of families) builds on the moral economy of the family and balances "public, formal, *zweckrational*" and "private, informal, *wertrational* economy"[2] (Aroldi and Vittadini, 2010, p. 3). Because "different families draw on different cultural resources, based on religious beliefs, personal biography, or the culture of a network of family and friends" (Silverstone, Hirsch and Morley, 1992, p. 19), the integration of technology and therefore its usage follow different patterns. The moral economy of the household includes regulations for and restrictions on young people's media use and also their "cultural capital, social capital (in terms of offline relations) and free-time capital (as a kind of scarce resource) emerged as key factor in the prediction of different styles of social networking on Social Networking Sites" (Trültzsch, Kõuts-Klemm and Aroldi, 2014, p. 204). Related to this approach, relationships, social, system and recipient factors are of particular importance.

(4) Other research is based on variations of the uses and gratification approach (Katz, Blumler and Gurevitch, 1973; McQuail, 2010, pp. 423–430), according to which users decide about their media choices on the basis of needs, motives and more especially expected gratification (Leung, 2009, pp. 1329–1330; Thaddicken and Jers, 2011, pp. 149–150). Sought and achieved gratification can vary from "information and education, guidance and advice, social contact [. . .] value reinforcement, emotional release" to "identity formation and confirmation [or] lifestyle expression" (McQuail, 2010, p. 427; see relationship, social, information and recipient factors in this chapter). With regard to social media use, Leung (2009, pp. 1336–1337) examines four "gratifications" resulting from creating online content: cognitive needs (broader knowledge, being informed about society), entertainment needs, recognition needs (establish personality, gain respect

and support), and social needs (express feelings, communicate with family and friends). Recognition and social needs are significant motivations for creating online content, while the other two are categorised as non-significant in Leung's (2009, p. 1337) sample. Thaddicken and Jers (2011, pp. 150–151) refer to them as social and individual integration needs in their discussion of the motives for online disclosure of personal information. With regard to privacy issues and the so-called privacy paradox (Barnes, 2006; Utz and Krämer 2009; Joinson, et al., 2011), Thaddicken and Jers (2011, p. 143) ask whether users trade "loss of privacy for social web gratifications". Research differentiates between the user's general attitude to not disclosing private information, and his/her actual online privacy behaviour, highlighting the paradox (Barnes, 2006; Utz and Krämer, 2009; Joinson, et al., 2011). To benefit from SNS use, it is necessary to reveal personal information similar to what occurs in offline communication within friendship groups. A study by Lampe, Ellison and Steinfield (2007, cited in Thaddicken and Jers, 2001, p. 144) confirms that the more personal information the SNS user reveals, the higher the level of networking activity: "Evidently the disclosure of private information is rewarded with social gratifications" (Thaddicken and Jers, 2001, p. 144), especially social and individual integration, but also including transformation of latent into weak ties or maintenance of weak tie networks.

The four concepts discussed earlier are among the most common approaches to describing and understanding current social media usage. In what follows, we reflect on the state of the art in research on young people's social media usage according to sociality, information, system and recipient relationship factors.

YOUNG PEOPLE AND SNS

Although for many young people SNS have become "integrated into the daily lives" (Pempek, Yermolayeva and Calvert, 2009, p. 236; Livingstone, Ólafsson and Staksrud, 2011), there are various socio-demographic and context-specific factors that influence the decision about whether to engage in social networking or not. In this section we draw on the findings from various international studies, and provide a short overview of the main socio-demographic and context-specific factors influencing SNS use. We also introduce five additional factors suggested by Agosto, Abbas and Naughton (2012) that have an impact on how young people choose SNS and other platforms for personal communication.

Reasons for Using SNS

Previous studies suggest many different socio-demographic factors have an impact on young people's SNS usage practices. For instance, studies carried out in the US (Lenhart, et al., 2007; Hargittai, 2008; Hampton 2011), Australia and many European countries (Joinson, 2008; Kalmus, Runnel and Siibak, 2009; Trültzsch and Wijnen, 2012) indicate that young women are more active than young males in using SNS. Also, the motives for engaging in SNS and prevalent SNS practices differ (Lenhart and Madden, 2007; Kalmus, et al., 2009a; Pujazon-Zazik and Park, 2010; Davidson and Martellozzo, 2012; Trültzsch, 2012).

Age has an impact on SNS usage. According to the findings from the EU Kids Online study (Livingstone, et al., 2011, p. 13), 59 per cent of nine- to twelve-year-olds are non-users of SNS compared to only 21 per cent of non-users amongst thirteen- to sixteen-year-olds. A study conducted in Austria reveals similar trends—the highest rate of non-users (44.5 per cent) belongs to the ten-to-eleven-year-old age group, while the number of non-users amongst twelve- to thirteen-year-olds is 25.8 percent (Trültzsch and Wijnen, 2012).[3] For young people aged older than twenty-four years, the rate of non-users of SNS increases again—probably because this is a typical age for people to be focusing on their careers or raising children (ibid).

Several studies refer to engagement in a particular SNS being dependent on ethnicity. According to Hargittai (2008), for instance, Hispanic students in the US are less likely to use Facebook than white students, while Asians/Asian Americans are significantly less likely to use MySpace and more likely to use Xanga than Hispanics or whites (ibid).

The preceding would suggest that an individual's offline network influences the use of (a particular) SNS or not. As suggested by Agosto, Abbas and Naughton (2012), relationship factors are an important factor in the choice of which SNS to use.

Relationship Factors

Studies conducted in different cultural contexts (e.g. the US, Australia, Europe, Asia, etc.) suggest that young people use SNS primarily to connect and re-connect with existing contacts, and much less to find new ones (e.g. Lenhart, et al. 2007, Kalmus, Runnel and Siibak, 2009; Pempek, Yermolayeva and Calvert, 2009). In other words, SNS are readily available, easy-to-use platforms that facilitate 'keeping in touch' with both close (strong ties) and more distant 'friends' (weak ties). The latter opportunity, however, may be associated with building social capital and gratification—engagement in SNS allows users to invest in accumulation of bridging and bonding social capital. Research indicates that engaging in social networking helps to increase social capital and thus "could have strong payoffs in terms of jobs, internships, and other opportunities" (Ellison, Steinfield and Lampe, 2007, p. 1164; see also Peter, Valkenburg and Fluckiger, 2009; Rienties, et al., 2012).

Social Factors

Peers have a major influence on young people's intrinsic motivations for using the Internet (Zhao, et al., 2010). According to Baker and White (2011, p. 15), young people's "intentions to engage in frequent SNS use are likely to be greater when they perceive the behaviour to be normative among their friendship group".

Empirical work suggests that peers and close friends are most often viewed as reference points (Siibak, 2009); their preferences and practices are noted when selecting the "markers of cool" (Liu, 2007) worthy of inclusion in one's profile. Hence, it appears that the impression management strategies young people use on SNS build largely on the collective peer culture (Corsaro, 1997), whose values and norms help to frame the self-presentation process (Siibak, 2009).

Self-Protection Factors

To benefit from SNS it is necessary to disclose at least a minimum of personal data to be recognised by both friends (strong and weak ties) and people with similar interests (latent ties).

Young users seem to have awareness of what information they reveal and to whom. They decide what personal information to include in their profile, and who is allowed to access it according to the results in Trültzsch (2012) and those from other studies of online communication (for an overview see Weissensteiner and Leiner, 2011, 530–536). The profiles of most young Austrian SNS users (79.3 per cent) include full names, and 80.7 per cent include a recognizable profile image (Trültzsch, 2012; see also Debatin, et al., 2009; Autenrieth, 2010). The findings based on the Austrian sample reveal also that those who do not use the Internet daily are less likely to upload a good likeness (a good photograph) for their profile image and that those who use the Internet less often are more likely try to be anonymous.

Information/Communication Factors

Recent research (Agosto, Abbas and Naughton, 2012; Vitak and Ellison, 2012) indicates that many young SNS users claim that they have benefited from access to a diverse network of contacts enabled by SNS. One such benefit is to obtain advice or information, or to receive support from a friend (ibid). Empirical research on three-generation families in Estonia reveals that although public postings on Facebook are not used much for communication within the family, the opportunity to exchange private Facebook messages and to use Facebook chat options are popular for parent–child interactions (Siibak and Tamme, 2013).

Systems Factors

Several studies suggest that the adoption of SNS is dependent on the users "confidence in their ability to successfully understand, navigate, and evaluate content online" (Daugherty, Eastin and Gangadharbatla, 2005, p. 71), or their Internet self-efficacy (e.g. Gangadharbatla, 2008). In other words, the greater the individual's facility to navigate on the site and perform the necessary tasks online, the greater will be their ability to join and engage in the service (ibid). Interviews with Facebook non-users for example suggest that non-users often "position themselves with respect to the discourse of technophobia, either admitting or denying that they were averse to new technology in general" (Portwood-Stacer, 2012, p. 13).

Recipient Factors

Some studies suggest that schools and higher education institutions are making more and more use of SNS for education-related reasons. According to Madge, et al. (2009), Facebook has become an important social tool or the 'social glue' required to help freshmen college students settle into the university system, feel part of the community and access important information (e.g. about social events).

Reasons for Not Using or Dropping Out of SNS Use

There is a lack of research on the reasons why some young people decide not to use SNS. So far only a few empirical studies have investigated non-use of SNS and even fewer analyse the phenomenon of dropout, that is the phenomenon of one-time users of SNS either deleting their profiles or no longer using the site. More research is needed on these aspects. However, the findings from the few studies that have been done so far provide us with a first glimpse of the lifestyle practice, which Portwood-Stacer (2012, p. 2) refers to as "media refusal". We can illustrate these findings using qualitative data from Austria. The study referred to by Trültzsch and Wijnen (2012) formed the basis for further qualitative research on forty-six young people aged between twelve and seventeen years (interviews and think-aloud technique), in the period November 2012 to February 2013 (Wijnen, 2013). The focus was on the relation between young people's SNS usage, media literacy and the habitus (Bourdieu, 1979). Although the majority were SNS users there were also some non-users. Their reasons for avoiding SNS are described in the following together with the findings from other studies on the topic.

Time Management and Media Use Preferences

There are various personal reasons for not using SNS, especially Facebook. For instance, several studies suggest that non-users of SNS "position themselves as above the 'time-wasting', 'artificiality' and 'narcissism' that they see as characterising Facebook use" (Portwood-Stacer, 2012, p. 11). Eleven- to eighteen-year-old Estonian non-users of the national language-based SNS, Rate, made similar references to it, stating that Rate SNS "is pointless", "sucks" or is just boring (Kalmus, Runnel and Siibak, 2009). In other words, the dominant reason for not adopting SNS among young non-users—regardless of the cultural context (e.g. the US, Saudi Arabia, Estonia, Australia), is a general lack of interest in the site (Kalmus, Runnel and Siibak, 2009; Baker and White, 2011; Aljasir, Woodcock and Harrison, 2012; Lampe, Vitak and Ellison, 2013).

Because non-users of SNS are more familiar with using the Internet for practical reasons—banking, research, shopping and so on—rather than expressive reasons, for example entertainment, they are not inclined to look looking around "just for fun", which is a normal activity on SNS (Tufecki, 2008). This applies to non-users in the Austrian sample. Most were not intensive media users and were very conscious of different media uses for different reasons; computers and the Internet are mostly classified as tools for research and doing homework but not for fun (e.g. using SNS; Wijnen, 2013).

D: [I]nternet? Well, I'm using it for homework because we have to.
I: And what about using it for private interests—for fun?
D: No, computer is not so much for fun.
I: And Facebook and something like that?
D: I don't need that.
I: But your friends are using it?
D: Yes, but I don't need that. I use my computer for work.

(girl, aged thirteen)

The preceding examples suggest that SNS may simply not fit with the specific media needs and preferences of non-users (e.g. Aljasir, Woodcock and Harrison's 2012 study of Facebook non-users in a group of Saudi Arabian students). In addition to engaging in more practical and task-oriented online activities, young non-users of SNS also tend to prefer to devote spare time to offline interests and commitments. For instance, many Australian teen non-users of Facebook stated that they had other interests (e.g. reading, watching TV series, etc.) or commitments (e.g. sports) which they preferred to spending time on SNS; they considered SNS use to be "too time-consuming or detracted from the time they could be spending on alternate activities" (Baker and White, 2011, p. 397).

In fact, according to Rainie, Smith and Duggan (2013, p. 4), 42 per cent eighteen- to twenty-nine-year-old Facebook users in the US who had taken a break from using the site in the past (N = 316), reported decreasing Facebook usage in the previous year, and 38 per cent of the sample expected to spend less time on the site in 2013. One of the main self-reported reasons for a 'Facebook vacation' was the need to deal with other life demands and not having time to spend on the site (21 per cent), followed by general lack of interest in the site (10 per cent) and the absence of compelling content (9 per cent). This last reason (lack of compelling content) is in line with the findings from a study by Pew Internet Research, which suggests that young Facebook users have started "to migrate their activity and attention to other sites" (Madden, et al., 2013, 7), such as Twitter or Instagram, mainly because these sites appear to be freer of negative social interactions (less 'drama' and fewer adults) and focused more on personal content creation than self-presentation.

Social Factors

Non-users of SNS are less interested in those activities referred to as social grooming (Portwood-Stacer, 2012). Hence, non-users of SNS are not only less interested in keeping in touch with their friends, especially friends from the past; they also are less curious about other people in general than SNS users (ibid). Ljepava, et al. (2013) show that non-users of Facebook may also be less committed to intimate friendships compared to frequent users of the site.

On the other hand, Portwood-Stacer (2012, p. 14) argues that only individuals whose "social standing will endure without" a SNS such as Facebook, can actually afford what has been described as the "cost of opting out" (Marwick, 2011). That these costs can be very high is shown by the example of a twelve-year-old boy and a thirteen-year-old girl in the Austrian sample (Wijnen, 2013) who do not use Facebook because their parents forbid it. (Baker and White [2011] refer to this as one of the reasons for teens in Australia not using Facebook). Both children suffered because their schoolmates were intensive Facebook users. Both were unable to participate in quick chat communications, missed out on invitations for leisure time activities and were unable to keep up to date with what their friends were doing and talking about (Wijnen, 2013). These results are confirmed by Madden, et al. (2013, p. 26), who suggest that although many teens have "widespread negative feelings about the interactions on Facebook", they still feel the need to stay on the site so as not to "miss out" (ibid, p. 7). Hence, although there is some evidence of attrition we are currently witnessing "lagging resistance", that is "a sense of wanting to quit but not doing so just yet" (Baumer, et al. 2013, p. 8) among young Facebook users in particular, the fear of being isolated and excluded from various social events is maintaining SNS use.

Privacy and Self-Disclosure Factors

In several studies, privacy concerns are cited as one of the aspects playing a role in non-users' decisions (Baumer, et al. 2013; Lampe, Vitak and Ellison, 2013; Madden, et al., 2013). Although the students in Tufecki's (2008) sample did not regard SNS as dangerous platforms, they were concerned about their privacy in general. Recent studies refer to the fact that many non-users are concerned about the need to share private information on a platform they consider to be public, regardless of the opportunity to use privacy settings (Lampe, Vitak and Ellison 2013; Madden, et al., p. 2013). Furthermore, comparisons between Facebook non-users and frequent users reveal that non-users are less interested in sharing personal information (Ljepava, et al., 2013). For instance, some of the non-users in Baumer, et al.'s (2013, p. 3) sample (N = 410) stressed that they not only did "not want to be on display or live 'life in a global aquarium', but also cited their concerns about privacy violations in professional relationships e.g. with employers, and were concerned about the (mis)use of personal data by Facebook itself."

Young non-users of SNS in the US (Tufecki, 2008; Madden, et al., 2013) also did not like the idea of using SNS for self-presentation reasons; that is they often believed people were "only fishing for affirmation" (Tufecki, 2008, 559) by including the names of their favourite movies and bands on their profiles either to impress or match the expectations of their online peer group. Similar dislike of the importance of self-presentation on Facebook was expressed by young non-users in Australia (Baker and White, 2011).

Although the above demonstrates that non-users of SNS are generally against the idea of using SNS as a self-presentation tool, several scholars argue that, regardless of non-users being conscious of the fact or not, such "performances of resistance" (Portwood-Stacer, 2012, 9) can also be regarded as "an alternative form of self-expression" (Kalmus, et al., 2009a, p. 1269). Portwood-Stacer's (2012, p. 3) interviews with non-users of Facebook indicate that their decision not to use the site can often be interpreted as a "wish to demonstrate one's superiority to the abstract 'mainstream', or even one's superiority to the friends one leaves behind in the Facebook network." Similarly, analysis of open-ended responses from non-users of SNS Rate suggest that non-users often revel in their difference from the mainstream, for instance by stating that SNS such as Rate represent "mass hypnosis and idiot culture" (Kalmus, et al., 2009a, p. 1269). Because non-users appear to be consciously critical of SNS, and open about their stance, they can be described as engaging in 'conspicuous non-consumption', that is "they make their refuser status visible through performance of non-consumption which [is] also on display" (Portwood-Stacer, 2012, p. 7).

This alternative self-expression is exemplified by a seventeen-year-old boy in the Austrian sample who had a Facebook profile but rarely used it because he believed himself superior to his class mates and peer group whose members he considered 'mainstream'. He aspired to being like his idol, Albert Einstein, and used his Facebook profile only to position himself as an intellectual non-user who does not need SNS. He never communicated with others and only sometimes posted "something intellectual" as his status update, in order to show off. However, despite his protestations that he wanted to be regarded as a non-user, he secretly and carefully watched others' reactions to his postings (Wijnen, 2013).

Ideological and Outside Factors

In addition to the previously mentioned personal reasons for not adopting SNS, some non-users gave ideological reasons for their decision. These were usually connected to "dissatisfaction with Facebook's corporate practices, and more broadly, voice[d] an overall ideology tinged with anti-capitalist sentiment" (Portwood-Stacer, 2012, p. 7) and to positioning "themselves with respect to the discourse of technophobia, either admitting or denying that they were averse to new technology in general" (ibid., p. 13).

Alongside these value-related reasons, lack of regular computer access was identified as one of the factors contributing to non-use of SNS among college students in the US and in Saudi Arabia (Ajasir, Woodstock and Harrison, 2012). Economic reasons (47 per cent) were also mentioned by non-users (only 3 per cent in this sample) in Italy (ISFOL, 2011; see Trültzsch, Kõuts-Klemm and Aroldi, 2014, pp. 201–202). In addition, lack of computer skills and knowledge about Facebook (Ajasir, Woodstock and Harrison, 2012), or lack of interest in the Internet and ICTs in particular, and lack of curiosity related to culture may have an impact on the decision not to adopt to SNS (ISFOL, 2011, p. 106).

CONCLUSION

In this chapter four of the most common approaches used to describe current social media usage have been discussed. However, are these theories applicable also to non-usage of SNS? Impression management–based theories that focus on personality items, such as the Big Five, have been shown not to be coherent in relation to SNS use (Weissensteiner and Leiner, 2011, p. 530). They suggest that extraverts behave in more extraverted ways online in personal networking and self-presentation. This might imply that introversion is a reason for not using SNS because introverts have no need for intensive communication—either online or offline. However, in light of the motives for and factors related to non-usage identified by the studies referred to in this chapter, this would seem to be a less than convincing explanation.

More promising seems the focus on social capital in the sense of Bourdieu (1979). Ellison, Steinfield and Lampe (2011, p. 5) and others argue that SNS can be used to build social capital. This is in line with recipient and relationship factors highlighted by many studies of SNS use. According to this research, young people use SNS mainly to connect, to reconnect and communicate with others, to stay in contact with geographically distant friends and family, to get settled into new environments (e.g. university), for education-related collaborations and so on. However, this does not explain why some people decide not to use SNS despite these advantages.

One factor in non-usage is the habitus of an individual whose other behaviour is also linked to media usage (Biermann, 2009; Bourdieu, 1979; Kommer, 2010). In this sense, an individual's values and behaviour provide a means of differentiation from others. This may explain why some young people do not need SNS either because these platforms do not fit with their individual media needs and preferences or because non-usage is part of an alternative form of differentiation from the mainstream. Silverstone's (2006) concept of the moral economy of the household is in line with this explanation. As the integration of technologies into everyday life follows the moral economy of the family, it also involves media education including regulations and restrictions on SNS use by young people.

The uses and gratifications approach (Katz, Blumler and Gurevitch, 1973) may also be useful to explain non-usage. The decision not to use SNS may be the result of weighing up gratifications such as entertainment and social needs, against potential risks such as privacy concerns or time constraints. For these reasons perhaps young people decide not to 'waste' their time on SNS and to use the Internet instead for homework or engaging in something they see as more valuable.

More research is needed to provide a more detailed insight into young people's decisions not to follow their peers onto SNS and to enable a better theoretical discussion of non-usage. There is no clear theoretical explanation, in part because of the focus in existing research on users, but also the implicit assumption that the level of competences and skills is connected to use and that non-use is related to an absence of these skills. This explanation builds on the earlier digital divide discussion. It seems clear that non-usage is not simply the result of lack of access or a lack of digital skills and poor media literacy. However, not using SNS should be seen as a well-thought-out decision based on rational choices and weighing the benefits and risks of disclosure of private information. With regard to communicative competence and media literacy, this choice can be considered as indicative of both because opting out and going against the peer group requires more justification, discussion and explanation than does using SNS according to group norms.

The literature review in this chapter shows that information on non-users is incidental to research on SNS usage. The small amount of data available is mostly the result of quantitative studies that do not investigate in depth reasons for and types of non-usage. We need more quantitative studies to identify a certain population of non-users and more qualitative research to enable an in-depth examination of the individual reasons for such behaviour. At the theoretical level, we need to consider and discuss the reasons for not using certain media—not just SNS but media in general (e.g. TV, newspapers) as well. This will involve questioning and retesting traditional theories from this new perspective because an active audience, central to modern audience research, means people who make active and conscious decisions about their usage as well as non-usage of media.

NOTES

1. The Big Five personality traits are dimensions to describe individuals personality, regarding *openness, conscientiousness, extraversion, agreeableness* and *neuroticism*. For a survey these are typically operationalised with questions such as "I am open to new experiences" (openness), "I am spontaneous" (conscientiousness) and so on. The Big Five address in detail *openness*: appreciation for new experiences, art and so on; *conscientiousness*: tendency to planned or spontaneous behaviour, self-discipline; *extraversion*: positive emotions, seeking the company of others or prefer to stay alone; *agreeableness*: being cooperative towards other or be suspicious and antagonistic; and *neuroticism*: the tendency to negative emotions like anger or stable and vulnerable.
2. The terms refer to Max Weber's typology of social action; *zweckrational* actions are goal oriented and more instrumental and *wertrational* are ones based on specific values.
3. These data refer to an online survey of social media usage (N = 2,492; age: 10–30 years) conducted in Austria during December 2011 and February 2012 (Trültzsch and Wijnen, 2012). The results were used as the basis for further analysis on privacy issues and the publication of photos on SNS (Trültzsch, 2012) and media literacy, SNS usage and its relation to the habitus of young people (Wijnen, 2012).

REFERENCES

Agosto, D. E., Abbas, J. and Naughton, R., 2012: Relationships and social rules: teens' social network and other ICT selection practices. *Journal of the American Society for Information Science and Technology* 63(6), pp. 1108–1124.

Aljasir Abdulrahman, S., Woodcock, A. and Harrison, S., 2012. Facebook non-users in Saudi Arabia: why do some Saudi college students not use Facebook? In: *International Conference on Management, Applied and Social Sciences*, Dubai, 24–25 March. Available at: <http://psrcentre.org/images/extraimages/312713.pdf>

Allport, G. W. and Odbert, H. S., 1936. Trait-names: a psycho-lexical study. *Psychological Monographs* 47(1), p. 211.

Aroldi, P. and Vittadini, N., 2010. Transnational digital audiences? 'Moral economy of the households' and digital television. In: *Ecrea Conference 2010*, Hamburg, 12–15 October.

Autenrieth, U. P., 2010: MySelf. MyFriends. MyLife. MyWorld: Fotoalben auf Social Network Sites und ihre kommunikativen Funktionen für Jugendliche und junge Erwachsene. In: K. Neumann-Braun and U. Autenrieth, eds. 2010. *Freundschaft und Gemeinschaft im Social Web. Bildbezogenes Handeln und Peergroup-Kommunikation auf Facebook und Co*. Baden-Baden: Nomos. pp. 123–161.

Back, M. D., Stopfer, J. M., Vazire, S., Gaddis, S., Schmukle, S. C., Egloff, B. and Gosling, S. D., 2010. Facebook profiles reflect actual personality, not self-idealization. *Psychological Science* 21(3), pp. 372–374.

Baker, R. and White K. M., 2011. In their own words: why teenagers don't use social networking sites. *Cyberpsychology, Behavior and Social Networking* 14(6), pp. 395–398.

Barnes, S. B., 2006. A privacy paradox: social networking in the United States. *First Monday* [e-journal] 11(9). Available at: <http://firstmonday.org/htbin/cgiwrap/bin/ojs/index.php/fm/article/viewArticle/1394>.

Baumer, E. P. S., Adams, P., Khovanskaya, V. D., Liao, T. C., Smith, M. E., Sosik, V. S. and Williams, K. 2013. Limiting, leaving, and (re)lapsing: an exploration of Facebook non-use practices and experiences. In: CHI '13, *Proceedings of the SIGCHI Conference on Human Factors in Computing Systems*, Paris, 27 April–2 May. pp. 3257–3266

Baym, N., 2010. *Personal connections in the digital age.* Cambridge: Polity Press.

Biermann, R., 2009. *Der Mediale Habitus von Lehramtsstudierenden: Eine quantitative Studie zum Medienhandeln angehender Lehrpersonen.* Wiesbaden: VS-Verlag.

Bourdieu, P., 1979. *La distinction: critique sociale du jugement.* Paris: Éds. de Minuit.

Bourdieu, P., 1986. The forms of capital. In: J. E. Richardson, ed., 1986. *Handbook of social research for the sociology of education.* New York: Greenwood Press. pp. 46–58.

boyd, d., 2008. *Taken out of context: American teen sociality in networked publics.* Ph.D. dissertation. University of California-Berkeley, School of Information.

boyd, d., 2009. Friendship. In: M. Ito, S. Baumer, M. Bittanti, d. boyd, R. Cody, B. Herr-Stephenson, H. A. Horst, P. G. Lange, D. Mahendran, K. Z. Martínez, C. J. Pascoe, D. Perkel, L. Robinson, S. Sims and L. Tripp, eds. 2009. *Hanging out, messing around, and geeking out. Kids living and learning with new media.* Cambridge: MIT Press. pp. 79–115.

boyd, d. and Ellison, N.B., 2007. Social network sites. Definition, history, and scholarship. *Journal of Computer-Mediated Communication* 13(1), pp. 210–230.

boyd, d. and Marwick, A., 2011. Social privacy in networked publics. Teens' attitudes, practices, and strategies. In: Oxford Internet Institute and *Information, Communication and Society*, *A decade in internet time: Symposium on the dynamics of the internet and society*, Oxford Internet Institute, Oxford, UK, 22 September. Available at: <http://www.danah.org/papers/2011/SocialPrivacy-PLSC-Draft.pdf>.

Correa, T., Hinsley, A. W. and de Zuniga, H.G., 2010. Who interacts on the web? The intersection of user's personality and social media use. *Computers in Human Behavior* 26(2), pp. 247–253.

Corsaro, W., 1997. *The sociology of childhood.* Thousand Oaks, CA: Pine Forge Press.

Daugherty, T., Eastin, M. and Gangadharbatla, H., 2005. e-CRM: Understanding Internet confidence and implications for customer relationship management. In: I. Clark III and T. Flaherty, eds. 2005. *Advances in electronic marketing.* Harrisonburg: James Madison University, Idea Group Publishing, Inc. pp. 67–82.

Davidson, J. and Martellozzo, E., 2012. Exploring young people's use of social networking sites and digital media in the Internet safety context: A comparison of the UK and Bahrain. *Information, Communication and Society* 16(9), pp. 1456–1476.

Debatin, B., Lovejoy, J.P., Horn, A. and Hughes, B.N., 2009. Facebook and online privacy: Attitudes, behaviors, and unintended consequences. *Journal of Computer-Mediated Communication* 15, pp. 83–108.

Dehne, M. and Schupp, J., 2007. *Persönlichkeitsmerkmale im Sozio-oekonomischen Panel (SOEP)—Konzept, Umsetzung und empirische Eigenschaften* [online. DIW Research Notes 26. Berlin: DIW Berlin. Available at: <http://www.diw.de/documents/publikationen/73/diw_01.c.76533.de/rn26.pdf>.

Donath, J. and boyd, d., 2004. Public displays of connection. *BT Technology Journal* 22(4), p. 71.

Ellison, N.B., Steinfield, C. and Lampe, C., 2007. The benefits of Facebook 'friends': exploring the relationship between college students' use of online social networks and social capital. *Journal of Computer-Mediated Communication*, 12, pp. 1143–1168.

Ellison, N.B., Steinfield, C. and Lampe, C., 2011. Communication practices, connection strategies: social capital implications of Facebook-enabled. *New Media & Society* 13(6), pp. 873–892.

Gangadharbatla, H., 2008. Facebook me: collective self-esteem, need to belong, and internet self-efficacy as predictors of the iGeneration's attitudes toward social networking sites. *Journal of Interactive Advertising* 8(2), pp. 5–15.

Gerlitz, J. and Schupp, J., 2005. Zur Erhebung der Big-Five basierten Persönlichkeitsmerkmale. In: *SOEP, DIW Research Notes* 2005–4. Berlin: DIW Berlin. pp. 36.

Granovetter, M.S., 1982. The strength of weak ties: a network theory revisited. In: P.V. Mardsen and N. Lin, eds. 1982. *Social structure and network analysis*. Thousand Oaks, CA: Sage. pp. 105–130.

Hampton, K.N., 2011. Comparing bonding and bridging ties for democratic engagement. Everyday use of communication technologies within social networks for civic and civil behaviours. *Information, Communication & Society* 14(4), pp. 510–528.

Hargittai, E., 2008. The role of expertise in navigating links of influence [online]. In: J. Turow and L. Tsui, eds. 2008. *The hyperlinked society*. Available at: <http://www.eszter.com/research/hyperlinkedsociety.html>

Hernwall, P. and Siibak, A., 2011. Writing identity. Gendered values and user content creation in SNS interaction among Estonian and Swedish tweens. *Global Studies of Childhood*, 1(4), pp. 365-376.

ISFOL. 2011. *Il divario digitale nel mondo giovanile. Il rapporto dei giovani italiani con le ICT*. Roma: ISFOL.

Ito, M., Horst, H, Bittanti, M, boyd, d., Herr-Stephenson, B., Lange, P. G, Pascoe, C. J., Robinson, L., 2008. *Living and learning with new media: summary of findings from the digital youth project* [online]. Berkeley: University of Southern California and University of California, Berkeley. Available at: <http://www.macfound.org>

Joinson, A. N., Houghton, D. J., Vasalou, A. and Marder, B. L., 2011. Digital crowding: privacy, self-disclosure and technology. In: S. Trepte and L. Reineckeeds. 2011. *Privacy online: perspectives on privacy and self-disclosure in the social web*. Heidelberg: Springer. pp. 33–46.

Joinson, N. A., 2008. 'Looking at', 'looking up' or 'keeping up with' people? Motives and uses of Facebook. In: CHI '08, *CHI 2008 Proceedings*, Florence, 5–10 April. ACM, New York. pp. 1027–1036.

Kalmus, V., Pruulmann-Vengerfeldt, P., Runnel, P. and Siibak, A., 2009a. Mapping the terrain of "Generation C": places and practices of online content creation among Estonian teenagers. *Journal of Computer-Mediated Communication* 14(4), pp. 1257–1282.

Kalmus, V., Pruulmann-Vengerfeldt, P., Runnel, P. and Siibak, A., 2009b. Online content creation. Practices of Estonian schoolchildren in comparative perspective. *Journal of Children and Media* 3(4), pp. 331–348.

Kalmus, V., Runnel, P. and Siibak, A., 2009 Opportunities and benefits online. In: S. Livingstone and L. Haddon, eds. 2009. *Children online: opportunities and risks for children*. London: Policy Press. pp. 71–82.

Kalmus, V., Siibak, A. and Blinka, L. (2014). The Internet and child well-being. In: A. Ben-Arieh, I. Frones, F. Casas and J.E. Korbin, eds. *Handbook of child well-being*. Delhi: Springer. pp. 2093–2133.

Katz, E., Blumler, J. G. and Gurevitch, M., 1973. Uses and gratifications research. *The Public Opinion Quarterly* 37(4), pp. 509–523.

Kommer, S., 2010: *Kompetenter Medienumgang? Eine qualitative Untersuchung zum medialen Habitus und zur Medienkompetenz von SchülerInnen und Lehramtsstudierenden*. Opladen: Budrich UniPress.

Krämer, N. C. and Haferkamp, N., 2011. Online self-presentation: balancing privacy concerns and impression construction on SNS. In: S. Trepte and L. Reinecke, eds. 2011. *Privacy online: perspectives on privacy and self-disclosure in the social web*. New York and Heidelberg: Springer. pp. 127–142.

Krämer, N. C. and Winter, S., 2008. Impression management 2.0: the relationship of self-esteem, extraversion, self-efficacy and self-presentation within social networking sites. *Journal of Media Psychology* 20(3), pp. 106–116.

Lampe, C., Ellison, N. and Steinfield, C., 2007. A familiar Face(book): profile elements as signals in an online social network. In: CHI '07, *Proceedings of the SIGCHI Conference on Human Factors in Computing Systems*, San Jose, CA, 28 April–3 May. ACM, New York. pp. 435–444.

Lampe, C., Vitak, J. and Ellison, N. 2013. Users and nonusers: Interactions between levels of adoption and social capital. In: CSCW '13, *Proceedings of the 2013 conference on Computer supported cooperative work (CSCW '13)*, San Antonio, TX, 23–27 February. New York: ACM. pp. 809–820.

Lenhart, A., Madden, M., Macgill, A. R. and Smith, A., 2007. *Teens and social media* [online]. PEW: Internet & American Life Project Report. Washington, DC: Pew Research Center. Available at: <http://www.pewinternet.org/pdfs/PIP_Teens_Social_Media_Final.pdf>.

Lenhart, M. and Madden, M., 2007. *Teens, privacy and online social networks. How teens manage their online identities and personal information in the age of MySpace* [online]. Pew Internet & American Life Project Report. Washington, DC: Pew Research Center. Available at: <http://www.pewinternet.org/~/media//Files/Reports/2009/PIP_Adult_social_networking_data_memo_FINAL.pdf>.

Leung, L., 2009. User-generated content on the Internet: An examination of gratifications, civic engagement and psychological empowerment. *New Media & Society* 11(8), pp. 1327–1347.

Lewis, K., Kaufman, J. and Christakis, N., 2008. The taste for privacy: an analysis of college student privacy settings in an online social network. *Journal of Computer-Mediated Communication* 14, pp. 79–100.

Liu, H. 2007. Social network profiles as taste performances. *Journal of Computer-Mediated Communication* 13(1), pp. 252–275.

Livingstone, S., 2008. Taking risky opportunities in youthful content creation: teenagers' use of social networking sites for intimacy, privacy and self-expression. *New Media & Society* 10(3), pp. 393–411.

Livingstone, S., 2009. *Children and the Internet*. Cambridge: Polity Press.

Livingstone, S., Haddon, L., Görzig, A. and Ólafsson, K., 2011. *Risks and safety on the Internet. The perspective of European children: full findings* [online]. London: EU Kids Online, LSE. Available at: <http://www.eukidsonline.net>.

Livingstone, S., Ólafsson, K. and Staksrud, E., 2011. *Social networking, age and privacy*. London: EU Kids Online Network.

Ljepava, N., Orr, R.R., Locke S. and Ross, C., 2013. Personality and social characteristics of Facebook non-users and frequent users. *Computers in Human Behaviour* 29(4), pp. 1602–1607.

Madden, M., Lenhart, A., Cortesi, S., Gasser, U., Duggan, M., Smith, A. and Beaton, M., 2013. *Teens, social media, and privacy. Full report* [online]. Pew Institute Center and the Berkman Center for internet & Society at Harvard University. Washington, DC: Pew Research Center. Available at: <http://www.pewinternet.org/~/media//Files/Reports/2013/PIP_TeensSocialMediaandPrivacy_FINAL.pdf>.

Madge, C., Meek, J., Wellens, J. and Hooley, T., 2009. Facebook, social integration and informal learning at university: it is more for socialising and talking to friends about work than for actually doing work. *Learning, Media and Technology* 34(2), pp. 141–155.

Marwick, A., 2011. '*If you don't like it, don't use it. It's that simple.' ORLY?* [online]. Available at: <http://socialmediacollective.org/2011/08/11/if-you-dont-like-it-dont-use-it-its-that-simple-orly/>.

McQuail, D., 2010. *McQuail's mass communication theory*. 6th ed. London: Sage.

Pempek, P. A., Yermolayeva, Y. A. and Calvert S. L., 2009. College students' social networking experiences on Facebook. *Journal of Applied Developmental Psychology* 30(3), pp. 227–238.

Peter, J., Valkenburg, P. M. and Fluckiger, C., 2009. Adolescents and social network sites: Identity, friendship and privacy. In: S. Livingstone and L. Haddon, eds. 2009. *Kids online: opportunities and risks for children*. Bristol: Policy Press. pp. 83–94.

Portes, A., 1998. Social capital: Its origins and applications in modern sociology. *Annual Review of Sociology* 24(1), pp. 1–24.

Portwood-Stacer, L., 2012. Media refusal and conspicuous non-consumption: the performative and political dimensions of Facebook abstention. *New Media & Society* 10(1), pp. 1041–1057.

Pujazon-Zazik, M. and Park, J., 2010. To tweet or not to tweet: gender differences and potential positive and negative health outcomes of adolescents' social internet use. *American Journal of Men's Health* 4(1), pp. 77–85.

Putnam, R. D., 1995. Bowling alone: America's declining social capital. *Journal of Democracy* 6(1), pp. 65–78.

Putnam, R. D., 2000. *Bowling alone: the collapse and revival of American community*. New York: Simon & Schuster.

Rainie, L., Smith. A. and Duggan. M., 2013. *Coming and going on Facebook* [online]. Washington, DC: Pew Research Center's Internet & American Life Project. Available at: <http://www.pewinternet.org/˜/media/Files/Reports/2013/PIP_Coming_and_going_on_facebook.pdf>

Rienties, B., Beausaert, S., Grohnert, T., Niemantsverdriet, S. and Kommers, P., 2012. Understanding academic performance of international students: the role of ethnicity, academic and social integration. *Higher Education* 63(6), pp. 685–700.

Ryan, T. and Xenos, S., 2011. Who uses Facebook? An investigation into the relationship between the Big Five shyness, narcissism, loneliness, and Facebook usage. *Computers in Human Behavior* 27(5), pp. 1658–1664.

Schmidt, J., Paus-Hasebrink, I. and Hasebrink, U., 2011. *Heranwachsen mit dem Social Web: Zur Rolle von Web 2.0—Angeboten im Alltag von Jugendlichen und jungen Erwachsenen*, Münster: Vistas.

Siibak, A., 2009. *Self-presentation of the 'digital generation' in Estonia*. Tartu: Tartu University Press.

Siibak, A., 2011. Online peer culture and interpretive reproduction on the social networking site profiles of the tweens. In: F. Colombo and L. Fortunati, eds. 2011. *Broadband society and generational changes*. Berlin: Peter Lang, pp. 121–132.

Siibak, A. and Tamme, V., 2013. Who introduced granny to Facebook?: an exploration of everyday family interaction in web-based communication environments. *Northern Lights* 11, pp. 71–89.

Silverstone, R., 2006. Domesticating domestication: reflections on the life of a concept. In: T. Berker, M. Hartmann and Y. W. Punje, eds. 2006. *Domestication of media and technologies*. Maidenhead: Open University Press. pp. 229–248.

Silverstone, R. and Haddon, L., 1996. *Television, cable and AB households. A report for Telewest*. Falmer: Sussex University.

Silverstone, R., Hirsch, E. and Morley, D., 1992. Information and communication technologies and the moral economy of the household. In: R. Silverstone and E. Hirsch, eds. 1992. *Consuming technologies: media and information in domestic spaces*. London: Routledge. pp. 15–31.

Subrahmanyam, K., Reich, S. M., Waechter, N. and Espinoza, G., 2008. Online and offline social networks: use of social networking sites by emerging adults. *Journal of Applied Developmental Psychology* 29, pp. 420–433.

Thaddicken, M. and Jers, C., 2011. The uses of privacy online: trading a loss of privacy for social web gratifications? In: L. Reinecke and S. Trepte, eds., 2011.

Privacy online: perspectives on privacy and self-disclosure in the social web. Heidelberg: Springer. pp. 143–156.
Tidwell-Collins, L. and Walther, J . B., 2002. Computer-mediated communication effects on disclosure, impressions, and interpersonal evaluations: getting to know one another a bit at a time. *Human Communication Research* 28(3), pp. 317–348.
Trültzsch, S., 2012. *Privacy, photographs and SNS.* Unpublished research paper.
Trültzsch, S., Kõuts-Klemm, R. and Aroldi, P., 2014. Digital divide in transformation: From first to second level digital divide: missing links and perspectives to overcome them. In: N. Carpentier, K. C. Schrøder and L. Hallett, eds. 2014. *Audience Transformations.* New York: Routledge. pp. 191–209.
Trültzsch, S. and Wijnen, C. W., 2012. *Social web use of children, youth and young adults in Austria.* Unpublished research.
Tufecki, Z., 2008. Can you see me now? Audience and disclosure regulation in online social network sites. *Bulletin of Science, Technology & Society* 28, pp. 20–35.
Utz, S. and Krämer, N. C., 2009. The privacy paradox on social network sites revisited: the role of individual characteristics and group norms. *Cyberpsychology: Journal of Psychosocial Research on Cyberspace* [e-journal], 3(2). Available at: <http://www.cyberpsychology.eu/view.php?cisloclanku=2009111001&article=2>.
Vitak, J. and Ellison, N. B., 2012. 'There is a network out there you might as well tap': exploring the benefits of and barriers to exchanging informational support-based resources on Facebook. *New Media & Society* 15, pp. 243–259.
Weissensteiner, E. and Leiner, D., 2011. Facebook in der Wissenschaft: Forschung zu sozialen Onlinenetzwerken. *Medien- und Kommunikationswissenschaft* 59(4), pp. 526–544.
Wijnen, C. W., 2012. Media literacy, participation and citizenship in the social web. In: ECREA, *ECC 2012*, Istanbul, 24–27 October.
Wijnen, C. W., 2013. *SNS use, media literacy and the habitus of young people.* Unpublished research paper.
Zhao, L., Lu, Y., Wang, B. and Huang, W., 2011. What makes them happy and curious online? An empirical study on high school students' Internet use from a self-determination theory perspective. *Computers & Education* 56(2), pp. 346–356.

11 Audiences as Socio-Technical Actors
The 'Styles' of Social Network Site Users

Piermarco Aroldi and Nicoletta Vittadini

INTRODUCTION

During recent decades a number of different studies have highlighted the characteristics of contemporary audiences. People act as audiences in their everyday life through both traditional media consumption (i.e. watching television) and by producing, commenting, sharing and using media content in their communication activities. Moreover, the inhabitants of the connected socio-technical environment provided by social media act as a networked audience, group and public (Livingstone, 2005; Varnelis, 2008).

In this chapter we discuss the need to broach the subject of the differentiation of digital audiences and especially of users of social networking sites (SNS) as a consequence of their agency. The relevance of this topic lies in our attempt to distance ourselves from two divergent kinds of reductionism: on one hand, the design of interfaces and affordances of SNS platforms are seen as instrumental guides that lead users to act in a—more or less—predictable manner, whereas on the other, the users' social position (age, gender, class, education, ethnicity and so on) is interpreted as the key factor in the production of their online behaviour. In this chapter we try to avoid this kind of polarisation by introducing the concept of 'style' as a form of personal agency that mediates between the constraints of technological affordances and the structure of opportunity in which the actor is rooted and which in turn directs and restricts his/her action. The validity of the concept of style is also discussed in terms of the results of a qualitative research project titled 'Online Social Relations and Identity: Italian Experience in Social Network Sites',[1] which was carried out in Italy in 2012 and 2013.

The constantly changing, fast-paced evolution of the digital environment suggests that we need to understand the (new) ways in which agency is implicated in both face-to-face and mediated relations, and to what extent the users' identity is intertwined with their both offline and online performances, against the (new) possibility to act in—and be controlled by—social networks. Indeed, this may not appear to be a dramatic innovation in terms of audience research, as this topic has featured at the core of a long-standing tradition initiated by the Nationwide study (Morley, 1980); however, this approach could be seen as an innovative approach in the study of the differentiation of 'digital' audiences, namely SNS users.

DIFFERENTIATING THE AUDIENCES

The shift from an undifferentiated mass 'audience' to a plurality of different 'audiences' has been a main concern, and a turning point, in media studies since the 1980s. This shift introduced the existence of 'audiences'—in the plural—to emphasise the fact that the public is actually made up of many groups, which are differentiated from one another according to their genre preferences and specific cultural and social positions. Audiences were thus understood as a plurality of social groups, made up of people from certain social contexts whose daily activities include media consumption (Moores, 1993). As a consequence, audience theory has become more and more concerned with the way that active audiences contribute to the negotiation and construction of meanings (Livingstone, 1990).

To understand these plural, diverse and sometimes conflicting audiences, at first media studies—and especially media ethnography in family contexts—focused on class differences (Morley, 1980), gender (Hobson, 1982; Radway, 1984; Ang, 1985), age (Buckingham, 1987) and ethnicity (Liebes and Katz, 1990; Gillespie, 1995). Viewers' interpretations of the texts differed depending on the "symbolic resources associated with their socioeconomic position, gender, ethnicity and so forth" (Livingstone, 2004, p. 79).

Also, identity processes involved in being part of an audience as part of a subculture or a participatory culture have been studied from different points of view, for example from the perspective of fandom (Jenkins, 1992; Lewis, 1992) as a phenomenon "associated with the cultural tastes of a subordinated formations of the people, particularly with those disempowered by any combination of gender, age, class and race" (Fiske, 1992, p. 30). To explain the role played by this kind of variable in producing cultural tastes, audience studies often used Bourdieu's concept of 'habitus' as a generator of "representations and practices which are always more adjusted than they seem to be to the objective conditions of which they are the product" (1984, p. 244). Taste is thus the main form of *amor fati* because it is strictly connected to the audience' social position and its cultural context.

When shifting from old media to new media, and especially to the realm of the internet, audience research experienced both the need for the radically 'new' and to ask whether there were lessons to be learnt from the study of mass television and its audience which could guide the analysis of the new media environment. Sonia Livingstone, contending the latter stand, noted that "audiences and users of new media are increasingly active—selective, self-directed, producers as well as receivers of texts. And they are increasingly plural, whether this is conceptualized as multiple, diverse, fragmented or individualized" (2004, p. 79). On one hand, some scholars have approached the internet as a whole due to its new interactivity; they also approached its users as increasingly uniform, less differentiated audiences, because of the growing penetration of digital technologies in everyday life and the wide diffusion of some platforms, such as SNS. On the other hand, both theories and empirical evidence are forced to acknowledge an increasing differentiation in internet uses and practices.

Two of the main debates in the field of internet studies made this process of audience differentiation especially noticeable: that of digital divide and that of digital natives. In both discussions, one can say that the emerging trend has shifted from an undifferentiated approach to users to a more nuanced and varied conceptualisation.

In terms of the debate surrounding the question of the digital divide, two major paradigms have arisen: that of the 'disappearing digital divide', which predicted "homogeneous internet use patterns irrespective of socio-economic, cognitive, and cultural resources once internet access gaps are bridged" (Peter and Valkenburg, 2006, p. 294; see also van Dijk and Hacker, 2003) and that of the 'emerging digital differentiation', which observed new differences and rising inequalities as Information and Communication Technologies (ICTs) have spread to reach the majority or almost all of the populations of Western nations, opening up new gaps just as previous gaps were being closed (Peter and Valkenburg, 2006). A number of meta-studies revealed that even after people gain access to the internet, the ways in which they incorporate the internet into their everyday lives differ, thus reflecting disparities "in the multiple dimensions of the social context in which individuals are situated" (Jung, 2008, p. 322; see also Barzilai-Nahon, 2006; van Dijk, 2006).

Besides the economic and easily quantifiable reasons for the formation of divides, such as socio-demographics, this so-called second-level digital divide has also been studied in order to broaden the analysis of differences in internet uses. Examples of these studies' focus points include internet skills, autonomy and literacy in relation to gender, age, digital experience (Hargittai, 2002), educational background (Hargittai and Hinnant, 2008), social and cultural capital (van Dijk and Hacker, 2003) and motivations or attitudes (Kalkun and Kalvet, 2002).

Furthermore, the narrative that describes digital natives as a brand new generation (Tapscott, 1998; Prensky, 2001) has been questioned and criticised based on both the technological determinism of the theoretical approach (Buckingham and Willett, 2006) and the heterogeneity of young people as internet users. A far from undifferentiated audience, children and teenagers are in fact more likely to use internet and SNS in a broadly diversified set of practices. As a reminder of a few examples we note how some "gradations in digital inclusion" have been postulated by Livingstone and Helsper (2007, p. 671) based on a 'continuum' of uses that maps the nature, quantity and quality of internet practices and the resulting opportunities; how internet use and skills do not seem to be equally distributed in the youth population and depend on higher levels of parental education, being a male, white or Asian American and on certain types of uses (Hargittai, 2010); how unequal socio-economic and varying cognitive resources in formal education have been connected to diverse tendencies towards ubiquitous internet use, whereas these variables are less relevant for the use of internet as a social medium (Peter and Valkenburg, 2006); and, last, how the plurality of young people's experience of technology has been linked by Bennett and Maton to "the various and varied, relatively autonomous social worlds in which they are situated" (2010, p. 326).

The debate on the digital divide and the concept of digital natives has highlighted differences that have been defined—more or less strictly—as being determined by the social position of the users: "Age, gender, the quality of the technical access, digital experience, topic-specific interest and something status related issues that we—following Bourdieu (1984)—can perhaps call Status-Specific Types of Internet Usage habitus" (Zillien and Hargittai, 2009, p. 289).[2] Hence, scholars have shifted from binary oppositions, through a gradation (of skills, inclusion, literacy, etc.) to different kinds of typologies (of patterns, uses and users) linked to demographic, socio-economic or socio-cultural variables, as well as to technological affordances and platform design.

FROM PATTERNS TO STYLES

It is noteworthy that different patterns of internet usage among young people have been framed either in degrees on a continuum of (improving) frequency of access, according to the number of activities and control of digital skills, or as a plurality of divergent typological models that describe very different groups of users on the basis of their differing use patterns; for example Holmes (2011, p. 1117), in his study of one group of users that "was more likely to be engaging in online recreation and communication" and a second group that "was more likely to use the internet for informational purposes", noted that "there appeared to be no evidence that this reflected a continuum of use" between the diverse user types.

Other typological descriptions of the patterns of user activities have been defined using terms that include 'Sporadics' (low-level SNS users), 'Lurkers' (people who use SNS but do not contribute or interact), 'Socialisers' (people who use SNS mainly for social interaction with friends and family), 'Debaters' (people who use SNS mainly for debating and discussion) and

'Advanced' (people who use SNS frequently for almost all purposes, such as socialising, debating and contributing; Brandtzaeg, 2010).

This kind of typology thus poses two main questions; the first relates to the indicators used to describe the patterns of usage and the theoretical approach assumed to interpret them as either a converging continuum or as a differentiated set of diverging models of users; the second questions the reasons that would seemingly account for this typological diversity and attempts to explain why users become, or choose to be, a Sporadic user rather than a Debater.

In relation to the first question, the continuum approach seems to duplicate that of the 'disappearing digital divide' and may sound as if it creates "a set of imperatives about what [young people] should be or what they need to become" (Buckingham, et al., 2006, p. 11) that underestimates differences and nonconformity, in a softly normative way.

As far as the second question is concerned, in acknowledging and interpreting diversity in young SNS users, different studies emphasised—besides socio-demographic variables—the relevance of digital literacy or the composition of households (e.g. young people who live alone or with their parents; Hargittai, 2010). Generally, little attention seems to be paid to the individual motivations and cultural dispositions of the user, to his or her family contexts and socialisation processes, to social groups and subcultural interests, to dispositions towards technology and the perception of its utility. To conclude, a "more refined approach is needed which properly accounts for diversity in engagement" with digital technologies (Holmes, 2011, p. 1109). An example of one such approach may be the concept of digital identity proposed as a theoretical framework by J. Goode, which mentions the relevance of "beliefs about one's own technology abilities; beliefs about the importance of technology; beliefs about participation opportunities and constraints that exist; and one's sense of motivation to learn more about technology" (2010, p. 502).

When looking for these kinds of approach, lessons from audience studies regarding both plurality and the audiences' activities prove to be relevant: audience studies have always stressed the relevance of social contexts to the shaping of the publics' activity, both in terms of everyday media habits or uses and in terms of the interpretation of texts' meanings; furthermore, they often counterposed the viewers' agency as a form of resistance and creativity.

If, according to Livingstone, "key terms in audience research are more, not less, significant in the new media environment—choice, selection, taste, fandom, intertextuality, interactivity" (2004, p. 89), in the shift from old media to new media this balancing of 'structure' and 'agency' remains not only an open question, but it also becomes more and more relevant. Active audiences are, in fact, more and more 'active', thanks to the Web 2.0, user-generated content (UGC) and participatory cultures. At the same time, their activity is more and more socially oriented, thanks to SNS and sharing. To fully grasp the implications of these audiences' increasing social activity we probably need to refer more directly to their agency as the possibility to act—meaningfully, responsibly, ethically and politically, even if not always rationally—in their mediated social relations (Livingstone and Das, 2009).

In other words, there is great need for a more 'actor-centred' approach that could combine the individual position in the structure of opportunities and the related capitals (economic, social, cultural and time capitals) with other personal resources or constraints, such as life-course stages, values, participatory attitudes and interests. A combination of this kind could be seen to affect internet use as a part of what Roger Silverstone calls the "private, informal, 'wertrational moral economy'" (2006, p. 237) that "enables users to produce something of their own as a result of their engagement with the formal economy of the media system" (Trültzsch, Kõuts-Klemm and Aroldi, 2013, p. 195); at the same time, when using this kind of approach one must be careful not to fall into a merely psychological or idiosyncratic account of individual choices and preferences, and focus on connecting the patterns of media consumption and their media incorporation to the personal agency of the actors.

To avoid overstating this agency as a utopian willingness and capacity to contrast and resist the (social or media) power, it could be useful to refer to the distinction suggested by Colin Campbell (2009), which differentiates between "power of agency" and "agentic power": Whereas "the first refers to an actor's ability to initiate and maintain a program of action [. . .] the second refers to an actor's ability to act independently of the constraining power of social structure" (p. 407). We now refer to the first concept of agency, as a form of power that is possessed by individuals and enables them to engage in actions with a certain degree of freedom and responsibility. According to Campbell, because there is no given logical relationship between these two forms of agency, it is possible to have 'power of agency' but no 'agentic power', or vice versa.

Some features of the concept of style—which we discuss in the following—suggest how we can grasp this kind of power of agency in the activities of SNS users.

A MATTER OF STYLE

In reference to digital and convergent media, Ito (2008) describes different "participation styles" or "media engagement styles", and both definitions refer to individuals' styles of relationship with digital media. The definition of these relationship styles using the notions of participation and engagement, according to Ito, avoids invoking "one end of a binary between structure and agency, text and audience" (2008, p. 401); at the same time it forces to focus one's attention on the practices and the broader social and cultural context in which these activities are conducted (structures of participation) including for example peer networks. Ito also suggests the complementary notion of "genres of participation", defining different modes or conventions for engaging with technology as "a nod to cultural context and normative structures of practice" (2008, p. 401).

When referring to SNS use, Papacharissi (2009) describes different "self-presentation styles" and "taste-performances styles". The first description relates to the individual's performance, or expressive plan for the self, on the SNS stage, including both the 'face' (Goffman, 1959) and the 'public display of connections' (Donath and boyd, 2004). The second notion relates to "the cultivation of taste performances as a mode of sociocultural identification" (Papacharissi, 2009, p. 199). The notion of taste-performance comes from Liu's (2007) definition of SNS profiles as a place where taste-performances emerge through the presentation of "a carefully compiled selection of interests, likes and dislikes, affiliations and preferences" (Papacharissi, 2009, p. 212). This presentation situates individuals "within a particular taste culture, adopting a specific taste ethos" and "separates them from those with differences in matters of taste," whereas conveying a stylistic impression (Papacharissi, 2009, p. 212).

Both authors describe styles as being influenced by the affordances of the media used. Ito suggests that "engagement with particular media types relates to differences in [. . .] agency" (2006, p. 398), for example in the form of hypersociality as a style/genre of social participation. Papacharissi (2009) states that self-presentation styles of digital users are influenced by the spaces in which they act (e.g. different SNS), and in particular by the way in which each platform rearranges the boundaries between public and private, leading "individuals to different styles of interaction" (p. 207).

In accordance with this first discussion, we can say that style can be defined as a specific form of interaction or engagement with digital media (and SNS).

Different forms of engagement (different styles) thus emerge in expressive practices (as self-performance or taste-performance) that are related to the structures of individuals' participation (for example the cultural context or social networks in real life). Styles of interaction (or engagement) also acquire the form of 'genres of participation' when they stabilise in modes or conventions that negotiate with normative structures of practice. Furthermore, styles (and especially taste-performance styles) are an expression of individuals' placement in specific (taste) cultures and their adoption of a specific (taste) ethos.

The process of defining a style is both individual and social. On one hand, individuals are proactive in the definition of their style. Proactivity is implied in the notion of participation used by Ito (2006), and boyd underlines the individuals' proactivity whereas performing their persona online, saying that they "must determine how they want to present themselves to those who may view their self-representation" (2011, p. 43). This proactivity results in a self-performance that is built gradually, and in time accumulates different communication activities (e.g. Facebook updates that contribute to the timeline). Thus, online self-performances are a part of or a parallel process to the offline activity of selectively organising one's experiences into a coherent sense of self and imply a coherent plan and sense-making project (Ricoeur, 1985; Giddens, 1991). As Jansson (2008) suggests—in reference to late modern societies—this coherent composition of choices and routines allows different kinds of practices and individual attributes to fit together (Jansson defines it as a lifestyle), and it is useful to preserve ontological security in a context that is 'rich in choices and poor in rules'. Some correlations can be found between late modern societies defined by Jansson and the SNS environment, and especially in relation to the need to situate oneself as a 'self' in a digital social environment.

On the other hand, the process of defining a style is a social activity. First, due to the fact that individuals do not have complete control over their self-presentations, which are co-produced with SNS friends (e.g. through the practice of tagging), their style is negotiated on an interpersonal level and the presence of Facebook friends whose style contrasts with the individual's style can be problematic. Second, given that the network of SNS friends forms part of any self-presentation as a "public display of connections" (Donath and boyd, 2004), one's style is also expressed by the friends' network.

Last, and as we have already mentioned, the definition of one's style locates the self in a social environment and is thus related to the definition of one's belonging to one (or more) social groups. As Jansson (2008) states, the (life)style creation is essentially a matter of being like some people and unlike others. We can therefore say that style is the expression and the sharing of a certain cultural taste and ethos that defines the individual's sense of belonging to groups of people.

Thus, we see how the definition of one's style also acts on the cultural level. Different studies on digital technologies have highlighted the relationship between the 'cultural styles' of belonging in real networks and the relative 'engagement styles' with digital technologies. For example, Castells (2007) states that culturally based communication styles affect the appropriation of mobile technologies in terms of the ethno-cultural belonging of digital users. Studies on subcultures (Hebdige, 1979) have highlighted how cultural belonging contributes to the definition of shared styles in the adoption of new technologies. Whereas subculture studies define codified cultures within the wider frameworks of class, gender and race, these studies have clearly identified that styles (of leisure or technology use) are both produced by and the producers of the culture of a group that shares a common consciousness.

At this point, we also have to take into account the networks of belonging that are ascribable to an "offline sphere of taste and culture" (Papacharissi, 2009, p. 213), in other words, social groups that are formed by individuals who are linked by common tastes and cultural consumption habits. These groups differ from subcultures in terms of the weakness of their ties and their often imaginary nature. Individuals who participate in these groups are bound together by a lifestyle or a "collective way of life [. . . which] points to common orientations of taste and interpretations" (Ziehe, 1994, p. 2).

According to these premises, the process of one's definition of style also implies the reflexivity of the self. As the late modern definition of (life)styles highlights, reflexivity is one of the three crucial features: self-attention or the orientation towards the fulfilment of a successful life; stylisation or the placement of objects, situations and actions in a coherent presentation; reflexivity or an "everyday semantic of self-observation and self-assessment" (Ziehe, 1994, pp. 11–12). Thus, (life)styles include the expressive plan "of the self represented according to intricately coded cultural conventions (including technological interfaces) and social preferences (embedded in the norms of consumer culture)" (Livingstone, 2008, p. 9).

Through our discussion of the definition of engagement styles (Ito, 2006) with SNS, some crucial features emerged. First, styles are expressed through the SNS self-performances which include both the individual and the social level (the structure of the networks of connections). On both levels this is characterised by the need for a coherent project. Second, the definition of styles situates individuals in the digital environments by defining their belonging to social groups through a set of cultural tastes, ethos and consumptions choices.

Finally, the definition of styles involves cultural aspects including "offline spheres of taste and culture" (Papacharissi, 2009, p. 213) and both online and offline cultural conventions.

Hence, style can be defined as an expression of agency negotiating with social positions, structures of participation and technological affordances. According to the distinction between the agentic power and the power of agency that we referred to previously, style can be defined as an expression of the power of agency because it is the result of a coherent programme of action involving the responsibility of the individual and a sense-making process that affects the composition of choices and routines.

To describe how one can detect styles by observing individual's behaviour in SNS, we can also refer to the idea that individuals are "acting and interacting as a certain kind of person" (suggested by Gee, 2000, p. 99), and in so doing, they build their self-presentations in an attempt to be recognised by others. This activity refers to the two levels that Gee (2000) defines the 'discursive' and 'affinity' levels.

The first level refers to the features that compose self-definition (e.g. to be 'charismatic'). These features form part of one's individuality whereas they cannot be achieved without the recognition of others. These individual traits are a result of discursive practices involving individual actions (that are coherent with self-definition) and other individuals' recognition thereof (expressed through dialogue).

The second level refers to traits defined in terms of a shared culture within an affinity group. In Gee's words, an affinity group can be dispersive. Members of this group share a set of "distinctive experiences" (including online experiences) and "little besides their interests" (2000, p. 105). Affinity is built through forms of participation and sharing that represent a crucial activity when using SNS. These groups can also be identified as 'morally heated affinity groups' (Beck, 1992; 1994)—as 'greens'—who share a set of practices and experiences that constitute a style with other people.

Styles are thus reflexively stylised and objectified (Ziehe, 1994) in mediated communication practices (posting, sharing, liking and so on). In the following paragraphs we describe some examples of how SNS users perceive, define and perform their engagement' styles through Facebook.

VOICES FROM THE FIELD

In order to reach a better understanding of style as a form of agency based on the personal interpretation of SNS affordances we will present some examples from the interviews collected during a qualitative study held in Italy in 2012 and 2013. The project—titled 'Online Social Relations and Identity: Italian Experience in Social Network Sites'—consisted of the collection of 120 in-depth interviews with Facebook users to investigate how identities and social relations are re-shaped and constructed online through SNS. The chosen informants included individuals aged between thirteen and fifty-four (50 per cent male and 50 per cent female) from different socioeconomic statuses (SESs), from both major cities (Milano, Rome, Palermo) and small towns (Bergamo, Pesaro, Cosenza) in different parts of the Italian territory, and were asked to give personal accounts about their daily practices on Facebook. The in-depth interviews were designed from an open, inclusive perspective to collect a thick description of the routines that gave insight into when and where SNS are used, the frequency, the intensity and the duration of SNS sessions; the users' preferred devices, activities and content; and the strategies adopted in the management of friend networks, habits, tastes and rules in social interaction, both online and offline. Second, the interviewer and informant sat side by side in front of the interviewee's Facebook Timeline, going through all the verbal and visual stratified materials in order to produce a sort of digital biography of the user; each interview lasted one and a half to two hours.

The preliminary analysis of the accounts shows that they are characterised by a variable but relevant degree of self-consciousness and reflexivity; this is not surprising because both the adopted methodology and the researched topic lead to enhance self-observation. The narrative set of the interview asks the informant to take part in an activity of self-narration that brings to light what is usually taken for granted, whereas also contributing to a retrospective perception of order and meaning in everyday habits and practices. For example Carlo, et al. (2013), in their presentation of an analysis of some of the interviews from the same research project, noticed that interviewed users consciously adopt different kinds of engagement with Facebook depending on the space-time context that frames their daily use of the SNS. The authors refer to Lull's (1990) styles of TV viewing—focused viewing, monitoring and idling—to characterise three different ways of acting on Facebook, which were seen to be widely distributed regardless of gender, age or SES variables.

In order to highlight how some styles emerged as a form of agency, here we focus on the forms of self-expression, self-representation and self-performance produced when interacting within a social networking environment, which require (and enhance) high levels of self-awareness (Gergen, 1991; Papacharissi, 2012). Obviously, it is a sort of limited or near-sighted reflexivity, because our informants always talk about their perceived style of online performance.

In particular, we describe how the interviewees give an account of their personal style in SNS use. We highlight recurrent topics and forms in these accounts, showing how the same expressions and forms of reflexivity are repeated in interviewees of different age and gender.

This kind of reflexive account is especially active when describing one's own habits, practices, activities and tastes; when reporting on their patterns of daily use of Facebook, the informants often include some kind of explanation or justification that refers to his or her personal identity, as well as to the social context in which he or she is rooted.

They thus introduce their imagined selves as "expressive creations and recreations of the performed self" (Bauman, 2004, p. 107). Typically, this kind of self-account is launched by the wording 'I'm/I'm not the guy who...', linking this self-declaration to a certain mode of interaction:

> I'm not the guy who feels ashamed, but . . .
> (Daniele, M. 13–18)

> Because I'm the guy who doesn't give a shit about anything.
> (Alessandro, M, 45–54)

> I'm not a girl who writes stupid things.
> (Laura, F, 45–54)

Sometimes the interviewees refer to their personal disposition, calling for a sort of consistency between their online and offline (imagined) self:

> I consider myself quite shy [. . .]. Generally, I try to post on Facebook things that I really like and I believe in. I do not like putting common phrases etc. . . I'm a minimalist in my communication.
> (Massimo, M, 25–34)

> I am a person who tends to build relationships and I am an extrovert, even my setting on Facebook is open.
> (Anna, F, 35–44)

Sometimes one feels that a contingent stage in one's own biography is under discussion:

> I was in a phase of life when I was not very satisfied, like two years ago. I did not feel good about myself, and I felt alone, and so I represented my mood. I remember that I published some very depressed updates [. . .]. Now, however, I'm okay with myself and now I post what I want to post.
> (Angela, F, 25–34)

Another strongly reflexive account is based on online and/or offline reputation; acting or refraining from acting in a certain way is thus explained referring to the impression that might be produced on one's own audience, both on Facebook and in real life, in a very unpredictable way because of the "context collapse" (Marwick and boyd, 2010). What is at stake is the possibility that one will be considered in terms of one's imagined self or public self:

> Once upon a time, I was commented on in front of everyone, and I feel ashamed because this may give the false impression that I am like them, and I do not like this.
> (Daniele, M, 13–18)

> [on Facebook] there is my public and artistic image, it is clear that I am neither a right-winger nor a left-winger; my anarchism shines through.
> (Alessandro, M, 45–54)

At any rate, the interviewees seem to be very conscious of the performative dimension of their cumulative self-expression on Facebook, as well as being well aware of the many rules that contribute to shaping the performed self:

> On Facebook, [. . .] certain things are not 'super true'; however, something shines through from photos, 'likes', your friendships, your groups; one can understand your personality, who you are, where you come from, what you think [. . .] and then it becomes a sort of identity card that tells you who you are.
>
> (Massimo, M, 25–34)

Some rules are local and binding within the main network of friends, and act as a sort of common language, or a style of conversation that defines what can be said and what cannot:

> There is not all of me there. You put things that give a plastic impression of you. It's not that I do not put the truth, but I put only the positive things. If I have a personal problem or I'm sad . . . I do not publish it. I publish what is socially expendable. This way the image that emerges is bubbly and cheerful person. Also because the network that I use is fun, we're messing around, making jokes, teasing each other.
>
> (Francesca, F, 35–44)

Other rules seem to be more general, affecting what is perceived to be the 'right' way to act with regard to and in full view of other people:

> It has almost never happened to me to write about sad things. Maybe it's a matter of your character, because it seems as if you are looking for the compassion of the people who read your posts.
>
> (Massimo, M, 25–34)

This normativity has a more superficial dimension which is connected to a sort of stylisation of the performance. Here, the 'right' thing to do is nothing but the 'cool' thing to do or 'the same way that other people act' in the same situation with the same tools for expression. Sometimes, it is a matter of aesthetics and tastes. On the other hand, some of these rules seem to be more deeply rooted in an ethical or political evaluation, and the 'right' thing to do becomes a matter of moral judgement, involving the need to establish a certain grade of consistency between online and offline self-perceptions or performances.

As stated before, the style adopted in SNS use also involves the shared lifestyles reflexively expressed through discursive practices and activities (e.g. the deleting of friends or subscription to causes).

The interviewees often give detailed descriptions of people that they dislike because of their communications styles on SNS. These topics emerge both as part of interviewees' self-descriptions and as a justification of the deletion of Facebook friends.

The main differences between 'my style' and 'the style of people that I dislike' are attributed to the public/private dichotomy (involving both the externalisation of sentiments, intimate images of oneself and the detailed account of everyday activities) and the dichotomy of the quantity/quality of the content posted:

> It bothers me, especially when it involves children. It's exaggerated. What bothers me is the excessive manifestation of sentiments, which often emerges from pictures and sentences. It is annoying.
> (Martina, F, 25–34)

> I think it's exhibitionism when one writes: 'finished work, time for the gym.' Omnipresence. Wanting to be the centre of attention.
> (Emanuela, F, 25–34)

> Two reasons [to delete friends]: people who clog up your wall [. . .], or people who do not publish anything as if they weren't there. Go away!
> (Massimo, M, 25–34)

Deleting Facebook friends who publish conflicting updates is an activity aimed mainly at protecting the coherence of one's own self-description and the style of his/her wall without an explicit reference to 'reputation' problems. To summarise what the interviewees said, 'I would like to read on my wall only updates that are coherent with my style'.

> People who often publish updates about dogs, children, vulgar or political messages, or messages that annoy me when I scan my wall, are too redundant. Maybe I have no real bad sentiments against them, but they posts things that bother me and so I take them off from my wall.
> (Marina, F, 25–34)

> Those who write 'I'm sad', 'depressed', 'unlucky with men', or 'my girlfriend left me', bother me because this not the way I use [Facebook].
> (Francesca, F, 35–44)

> It tends to bother me to see that other people can post, 'today I'm sad because . . . ' I don't take it seriously. I think it comes from my character. I do not consider it to be appropriate.
> (Giulia, F, 19–24)

Interviewees confirm the homogeneity of Facebook networks (boyd and Ellison, 2008; Papacharissi, 2011). They tend to include or exclude people according to their style. At the same time, these networks contribute to defining and reinforcing common rules (or 'netiquettes') that influence the choice of topics or—again—the level of activity and publicity of personal profiles.

> Just to say, I do not have as great a knowledge of classical music as many of the people with whom I hang out [on Facebook], I like pop music. So on Facebook I don't post about pop music. Some time ago I posted about pop music, but now I do this less frequently. This is a kind of selection . . . the group counts in the selection of things that you choose to publish.
>
> (Francesca, F, 35–44)

At the same time—for different interviewees—Facebook networks overlap with social networks in real life and some rules are defined on the base of offline expertise.

> [In Facebook] and in real life we tend to hang out with people who reflect our ideas on reality [. . .]"
>
> (Biagio, M, 25–34)

> For example, [after] my sister had had her baby, I met a friend of mine who I know is [also] one of my sister's Facebook friends. I knew that she had made a comment [on Facebook] on the photo of the child, but when I told her that the child had been born she pretended to be surprised. There is still the rule that is unsuitable that one has found out something from Facebook. That it is improper to peek at someone's photo on Facebook.
>
> (Marina, F, 25–34)

> If my daughter takes pictures with her best friend I don't tag her because her mom is my friend on Facebook and I do not know if she likes the fact that her daughter is on Facebook.
>
> (Anna, F, 35–44)

The affiliation style characterised by updates aimed primarily at describing networks of belonging is not only criticised as being superficial—a kind of mask—but is also chosen as a trait of personal style. In some cases this style is referred to as 'communities of practices' (sports, hobbies), whereas in other cases, it is referred to Facebook-based 'communities of interests' (topics, causes):

> A thing that annoys me when I open my Facebook are photo albums [. . .] that are all so similar [. . .] and which legitimize one's belonging to a group, or a certain identity, like that of the teenager who goes dancing every Saturday evening and then every Sunday morning posts the pictures of the club.
>
> (Giulia, F, 19–24)

My dad is from Lombardy and my mom is from Lunigiana. I have a lot of friends from Lunigiana and one of them introduced me to this network because he's a bookseller and a great fan of comics, a great reader of *Il Vernacoliere* and through him I met this network of very funny people.

(Francesca, F, 35–44)

CONCLUSION

In this chapter we presented some major issues related to SNS users as digital audiences. The first issue we confronted was the need to add layers to our understanding of the fragmentation of digital audiences to complement differentiations based on social position, affordances and constellations of practices, whereas the second is the need to take into account some key concerns highlighted by audience studies when approaching SNS users, in particular meaning and agency.

On one hand, SNS users are committed to negotiating with the social structure in which they are located and on the other, with the constraints of online environments. In this double-sided negotiation, the agency of the user creates space for the self-expression of a personal identity that is characterised more or less consciously by values, tastes and styles of relationship.

These identities are defined both on an individual level (individual agency) and on a group level (i.e. group affiliation). They thus become social identities that are played out on a relational level, both on- and offline, as a 'way of being' or 'to inhabit' the internet, a moral option that is often the result of a process, a kind of 'digital biography' in which the subject assumes (albeit on a temporary basis) a 'voice' and a 'face'. We suggested that style could be used as a concept through which to understand how users 'act as a certain kind of person' that interprets digital affordances on the base of his or her contextualised self-definition.

The examples provided in this chapter describe how style appears as a form of self-reflexivity. In particular, we highlighted that styles emerge in relation to the imagined self, the individual's online and offline self reputation and his or her group affinity and affiliation. Style is thus the result of a reflexive process related to the (imagined) self and its relations with both technology and (online and offline) social relations. At the same time, style is also the product and the producer of both self-performances and of the set of rules affecting SNS activities as a form of power of agency.

This kind of analysis suggests that style—as defined above—can cross the boundaries of different social positions and seems rather to characterise people who share values, lifestyles and rules. Further research on SNS users could proceed—and perhaps from a cross-country perspective—to define different style typologies and expand on the analysis of the variables that affect them, thus facilitating an exploration of the process through which SNS platforms tend to both adapt to and shape users' styles.

NOTES

1. 'Online Social Relations and Identity: Italian Experience in Social Network Sites' is a PRIN (Research Project of National Interest) funded by the Italian Ministry of Education, University and Research (http://snsitalia.wordpress.com/). When this chapter was written (September 2013), the analysis of the collected data was still in progress; the authors quoted parts of the interviews, namely those collected in Milan, to exemplify some evidences, without the aim to present the whole research results. The presentation of other preliminary results of this research can be found in Boccia Artieri, et al. (2013).
2. For other references to the work of Bourdieu and his theoretical concepts in the digital divide debate see also Bennett and Maton (2010), Livingstone and Helsper (2007), Peter and Valkenburg (2006), Selwyn (2004) and van Dijk and Hacker (2003).

REFERENCES

Ang, I., 1985. *Watching Dallas: soap operas and the melodramatic imagination.* London: Methuen.
Barzilai-Nahon, K., 2006. Gaps and bits: conceptualizing measurements for digital divide/s. *The Information Society* 22(5), pp. 269–278.
Bauman, R., 2004. *A world of others' words.* Blackwell: Oxford.
Beck, U., 1992. *Risk society: towards a new modernity.* London: Sage.
Beck, U., 1994. *Reflexive modernization: politics, tradition and aesthetics in the modern social order.* Stanford: Stanford University Press.
Bennett, S. and Maton, K., 2010. Beyond the "digital natives" debate: towards a more nuanced understanding of students' technology experiences. *Journal of Computer Assisted Learning* 26(5), pp. 321–33.
Boccia Artieri, G., Carlo, S., Farci, M., Gemini, L., Pasquali, F., Pedroni, M. and Scifo, B., 2013. Relazioni sociali ed identità in Rete: Vissuti e narrazioni degli italiani su Facebook [online]. In: Università Cattolica del Sacro Cuore, *So close, faraway. The Italian way to social network sites*, Milan, 26–27 September. Available at: <http://snsitalia.wordpress.com/>.
Bourdieu, P., 1984. *Distinction: a social critique of the judgement of taste.* London: Routledge & Kegan.
boyd, d., 2011. Social network sites as networked publics. In: Z. Papacharissi, ed. 2011. *The networked self: identity, community and culture on social network sites.* London: Taylor & Francis. pp. 39–58.
boyd, d. and Ellison, N., 2008. Social network sites: definition, history, and scholarship. *Journal of Computer-Mediated Communication* 13(1), pp. 210–30.
Brandtzaeg, P.B., 2010. Toward a unified media-user typology (MUT): a meta-analysis and review of the research literature on media-user typologies. *Computers in Human Behaviour* 26(5), pp. 940–956.
Buckingham, D., 1987. *Public secrets: "Eastenders" and its audience.* London: BFI.
Buckingham, D. and Willett, R. eds., 2006. *Digital generations. Children, young people and new media.* Mahwah: Erlbaum.

Buckingham, D., Banaji, S., Burn, A., Carr, D., Cranmer, S. and Willett, R., 2006. *The Media literacy of children and young people: a review of the research literature on behalf of Ofcom* [online]. London: Centre for the Study of Children Youth and Media Institute of Education University of London. Available at: <http://eprints.ioe.ac.uk/145/>.

Campbell, C., 2009. Distinguishing the power of agency from agentic power: a note on Weber and the "black box" of personal agency. *Sociological Theory* 27(4), pp. 407–418.

Carlo, S., Pasquali, F., Pedroni M. and Scifo, B., 2013. 'My friends are my audience': mass-mediation of personal content and relations in Facebook. In: IAMCR, *Crises, 'creative destruction' and the global power and communication orders*, Dublin, 25-29 June.

Castells, M., 2007. *Mobile communication and society: a global perspective*. Boston: The MIT Press.

Donath, J. and boyd, d., 2004. Public displays of connection. *BT Technology Journal* 22(4), pp. 71–82.

Fiske, J., 1992. The cultural economy of fandom. In: L.A. Lewis, ed. 1992. *The adoring audience: fan culture and popular media*. London: Routledge. pp. 30–49.

Gee, P., 2000. Identity as an analytical lens for research in education. *Review of Research in Education*, 25, pp. 99–125.

Gergen, K.J., 1991. *The saturated self: dilemmas of identity in contemporary life*. New York: Basic Books.

Giddens, A., 1991. *Modernity and self identity: self and society in the late modern age*. Cambridge: Polity Press.

Gillespie, M., 1995. *Television, ethnicity and cultural change*. Oxon: Routledge.

Goffman, E., 1959. *The presentation of self in everyday life*. Garden City: Doubleday & Co.

Goode, J., 2010. The digital identity divide: how technology knowledge impacts college students. *New Media & Society* 12(3), pp. 497–513.

Hargittai, E., 2002. Second level digital divide. Differences in people's online skills. *First Monday* [e-journal] 7(4). Available at: <http://www.firstmonday.dk/issues/issue7_4/hargittai>

Hargittai, E., 2010. Digital na(t)ives? Variation in internet skills and uses among members of the "net generation". *Sociological Inquiry* 80(1), pp. 92–113.

Hargittai, E. and Hinnant, A., 2008. Digital inequality: differences in young adults' use of the internet. *Communication Research* 35(5), pp. 602–621.

Hebdige, D., 1979. *Subculture: the meaning of style*. London: Taylor & Francis.

Hobson, D., 1982. *"Crossroads": the drama of a soap opera*. London: Metheun.

Holmes, J., 2011. Cyberkids or divided generations? Characterising young people's internet use in the UK with generic, continuum or typological models. *New Media & Society* 13(7), pp. 1104–1122.

Ito, M., 2008. Mobilizing the imagination in everyday play: the case of Japanese media mixes. In: S. Livingstone and K. Drotner, eds. 2008. *The international handbook of children, media and culture*. London: Sage. pp. 397–412.

Jansson, A., 2008. Contested meanings: audience studies and the concept of cultural identity. *Intexto* [e-journal] 1(5). Available at: <http://www.seer.ufrgs.br/intexto/article/view/3383>

Jenkins, H., 1992. *Textual poachers: television fans and participatory culture*. London: Routledge.

Jung, J.-Y., 2008. Internet connectedness and its social origins: an ecological approach to postaccess digital divides. *Communication Studies* 59(4), pp. 322–339.

Kalkun, M. and Kalvet, T., 2002. *Digital divide in Estonia and how to bridge it* [online]. Policy Analysis Paper 1/2002. Tallinn: Praxis. Available at: <http://econpapers.repec.org/paper/wpawuwpdc/0401004.htm>.

Lewis, L.A., ed., 1992. *The adoring audience: Fan culture and popular media*. London: Routledge.

Liebes, T. and Katz, E., 1990. *The export of meaning*. Oxford: Oxford University Press.

Liu, H., 2007. Social network profiles as taste performances. *Journal of Computer-Mediated Communication* 13(1), pp. 252–275

Livingstone, S., 1990. *Making sense of television: the psychology of audience interpretation*. Oxford: Pergamon.

Livingstone, S., 2004. The challenge of changing audiences. *European Journal of Communication* 19(1), pp. 75–86.

Livingstone, S., 2005. *On the relation between audiences and publics: why audience and public?* [online]. London: LSE Research Online. Available at: <http://eprints.lse.ac.uk/archive/00000437>.

Livingstone, S., 2008. Taking risky opportunities in youthful content creation: teenagers' use of social networking sites for intimacy, privacy and self-expression. *New Media & Society* 10(3), pp. 393–411.

Livingstone, S. and Das, R., 2009. *The end of audiences? Theoretical echoes of reception amidst the uncertainties of use* [online]. London: LSE Research Online. Available at: <http://eprints.lse.ac.uk/25116/>.

Livingstone, S. and Helsper, E., 2007. Gradations in digital inclusion: children, young people and the digital divide. *New Media & Society* 9(4), pp. 671–696.

Lull, J., 1990. *Inside family viewing*. London: Routledge.

Marwick, A.E. and boyd, d., 2010. I tweet honestly, I tweet passionately: Twitter users, context collapse, and the imagined audience. *New Media & Society* 13(1), pp. 114–133.

Moores, S., 1993. *Interpreting audiences: the ethnography of media consumption*. London: Sage.

Morley, D., 1980. *The Nationwide audience: structure and decoding*. London: British Film Institute.

Papacharissi, Z., 2009. The virtual geographies of social networks: a comparative analysis of Facebook, LinkedIn and ASmallWorld. *New Media & Society* 11(1–2), pp. 199–220.

Papacharissi, Z. ed., 2011. *The networked self: identity, community and culture on social network sites*. London: Taylor & Francis.

Papacharissi, Z., 2012. Without you, I'm nothing: performances of the self on Twitter. *International Journal of Communication* 6, pp. 1989–2006.

Peter, J. and Valkenburg, P.M., 2006. Adolescents' internet use: testing the "disappearing digital divide" versus the "emerging digital differentiation" approach. *Poetics* 34(4–5), pp. 293–305.

Prensky, M., 2001. Digital natives, dimmigrants part 1. *On the Horizon* 9(5), pp. 1–6.

Radway, J., 1984. *Reading the romance: women, patriarchy and popular literature*. Chapel Hill: University of North Carolina Press.

Ricoeur, P., 1985. *Time and narrative*. Chicago: Chicago University Press.

Selwyn, N., 2004. Reconsidering political and popular understandings of the digital divide. *New Media & Society* 6(3), pp. 341–362.

Silverstone, R., 2006. Domesticating domestication: Reflections on the life of a concept. In T. Berker, M. Hartmann, and Y.W. Punje, eds. *Domestication of media and technologies*. Maidenhead: Open University Press. pp. 229–248.

Tapscott, D., 1998. *Growing up digital: the rise of the net generation*. New York: McGraw-Hill.
Trültzsch, S., Kõuts-Klemm, R. and Aroldi, P. 2014. Transforming digital divides in different national contexts. In: N. Carpentier, K.C. Schrøder and L. Hallett, eds. 2014. *Audience transformations*. London: Routledge. pp. 191–209.
van Dijk, J., 2006. Digital divide research, achievements and shortcomings. *Poetics* 34(4–5), pp. 221–235.
van Dijk, J. and Hacker, K., 2003. The digital divide as a complex and dynamic phenomenon. *The Information Society* 19(4), pp. 315–326.
Varnelis, K. ed., 2008. *Networked publics*. Cambridge: MIT Press.
Ziehe, T., 1994. From living standard to life style. *Young: Nordic Journal of Youth Research* 2(2), pp. 2–16.
Zillien, N. and Hargittai, E., 2009. Digital distinction: status-specific types of internet usage. *Social Science Quarterly* 90(2), pp. 274–291.

12 The Intermediality of Cross-Media Audiences
The Case of Digital Television

Taisto Hujanen and Seppo Kangaspunta

INTRODUCTION

The purpose of our chapter is to analyse and discuss the relevance and nature of specific media identities and the consequent audience orientations in a cross-media environment supposedly leading to the convergence of media forms and identities. Following our approach to intermediality, we presuppose that differences between various media are still relevant, but, parallel to that, there is a continuous re-articulation of differences and similarities taking place due to the changing contexts of mediation. What is supposed to constitute a medium or the media more generally has become in many ways fluid because of continuous changes in technology and the related changes of circulation and reception practices. These changes will then gradually affect the way we understand the media as cultural forms and aesthetics. In the present cross-media environment we should approach the media and their intermedial audience practices as a process of continuous change. Consequently, we cannot approach the media by emphasising their historical nature or essence but, rather, can look at the ongoing processes of mediation (and remediation) which construct such differences and similarities. It is easy to agree with Nick Couldry's (2004; see also 2009; 2010) conclusion that in order to understand the changing character of audiences one should concentrate on a detailed, concrete analysis of audience practices. We believe, following Bjur, et al. (2014), that cross-media use is increasingly characteristic of the construction of contemporary media audiences. We demonstrate such a change of audiencehood through a concrete analysis of a case of transformation which is described in the following as an intermedial redefinition of television, characterised by the switchover from analogue to digital.[1]

The concept of intermediality is taken from a major research project (the Intermedia project) in which both authors of this chapter, along with a number of researchers from two other Finnish universities, participated. Intermediality was defined as social and cultural relationships in which different media are articulated in relation to and exercise power over one another

(Herkman, 2012, pp. 13–14). In the analysis of current media change, intermediality was applied as a methodology which focuses on the interfaces and interrelationships between different media. In addition to technological developments, intermediality was used to pay attention to the continuity of media forms and the articulation and re-articulation of media through shifts and adjustments in their social and cultural contexts (Herkman, 2012, pp. 19–20). If applied to media use in a cross-media context, the innovative dimension of the intermedia approach is pointing out how specific media practices and consequent identities are negotiated and redefined and how all that contributes to new hybrid forms of mediation.

Through the concept of intermediality the chapter raises questions about the interplay between different media identities and content in cross-media audience practices. The point of departure is that in the present cross-media environment media, use and 'user' practices are basically intermedial, and consequently, the development and maintenance of specific media identities becomes problematic. This creates a contrast between conceptions of audiences in mass communication research tradition, emphasising a media-specific audiencing and intermedially oriented qualitative approach to audiences, pointing to a continuous interplay and re-articulation of user practices and identities. We suppose that some form of mass or target orientation remains relevant for traditional media like television, at least in the context of production and distribution. The question is whether that requires the recognition and maintenance of television as a specific identity in cross-media-oriented user practices.

Our research questions are as follows:

1. How do media users express and perform their media relationships and identities in a cross-media context?
2. Is there any future for media specific audiences in a cross-media context?
3. How to connect mass communication or target-oriented audiencing with a cross-media-oriented medium relationship? How does that connect with the individualising tendencies of media use and the emergence of social and participatory forms of networking?
4. What constitutes a medium/media in cross-media-oriented user practices?

RESEARCH DATA AND METHODOLOGY

The research data to be analysed and discussed in this chapter were collected shortly prior to and following the digital switchover of terrestrial television in Finland in September 2007. The data consist of interviews with thirty different families (including seventy family members) in six communities, and with four mentor groups assisting people with digitalisation problems. The data can be characterised as a reception study with a focus on consumers' intermedially oriented media use and media relationships. Question topics included the ways in which people experienced the switchover and how they constructed intermedial relationships in their discourse. The approach was qualitative in nature.

Intermedial user practice as a point of view opens a connection with what we term the intermedial redefinition of television. The idea of redefinition is taken from Urrichio (2004, pp. 30–31), who characterises the digital transformation of television as "intermedial redefinition". We also appreciate his conclusions about the relevance of such moments of transformation as research objects. As he said, such moments may offer rich discursive evidence regarding perceived media capacities, anticipated use patterns and intermedial relations (Urrichio, 2004, p. 31). In this spirit, we have tried to carry over to a concrete analysis of the digital switchover of television reported in this chapter (see also Kangaspunta, 2008; 2013; Kangaspunta and Hujanen, 2013).

A useful approach for understanding the kind of discursive evidence considered in the following is offered by Moscovici's (1984) notion of social representations, which refer to joint, everyday understandings of objects among a community of people. The issues raised in this approach concern systems of values, ideas and practices. According to Moscovici, thinking is not only an internal activity of the human brain but also, or rather, communal communicative action. He speaks of a "thinking society" in which its members play an active and intelligent role. (Moscovici, 1984)

The basic function of a social representation is to make a new, alien and unknown thing or object familiar and close to people. This comprises two central processes: "anchoring" and "objectification" (Moscovici, 1984, pp. 3–39). In anchoring, an unknown item is connected to (as part of) the old way of understanding by linking it through familiar concepts and categories with known contexts. With objectification, sensory experiences and sensory as well as symbolic interpretations are linked with an originally alien and abstract concept, and through that concept, the item made into an object of concrete thinking. Moscovici points out that representations are not only verbal (or, more widely, depictions using words and images [at least], and by more literal-realist or metaphorical-symbolic means) but are materialised in social practices and rituals. Anchoring and objectification, as defined by Moscovici, are useful tools for analysis for this study when considering the intermedial redefinition of television in people's media practices.

ABOUT THE DIGITAL SWITCHOVER OF TELEVISION IN FINLAND

After a period of tests, the digitalisation of distribution and reception of television in Finland started in August 2001. That introduced a process of transition and transformation that lasted altogether for six years. In

September 2007, terrestrial distribution and reception turned fully digital, and Finland became the first country in the world to switch off its terrestrial (broadcast) analogue transmissions. Parallel to that, cable companies started reducing their analogue channel supply. By March 2008, cable distribution and reception had also gone fully digital.

The Finnish model of digitalisation did not follow the normal process of media evolution. Like many states and international organizations, the Finnish government and authorities were active in making decisions that aimed in particular at enforcing the digitalisation of terrestrial television. More than half the population in Finland received television through terrestrial distribution, and this is why digitalization was seen necessary to safeguard the future of domestic programming and production.

As an action, the Finnish model of a total digital transition represented a hard form of media policy, especially, with respect to a media technology that was still highly incomplete and untested. A lot of defective equipment was available in the market. More than 70 per cent of households had some sort of technical problems in digitalisation. State authorities and other decision makers with respect to digitalisation did not listen to consumers' problems. User research showed that digitalisation as such was seen as reasonable, but people were critical of the way the process was implemented. A section of consumers responded by just fully abandoning television. Because of the switchover, the share of households without a television set grew from 5 to 8 per cent (Finnpanel, 2009).

Digital television was considered part of the Finnish information society project and was marketed as an important new dimension of information society. Digital television was characterised as an interactive medium in which television and the internet go hand in hand. Promises were big and expectations high. The new media hype made 'interactivity' a key slogan for digital television which, however, turned out to be misleadingly utopian and illusory.

This kind of marketing of digital television represents a dominant version of the transformation discourse typical of so-called digital convergence, more generally. We turn now to analysing how interviewees in our research data positioned themselves in relation to that discourse. The analysis focuses on the following three dimensions of intermediality: the intermedial redefinition of television in comparisons between the 'old' and 'new', television in the context of intermedial user practices and television in the context of an intermedially oriented medium relationship.[2]

THE INTERMEDIAL REDEFINITION OF TELEVISION

The interviews demonstrated a strong continuity between television in its old and new forms. Digital television was still recognized as television, although it had clear potential to enhance the experience of television. The numerous problems encountered by many people in their efforts to manage the switchover created, however, a lot of pessimism about the consequences of the change. Against such concerns, it is interesting to note that the research data offers also clear evidence of people's readiness to rethink the medium in terms of the larger context of digitization. In this way the data demonstrated a variation on the kind of transformation discourse that Urrichio (see the earlier discussion) considered typical of certain periods of media change. Although current changes in television did not appear revolutionary, the potential for change was seen as more dramatic when considering it as part of a major process of digital transformation.

The representation of television as part of media change shows an interesting difference of time perspectives. When looking at television and broadcast media more generally people are used to considering such changes from a longer-term media development perspective in contrast with the case of computers or mobile technology. From such a perspective it seems natural that the identity of television will be maintained across its digital transformation. The conclusion is that after the current period of transition, no special emphasis on digital is needed any more. The identity of television will again signify the medium, although it might incorporate a number of features from new digital media.

Interview data imply, however, that the typical emphasis of the current transformation discourse in characterizing media change as rapid and continuous may affect the time perspectives of television. For example, people's comparisons between old and new television pointed out that the analogue receivers often lasted fifteen to twenty years. Today, television sets are like computers and mobile phones. To keep pace with new technical capabilities, you need to be ready to invest in new equipment more often. The reliability of technology is also worse, and the repair costs may be more than the cost of buying new equipment. So, if one emphasizes the continuity of television, it is more about television as a social and cultural institution than a technology. The technological determinism of the overall transformation discourse has had a strong impact on how people understand media change. Discontinuity and the rapid pace of change are taken for granted. The question is whether this kind of determinism will finally ruin the belief in the cultural continuity of television as a medium.

Further analysis of the research data showed that the way interviewees described digital television in relation to analogue television was dependent on their age, or place in the life cycle and, in particular, on the periods of television that they had experienced. Ellis (2000) characterises the historical periods of television as three eras, named "scarcity", "availability" and "the era of plenty". How much of this history the interviewees had lived through clearly affected their interpretations of the present. Older generations were suspicious of the reform, while younger ones had more positive expectations. Another division related to whether people lived in antenna or cable households. The former experienced the change as more significant.

The change of standards in the distribution and reception of television forced users to deliberate not only about digitalisation but also the relationship between its new and old forms. For many older people and for those who can be identified as 'late adopters'—the two groups coincided to a significant degree, for older people tended to hold out against digital later and vice versa—digital technology appeared problematic, mysterious and unnecessary. They were anguished by continuous technological change, and their answers reflected a distancing: "I should not bother myself with this." Like a seventy-year-old lady from the town of Nokia, they said that they were "not keen on new things", there was "no need for such fine things" and it was "good enough when things work like now."

This attitude reflects outsider experience and distancing. Older people and late adopters[3] were most often negative about the digital switchover. They described the switchover in terms of enforcement and too rapid a speed of development. Even the need for a change was questioned (Kangaspunta, 2008, pp. 7–8). For these people, the old was simply better. Their fatalism and fear of technology were expressed in the attitude 'Whatever's done, everything will change'. Fears of learning and mastering new technology intensified the problems of adoption. The mentor groups consulted for the research stated that they often met older people with this kind of technology fear.

In a study of the British digital switchover, the most problematic consumer group was identified as the "reluctant 50 per cent". This group consisted of older people, late adopters and the reluctant (Mackay, 2007, pp. 33, 43–45). Also in Finland, late adopters have been characterised by different attributes, such as with the notion of *hidastelijat* (hangers-back) in a report for the Ministry of Communication (LVM, 2002).

In our research, a seventy-six-year-old lady, a late adopter from the community of Pälkäne, reported experiencing digital television as difficult because "the set was allowed to make tricks." Her relationship with the television equipment became insecure and the whole reform became, as she put it, "worsening". The reason behind this was that there was no control over the retail sale of set-top boxes in Finland, and as a consequence, there were a lot of unsuitable devices on the market—and this state of affairs continued throughout almost the whole transition process. The loose policies and practices of actors in the digital television market and failure to intervene or regulate on the part of the authorities ensured that consumers suffered. Problems appeared in 71 per cent of households, altogether. Nevertheless, and somewhat surprisingly perhaps in the light of these implementation difficulties, research conducted by the Office of Communication found that users rated digitalisation positively (Viestintävirasto, 2007).

The evidence gathered by our research also showed that late adopters in particular protested by abandoning television viewing altogether, at least for a while. Another (no doubt intersecting) group of consumers was identified as those who (illegally) stopped paying the television license fee (again, at least for a while). The share of people who completely opted out and did not watch or even (necessarily) own a television was reported to have grown from 5 per cent in 2002 to 8 per cent in 2008 (Finnpanel, 2009). The figure has grown to 9 per cent in 2012, but one should notice that watching television does not require the use of a television set any more.

To summarise the views of respondents in this study, technical problems of digital television strongly characterized their dissatisfaction. Some respondents considered digital switchover as part of a major process of convergence. One sixty-year-old lady was critical of the enforced buying of "these digital miracle devices" and compared it with the electricity company that delivered an automatic electricity meter free of charge to her house—a comparison representing what can be characterised as 'inter-technological' argumentation.

The Promise of Interactivity Became a Disappointment

In the beginning, digital television was marketed in Finland as a multimedia centre for the home—an interactive, converged medium, delivering internet services through television. The new media hype raised 'interactivity' as the key word for digital television (Kangaspunta, 2006)—just as, it may be noted, 'interactive' has become a buzzword generally, including outside the media world.[4]

Many adult interviewees saw only minor improvements through digital reform, contrary to expectations, a feeling that seemed to be generalised irrelevant of adopter category. Innovators and early adopters were more interested about the reform and enthusiastic about the new kind of interactive television, but they were doomed to disappointment. An example is the forty-five-year-old father in the Pälkäne community who had had strong expectations of digitalisation but felt that these were realised by the internet, not television. His family generally had a positive attitude towards technical innovation and demonstrated what might be termed a pragmatic relationship to media; new technologies made life easier, and they tended to adopt them early on. They owned several television sets including the so-called second-round set-top boxes, one of which could record. The man thought that a major reform was on its way that would concern most of all the intermedially oriented user practices of television and the internet (or computers).

Digital television was mis-marketed, said many interviewees. A thirty-year-old woman from the town of Porvoo thought that the interactivity argument was misleading, because one could not send information back directly, in the absence of a built-in return channel.

Many informants had been keenly waiting for added interactive services, but to no avail. The marketed digital vision included three phases: enhanced television, interactive television and television as a gateway to the internet. In Finland, marketing concentrated on the two latter phases, which were also what captured the attention of the mass media. The third phase, digital television, represented a vision of a new kind of media combination, hybrid in nature. The hype over these digital visions lasted a few years, with public and consumer enthusiasm falling flat with the delay of functioning mhp-boxes and the lack of a functioning return channel. Digitalisation of television remained at the first phase, enhanced television (Kangaspunta, 2006).

In the middle of the digital switchover, expectations of interactivity were still strong. A thirty-four-year-old man from Porvoo thought that the fate of interactivity might be like that of 3G mobile services. The WAP technology remained something of a bubble because of missing services and content, although the technology was working. In contrast, ready, tailored interactive services for digital television were developed, but the technology and the television operators were not ready to make use of them.

For a couple from Nokia, aged twenty-six and twenty-nine years, interactivity seemed to be lost, although they thought that sending SMS messages to the *Big Brother* programme represented well-functioning interactivity. They would not use interactive services based on a direct return channel in the digital television, because they already had a broadband connection at home. Having internet services in digital television was a foolish idea, they thought. They only occasionally used even teletext services.

A thirty-four-year-old man from Porvoo with work experience in television had given up on interactivity, because he saw it as "huuhaa", a strong, disparaging expletive (something like *rubbish* in English). Who would like to hang around teletext pages, when the internet was available? The next feedback technology for him would be a set combining an ADSL box (giving internet and television feeds) and a computer with a big screen and keypad. He had a friend who had constructed just such a combination for himself.

Videotape Destroyed

According to Robert Allen (2004), the new millennium brought with it new characteristics for television such as a quantitative and qualitative proliferation of channels, availability of international channels, and, especially, the dimension of theme and group-targeted channels. In addition, the new television enabled prolonged viewing, supplied on-demand and pay-TV services and offered new options for recording and archiving. Also, television viewing outside the home, in public spaces, increased. The dominant feature in Allen's view was a "constant, rapid, and unpredictable technological, institutional, and economic change" (Allen, 2004, p. 16).

Allen (2004) asserted that (in the US) not until 2001 were sales of videotape recorders surpassed by DVD. A similar change took place in Finland a little bit later between 2002 and 2003. The main commercial development of DVD came in the late 1990s and was much quicker than in the case of VCR (although acknowledging that the technologies serve different functions). In five years between 1997 and 2002, more than 30 million households in the

US purchased a DVD player. When this was complemented by a computer-like recording capacity in digital television, the era of VCR/VHS ended. In addition to recording, the digital set-top box enabled prolonged viewing even in boxes without a recording capacity.[5]

VCR/VHS had a major impact on television viewing on its arrival in Finnish homes (Kortti, 2007). The rapid displacement of video tapes by recording set-top boxes, computers and DVDs surprised many people, and several interviewees regretted the change. A videotape archive or a small video library had appeared in many homes. Tapes were actively used for both recording and viewing. A young couple in Nokia estimated that they had in their cupboard more than 100 cassettes; they also had a list of videos on their computer. The twenty-nine-year-old man thought that (pre-recorded, television company produced) videos could be completely skipped once one could search and watch the series in the net or DVD. They were waiting for more highly developed recording set-top boxes.

Although interviewees had hardly any knowledge of digitalization in other countries, many wondered about the curiosities of Finnish media policy in the digital switchover. A forty-four-year-old father of three from Porvoo was irritated by the solution of one set-top box per television, which became expensive and bothersome for a larger family. He preferred the solution of one set-top box per household (i.e. linking several TV sets) and thought that it should be technically possible: "If man goes to the moon, why shouldn't such a set-top box be possible?" He pointed out that manufacturers of home appliances had an interest in speedy returns.

Enthusiasm for Prolonged Viewing

According to Hirsch (2004), there are both established and new forms in the domestication of consumption of technologies. Domestication normally encourages people to apply both strategies. With regard to the digitalisation of television, therefore, it is important to evaluate the extent to which this changed old practices and how much it brought in new ones.

The Finnish data introduced here shows that the use of universal channels changes slowly. At the time of the interviews of this research (in the summer of 2007), the older age groups typically followed four main channels, but the younger ones also watched more target-oriented channels such as Subtv and Voice. There is a big cultural gap between the generations in media consumption and competence. Media use is in the middle of a major transition, of which the practice of prolonged viewing, which makes it possible to pause viewing and continue later, is a good example. The Finnpanel (2009) survey titled the result "Recording Set-Top Boxes Increase Television User Comfort". In households with a recording set-top box or IPTV, the share of prolonged viewing is now 15 per cent, and the trend is moving upward.

The main share of television viewing continued to consist of live programming, with news, current affairs and sport as main examples. According to

Finnpanel's evaluation, in the case of some programmes, watching recorded material had already increased total viewing time by 30 to 50 per cent. The most popular recorded materials were foreign and domestic series. Typically the recorded programmes were viewed within twenty-four hours of the original transmission. The practice was most popular among those aged twenty-five to forty-four and in families with children.

In our research data, there were few direct references to the preceding kind of changes in viewing practices. But the visions and expectations expressed demonstrated that one could forecast a change in a similar direction. The most common vision was to connect television and the computer. Many families interviewed had considered the idea of watching television through the computer and, indeed, expected to do so. Many hoped for the option of an on-demand subscription to programmes, particularly through the internet. The connection of television and the internet would also enable the creation and use of personal programme archives.

Towards Intermedial User Practices

The references to 'intermedial' user practices with a number of attributes were common in our research data. For example in a family from Porvoo, a thirty-four-year-old man and thirty-year-old woman, representing late adopters, used to check the TV pages of newspapers and the web page of *Big Brother*. Both said that they had stayed with *Big Brother* despite skipping watching the programme itself. They also read about the key events in this reality show in a free-circulation newspaper, *Metro*; the popular afternoon papers; and the weekend appendix to the biggest newspaper in Finland, *Helsingin Sanomat*. The woman pointed out that it was important to know about *Big Brother* for making friends and following things generally. The web page information about almost all programmes was enough, she thought, to keep one up-to-date and able to join in coffee-table chats, even if one skipped actually watching the programmes themselves.

Using the internet for watching television was common among interviewees, but only one reported having tried digital streaming of television channels by inserting a TV card into a PC. Following television through the internet offered clear bonuses, such as background information about programmes. The couple from Porvoo was an interesting case of intermedial use; they followed television but did not own a television set prior to the switchover. When contacted later in February 2008, they reported having purchased a TV set. Since spring 2013, the Finnish public service broadcaster (YLE) offers direct streaming of its television channels through the internet.

It seems that television is an important factor in motivating people toward intermedial use. In this sense, the data reflect televisualisation, a factor, which Herkman (2005, pp. 264–269) connects with television's impact on newspapers, in particular, the popular papers which in Finland are identified as afternoon papers. Televisualisation and audiovisualisation of the internet are also apparent, including web versions of the newspapers. Some newspapers characterize their web pages as 'web television', but others avoid reference to television, although the content might consist of only moving images, videos or video portals (Mäenpää and Männistö, 2009, pp. 101–102). Most newspapers describe the audiovisual supply of their web pages as 'net TV' or simply 'videos'.

In our research data, the discourse on intermedial use was frequent. Television channels have brought and created services for the internet that have accelerated the use of television through the internet. The consequent new user practices reflect that television as a technological device has lost some of its previous importance. Interesting programmes and related content are followed independent of source and technology.

The web pages of *Pikku Kakkonen* (*The Little Two*), one of the most traditional public service children's programmes on TV2, were known to many young families. For example one was a three-member family from Nokia that lived in a terrace house but dreamed of a villa. Their interest in house construction programmes and associated web pages had turned almost into a hobby, reminiscent of the cross-media interest orientation of the Porvoo family without a television (mentioned earlier).

The twenty-nine-year-old woman in the family said that she visited the web page of the television programme *Sillä silmällä* (*Queer Eye for the Straight Guy*) just for a quick look. The man (thirty years old) explained about the web pages of the house construction programmes, such as *Remontti Reiska*.[6] He had also found a good construction programme (*Paikat kuntoon*[7]) on the web page of the local TV station TV-Tampere. In *Remontti Reiska* a house is built and viewers can vote on the selection of roof material, for example. The couple also used the web pages of food and cooking programmes when looking for recipes.

Situation in Life Influences Viewing

In interviewed families with children, the youngest watched *Pikku Kakkonen* (*The Little Two*) and somewhat older *The Simpsons* with adults. Digital television brought more channels and target group channels in particular. The web pages of many channels and programmes offer archives and links. In this way, the internet extends channels and programmes to cross-media, and consequently, digitalisation increases intermedial use.

The middle-aged parents of a family in Pälkäne did not read print newspapers but occasionally followed web versions of newspapers. Television was their dominant medium, and it was on continuously. The woman watched all the soaps. They actively visited the web pages of television channels and programmes. Their use of the internet at home changed in part because of the increased internet use of their teenage children (fourteen- and seventeen-year-old sons). Both parents had a college education and used a computer and the internet at work.

Consumers are inventive and creative. They employ devices for several uses and make combinations of them to suit their own purposes. An example is a retired woman from Helsinki who not only was keen to use her computer to chat with friends through Skype connection but was also able to link her computer to the television to screen photos of a joint event for her hobby community.

The above example not only demonstrates intermedial use but also the new role of women in the domestication of media technology. For instance, the thirty-year-old woman from Porvoo felt ready to abandon the television set and purchase instead a digital stick for her computer. She took care of all the media equipment in the home and was considering setting up a separate media room where the family would be able to watch programmes with a video projector. The idea reflected criticism towards the viewing routines of her family; television was on all night regardless of whether anyone was watching it. Her media use was divided according to content. When searching for daily news she turned to the web version of the newspaper *Helsingin Sanomat* and to the public service broadcaster YLE's web page, but for more background, she looked in the print newspaper.

ABOUT THE CONSTRUCTION OF MEDIUM RELATIONSHIP

The background to people's medium relationship lies in their life history and, as with life itself, continuously changes and transforms. The interviews reported here showed that people's relationship to media was challenged by the launch of a new medium for the market. The same person and family might turn out to be an early adopter of one medium but a late adopter of another. The consumption culture of each generation frames their medium relationship. Our data point out that the articulation of a medium relationship varied not only by age but also by life situation. The clearest peak of television viewing appeared with the birth of the first child in a family, when the child acted as a mediator and gave a rhythm for viewing. Another peak was brought on by retirement, when the viewing became ritualised and gave a rhythm to everyday life.

Historically, the eras characterised by the long history of newspapers, radio and television each resulted in a certain level of dominant identification with a specific medium. Media-related rituals and fan relationships were formed. Consumers identified themselves as newspaper people, radio freaks and fans of television, consciously and unconsciously. In their study of changes in media literacy, Herkman and Vainikka (2012, p. 26) characterised these historical links with a typology of media generations. The two older generations are named as the newspaper generation (people born in during the 1930s through the 1950s) and the television generation (born in the 1960s and the 1970s). The two younger generations are termed as the internet generation (people born in the 1980s or later) and as digital natives (born after 2000).

With new media and digitalisation, however, the variety of media proliferated and the identification changed character. It is not only, any more, about identification with a particular medium but rather with certain programmes, content, services and activities. Users follow their favourite content across different media, and the medium itself remains a pure mediator. This corresponds to what the Danish media scholar Klaus Bruhn Jensen argues about the increased importance of modalities like genres in the context of networked media and communications (Jensen, 2010, pp. 85–87).

The preceding transformation applies in particular to children, young people and young adults (people younger than thirty-five). In the earlier typology of generations they represent the two younger categories. They follow their favourite genres and objects of interest and search for information across several media, according to varying situations and needs. Their media use is dominantly cross-media oriented and only secondarily intermedial, the latter emphasising the interplay and relevance of particular media identities. The establishment of a new medium relationship requires continuous use. The younger generations use the internet continuously, albeit sometimes irregularly. The signs of their changing medium relationship are clear and numerous.

A special feature of the argumentation among younger generations was spatiality, particularly in relation to the internet. They visited services such as You Tube, IRC Gallery and Habbo Hotel and identified as spaces, including chat rooms and hobby groups. Their media relationship was characterised by communication, messaging, playing games and activity on social media. The fact that for example Facebook did not appear on this list of spaces illuminates the fast pace of change; Facebook started spreading in Finland just after the digital switchover in the autumn of 2007. Among older adults, the relationship with new media technology depended most clearly on whether they used a computer in their work. For young people, the most apparent factors were their relationships with parents, school and friends and the income level of the family. In school, young people learnt basic knowledge and practice about computers, but playing games, net surfing and similar activities opened up their circle of friends. In our research data, all young people interviewed had that opportunity.

A typical cross-media user seemed to be acquainted and felt safe with the new media technology. Discursively the relationship was relaxed, despite the technical problems of the digital switchover and particularly in cases of self-critical understatements, typical of many female interviewees. Use and competence defined the relationship with media technology. If computer competences were low, the relationship with technology was distant. On the other hand, cross-media use increased competence and resulted in a stronger relationship with the new media, which again reduced the resistance to and/ or difficulty of adopting ever more new media and technologies.

From the point of view of children's information technology competences, the media environment of the interviewed families was rather rich and multifaceted. Children generally had good competencies, and their role in the family turned upside down compared to the family viewing, during which the father mastered the remote control and dominated knowledge of technology. As our data illuminate, today the dominant role may go to the woman in the family or even more probably to the younger generation.

CONCLUSION AND DISCUSSION

The preceding analysis of media users' response to the digital switchover of television points out that the interpretations of the reform emphasised the historical continuity of television as a medium and a social and cultural institution. In people's minds the groundbreaking transition of the medium through digitalisation was anchored to the old institutional form and practices of television. In this sense the reform seemed to shrink to a minor extension of the old television, an enhanced television. On the other hand, the data demonstrated that in particular, younger generations were keen to objectify the potential of the reform to a number of intermedial user practices which pointed to a major change of their media use and relationships.

When looking at the present situation, more than half a decade after the digital switchover, the consequences of the reform are clearly visible. Already in the early phase of digitalisation it was clear that the available output in terms of channels and services would increase enormously. We not only have a television of plenty but, rather, of a super or maximum plenty. In a small market such as Finland even the terrestrial network offers now in addition to the main generalist channels tens of niche channels targeted to special interest audiences. The huge increase of output as such affects the nature of television audiences as pointed out by Napoli (2011) in his conclusions about audience evolution in the context of new technologies. Fragmentation of audiences and their increased autonomy can be listed among the most immediate consequences of the increased output. One should, however, emphasise that the increased autonomy is probably even more based on the participatory potentials of new media technologies. As pointed out in the growing amount of literature, this change includes a possibility for media users to mix the roles of receiver and producer.

Finnish statistics on television audiences show a clear increase in the popularity of niche-oriented pay-TV services. The main generalist channels accounted for a 95 per cent share of television viewing in the early phase of digitalisation in 2001. That share went down to 80 per cent in 2008 following the digital switchover and down further to 67 per cent in 2012. The average Finnish viewer followed more than five channels daily in 2012 and some ten channels a week. Besides these changes many other factors contribute to the transformation of television audiences. Recording set-top boxes are now available in half of all households. The computer-like capacities of interactivity are becoming increasingly typical in set-top boxes and television receivers, including smart TV and IPTV applications. Parallel to that, television viewing through the internet is expanding; the growth was 50 per cent in Finland from 2011 to 2012.

The traditional TV institutions meet increased competition not only from the side of telecommunication companies but also from the internet-based service operators such as YouTube, Google or Netflix. The new players of the market complicate the game about audiences simply because of increasing difficulties to agree on an institutional definition of television. As proposed by Napoli (2011, pp. 2–3), from the point of view of media industries the audiences can be characterised as institutional audiences. He also points out that the reference to institutions can be understood in two interrelated ways; it deals with the particular sets of practices, behavioural patterns and analytical orientations and priorities that characterise the operation of media industries, but it can also more generally refer to established social norms, formal procedures and practices. Accordingly, the institutional transformation of television has the potential to challenge the operation of media industries, and in parallel, may also affect the social and cultural norms and practices of the audience game. The rapid growth of pay-TV and on-demand-based services through the digital switchover is a good example of such potential. The new services do not only affect the funding options of the old players, but they also strengthen the consumer orientation of media users through the emphasis on individual choice of interests and gratification (Napoli, 2011, p. 151).

In the light of these conclusions we briefly summarize our answers to the four research questions listed in the beginning.

Research Question 1: How do media users express and perform their media relationships and identities in the cross-media context?

Media use is changing remarkably through digitalisation. The repertoire of media use expands continuously towards a more cross-media oriented use. Our data show that the use of digital television is still based on established conventions but that intermedial use and orientation increases parallel to that. There are big differences in the media practices of different generations. Older people act according to traditional conventions, whereas young audiences change their practices continuously. The latter follow television programmes through several media, side by side. The televisualisation of afternoon papers makes it easy to follow the events and characters of TV shows through newspapers. The use of the web pages of channels and programmes also becomes more common. In addition to age, the life situation of the interviewed families strongly framed their media practices.

The circulation of media content is increasingly participatory of nature (Jenkins, 2006, p. 3). Rather than talking about media producers and consumers as occupying separate roles, writes Jenkins, we might now see them as participants who interact with each other according to a new set of rules that none of us fully understands. The new participatory media culture contrasts with older notions of passive media spectatorship (ibid.). This kind of participatory culture was clearly visible in the research data. The younger generations objectified digital television by linking it with attributes, images and visual as well as symbolic interpretations of the new media conventions and practices. This kind of articulation was central in their intermedial orientation. Media were used in a crossover fashion, side by side, simultaneously and with a continuous comparison of uses and content.

Digital television was articulated as an 'intermedial hybrid'. The use of and talk about digital television reflected its hybrid nature in several ways; it was used for viewing and listening, as a teletext service and as game equipment and for screening DVDs. The hybrid dimensions characterised the cross-media-oriented medium relationship. Television was followed not only through a television set but also through PC and the internet and intertextually on radio and on the web pages of newspapers. The time shift dimension of television viewing is increasing with the use of recordings, prolonged viewing and video-on-demand services as well as through DVDs. The ritualistic use of television based on the daily rhythm of the programme flow is breaking down.

Cross-media use demonstrated a relaxed medium and technology relationship. The so-called Diderot effect, of good competences in one technology making it easier to master another, was reflected in the articulation of the interviewees. The constitution of cross-media oriented media relationships and the consequently relaxed relationship with technology increased the users' information society competence. Insofar as people managed to deal with the challenges of the new technology, they remained connected, as it were, on the safe side of the digital gap which threatens to widen because of the growing speed of changes.

Research Question 2: Is there any future for media specific audiences in a cross-media context?

Yes, but it will be more difficult to define and expose such audiences. As demonstrated above through the analysis of the digital switchover of television, the discussion on institutionalized media audiences cannot avoid paying attention to the increased importance of intermedial user practices and the consequent change of media relationships. Institutional practices and identities are contested by the increased autonomy of media users, and they may even close their eyes and ears to the temptations of institutional engagement and select their own priorities. One should not, however, overestimate the change and think that only individuals matter in the future; even in the context of a more individualized media use, culture and society in terms of values and norms, social bonds and practices still matter. And the billions used for the services of media institutions and industries will guarantee that even those institutions matter in the future.

There is continuing evidence that traditional media institutions such as television are considered to be the most trustworthy and reliable sources of public information. That is an asset in the context of network communication where building and maintaining trust and credibility is in many ways problematic. Our data support also the continuing importance of television as a medium of social sharing and common interests. For younger generations, television as such may be less important. But its programmes and content remain important reference points in their construction of identity, taste and lifestyle in the framework of broader cultural consumption. For television as institution, the problem is how to incorporate such processes and practices into the planning of their operations and, in particular, into their conception of audiences. The traditional head counting of audiences, the exposure model, as Philip Napoli (2011) calls it, is not working in the context of cross-media use. Basically one should be able to develop measures and practices of audience research which make it possible to identify and track different forms of people's interaction with television and its content, the search for and the use of content on several parallel platforms and the participation of people in production and distribution of that content.

Research Question 3: How to connect mass communication or target-oriented audiencing with cross-media oriented medium relationship? How does that connect with the individualising tendencies of media use and the emergence of social and participatory forms of networking?

We think that increasing cross-media use and the consequent autonomy of users do not as such exclude mass communication or target-oriented audiencing. At this point we would like to refer to the conclusions of a recent research project which analysed the meanings of journalism in the social networks of media users (Heikkilä, et al., 2012). The conclusions of the project point out that the autonomy of users could be interpreted as a possibility to select different sorts of audience practices which cover a continuum from mass orientation to acting as a public, this last option referring to the distinction between audience and public in English language. Increased cross-media use together with the potential for interactivity naturally encourages people to act as a public which is additionally supported by the social networking capacity of digital media. This kind of model points out that media users can select between several parallel identities, including institutionally affiliated mass and target audiences.

When applied to television the preceding kind of model about optional audience identifications might be interpreted as follows. The television of (maximum) plenty with the consequent commercialization has made individual choice the dominant ideology of cultural consumption. From the point of view of television as an institution, the options of choice invite people to become members of institutional audiences which represent people's individual interests and gratifications. Making choices and becoming an audience through these choices represents an audience practice which emphasizes awareness of other people's similar orientations. This is the essence of the institutional target orientation of television and is qualitatively different from the earlier mass orientation, based on a simple exposure to the mass-mediated messages.

Acting as a public, then, is a user practice which is not only about choices but also represents active involvement and participation with other people in their existing social networks or in the new networks created to support common interests and joint engagements. These practices may connect with institutional audience identities, but they may equally represent social sharing and practices based, for example, on the potentials of the new social media. As a practice of media use, participation in a public is more than becoming a receiver of certain contents; it requires sharing and distribution of contents through mediated interaction, but one might equally include participation in the production of contents.

> *Research Question 4*: What constitutes a medium/the media in cross-media oriented user practices?

We have already referred to how the new digital platforms challenge the institutional definition of television as a medium. Following the emphasis of our Intermedia project on the continuities of media development, we defined the transformation of television in terms of intermedial redefinition. As pointed out by our research data, redefined digital television was still recognizable as television with certain technical capacities and institutional features. The Intermedia project as a whole argued against the interpretation of media change in the form of a convergence model that made the differences between media forms irrelevant. But we also acknowledged that in the context of continuous change it may be impossible to capture any single universal definition of the media in terms of a general media theory or of more specific theories such as television theory. However, we felt that a critical analysis of media change required that we tried to become aware of our implied understanding of the media.

In his critique of the discussion on the universal features of the media, Arild Fetveit, our Danish colleague on the Intermedia project (Fetveit, 2012), opted to change the focus from definitions of the media to the process of mediation. This is how he formulates the change of focus:

> The move to seeing media from the vantage point of mediation could be construed as one that provides us with a more stable point of observation,

but it may be even more productively considered as a move that can help us understand the institutional solidification of something into a medium. If something can solidify into a medium, a reversal of the process may also take place whereby a medium is de-solidified.

(Fetveit, 2012, p. 62)

This kind of focus on mediation processes would result in two kinds of research approaches. On one hand, one could critically analyse the mediation processes in their constitution, the development towards "fully fledged media"; on the other, one could look at mediation in reverse, in the process of de-solidification. Our particular case on the digital switchover of television represents the study of mediation in reverse. That is evaluated as an aspect of increasing intermedial use and the consequent changes in media relationships. But on the other hand, intermedial use offers a potential to capture the mediation processes in their constitution, on their way towards more institutionally established forms of mediation; and, as such, recognizable and identifiable only in the emerging user practices. If one relates this kind of approach to Couldry's idea of media as practices, one could conclude that mediation is about media practices that through continuous repetition may become institutionalized or which through redefinition or dissolution may lead to new kinds of media practices. Whatever direction one selects, the idea is to consider the media as basically 'fluid' in nature (Fetveit, 2012, pp. 66–67).

To summarise our answers to the four research questions of this chapter, we conclude that the digitalisation of television encouraged an intermedial user practice which made people reconsider and rethink their relationships to media. Television was characterised as an intermedial hybrid but still maintained its identity as television. But our data support also the evidence that the traditional institutional dimensions of audiences are losing relevance, and particularly younger generations are opting towards a medium relationship that emphasises more content and modalities such as genres instead of the media as institutions.

However, based on the conclusions from our Intermedia research more generally, we would like to pay attention to the relevance of mediation processes when studying the constitution of cross-media audiences. These processes can represent redefinition of established media such as in the case of digital television, but they can also tell us about the dissolution of institutional identities. But as proposed by Fetveit (2012), emergent cross-media practices create, on the other side, a possibility to follow up "the institutional solidification of something into a medium". We would like to add that although cross-media audiences increasingly could be characterised in terms of content and modalities, institutional dimensions remain potentially relevant in the study of media use. If not, there is a risk of conceptualising media use as a purely individual practice without any social and cultural connections.

NOTES

1. Our understanding is that intermedia and cross-media are related concepts with different emphases. If applied to media use, intermediality refers to the interplay between different media identities and their consequent redefinition. For its part, cross-media use is an expression of a new kind of medium relationship which orientates more to contents and modalities than the use of specific media.
2. This analysis of the research data is updated from an earlier version published in Kangaspunta and Hujanen (2012).
3. The category 'late adopter' is taken from Rogers's (2003, pp. 155–157, 282–286) model concerning the diffusion of innovations.
4. Activities for the public to engage with at museums for example are regularly termed 'interactive'—indicating the transposition of digital culture to the framing role of a medial discourse of society.
5. Today, TV Everywhere, a new form of Digital Video Recording (DVR) is spreading based on ideas of cloud computing. It enables distant viewing of centrally stored personal video recordings through an internet connection.
6. The name can be translated to *Renovation Reiska*—the notion of Reiska characterises a male who is skilled to fix things.
7. The name could be translated to *How to Fix Your Places*.

REFERENCES

Allen, R., 2004. Frequently asked questions: a general introduction to the reader. In: R. Allen and A. Hill, eds. 2004. *The television studies reader*. London: Routledge. pp. 1–25.

Bjur, J., Schrøder, K.C., Hasebrink, U., Courtois, C., Adoni, H. and Nossek, H., 2014. Cross-media use: unfolding complexities in contemporary audiencehood. In: N. Carpentier, K.C. Schrøder and L. Hallett, eds. 2014. *Audience transformations*. New York and London: Routledge. pp. 15–29.

Couldry, N., 2004. Theorising media as practice. *Social Semiotics* 14(2), pp. 115–132.

Couldry, N., 2009. Does "the media" have a future? *European Journal of Communication* 24(4), pp. 437–450.

Couldry, N., 2010. The necessary future of audience, and how to research it. In: V. Nightingale, ed. 2010. *The handbook of media audience*. Malden: Blackwell. pp. 213–229.

Ellis, J., 2000. *Seeing things. Television in the age of uncertainty*. London: I.B. Tauris.

Fetveit, A., 2012. The concept of medium in the digital era. In: J. Herkman, T. Hujanen and P. Oinonen, eds. 2012. *Intermediality and media change*. Tampere: Tampere University Press. pp. 45–71.

Finnpanel, 2009. *TV-taloudet Suomessa* [online]. Helsinki: Finnpanel Oy. Available at: <http://www.finnpanel.fi>.

Heikkilä, H., Ahva, L., Siljamäki, J. and Valtonen, S., 2012. *Kelluva kiinnostavuus: journalismin merkitys ihmisten sosiaalisissa verkostoissa*. Tampere: Vastapaino.

Herkman, J., 2005. *Kaupallisen television ja iltapäivälehtien avoliitto: median markkinoituminen ja digitalisoituminen*. Tampere: Vastapaino.

Herkman, J., 2012. Introduction: intermediality as a theory and methodology. In: J. Herkman, T. Hujanen and P. Oinonen, eds. 2012. *Intermediality and media change*. Tampere: Tampere University Press. pp. 10–27.

Herkman, J. and Vainikka, E., 2012. *Lukemisen tavat: lukeminen sosiaalisen median aikakaudella*. Tampere: Tampere University Press.

Hirsch, E., 2004. New technologies and domestic consumption. In: P. Marris and S. Thornham, eds. 2004. *Media studies: a reader.* 2nd ed. Edinburgh: Edinburgh University Press. pp. 816–834.

Jenkins, H., 2006. *Convergence culture. Where old and new media collide.* New York and London: New York University Press.

Jensen, K.B., 2010. *Media convergence: the three degrees of network, mass, and interpersonal communication.* London and New York: Routledge.

Kangaspunta, S., 2006. *Yhteisöllinen digi-tv: digitaalisen television uusi yhteisöllisyys, yhteisöllisyyden tuotteistaminen ja yhteisötelevision vaihtoehto.* Tampere: Tampere University Press.

Kangaspunta, S., 2008. *Keskeneräistä pakolla: tutkimus digi-tv: n ja mediateknologian kotouttamisesta.* Tiedotusopin laitoksen julkaisuja, C42. Tampere: Tampereen yliopisto, Journalismin tutkimusyksikkö.

Kangaspunta, S., 2013. *Sekakäyttöä ja salarakkautta: digi-tv ja monimediaisuuden murros Suomessa.* Tampere: Tampere University Press.

Kangaspunta, S. and Hujanen, T., 2012. Intermediality in user's discourses about digital television. In: J. Herkman, T. Hujanen and P. Oinonen, eds. 2012. *Intermediality and media change.* Tampere: Tampere University Press. pp. 145–169.

Kortti, J., 2007. *Näköradiosta digiboksiin: suomalaisen television sosiokulttuurinen historia.* Helsinki: Gaudeamus.

LVM, 2002. *Digi-TV Suomessa: Suomalaisten toimijoiden näkemykset digitaalisen television nykytilasta ja suositukset etenemisstrategiasta 2002–2004.* Liikenne- ja viestintäministeriön muistio.

Mackay, H., 2007. Analogue switch-off: multi-channel viewing by "the reluctant 50%". *International Journal of Cultural Policy* 13(1), pp. 33–48.

Moscovici, S., 1984. The phenomenon of social representations. In: R.M. Farr and S. Moscovici, eds. 1984. *Social representations.* Cambridge: Cambridge University Press. pp. 3–69.

Mäenpää, J. and Männistö, A., 2009. *Kun kaikki videoivat kaikkea: liikkuva kuva sanomalehden sivuilla.* Tiedotusopin laitoksen julkaisuja, B53. Tampere: Tampereen yliopisto, Journalismin tutkimusyksikkö.

Napoli, P., 2011. *Audience evolution: new technologies and the transformation of media audiences.* New York: Columbia University Press.

Rogers, E.M., 1962. *Diffusion of innovations.* Glencoe: The Free Press.

Uricchio, W., 2004. Historicizing media in transition. In: D. Thorburn, H. Jenkins and B. Scawell, eds. 2004. *Rethinking media change: the aesthetics of transition.* Cambridge: MIT Press. pp. 23–38

Viestintävirasto, 2007. *Digi-TV: n käytettävyystutkimus 2/2007.* Viestintäviraston julkaisuja, 10/2007. Helsinki: TNS-Gallup. Available at: <http://www.ficora.fi/attachments/suomiry/5tmETS9M5/ViestintavirastonJulkaisuja102007.pdf>.

13 Exploring Audience Activities and Their Power-Relatedness in the Digitalised City
Diversity and Routinisation of People's Media Relations in the Triply Articulated Urban Space

Seija Ridell

INTRODUCTION

Since the early days of city life, the street and the square have been the central stages for public appearance and interaction, permeated by intricate codes that govern urban modes of (self-)presentation and audiencing (Goffman, 1963; Sennett, 1974). Today, because of the overwhelming presence of audiovisual media, big cities, in particular, resemble department stores or commercial television rather than *theatrum mundi* in their overall rhetoric. In recent years, the digitalisation of material infrastructures, and the proliferation of networked Information and Communication Technologies (ICTs) have augmented media saturation and deepened the commodification of cityscapes, thereby multiplying instances of urban mass media audiencehood. At the same time, mobile ICTs have diversified people's activities as urban audiences; we now also receive constantly—in both voluntary and forced audience positions—other people's technology-enabled presentations while on the move in the physical city. In addition, through our smart gadgets, we can audience performances 'virtually elsewhere'. Hence, the history and the transformations of both face-to-face and (mass-)mediated audience practices as well as their multiple intertwinements, particularly in contemporary urban environments, offer a multifaceted topic for theoretical and empirical attention.

Despite this richness, there has been only scant interest in the field of media audience research concerning how people act as media audiences as well as how they audience other people's media-related presentational acts in the urban context. Only during the past decade has one been able to see examples of studies that extend their gaze to people's media reception beyond the domestic space (see e.g. Drotner, 2005; Morley, 2006; de la Garde, 2010). As such, the proliferation of mobile media in particular has made the outdoor and the urban increasingly fascinating for scholars in different disciplines, including those involved in communication and media studies. From the end of 1990s onwards, there has been a growing body of studies on mobile communication (see Brown, Green and Harper [2001] as well as Katz and Aakhus [2002] for examples of the start of the publication boom) and one also finds research that discusses urban localities as mediat(is)ed communicative environments (see e.g. McCarthy, 2001; Couldry and McCarthy, 2004; Falkheimer and Jansson, 2006). Regarding research with a specific focus on audience activities, however, the spatial expansion of scholarly purview has remained thus far rather tentative.

Without too much exaggeration, it can be argued that for media audience researchers, the household is still the primary context of people's relations with the media, and questions concerning (mass-)mediated audience activities in urban settings tend to be more commonly posed by scholars in other fields (see e.g. Rieser, 2011). For example, with regard to viewing television—by far the most popular object of empirically oriented media audience studies— the overall situation has not changed too drastically since the beginning of the 1980s, when Dafna Lemish (1982, p. 757) suggested that scholarly attention should be directed at the phenomenon of 'television viewing done in public places'. Lemish's suggestion was taken up from different starting points by Krotz and Eastman (1999) in their empirical study at the end of the 1990s, but the main focus in the field remained on media reception and use in the home. The same is true of ICTs once they were brought onto the agenda of British cultural media studies at the end of the 1980s and in the early 1990s by ethnographically oriented researchers (see e.g. Morley and Silverstone, 1990; Silverstone and Morley, 1990; Silverstone, Hirsch and Morley, 1991; Silverstone and Hirsch, 1992; Silverstone, 1996). In more recent studies that are mostly interested in children and young people as users of these technologies the household continues to be the spatial locus of ICT relations (see e.g. Livingstone, 1998; 2002; Livingstone and Bovill, 2001; Livingstone and Drotner, 2011). Some of this research, however, takes note of how portable devices are used outside of the domestic space and it also even pays attention to related audience activities (see e.g. Drotner, 2005). Goggin (2011, p. 143), for one, stated more generally that "'going mobile' has become central to the processes of contemporary audience engagement".

Overall, a sub-disciplinary myopia seems to persist in the field of media studies concerning the spatial contexts of audience activities. In this chapter, I suggest that to 'revitalise' media audience research, it is necessary to broaden the analytic horizon in this respect through an exploration of people's activities as urban audiences. Given the increasing software sustenance of cities, this also means that the radical transformation of urban spatiality in recent years needs to be taken into account—indeed, taken as a starting point. It is my contention that a systematic theorisation and theoretically informed empirical studies of audience activities in contemporary urban settings will allow, among other things, for a more nuanced grasp of how people, in their daily media relations, continue to negotiate the still normatively charged boundaries of the private and public spheres of life. At the

238 *Seija Ridell*

same time, fresh perspectives would open on domestic media reception and the ways in which it, too, extends to other spatial contexts. Furthermore, a focus on urban audience activities would help us to understand and analyse how the uses and reception of media partake in the constitution of spaces in which people today lead their public social lives. All of this, then, would connect media audience research to discussions in other disciplinary fields on the nature and dynamics of power in an era of pervasive technology mediation.

Before probing these directions of 'revitalisation' in more detail, a few starting points, based on key conceptual clarifications, need to be outlined.

SKETCHING THE ANALYTIC SCENE

The first clarification concerns no less than the definition of 'audience'. With this notion, I refer to a culturally specific mode of action and the related actor position—one that in its basic form involves the following of a performance or a representation that is voluntarily or involuntarily, by design or accidentally, offered—presented—to others for interpretation (Goffman, 1974, chap. 5). With regard to people's media-related activities, this definition means that not each and any form of these activities can be fruitfully subsumed under the notion of 'audience'—a tendency that presently appears to be rather strong in media audience research as a reaction to the upsurge in digital networked media (for a critical discussion see Ridell, 2012). To properly discern what is specific about acting as an audience (media related or not), then, an analytic distinction needs to be made between it and certain other modes of action, say, acting as a 'user', a member of the 'public' or as a 'community member'. All these activities have their specific characteristics that differentiate them from the activity of audiencing (ibid.). At the same time, it is also important to keep in mind that the actual variety of audience activities, especially in the present-day urban environments, is huge, as these activities range from interpersonal to mass-mediated instances and are enacted in diversely technology-mediated forms. In summation, the definition of 'audience' employed in this chapter is deliberately distanced from the common-sense conception and overly simplistic way of talking about the audience as a group-like entity, which, in itself, acts (for a detailed discussion and critique of the essentialist view of audience as it prevails in the field of media audience research, see Ridell, 2012; cf. Fiske, 1994; Fiske and Dawson, 1996; see also Tosoni and Tarantino, 2013). Instead, understanding 'audience' in terms of mode of action directs attention to *people's* activities.

Second, I proceed from the observation that people's activities as audiences occur in multiple situations, overlapping and intertwining with a variety of other activities in many different ways. In actual practice, people shift constantly and swiftly back and forth between audiencing and various other actor positions such as performer, public member or community member. In addition, in the uses of smart mobiles, these shifts cut through various spaces and spatial scales, interlacing distinct social situations in the process. This, in turn, may affect, quite profoundly, the codes of communication that structure the situations (cf. Goffman, 1963; Meyrowitz, 1985). Hence, the *differentia specifica* of audience activities can be perceived and understood adequately only if we take into account that these activities are interwoven in the complex and ever-more technology mediated fabric of social life in general and of life in the cities in particular.

The third clarification relates to the multilayered nature of urban space brought about by digitalisation and the proliferation of location-aware networked portables. Not only does the sphere of urbanism expand beyond the physical city in people's uses of portable devices, but through these gadgets, the material infrastructure literally becomes connected to human bodies as well. Indeed, this development has involved people corporeally in the moving (re)production of urban infrastructures. Thus, to describe adequately the nature of urban spatial transformation, it is necessary to update Henri Lefebvre's (1974 [1991]) well-known relational notion of space and take note of the *inter*relationality of space (see Ridell and Zeller, 2013, pp. 439–441; also Ridell, 2010). The latter notion not only directs attention to the hybridity of urban space but also raises the issue of people's complicity with the intricate dynamics of spatial power in the software-sustained cities onto the agenda.

To capture people's urban activities in terms of their elusively reciprocal power-relatedness, an analytic distinction—and this is my fourth clarification— between the presentational, representational and non-representational aspects of space is useful. All three aspects (and their interrelations) are of importance for understanding the characteristics of urban audience activities and their power-relatedness. The notions of presentation and representation are attached, in their analytically distinct ways, to the visible or otherwise perceivable dimensions of the cityscape: to physical objects and people's gestures and movements in the case of presentation and to the abundance of symbolic elements in the case of representation. With non-representation, in turn, I refer—in resonance with the view of some critical geographers—to how the daily uses of mobile technologies engage people as co-producers of infrastructures in invisible and easily automated ways (see Thrift and French, 2002; specifically on non-representation, see Thrift 2007; Anderson, 2009; Cadman, 2009; on the relationality of infrastructures, see Star, 1999; Star and Bowker, 2002). More precisely, through the habituation of their technology-mediated activities in the city, people become active participants in the processes that structure and condition their own agency in the urban space (see Ridell, 2010). Hence, the notion of non-representation encapsulates the dynamics of power that some scholars have coined 'posthegemonic' (see e.g. Lash, 2007; Beer, 2009) and some others 'posthuman' (see e.g. Hayles, 2006; 2009; Gane 2006; Gane, Venn and Hand, 2007)—both camps wishing to put their finger on what can be seen to epitomise the processes of power in the pervasively digitalised condition. Given that we have at stake here a dynamic that affords and constrains people's possibilities to act beyond the level of the symbolic, the notion of non-representation challenges us not to restrict our analytical efforts merely to "whatever it is that people are doing with or around, media" (Couldry, 2011, p. 226) in the cities.

Proceeding from the preceding points of departure, in what follows, I explore the nature of mediated urban audience activities in terms of both their general multiplicity and simultaneous power-relatedness. In the next section, I begin by discussing what has been called a spatial turn in media studies. Apart from paying attention to people's spatially manifold relations with the media, studies that exemplify this spatial turn also take note (directly or indirectly) of the relevance of interdisciplinarity, which—as implicated in the introduction—can be considered as a prerequisite for the revitalisation of media audience research. Another stepping stone—which is especially fruitful for the theorisation of the power-relatedness of audience activities—is provided by the early 1990s media ethnography, most notably by the work of Roger Silverstone (see Silverstone, 2006; also Haddon, 2007). In the latter part of this section, I discuss and redefine, in the urban context, the notions of 'domestication' and 'double articulation' introduced to media studies by Silverstone and that were also dealt with by other ethnographically oriented researchers. Here, I follow Leslie Haddon's suggestion that 'domestication' can and should be extended "beyond its original base" and employed in the study of "life outside the home"; in this case, to the contemporary city, which I simultaneously conceive of as 'an object of study in its own right' (Haddon, 2003, p. 49; cf. Ridell, 2010; 2013). Through a rethinking of media ethnography's two central concepts, I formulate my own conceptualisation for the study of people's activities as audiences in contemporary cities and, more particularly, for critically reflecting on and analysing how mediated urban audience activities are involved in the dynamics of spatial power.

In the subsequent section, then, I develop the sensitising conceptualisation (cf. Blumer, 1969) of 'urban triple articulation', ensuing from my discussion on media ethnography. I do this with the aid of some examples from the more recent research literature that deals with the presence and uses of mass and personalised media in cities. In the section after that, I steer my discussion closer to the actual exploration of how people act as urban audiences by mapping potential topics for empirical research. I close the chapter by pointing to what I think presents one of the greatest theoretical–methodological and empirical challenges in terms of studying the power-relatedness of mediated urban audience activities.

TAKING OFF FROM DISCIPLINARY STEPPING STONES

The Blurring Spatial Contexts of Media Relations

During the past two decades, and particularly from the early 2000s onwards, one can detect certain scholarly developments in the field of media studies that relate and contribute, although often indirectly, to the study of audience activities in urban environments. We are talking about the entry of theories of spatiality in the mid-1990s, which have since gained a rather prominent position in the field—to the extent that some now consider it warranted to talk about a 'spatial turn' (see Couldry and McCarthy, 2004; Falkheimer and Jansson, 2006). Combining questions of media with issues of space has made the boundary line between media studies and human geography in particular increasingly fluid, inspiring cross-disciplinary discussion and collaboration (see e.g. Morley and Robins, 1995; Morley, 2000; Moores, 1993; 2000; 2006; 2012; Seamon, 2006).

One pertinent set of spatial questions, formulated as part of these discussions, concerns how the personalisation and mobilisation of networked ICTs have altered the notions of 'space' in general and 'home' as a space in particular. The concept of 'space' was seen to incorporate virtuality as one of its dimensions as well as covering the multilayered nature of the technologically mediated experience of different places (see e.g. Munt, 2001). As the Sussex Technology Group (2001) noticed in their early pilot study on people's perceptions of the mobile phone, place can mean many different yet interrelated things to users. It can be about "the public/private divide, it may mean a place inside or outside, a real place or an imagined place, a geographical space or a communication zone, or it may refer to mechanisms of creating space around oneself which criss-cross these divides" (Sussex Technology Group, 2001, p. 216). Over a decade later, one finds in the field a plethora of research that emphasises the 'hybrid' nature of space (see e.g. de Souza e Silva, 2006; de Waal, 2008; Gordon and de Souza e Silva, 2011; Mcquire, 2011). Smith (2013, p. 466), for one, describes the contemporary spatial complexity by pointing to how the digital cross-fertilises embodied environments and, conversely, how the physical social world acts as the reservoir of potentialities for virtual worlds.

In the case of 'home', portable media devices were seen to challenge the notion's socio-cultural attachment to a stable material location and the privacy created by the household's four walls. At the end of the 1950s, philosopher Hannah Arendt (1958, p. 71) located privacy emphatically in the home in this pre-digital sense by arguing that it offers "the only reliable hiding place from the common public world [. . .], from its very publicity, from being seen and being heard". With new media technologies, as John Sloop and Joshua Gunn (2010, p. 294) remind us more than fifty years later, the physical markers of "all things home" have eroded, and "the real *and* metaphorical governance of the door" has disappeared. We live in a world of doorless domesticity where your networked portable defines where your home is. More specifically, as Silverstone (2006, p. 242) points out, technological development has brought about a shift from the physical to the phenomenological in experiencing 'home'—a shift that emphasises the analytical separation of the home from the material stability of the 'household'. Today, 'home' refers to a sense of belonging and personally meaningful locatedness "that can be carried with you" as "a technological extension of the self, and one which means that you are never out of reach, never disconnected" (Silverstone, 2006, p. 242; cf. Owen and Imre, 2013). In this sense, the 'spatial turn' has already been followed by a 'mobilities turn' in media studies, too (see e.g. Sheller and Urry, 2006; Wiley and Packer, 2010). Yet it seems that both 'home' and 'household' remain indispensable. As Silverstone (2006, p. 243) formulates their persistence, "to be homeless is to be beyond reach", and if deprived of a material structure, our "lives would be impossible".

The dislocation of the household as the primary spatial node of media reception has meant, as David Morley (2006, p. 33) paraphrases Abercrombie and Longhurst's (1998, pp. 68–76) idea of 'dispersed audiences', that "we are all now, in effect, audiences to some kind of media almost everywhere and all of the time". Given the popularity of portable ICTs, it is necessary to add that we also constantly (are able to or are forced to) audience other people's media use and their related performances almost everywhere and all of the time. The ubiquitousness of audience activities, however, should not mislead us into thinking that people's relations with media could be reduced to acting as an audience or, reversely, that each and any media-related activity could be labelled as audience activity (cf. Ridell, 2012). In any case, to understand the mobile and networked multiplicity of contemporary audience activities, it is crucial that we take account of the technologically mediated nature of different spatial contexts in which people act as audiences, including the household and the city.

Regarding the household as a place for media audience activities, the space-binding and scale-adapting capacities of mass communication technologies were noted quite early on by cultural media scholars. Mass media, first the newspaper, but most notably broadcast radio and television, have long been discussed as intermediaries between the private space of the household and the public sphere of social life. In the European context, public broadcasting is seen to have played a central part in synchronising the domestic rhythms and routines with collective national rituals (see e.g. Cardiff and Scannell, 1987; Scannell, 1989; 1996; Morley 1994; 1996). It is noteworthy here that also in the early 1990s' ethnographically oriented research, these mass media–framed views of the (inter)mediating specificity of media technologies shaped the way in which the key concepts of 'domestication' and 'double articulation' were defined.

Domestication and Double Articulation beyond the Household

In his review of "the life of a concept", Silverstone (2006, p. 231) describes that, originally, the notion of domestication "was an attempt to grasp the nettle of socio-technical change where it could be seen to be both mattering most and where it was almost entirely taken for granted: in the intimate spaces of the home and the household". In a more general sense, the concept was meant to link the objects and forces beyond people's immediate control to the consistencies of their daily existence. Having obvious resonance with Anthony Giddens's (1984) theory of structuration, 'domestication' refers to a process through which human beings define the stability of their everyday lives and attempt in this way to sustain their ontological security in the world (Silverstone, 2006, p. 231, p. 233). At the core of 'domestication' thus is, in Silverstone's (2006, p. 232) words, its reference to "practice. It involves human agency". From these more general and partly rather sociological starting points, the early domestication studies then focused on the accommodation of ICTs in the daily life of households. Indeed, in spatial terms, domestication was literally seen "as a process of bringing things home" (Silverstone, 2006, p. 233; see also Haddon, 2006, p. 118). At the same time, the households' connections with the surrounding social world were considered as crucial. This meant, both spatially and socially, that the process of domestication was seen to always involve the crossing of boundaries and of constant boundary renegotiation: "above all those between the public and the private, and between proximity and distance" (Silverstone, 2006, p. 233).[1]

All in all, then, and despite its actual focus on the household, the notion of domestication is helpful in understanding how people in today's spatially hybrid cities, too, attempt to secure the sensibility of their everyday existence through 'domestication', that is through the creation of consistencies around their usage of media and technologies. In the contemporary urban context, however, it makes more sense to talk about this process in terms of habit formation or routinisation rather than of domestication. Here, in fact, the early 1980s' ethnographically inclined research that paid attention to the routines of media use in the household is still relevant (see e.g. Bausinger, 1984). This strand of research preceded domestication studies and paved the way for them (cf. Hartmann, 2006, p. 98).

Within the domestication frame, 'double articulation' offered a notion for getting to grips with "the dynamics of the distinctive appropriation of information and communication technologies and media technologies, as both material and symbolic objects and as content, into domestic space" (Silverstone, 2006, p. 239). What was seen as specific to these technologies was that while being incorporated into "the fabric of everyday life" of households, they "brought, through the communications they enabled, a range of content-based claims", and this was "their second articulation" (Silverstone, 2006, p. 239). In the early media ethnographic view, precisely this extra dimension of bridging the public and private spaces through communicative contents differentiates media from other technologies. The first articulation, in turn, referred to the materiality of technological objects, but as Silverstone (2006, p. 234) is quick to add, machines come to the household not only in packages but packaged with "dreams and fantasies, hopes and anxieties". In other words, as material objects ICTs and media are always imbued with symbolic meanings and therefore can be conceived of as 'cultural texts' in themselves. This characteristic of media technologies as simultaneously physical and semiotic objects is taken up by Morley (2006, p. 28) in relation to mass media, when he states that television provides a flow of images for us to "look through", being simultaneously "a totemic object of enormous symbolic importance in the household" (see also Morley, 1995).

Interestingly, Silverstone (2006, p. 240) points to the possibility of a third dimension in the way ICTs and media technologies articulate—even though he says to be "nervous about such a proliferation". According to him, if there is to be a third articulation, "it lies in the activities of the household itself" (Silverstone, 2006, p. 240). To summarise Silverstone's (hesitant) view in his 2006 review, the triple articulation of media consists of the media technological objects (first articulation), the conveyed contents or messages that (inter)mediate public and private spheres (second articulation) and the activities of the household as the microcosmic communicative location at the interface with technology (third articulation). Maren Hartmann, for one, is more confident in making, somewhat differently from Silverstone, a case for the media as triply articulated. She suggests that the present-day digital and mobile context has made it necessary to consider three dimensions of media: the technological objects, the symbolic environments to which the technologies give access and the single texts/messages they convey (Hartmann, 2006, pp. 96–97; see also Courtois, Verdegem and Lieven, 2012).

What catches one's attention in both Silverstone's and Hartmann's definition of the triple articulation of media is that they leave the level of the first articulation curiously obscure. Even if Silverstone does not explicitly formulate this, it becomes apparent in his discussion that as technological objects, media contain, in actual practice, two articulating aspects rather than one: the objects' material affordances, on one hand, and their characteristics as culturally meaningful 'texts', on the other hand. Hartmann, for her part, states that technology itself comes with certain affordances with which she refers to "pre-given limitations or directions—the technology suggests certain ways of how it should be used, what it is for and so on" (Hartmann, 2006, p. 84). However, similarly to Silverstone, she does not really pay attention to the material aspect of the object-level articulation but conflates it with the technological object's semiotic nature. My contention is that this conflation presents a problem for a sensitive exploration of people's relations with media and technologies more generally and for an analysis of their mediated urban audience activities more particularly.

For the purposes of theorising and studying how people act as audiences in contemporary cities, then, I find it necessary to formulate a notion of triple articulation that encapsulates the articulating aspects of media differently from the early media ethnographic view and that also places equal emphasis on all three aspects. My suggestion here is that it is fruitful to approach the triple articulation of media as consisting of analytically distinct yet inextricably intertwined dimensions as follows: media technologies as material objects with specific affordances (first articulation), media technologies as semiotic objects or 'texts' (second articulation) and media technologies as conveyors of meaningful messages (third articulation). It should be stressed that in this definition the (inter)mediating capacity of media is not confined to only one level but is seen to operate along all of the analytic dimensions of the triple articulation as well as at their interfaces.

As it is, the more recent research both on the presence of mass media in out-of-home environments and on the urban uses of personalised mobile media is helpful in illustrating the pervasively mediat(is)ed city as a spatial context for audience activities—simultaneously assisting in getting a grasp on the city itself as a triply articulated medium (see Ridell, 2010; 2013; cf. Bakardjieva, 2011, p. 76–77). Be the focus on mass media or on personalised media, these studies usefully illuminate the technology-mediated and media-saturated nature of urban environments. In addition, they deal with how people's (mass-)mediated activities in the cities are entangled with spatial power relations. In the following section, I discuss some of these studies in more detail in order to navigate the suggested formulation of triple articulation of media towards a framework for the study of mediated urban audience activities and their power-relatedness.

MEDIATED AUDIENCE ACTIVITIES IN THE TRIPLY ARTICULATED URBAN SPACE

One fruitful example is Anna McCarthy's (2001) study of the pervasive presence of television monitors and other display screens in public and semi-public urban settings, such as bars, waiting rooms, stores and airports. For McCarthy (2001, p. 14), television, as a piece of non-domestic furniture, has dialectical qualities "as an object in space and as a relationship between spaces". It is at once a connective and symbolically meaningful material object and a source of discursive meanings: both the technical device and the televisual representation are needed to bring together the local 'here' and the distant 'there' in one communicative instance. An important dimension in television's ability to create a synchronous link between physically remote locales is that its place-linking and scale-adapting dynamics are embedded in the relations of economic, social and cultural power. As a medium, television accommodates the macro level forces that define the contents circulated on individual TV screens into the routines of daily domestic and non-domestic spaces (McCarthy, 2001, p. 15).

From an audience studies perspective, it is noteworthy that McCarthy approaches the role of television in out-of-home settings in terms of (anticipated) reception and its power-relatedness. There is a critical rhetorical tendency in her conceiving of audiovisually mediating objects as having a strategic role to play in the construction of urban environments. The messages offered on media platforms, for their part, are seen to contribute to and strengthen the one-way, predominantly commercially framed mode of address that epitomises urban spatial rhetoric. For example McCarthy remarks that the positioning of television monitors in urban spaces is carefully planned in order to standardise certain patterns of perception for users who pass through those locations. Similarly, the commercial practices that guide the production of images circulating on the screens work to "commodify the spectator's position in space for sale to advertisers" (McCarthy, 2001, pp. 11–12).

It is pertinent to notice in this connection that the mass media dominated urban rhetoric is not 'readable' in any simple sense, but is strongly embodied and sensational. McCarthy (2001, p. 93) points to the ongoing corporate strategies of interweaving "television with the habits and protocols of particular places", which makes dwelling in and passing through these locales "an imperceptibly sponsored experience" (McCarthy, 2001, p. 103). Or as urban sociologist Anne Cronin (2006a, p. 627) points out, "advertising attempts to target and inhabit everyday commuting routes and become part of the fabric of people's urban experience". Arguably, in the wake of location-aware networked portables, the attempts at the commercial control of people's dwelling within and moving about in urban places have become ever more sophisticated and intense (see e.g. Farman, 2012, p. 61). At the same time, audiovisual mass media platforms have become organically connected to the globally reaching technological machinery that produces and displays the moving images and augments the presence of mass-media representations in the urban spatial texture. Likewise, the buildings of media houses, which furnish the urban stage as site-specific architectural elements, are integrated into a global techno-network like fungi with their rhizomes.

With regard to how the proliferation of portable media devices has transformed the nature of cities, one of their most palpable effects has been on the overall urban rhetoric. As Zlatan Krajina (2009, pp. 410, 415) points out, in contemporary urban environments, the hailing by broadcasting and commercial display screens and panels is mixed with distractions coming from people's use of personalised media. Similarly, practices of mass media audiencehood are now interwoven with acting as an audience to other people's publicly perceivable interactions and presentations of self. Although both have been part of street life from early on (see e.g. Sennett, 1974), mobile media have made communication in the urban context more theatrical thereby affecting how people both perform to and audience with each other.

One way to describe the spatial effects of portable media in contemporary cities is to say that these devices have added an extra layer to the urban space: through them people may connect to and visit places 'elsewhere' while being present in the physical city. Indeed, along with networked mobile technologies, the city has become a multilayered spatial configuration and people keep shifting back and forth, not only between the spatial layers, but between different spatial scales (Ridell, 2010; cf. Mitchell, 2005, pp. 15–18). Both the reception of mass media and the diverse uses of portable personalised media are involved in this navigation, and the latter affords a multiplicity of 'virtual' audience activities in the process. At the same time, our acting as audiences in the spatially hybrid cities not only is itself diverse, but it also interweaves with many other technology and media-related urban activities. For example while sitting on a park bench with a laptop or an iPad, we may be moving swiftly back and forth between the offline and online positions of a spectating audience to acting as a community member, a player or a member of the public online.

Overall, the proliferation of networked and location-aware portables combined with the general digitalisation has turned cities themselves into multidimensional media environments where people are simultaneously present—and act as audiences—in many different, often overlapping, spaces and social situations. In addition, through these multi-spatial activities, people not only take an active role in the production of urban phenomenality but are also involved in and contribute to the (re)production of urban infrastructures.

In the field of communication and media studies, even spatially sensitive scholars have so far largely ignored the increasingly technology-mediated constitution of urban space. This is unfortunate, as the code-based material structures play an ever-more central role both in imperceptibly conditioning the symbolic dimension of cities and in shaping how people share physical public spaces and communicate in them. One can even argue that it has become impossible to understand the nature of urban space separately from technological networks and vice versa because their linkages are so intimate and recombinatory, as geographers Steve Graham and Simon Marvin (2001, p. 216) pointed out more than ten years ago (see also Cuff, 2003; Crang and Graham, 2007; Kitchin and Dodge, 2011).

Even less attention in the field has been paid to how people, by using their smart portables, have acquired an active role in urban spatial production in infrastructural terms. Indeed, along with digitalisation, city dwellers are now almost literally a part of the urban infrastructure, which moves with them when they travel in their cars, when they use their mobile media devices and walk along the streets with RFID-tagged[2] consumer products in their bags and pockets (see Hayles, 2006). People's participation, however, is rarely conscious or self-reflexive. The accommodation of new technologies as part of daily urban activities rather happens without much thinking. This, then, is a process that some critical spatial scholars have approached in terms of non-representation. By this notion, they refer to the mutely performative digital-material logic of the 'mechanosphere' of the city that makes things happen in the visible realm of the urban front stage; that is, at the level of urban representation (Thrift and French, 2002; also van Kranenburg, 2008).

It is pertinent to note in this connection that both the transformation of existing urban audience activities and the development of novel forms of these activities most intriguingly actualise at the interfaces between the invisible technostructure and the representation-filled physical cityscape. This, in turn, draws attention to the aspect of presentation, because it is both the presentational objects (such as mass media platforms) and people's presentational acts—their displaying and performative bodily gestures and the use of media as part of them—that make things 'appear' in the urban space and enable them to be publicly shared. Indeed, through the presentational aspect, as a metaphorical membrane between the non-representational and the representational, the symbolically meaningful dimension of urban space gains its visible existence in the first place.

At this point—by way of a provisional summary of what has been discussed so far—it can be suggested that the triplet of non-representation—presentation—representation in the contemporary urban context can be fruitfully combined with the view of media as triply articulated. We can talk about 'urban triple articulation', which is based on the view of the city as a highly mediat(is)ed spatial context—indeed, as a medium in itself. The notion of urban triple articulation, then, not only enables the sensitive exploration of mediated urban audience activities in all their multiple specificities but also the examination of the complex power-relatedness of these activities. In both respects, the notion wishes to sensitise us simultaneously to the levels of non-representation, presentation and representation and, importantly, to direct our attention to their interfaces. One set of power-related questions concerning audience activities in the triply articulated cities concerns—as exemplified indirectly by McCarthy (2001) and Cronin (2006a; 2006b)—people's reception of the persuasive strategies of mass media, understood as non-representationally embedded presentational objects that furnish urban space and simultaneously put meaningful representations on public display.

In the following section, I move closer to the actual research on mediated urban audience activities and their power-relatedness by pointing to potential topics for empirical study in the previous research literature. In the first part of the section, my mapping revolves around the interfaces between the representational and presentational dimensions of urban triple articulation, making visible the reciprocity of public appearance and forms of audience activity at these interfaces. In the latter part, I take up very briefly how the habituation of mediated urban audience activities contributes to the dynamic of power that has been called posthegemonic or posthuman. Here we have a problematic that requires us to focus our attention on the interfaces between the non-representational and presentational aspects of urban triple articulation.

MAPPING TOPICS OF RESEARCH FOR URBAN AUDIENCE STUDIES

The Representation–Presentation Interface

Day-to-day audience activities in contemporary cities can be characterised not only as predominantly captive but also as thoroughly (mass-)mediated, because people in urban settings are ceaselessly bombarded with advertising and other mass media signage. At the same time, portable digital technologies have provided commercial actors with tempting new possibilities to ambush city dwellers with smart marketing via their portable media devices. Paradoxically, though, these gadgets also make it possible for people to escape from the position of forced mass media audience by stepping into a more self-fashioned mobile audience position by using headphones, for example (see Bull, 2004). Hence, the ways in which people cope with mass media saturation in present-day urban milieus and the tactics that many develop to avoid it are an obvious case for urban audience studies.

Large electronic screens that appeared in the cityscape in the late 1990s have been central to the saturation of the contemporary urban environment with audiovisual mass media. In the context of geographical discussions on the media, Clayton Rosati (2007, p. 1003) goes so far as to refer to cities themselves as "massive public video screens". Indeed, the public screen as a metaphor for urban rhetoric epitomises the characteristics of the city itself as a mass medium in that the screen draws our attention as an audience without reciprocating (Gitlin, 2001, pp. 20–11).

According to Scott Mcquire (2008, pp. 130–131), the presence of large display screens in the urban 'mediatecture' together with mobile devices have been crucial in that today, "media consumption is increasingly occurring in public space". In Mcquire's (2008, pp. 131–132) view, this has made it necessary to re-examine the interplay between media and public space. And obviously, technological developments have reframed the whole set of spatial questions that concern the role of mass media in drawing the boundaries between private and public. While television at the beginning of the 1990s was seen, as summarised by Shaun Moores (2000, p. 96), to connect domestic units with public worlds, to enable the meeting of global and local in the living room and to make it possible to go to places via electronically transmitted sounds and images without actually leaving home, now the broadcast media have migrated to the streets. At the same time, it has grown increasingly difficult to delineate the specific position of mass media as signifying objects amidst the overwhelming audiovisuality of urban space. In effect, McCarthy (2001, p. 13) stresses that "when we search for TV in public places, we find a tense, ambient clutter of public audiovisual apparatuses". This, of course, presents a challenge for the empirical study of urban television viewing.[3]

Nevertheless, the importance of urban mass media audiencehood—and the need for its critically informed study—has not diminished, quite the contrary. Whereas screens have become ambient and mobile, appearing in all sizes and hailing people on the move in each and every locale from the tiny TV monitor in the corner of a local pub to laptop and iPad screens viewed on trains, all the way to huge video screens and digitally animated façades of buildings in city squares, the space-binding and scale-adapting dynamics of mass media machinery have grown to be equally globally flexible and centralised. As Mimi Sheller and John Urry (2003, p. 120) emphasise, the power to choose and shape what is displayed on these screens remains "a significant issue of political contestation".

Apart from furnishing public and semi-public spaces in the physical city, large electronic screens have become central elements in festive audience activities, such as attending live sports events and mega-concerts, adding to the intense atmosphere at the events. During these urban spectacles, viewers can follow not only what is happening on the stage, but they can also witness live projections of themselves watching the ongoing performance on huge multi-screens. The public showing of the audience to 'itself' is an essential part of spectacular outdoor audience activities and presumably intensifies the sense of engagement and collective belonging (cf. de la Garde, 2010, p. 197; also Kolamo and Vuolteenaho, 2013). Such instances of mass-mediated urban audiencehood provide a fascinating topic for empirical research.

An additional aspect and an issue for detailed analysis is the by now well-established use of portable media devices as a part of on-site public spectating, such as verifying and documenting one's participation in live events via camera phones. Moreover, the multimedia features of mobile phones allow the participants to step momentarily into the role of producer and publisher. They can send MMS snapshots to absent friends or upload images on their Facebook page or elsewhere on the web. In this way, they not only instantly share the high moments of live urban audiencing with their close and semi-close circles but also circulate public representations to be audienced by those who are not physically present. Obviously, in the virtual space of the internet these images may then reach people that the individual 'publisher' or circulator did not even imagine being part of his or her audience (see boyd, 2008).

It would be an interesting case for empirical audience research to explore how live collective spectatorship has evolved and in what ways networked portable devices are now embedded in its practices. At the same time, the use of the mobile phone's camera function has become a common activity in daily city life, and many users share these snapshots on the web, too. A fascinating feature of this more mundane photo-taking and online publishing is that the people who engage in these activities are acutely aware of having an audience and tune themselves towards pleasing it. As Dong-Hoo Lee (2009, p. 168) puts it, the uploading of camera phone photos to the web is "a part of the self-presentation process that tries to meet the audience's expectations".

With regard to technologically mediated interpersonal communication in the city, one interesting question for audience research is whether and to what extent people who use portable devices understand those in close physical proximity to be their audience and perhaps even intentionally perform or show off to them (see Drotner, 2005, pp. 196–198). It is also possible to formulate a related theoretical question and ask how the uses of mobile devices for interpersonal communication—with the (inter)related activities of performing and audiencing—mould the city as a spatial constellation and thereby affect its overall rhetoric. A more specific issue in this connection concerns the nature of the urban environment as a public space in its dual sense of visibility and collectivity (Arendt, 1958, chap. 2).

One way to start approaching these issues is through recent research on the use of portable media, especially the increasingly multifunctional mobile phones, in the city. Many of these studies report that mobile technologies construct individualised space capsules within which users socialise with remote but already familiar people and groups. Indeed, these personal space bubbles appear to be surrounded by invisible barricades that shield those inside from encounters with unknown others (see e.g. Harris, 2003; Kopomaa, 2004; Humpreys, 2005; Forlano, 2008; Hampton and Gupta, 2008; Ito, Okabe and Anderson, 2009). This phenomenon has been variably called 'public privacy' (Bull, 2004), 'portable public privacy' (Gumpert and Drucker, 2007) or 'public privatism' (Hampton and Gupta, 2008). These notions echo the term 'mobile privatization' coined by Raymond Williams (1974) in his study on television as a technology and cultural form. At the same time, the meanings of these more recent terms reflect the developments in the past four decades both in media technology and, concomitantly, in understanding the media-related spatial boundaries between the private and the public.

Based on the preceding studies, it seems that despite the ubiquitousness of (inter)personal uses of mobile media, the changes in the overall spatial rhetoric of the city have not been too dramatic in that the inward-directed 'telecocoons' coexist in their separation on the mass media dominated urban front stage. However, and pertinently to audience research, people in their apparently self-enclosed space bubbles are visible and audible to those physically around them—also rendering strangers as audiences to sometimes intimate self-disclosures. A related dimension in the use of portable devices for social interaction concerns the simultaneous diversity of modes of action and the multiplicity of audience positions within it. For example in a mobile phone conversation, the user not only appears, and potentially performs, to those around in the physical urban space, but he or she shifts back and forth from producing and circulating meaningful contents and responses to the person at the other end, to audiencing what that other person is saying. For young people in particular, Kirsten Drotner (2005, p. 198) remarks, the awareness of and interplay with the presence of both a physical and virtual audience can be a great source of fun.

Finally, one specific area for urban audience studies at the interface between the representational and the presentational would be to explore the reception of such subversive activities that deliberately challenge the strategies of the spatially powerful. These kinds of activities include countering the consumerist urban rhetoric through interventionist art projects and certain forms of pervasive gaming. There is, as yet, hardly any research on how people receive these subversive campaigns in the audience position and whether these activities are able to disrupt the embodied rhythms of mass media audiencehood or break the bubbles of (inter)personal media use.

Especially fascinating cases of spatial activism from the perspective of audience studies—and ones that start to steer our attention towards the interface between the non-representational and the presentational in contemporary cities—are those that attempt to make the presence of the imperceptible urban infrastructure visible to others and thereby bring it under critical scrutiny. One example is sousveillance, which seeks to uncover the disappearance of digital technologies into the fabric of buildings, objects and bodies and make their top-down surveilling role known to other people by means of photographing, videotaping or evoking counter-performances (see e.g. Mann, Nolan and Wellman, 2003). Urban internet crackers, for their part, are street-level activists who track points of corporate wireless broadband access and mark these hotspots of hidden digital infrastructure not only to be recognised by others but also to be more openly used (Graham, 2004, p. 16).

These forms of mediated urban activism clearly politicise the established urban spatial order and thereby challenge the position of the mass media audience, provoking other city dwellers to step instead into the role of a public. Equally important, these activist activities begin to formulate and voice questions of the complicity of urbanites themselves in the 'automatic production of urban space' (Thrift and French, 2002) through their technology-mediated and media-related interactions and audience activities.

The Non-Representation–Presentation Interface

As discussed in the previous subsection, the uses of networked and location-aware portables have been integrated as parts of mediated urban audience activities in multiple, diverse ways. The general diversity and heterogeneity of these activities, however, does not exclude the fact that they tend to take standardised forms. The enthusiastic on-the-spot football fans, for example, in their showy outfits and spectacularised performances, follow a rather strictly scripted pattern of celebratory sports audience behaviour, which at the same time stretches the public presentation of urban audiencehood to an extreme and expands it to discursive and virtual spheres (see Kolamo and Vuolteenaho, 2013). Likewise, the more mundane and frequent varieties of mediated urban audience activities are based on and rehearse often taken-for-granted codes of conduct and situational rules. Similar to urban fan activities, these activities, too, shape and are shaped by internalised norms of street life.

In terms of urban spatial power, the stabilisations of both spectacular and mundane audience activities into repetitive patterns are interesting and important, because both play a role in supporting the infrastructures of social life in cities. Regarding the dynamics of power that are seen to be characteristic of our digitalised condition, however, it is the general accommodation of smart portables as taken-for-granted parts of people's everyday activities and interactions in urban environments that is particularly pertinent. The habits formed around the uses of these devices have come to sustain the ordinariness—and thereby the ontological security—of public life in contemporary cities. A significant feature of these processes of habituation is that along with them, the operation of computer code becomes a self-evidently affording background for urban (co)existence, conditioning silently and beyond conscious recognition how urbanites (inter)act. It is precisely this sinking of software into our collective 'technological unconscious' (Thrift and French, 2002) that is seen to turn the dynamics of power posthuman or posthegemonic (see e.g. Hayles, 2006; 2009; Gane, Venn and Hand, 2007; Lash 2007; Beer 2009).

According to the latter views, power is most effectively enacted through the repetitions of activities that stabilise certain technology-mediated and media-related gestures and acts as parts of self-evident urban routines. From this perspective, power-related habituation that takes place at the bodily level can be argued to be more fundamental and acute than is the reception of urban representations, however thoroughly ideological their intended meanings are and however automated the actual meaning making is. The importance of the processes of routine formation more generally lies in the fact that once fully formed and established mediated urban routines function—as routines typically do—as institutions of social life; that is they appear to us and are lived by us as immutable and given (Gieryn, 2002; cf. Ridell, 2005). The taken-for-grantedness of these routines, in turn, further cements the structures of power that initially took form through negotiations and the stifling of potential struggle.

It is beyond the scope of this chapter to delve into any detail as to how, then, to study mediated audience activities and their power-relatedness and, more particularly, how to do this at the interface between the urban non-representational and presentational. In any case, as outlined earlier, a first step would be to direct attention to the pattern-forming aspects of embodied urban audience activities.

CONCLUDING REMARKS

I close my discussion by suggesting that precisely the issue of mediated urban audience routines presents one of the most demanding theoretical and, subsequently, empirical challenges for future media audience studies. Obviously, the notions of 'domestication' and 'triple articulation', in the sense in which these notions were defined in the early British media ethnographic work, are not potent and precise enough analytical tools for tackling this problematic and, even less, for cracking open the 'black box' of these routines. Regarding 'domestication', a fundamental reason for the inadequacy is that in the attempt to capture the technological change, the purpose of the notion was, as Silverstone (2006, p. 235) stresses, "to instate the human at its centre". Yet, in the contemporary pervasively digitalised condition, a resolutely human-centric point of departure effectively hinders us from recognising and critically reflecting on the elusive dynamic of power that works beyond representation—a dynamic that actualises not only in the mutely performative logic of the urban 'mechanosphere' but also equally in the technology-mediated corporeal urban repetitions, that is in the bodily rhythms and routines of people's presentational acts and interactions in the contemporary mediat(is)ed cities.

With regard to 'triple articulation', in the sense Silverstone and Hartmann defined it on the basis of the 'double articulation' of media, the problem with the notion is that it leaves the level of first articulation not only analytically unclear but quite undeveloped. The neglect relating to the material affordances of media technologies seems to be rooted in the emphatic human-centredness of early domestication studies. As it is, from this anthropocentric starting point, it appears crucial, first and foremost, to reject the putative threat of 'technological determinism' (see Silverstone 2006, p. 230). This rejection, however, is a double-edged sword, because it easily leads to ignoring the technological specificity and related affordances of different media. This, I contend, is what happens in both Silverstone's and Hartmann's definition of triple articulation. To word the problem differently, in restricting 'significance' on the level of the symbolic, their definitions exclude the possibility of being able to ask, 'How does the (invisible and visible) materiality of media articulate?' And this is a question that needs to be posed as a matter of urgency if we want to grasp and investigate how and to what extent mediated urban audience routines are integral to the dynamics of power that are enacted through our daily activities. Moreover, given the pervasive software sustenance and moving reproduction of urban infrastructures, an acute issue that rises to the fore concerns the first-level articulation and the related affordances of the city as a medium in itself.

I hope that the notion of the urban triple articulation outlined in this chapter will be helpful in addressing the conditions and power-relatedness of people's mediated urban audience activities in an age when it has become untenable to separate the technologies created by humans from the question of 'What is human?' in the first place.

NOTES

1. See Silverstone and Haddon (1996) for a discussion on domestication in the context of contemporary capitalism and the stimulation of consumption by design. For a review of empirical domestication research projects, see Haddon (2006).
2. RFID = *r*adio *f*requency *id*entification.
3. I want to stress here that the omnipresence of display screens and moving images in the present-day cityscape does not mean that printed words for example are no longer important regarding how the phenomenality of the urban environment is constituted and experienced (see e.g. Henkin, 1998; for a critique of the one-sided emphasis on audiovisual elements in Mcquire's

definition of the 'media city', see Chikamori, 2009). Likewise, the sounds of the city create a scape of their own to be experienced individually and shared collectively in specific ways. In addition, the significance of such site-specific objects as buildings, statues and monuments in the urban spatial fabric cannot be underestimated.

REFERENCES

Abercrombie, N. and Longhurst, B., 1998. *Audiences. A sociological theory of performance and imagination.* London: Sage.

Anderson, B., 2009. Non-representational theory. In: R.J. Johnston, D. Gregory, G. Pratt and M. Watts, eds. 2009. *The dictionary of human geography.* 5th ed. Oxford: Blackwell. pp. 503–505.

Arendt, H., 1958. *The human condition.* Chicago: University of Chicago Press.

Bakardjieva, M., 2011. Reconfiguring the mediapolis. New media and civic agency. *New Media & Society* 14(1), pp. 63–79.

Bausinger, H., 1984. Media, technology and daily life. *Media, Culture & Society* 6(4), pp. 343–351.

Beer, D., 2009. Power through the algorithm? Participatory web cultures and the technological unconscious. *New Media & Society* 11(6), pp. 985–1002.

Blumer, H., 1969. *Symbolic interactionism. Perspective and method.* Berkeley: University of California Press.

boyd, d., 2008. Why youth social network sites: the role of networked publics in teenage social life. In: D. Buckingham, ed. 2008. *Youth, identity, and digital media.* Cambridge: MIT Press. pp. 119–142.

Brown, B., Green, N. and Harper, R. eds., 2001. *Wireless world: social and interactional aspects of the mobile age.* London: Springer.

Bull, M., 2004. To each their own bubble. Mobile spaces of sound in the city. In: N. Couldry and A. McCarthy, eds. 2004. *Mediaspace. Place, scale and culture in a media age.* London & New York: Routledge. pp. 275–293.

Cadman, L., 2009. Non-representational theory/non-representational geographies. In: R. Kitchin and N. Thrift, eds. 2009. *International encyclopedia of human geography.* Vol. 7. London: Elsevier. pp. 456–463.

Cardiff, D. and Scannell, P., 1987. Broadcasting and national unity. In: J. Curran, A. Smith and P. Wingate P, eds. 1987. *Impacts and influences. Essays on media power in the twentieth century.* London and New York: Methuen. pp. 157–173.

Chikamori, T., 2009. Between the 'media city' and the 'city as a medium'. *Theory, Culture & Society* 26(4), pp. 147–154.

Couldry, N., 2011. The necessary future of the audience ... and how to research it. In: V. Nightingale, ed. 2011. *The handbook of media audiences.* West Sussex: Wiley-Blackwell. pp. 213–229.

Couldry, N. and McCarthy, A. eds., 2004. *MediaSpace. Place, scale and culture in a media age.* London and New York: Routledge.

Courtois, C., Verdegem, P. and Lieven, D.M., 2012. The triple articulation of media technologies in audiovisual media consumption. *Television & New Media* 20(10), pp. 1–19.

Crang, M. and Graham, S., 2007. Sentient cities. Ambient intelligence and the politics of urban space. *Information, Communication & Society* 10(6), pp. 789–817.

Cronin, A., 2006a. Advertising and the metabolism of the city: urban space, commodity rhythms. *Environment and Planning D: Society and Space* 24(4), pp. 615–632.

Cronin, A., 2006b. *Urban space and entrepreneurial property relations: resistance and the vernacular of outdoor advertising and graffiti* [online]. Lancaster: Department

of Sociology, Lancaster University. Available at: <http://www.lancs.ac.uk/fass/sociology/papers/cronin-advertisingandgraffiti.pdf>.
Cuff, D., 2003. Immanent domain. Pervasive computing and the public realm. *Journal of Architectural Education* 57(1), pp. 43–49.
de la Garde, R., 2010. The public manifestations of audience. *Matrizes* 4(1), pp. 193–202.
de Souza e Silva, A., 2006. Interfaces of hybrid spaces. In: A. P. Kavoori and N. Arceneaux, eds. 2006. *The cell phone reader: essays in social transformation*. New York: Peter Lang. pp. 19–44.
de Waal, M.C., 2008. From BLVD urbanism to MSN urbanism: locative media and urban culture. In: F. Eckardt, J. Geelhaar, L. Colini, K. S. Willis, K. Chorianopoulos and R. Hennig, eds. 2008. *Mediacity. Situations, practices and encounters*. Berlin: Frank & Timme. pp. 383–406.
Drotner, K., 2005. Media on the move: personalised media and the transformation of publicness. In: S. Livingstone, ed. 2005. *Audiences and publics*. Bristol: Intellect. pp. 187–211
Falkheimer, J. and Jansson, A. eds., 2006. *Geographies of communication. The spatial turn in media studies*. Göteborg: Nordicom.
Farman, J., 2012. *Mobile interface theory: embodied space and locative media*. London: Routledge.
Fiske, J., 1994. Audiencing: cultural practice and cultural studies. In: N. Denzin and Y. Lincoln, eds. 1994. *Handbook of qualitative research*. Thousand Oaks: Sage. pp. 189–198.
Fiske, J. and Dawson, R., 1996. Audiencing violence. Watching homeless men watch *Die Hard*. In: J. Hay, L. Grossberg and E. Wartella, eds. 1996. *The audience and its landscape*. Boulder: Westview Press. pp. 297–316.
Forlano, L., 2008. Anytime? Anywhere? Reframing debates around municipal wireless networking. *The Journal of Community Informatics* [e-journal] 4(1). Available at: <http://ci-journal.net/index.php/ciej/article/view/438/401>.
Gane, N., 2006. Posthuman. *Theory, Culture & Society* 23(2–3), pp. 431–434.
Gane, N., Venn, C. and Hand, M., 2007. Ubiquitous surveillance. Interview with Katherine Hayles. *Theory, Culture & Society* 24(7–8), pp. 349–358.
Giddens, A., 1984. *The constitution of society. Outline of the theory of structuration*. Cambridge: Polity Press.
Gieryn, T. F., 2002. What buildings do. *Theory and Society* 31(1), pp. 35–74.
Gitlin, T., 2001. *Media unlimited: how the torrent of images and sounds overwhelms our lives*. New York: Metropolitan Books.
Goffman, E., 1963. *Behavior in public places*. New York: The Free Press.
Goffman, E., 1974. *Frame analysis*. Boston: Northeastern University Press.
Goggin, G., 2011. Going mobile. In: V. Nightingale, ed. 2011. *The handbook of media audiences*. West Sussex: Wiley-Blackwell. pp. 128–146
Gordon, E. and de Souza e Silva, A., 2011. *Net locality: why location matters in a networked world*. West Sussex: Wiley-Blackwell.
Graham, S., 2004. Introduction: from dreams of transcendence to the remediation of urban life. In: S. Graham, ed. 2004. *The cybercities reader*. London: Routledge. pp. 3–29.
Graham, S. and Marvin, S., 2001. *Splintering urbanism: networked infrastructures, technological mobilities, and the urban condition*. New York: Routledge.
Gumpert, G. and Drucker, S., 2007. Mobile communication in the 21st century or 'everybody, everywhere, at any time'. In: S. Kleinman, ed. 2007. *Displacing place*. New York: Peter Lang. pp. 7–20.
Haddon, L., 2003. Domestication and mobile telephony. In: J. E. Katz, ed. 2003. *Machines that become us. The social context of personal communication technology*. New Brunswick and London: Transaction Publishers. pp. 43–55.

Haddon, L., 2006. Empirical studies using the domestication framework. In: T. Berker, M. Hartmann, Y. Punie and K.J. Ward, eds. 2006. *Domestication of media and technology.* Maidenhead: Open University Press. pp. 103–122.

Haddon, L., 2007. Roger Silverstone's legacies: domestication. *New Media & Society* 9(1), pp. 25–32.

Hampton, K. and Gupta, N., 2008. Community and social interaction in the wireless city: Wi-Fi use in public and semi-public spaces. *New Media & Society* 10(6), pp. 831–850.

Harris, K., 2003. Keep your distance: remote connection. *Journal of Community Work and Development* 4(4), pp. 6–28.

Hartmann, M., 2006. The triple articulation of ICTs. Media as technological objects, symbolic environments and individual texts. In: T. Berker, M. Hartmann, Y. Punie and K.J. Ward, eds. 2006. *Domestication of media and technology.* Maidenhead: Open University Press. pp. 80–102

Hayles, K., 2006. Unfinished work. From cyborg to cognisphere. *Theory, Culture & Society* 23(7–8), pp. 159–166.

Hayles, K., 2009. RFID: human agency and meaning in information-intensive environments. *Theory, Culture & Society* 26(2–3), pp. 47–72.

Henkin, D., 1998. *City reading. Written words and publics spaces in antebellum New York.* New York: Columbia University Press.

Humpreys, L., 2005. Cellphones in public: social interactions in a wireless era. *New Media & Society* 7(6), pp. 810–833.

Ito, M., Okabe, D. and Anderson, K., 2009. Portable objects in three global cities'. In: R. Ling and S. Campbell, eds. 2009. *The reconstruction of space and time: mobile communication practices.* New Brunswick: Transaction Publishers. pp. 67–87.

Katz, J.E. and Aakhus, M. eds., 2002. *Perpetual contact. Mobile communication, private talk, public performance.* Cambridge: Cambridge University Press.

Kitchin, R. and Dodge, M., 2011. *Code/space. Software and everyday life.* Cambridge, MA, and London: The MIT Press.

Kolamo, S. and Vuolteenaho, J., 2013. The interplay of mediascapes and cityscapes in a sports mega-event. The power dynamics of place branding in the FIFA World Cup. 2010 in South Africa. *The International Communication Gazette* 75(5–6), pp. 502–522.

Kopomaa, T., 2004. Speaking mobile: intensified everyday life, condensed city. In: S. Graham, ed. 2004. *The cybercities reader.* London: Routledge. pp. 267–272.

Krajina, Z., 2009. Exploring urban screens. *Culture Unbound* 1(1), pp. 401–430.

Krotz, F. and Tyler Eastman, S., 1999. Orientations towards television outside the home. *Journal of Communication,* 49(1), pp. 5–27.

Lash, S., 2007. Power after hegemony. Cultural studies in mutation? *Theory, Culture & Society,* 24(3), pp. 55–78.

Lee, D.H., 2009. Mobile snapshots and private/public boundaries. *Knowledge, Technology & Policy* 22(1), pp. 161–171.

Lefebvre, H., 1974 [1991]. *The production of space.* Oxford: Blackwell Publishing.

Lemish, D., 1982. The rules of viewing television in public places. *Journal of Broadcasting* 26(4), pp. 757–781.

Livingstone, S., 1998. Mediated childhoods: a comparative approach to young people's changing media environment in Europe. *European Journal of Communication* 13(4), pp. 435–456.

Livingstone, S., 2002. *Young people and new media.* London: Sage.

Livingstone, S. and Bovill, M. eds., 2001. *Children and their changing media environment.* Mahwah, N.J.: Lawrence Erlbaum Publishers.

Livingstone, S. and Drotner, K., 2011. Children's media cultures in comparative perspective. In: V. Nightingale, ed. 2011. *The handbook of media audiences*. West Sussex: Wiley-Blackwell. pp. 405–424.

Mann, S., Nolan, J. and Wellman, B., 2003. Sousveillance: inventing and using wearable computing devices for data collection in surveillance environments. *Surveillance & Society* 1(3), pp. 331–355.

McCarthy, A., 2001. *Ambient television. Visual culture and public space*. Durham and London: Duke University Press.

Mcquire, S., 2008. *The media city. Media, architecture and urban space*. Los Angeles: Sage.

Mcquire, S., 2011. Geomedia, networked culture and participatory public space. In: R. Hinkel, ed. 2011. *Urban interior: informal explorations, interventions and occupations*. Baunach: Spurbuchverlag. pp. 113–128.

Meyrowitz, J., 1985. *No sense of place. The impact of electronic media on social behavior*. New York and Oxford: Oxford University Press.

Mitchell, W.J., 2005. *Placing words. Symbols, space, and the city*. Cambridge: The MIT Press.

Moores, S., 1993. Television, geography and 'mobile privatization'. *European Journal of Communication* 8(3), pp. 365–379.

Moores, S., 2000. *Media and everyday life in modern society*. Edinburgh: Edinburg University Press.

Moores, S., 2006. Media uses & everyday environmental experiences: a positive critique of phenomenological geography. *Participations* [e-journal] 3(2). Available at: <http://www.participations.org/volume%203/issue%202%20-%20special/3_02_moores.htm>.

Moores, S., 2012. *Media, place & mobility*. Basingstoke, Hampshire: Palgrave Macmillan.

Morley, D., 1994. Between the public and the private. The domestic uses of information and communications technologies. In: J. Cruz and J. Lewis, eds. 1994. *Viewing, reading, listening*. Boulder: Westview Press. pp. 101–123.

Morley, D., 1995. Television: not so much a visual medium, more a visible object. In: C. Jenks, ed. 1995. *Visual culture*. Routledge: London. pp. 170–189.

Morley, D., 1996. The geography of television: ethnography, communications, and community. In: J. Hay, L. Grossberg and E. Wartella, eds. 1996. *The audience and its landscape*. Boulder: Westview Press. pp. 317–342.

Morley, D., 2000. *Home territories. Media, mobility and identity*. London and New York: Routledge.

Morley, D., 2006. What's 'home' got to do with it? Contradictory dynamics in the domestication of technology and the dislocation of domesticity. In: T. Berker, M. Hartmann, Y. Punie and K.J. Ward, eds. 2006. *Domestication of media and technology*. Maidenhead: Open University Press. pp. 21–39.

Morley, D. and Robins, K., 1995. *Spaces of identity. Global media, electronic landscapes and cultural boundaries*. London: Routledge.

Morley, D. and Silverstone, R., 1990. Domestic communication: technologies and meanings. *Media, Culture & Society* 12(1), pp. 31–55.

Munt, S. ed., 2001. *Technospaces. Inside the new media*. London and New York: Continuum.

Owen, S. and Imre, R., 2013. Little mermaids and pro-sumers. The dilemma of authenticity and surveillance in hybrid public spaces. *The International Communication Gazette* 75(5–6), pp. 470–483.

Ridell, S., 2005. Mediating the web as a public space. A local experiment in the creation of online civic genres. *Nordicom Review* 24(1), pp. 31–48.

Ridell, S., 2010. The cybercity as a medium. *International Review of Information Ethics* 12(3), pp. 12–20.

Ridell, S., 2012. Mode of action perspective to engagements with social media. Articulating activities on the public platforms of Wikipedia and YouTube. In: H. Bilandzic, G. Patriarche and P.J. Traudt, eds. 2012. *The social use of media: cultural and social scientific perspectives on audience research*. Bristol and Chicago: Intellect. pp. 17–35.

Ridell, S., 2013. The city as a medium of media. In: S. Tosoni, M. Tarantino and C. Giaccardi, eds. 2013. *Media and the city: urbanism, technology and communication*. Cambridge: Cambridge Scholars Publishing. pp. 32–50.

Ridell, S. and Zeller, F., 2013. Mediated urbanism: navigating an interdisciplinary terrain. *The International Communication Gazette*, 75(5–6), pp. 437–451.

Rieser, M. ed., 2011. *The mobile audience. Media art and mobile technologies*. Amsterdam and New York: Rodopi.

Rosati, C., 2007. Media geographies: uncovering the spatial politics of images. *Geography Compass* 1(5), pp. 995–1114.

Scannell, P., 1989. Public service broadcasting and modern public life. *Media, Culture & Society* 11(2), pp. 135–166.

Scannell, P., 1996. *Radio, television and modern life. A phenomenological approach*. Oxford: Blackwell.

Seamon, D., 2006. A geography of lifeworld in retrospect: a response to Shaun Moores. *Participations* [e-journal] 3(2). Available at: <http://www.participations.org/volume%203/issue%202%20-%20special/3_02_seamon.htm>.

Sennett, R., 1974. *The fall of public man*. London: Penguin Books.

Sheller, M. and Urry, J., 2003. Mobile transformations of 'public' and 'private' life. *Theory, Culture & Society* 20(3), pp. 107–125.

Sheller, M. and Urry, J., 2006. The new mobilities paradigm. *Environment and Planning A* 38(2), pp. 207–226.

Silverstone, R., 1996. From audience to consumers: the household and the consumption of communication and information technologies. In: J. Hay, L. Grossberg and E. Wartella, eds. 1996. *The audience and its landscape*. Boulder: Westview Press. pp. 265–296.

Silverstone, R., 2006. Domesticating domestication. Reflections on the life of a concept. In: T. Berker, M. Hartmann, Y. Punie and K.J. Ward, eds. 2006. *Domestication of media and technology*. Maidenhead: Open University Press. pp. 229–248.

Silverstone, R. and Haddon, L., 1996. Design and the domestication of information and communication technologies: technical change and everyday life. In: R. Mansell and R. Silverstone, eds. 1996. *Communication by design. The politics of information and communication technologies*. Oxford: Oxford University Press. pp. 44–74.

Silverstone, R., Hirsch, E. and Morley, D., 1991. Listening to a long conversation: an ethnographic approach to the study of information and communication technologies in the home. *Cultural Studies* 5(2), pp. 204–227.

Silverstone, R. and Hirsch, E. eds., 1992. *Consuming technologies. Media and information in domestic spaces*. London: Routledge.

Silverstone, R. and Morley, D., 1990. Families and their technologies: two ethnographic portraits. In: T. Putnam and C. Newton, eds. 1990. *Household choices*. London: Futures Publications. pp. 74–83.

Sloop, J. and Gunn, J., 2010. Status control: an admonition concerning the publicized privacy of social networking. *The Communication Review* 13(4), pp. 289–308.

Smith, D.H., 2013. Reflexive design of the recursive space of virtual worlds. macGRID art & cyberscience network as an example of mediated urbanism. *The International Communication Gazette* 75(5–6), pp. 452–469.

Star, S.L., 1999. The ethnography of infrastructure. *American Behavioral Scientist* 43(3), pp. 377–391.

Star, S.L. and Bowker, G., 2002. How to infrastructure. In: L. Lievrouw and S. Livingstone, eds. 2002. *The handbook of new media*. London: Sage. pp. 151–162.

Sussex Technology Group, 2001. In the company of strangers. Mobile phones and the conception of space. In: S. Munt, ed. 2001. *Technospaces. Inside the new media*. London and New York: Continuum. pp. 205–223.

Thrift, N., 2007. *Non-representational theory: space, politics, affect*. London: Routledge.

Thrift, N. and French, S., 2002. The automatic production of space. *Transactions of the Institute of British Geographers* 27(3), pp. 309–335.

Tosoni, S. and Tarantino, M., 2013. Media territories and urban conflict: exploring symbolic tactics and audience activities in the conflict over Paolo Sarpi, Milan. *The International Communication Gazette* 75(5–6), pp. 573–594.

van Kranenburg, R., 2008. *The internet of things. A critique of ambient technology and the all-seeing network of RFID*. Network Notebooks 02. Amsterdam: University of Amsterdam, The Institute of Network Cultures.

Wiley, S.B.C. and Packer, J., 2010. Rethinking communication after the mobilities turn. *The Communication Review* 13(4), pp. 263–268.

Williams, R., 1974. *Television. Technology and cultural form*. London: Fontana.

14 Big Data in Audience Research
A Critical Perspective[1]

Frauke Zeller

INTRODUCTION

What does big data[2] mean for contemporary and future audience research? Does it simply have methodological implications, such as giving up traditional methods for the sake of algorithms and large data sets? Does it mean that our audiences have changed, given that they can be seen as accessories to the big data wave by continuously feeding the data streams of social media usage? Does this in turn mean that we need to talk about agency versus "dataism" (Brooks, 2013) or "datafication" (Couldry, 2013)? Before being able to answer these questions, it is important to approach the concept holistically, that is to be cognizant of its implications, challenges, affordances and potentials for audience research and social sciences research in general. As a matter of fact, the omnipresence of big data not only in academic but also in business, political and private discourses does not necessarily foster a sound understanding of the term and concept. As it is, big data serves in all those discourses a multifaceted role—being discussed as a new discipline, movement, paradigm, promising utopia as well as implying dystopia, or even being viewed as a myth.

In the academic world, big data can be considered something of a 'buzzword' that has crossed disciplines. It thus has expanded from its original provenance in the MINT (Mathematics, Information Sciences, Natural Sciences and Technology) disciplines, to acquire increasing interest in the humanities and social sciences (Halevi and Moed, 2012). The disciplines differ in how they define big data and the relevant research questions and/or approaches connected to it. What they have in common though is the notion that big data bear the potential of opening up new research dimensions and opportunities. At the same time, big data is also said to bear risks and unforeseen challenges for researchers in any field or discipline, which calls for the development and critical discussion of new approaches and methods.

Since 2010, the number of publications and conference contributions about big data has risen exponentially. Furthermore, research programmes and university study programmes focusing on big data analytics have been initiated (Harris, 2013). Hence, within a few years big data has developed into one of the most popular and promising topics in the academic world. One major focus of most discussions about big data is social media.

Here, big data is often seen as a potential Achilles' heel of the participatory internet (Jenkins, 2006; Bruns, 2008). Discussions can range from recent espionage stories around intelligence services' procedures, which are made possible by big data technologies (Greenwald and MacAskill, 2013), to professional trends such as data analysts that are defined as the new "sexy job" (Davenport and Patil, 2012), and descriptions of big data as the new oil of the information economy (Mayer-Schönberger and Cukier, 2013). The last example usually refers to social media and the associated possibility of harvesting user data, which are generated by using interactive and participatory applications on the internet such as social platforms, blogs and so on. Harvesting these data are often directly connected with profit generation, with little or no attention to the difficulties that are connected with collecting, processing and finally using these data (Hey, Stewart and Tolle, 2009; Bollier, 2010; Manyika, et al., 2011; Barton, 2012; Baym, 2013).

However, the term *big data* does not refer exclusively to the data generated through social media usage. This also holds true for "data-ism" (Brooks, 2013), another term that is often mentioned in connection with big data. In fact, big data describes, first of all, different forms and kinds of large data records, which require special computer platforms and equipment for their analyses (Manovich, 2011). This means big data often cannot be handled with conventional techniques and methods. boyd and Crawford (2012, p. 663) also emphasize that there is indeed more that meets the eye than size:

> There is little doubt that the quantities of data now available are often quite large, but that is not the defining characteristic of this new data ecosystem. In fact, some of the data encompassed by Big Data (e.g. all Twitter messages about a particular topic) are not nearly as large as earlier data sets that were not considered Big Data (e.g. census data).

As a matter of fact, in academic and particularly scientific-oriented definitions of big data, size itself is rarely discussed. Instead, three core areas or challenges are mentioned in connection with big data: its capture, curation and analysis.

The following contribution offers an overview of big data from a social sciences and particularly audience research perspective. It begins with an attempt to align big data within social sciences and audience research, followed by a discussion of the research potential it offers as well as methodological aspects. Beside the potential of big data, the risks and the limitations of large data-driven research are also discussed.

CAPTURING BIG DATA: GENESIS OF A MISNOMER

Taking a closer look at big data, predominantly rather vague definitions prevail: "Big Data is a loosely defined term used to describe data sets so large and complex that they become awkward to work with using standard statistical software" (Snijders, Matzat and Reips, 2013, p. 1). Others discuss the phrase as not more than a descriptive feature: "The term Big Data is often invoked to describe the overwhelming volume of information [. . .]" (Lewis, Hermida and Zamith, 2013, p. 34). IBM on the other hand states that the term is "a bit of a misnomer since it implies that pre-existing data is somehow small" (Zikopoulos, et al., 2012, p. 2). Generally, defining big data means that it is less the quantity and size that demarcate the semantic meaning, but the actual handling of such, thus "the capacity to search, aggregate, and cross-reference large data sets" (boyd and Crawford, 2012, p. 663). In a similar vein, Miller's definition states that the term refers to analytic techniques, which "have existed for years but can now be applied faster, on a greater scale and are accessible to more users" (2013, p. 1, quoted in Park and Leydesdorff, 2013, p. 756). Park and Leydesdorff (2013, p. 756) apply on the other hand a methodological perspective: "[R]esearch driven by big data reflects a discipline that, to extract meaning from very large datasets, incorporates various techniques such as data mining and visualization into diverse fields, including the humanities and social sciences". Flew et al. (2012) summarise the inherent ambiguity of the word *data*:

> It is important to remember that data refers not only to numeric and statistical records, but to any form of information represented in a digitised format including text, audio, photographic, and video files. The application of computational processes and techniques to mine, categorise, filter, amplify and transform this data into discernable trends, patterns and accurate and meaningful summaries generates information.
> (p. 160)

According to a study conducted by Halevi and Moed (2012, p. 3), the term big data was used for the first time within academic discourse in 1970 in a publication on *Atmospheric and Oceanic Soundings*. The authors also found that, in its infancy, the term was used exclusively in natural sciences– and engineering-related publications. As to the country producing the most publications, Halevi and Moed cite the US as taking the lead, followed by China and Germany (although with significantly fewer publications).

In the social sciences, it took (maybe not so surprisingly) considerably longer for the first publications and conference contributions to explicitly mention or deal with big data. A 'big data' string term search in Scopus within the social sciences and humanities disciplines returned 129 hits (September 2013). However, this range covers also titles from academic fields only remotely connected to traditional social sciences and, in fact, more computer science–related fields. A more exact listing of the 129 hits shows that the majority originates from the social sciences and business and management studies (with approximately 25 per cent each) and an additional small portion of 6 per cent from the arts and humanities. More than half the publications originate from more scientifically oriented subjects such as engineering, chemistry or medicine.

The literature analysis also reveals that the term big data *per se* has not been used as frequently as today, whereas data-driven research relying on large data sets has been conducted since the 1970s. Also, the early usages of the term did not imply its current semantic broadness, ranging from an omnipotent *Über-data* perspective to a threat in traditional social sciences and humanities research.

Diebold (2012) attributes the first source of the term, reflecting its contemporary use and penetration, to a presentation by John Mashey, a scientist with the company Silicon Graphics (SGI) in the 1990s. However, not until later—with the introduction of the so-called fourth paradigm (Hey, Tansley and Tolle, 2009)—did big data was established with its current multifaceted meaning. According to Hey, Tansley and Tolle (2009), the fourth paradigm[3] of scientific research was coined by Jim Grey, who was one of the most influential computer scientists at Microsoft. It describes data-driven research as a novel approach to the analysis of new patterns, among others, and particularly stands as a contrast to the traditional hypotheses-led research (Park and Leydesdorff, 2013).

RESEARCH POTENTIALS AND CHALLENGES

In 2008, Anderson declared in the magazine *Wired* the end of scientific research:

> Forget taxonomy, ontology, and psychology. Who knows why people do what they do? The point is they do it, and we can track and measure it with unprecedented fidelity. With enough data, the numbers speak for themselves... There's no reason to cling to our old ways. It's time to ask: What can science learn from Google?
>
> (para. 6)

Statements such as this one surely contributed to the current popularity and utopian image of big data. They claim that theory-driven research, which often relies on lengthy processes of data collecting and preparation, allegedly has become obsolete in this era of big data and smart algorithms. Moreover, concerning audience research, big data research can be described as highly tantalizing, given that it seems to promise easy access to large studies simply because all the data are available through social media.

However, it is also important to be aware of the challenges of this 'brave new world'. IBM (Zikopoulos, et al., 2012) as well as Klein, Tran-Gia and Hartmann (2013) describe four main characteristics and core challenges of big data: volume, variety, velocity and veracity. The first characteristic—*volume*—refers to the size of big data. Indicative of this aspect are the many synonyms for big data, as for example the "Petabyte Age" (Anderson, 2008). Given that these size units are beyond human conception, big data is often also described by means of the individual data forms that are continually produced online. For example the sum of all active Facebook members produces more than 650,000 different content items per minute. Regarding the dispatching of messages, the almost 'antique' medium e-mail alone adds up to more than 200 million messages per minute, compared to 175 million short messages, which are dispatched daily, mainly over the micro-blogging service Twitter (Klein, Tran-Gia and Hartmann, 2013).

The *variety* challenge mainly refers to the fact that user data, which are generated through social media usage, come in many different forms and flavours. The pivotal problem here is the complexity of the data (or its variety) and the unstructured form of data. Structured data can be described in simple terms as database entries, which exhibit simple, unambiguous relations among themselves. Examples for structured data are to be found in questionnaire results, particularly in those entries such as name, address or sex, in which each case refers to one data point. However, data derived from e-mails are only half structured: whereas the e-mail header with the name, date and subject line is structured, the actual e-mail text can contain different communication modes such as text, pictures and URLs and is thus unstructured (Klein, Tran-Gia and Hartmann, 2013). Typical examples for fully unstructured sources of raw data are web pages, social media as microblogging platforms, news forums or search indices. Although unstructured data already represent a major challenge for analysis, this challenge is exacerbated in social media analysis projects in which the data sets usually come in mixed formats (Klein, Tran-Gia and Hartmann, 2013).

A positive side to these data varieties surely is that researchers have never before been able to gather such a great variety of user data for their studies. However, the apparent abundance and variety of available data tends to obfuscate what is called "dark data" (Burgelman, 2013), wherein *dark* describes less the quality of the data but, rather, the issue of non-used raw data. According to Burgelman (2013), dark data is frequently unused or not fully evaluated data which are generated by social media usage, web pages and mobile applications. Thus, data from social platforms that are connected to specific products or companies not only convey information about who the users/consumers of these companies or products are but also "how they feel about brands, what they are looking for, where they shop, their personal network" (Burgelman, 2013, para. 2). These aspects are often not addressed in typical market research studies, given their complexity and need for contextualization.

Velocity refers to the fact that data are produced constantly and with high speed, particularly by interactive social media. The *velocity* of data generation presents the challenge to develop methods and techniques to rapidly process and analyse data in real time in order to be able to react accordingly (Klein, Tran-Gia and Hartmann, 2013). For example so-called internet memes, which develop over individual short statements or pictures and videos on certain sides, spread extremely fast in online platforms through forwarding and linking of the respective URL. Should such a meme contain negative content/opinions about an enterprise, the company needs to be able to retrieve this meme and to react to it instantly. Velocity challenges traditional academic research methods adapted to queries of static data sets whereas big data analysis demands real-time processing and updating of raw data in short intervals, such as in research using GPS data. Hence, what is often needed is the ability to analyse raw data in real time, or "in motion" rather than "after it is at rest" (Zikopoulus, et al., 2012, p. xxix).

The fourth challenge—*veracity*—points to more critical interpretations of big data and was added at a later stage by IBM (Zikopoulus, et al., 2012). This aspect addresses the fact that it is almost impossible to verify big data. The reason for this is not so much due to a lack of goodwill or interest, but rather the result of the first three challenges of volume, velocity and variety.

Volume, variety, velocity and veracity also can be summarised as methical challenges. In addition to the issues regarding the handling and management of big data, challenges relating to societal questions and requirements as well as resources and affordances related aspects need to be taken into account. Figure 14.1 shows the different challenges and influences on research with big data, or large data sets in general. The societal aspect relates to questions regarding privacy and data protection concerns as well as ethical questions. The resources and affordances side integrates the aspects technology, personnel and budget. For the work with large data sets, not only is specific technological equipment needed to store, curate and

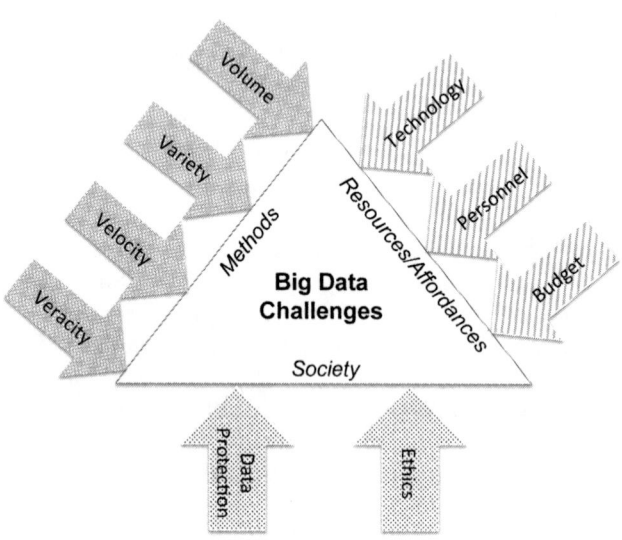

Figure 14.1 Influences and Challenges
Source: Adapted from Zeller (2014).

harvest the data, but specifically trained staff are also needed, both of which have budget implications.

LOCATING BIG DATA RESEARCH

Research with large data records represents a promising approach particularly in internet research[4]. According to Welker and Matzat (2009), internet research can be divided into two main areas: internet research as a research instrument, that is sociological research realized through the internet (e.g. online questionnaire) and, second, internet research as a research object *per se*. The latter area focuses on questions around the use of the internet, such as behavioural patterns in online networks, online news consumption and so on. Figure 14.2 shows a visual adaption for big data research, which was based on Welker and Matzat's (2009) concept of the binary distinction of internet research. The circular arrows depict the mutual influence of the two dimensions: big data as a research object and as a research instrument and/or apparatus. The term *apparatus* was added here by drawing on Foucault's use of the term, to describe the myriad of arguments and different discourses that coin big data in both scientific and public discussions.

Starting on the right-hand side of the figure, the topic big data is visualised as relating to the research object dimension. Big data is thus being employed here by researchers of different disciplines for studies on internet

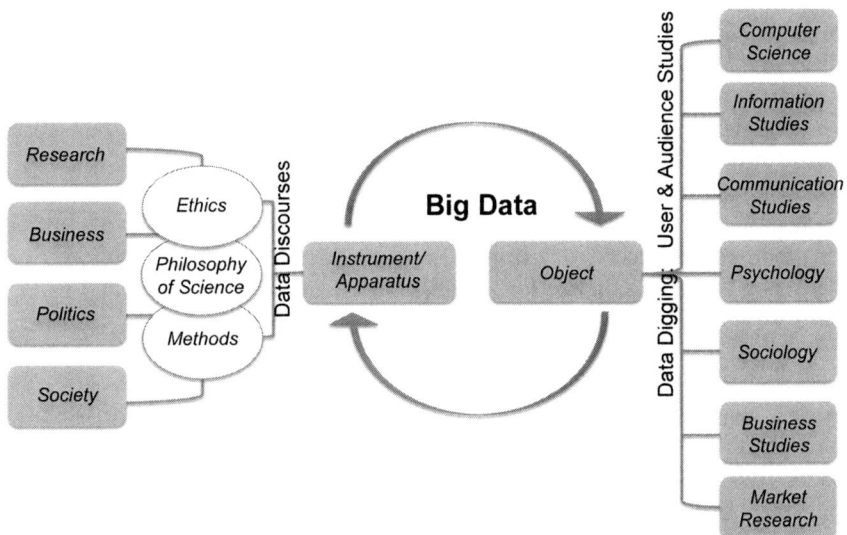

Figure 14.2 Big Data Dimensions
Source: Adapted from Zeller (2014).

or social media usage. User studies here refer to the integration of analyses of different forms and methods, conducted by a broad range of different academic and non-academic persons. The term *data digging*, on other hand, is rather popular in connection to big data debates and simply describes the act of using big data by 'digging' through large data records to discover patterns or relationships in the data.

The left-hand side of the figure acknowledges the fact that large data sets are not easily employed in our traditional research settings (neither practically nor ethically) and demand a critical discussion. Thus, a range of publications can be found that integrate critical theoretical elaborations, including also philosophy of science-inspired discussions. Ethical questions are also relevant and include, for instance, questions about how data-driven research as well as the computer affect and coin the results: "Big Data reframes key questions about the constitution of knowledge, the processes of research, how we should engage with information, and the nature and the categorization of reality" (boyd and Crawford, 2012, p. 665).

Finally, noteworthy methodological discussions can also be found. Beside Manovich's (2011) report on video analyses, there are also interesting elaborations concerning the influence of grid computing and high-performance computing (HPC, high-performance computer systems) on qualitative social science research. Fielding (2007) describes how data-intensive qualitative research can profit from high-performance computer systems and how big data and in general research supported by HPC infrastructures connects not just to quantitative research. The author provides in his overview on e-science projects in/with qualitative research multimedia-hypertext-ethnography (Fielding, 2007) as a very promising area that would benefit from HPC infrastructures and big data computing environments. Hence, Fielding, as well as Manovich (2011) and publications on data and information visualization (Fischer, et al., 2013; Fox and Hendler, 2011), mention visual data and information processing in connection with big data as a research tool.

Although modern information technologies enable research with big data, this does not mean that the data in 'big data' are only generated online (big data as a research tool), nor do they only focus on online behaviour (big data as a research object). For example census data can be labelled as big data or as major corpus studies that make use of vast textual and statistical resources such as those connected to the British National Corpus, which contains more than 100 million words. However, these studies do not necessarily need to be connected with research into online behaviour or social media usage. The evolving research area of 'Culturomics' provides an interesting example of new research areas and approaches made possible through big data but that are not exclusively connected to online or social media. In fact, whilst studies in Culturomics are enabled through internet technologies, they do not necessarily concern themselves with the use of social media: "The emerging field of 'Culturomics' seeks to explore broad cultural trends through the computerized analysis of vast digitally book archives, offering novel insights into the functioning of human society" (Leetaru, 2011, para. 1). Hence, studies in Culturomics are primarily interested in the quantitative data collection of cultural and social trends. One prominent example is the Google digital book project (Michel, et al., 2011).

BIG DATA IN AUDIENCE RESEARCH

The advent of big data in audience research has led to a long-needed revision of the concept of data in connection with social media, mark-up data and the myths connected with big data. Napoli (2011) underscores a new data perspective appropriate to the new audience information systems: "New streams of data can be gathered and analyzed about audience members' media consumption habits, content preferences, degree of engagement, and levels of interest in, anticipation about, and appreciation of the content they consume. All of these dimensions of audience behaviour are fundamentally different from the traditional exposure metric".

Taking a closer look at data, Jensen pointedly argues that "data are either *found* or *made*" (2014, p. 224); humanities researchers study what they *find*, such as texts, documents or any kind of artefact, whereas social scientists are more involved in the *making* (of data) "through interviewing, experimenting and observing" (Jensen, 2014, p. 224). However, when it comes to digital communication systems, Jensen speaks of "a new type and scale of data [. . .]: big data or *metadata* that indicate who did what, with which information, together with whom, when, for how long and in which sequences and networks" (2014, p. 224). This new kind of data, he argues, calls for a reconsideration or a discussion regarding our understanding of data, specifically regarding 'the nature of data'. One reason for this being that big data and metadata are both *found* and *made* at the same time: "They can be found online, as they are being generated through our social media usage. However they also integrate the 'making' aspect, given that one would have to 'make' the corresponding algorithms, hence programming, and then extracting, etc. in order to get them" (Jensen, 2014, p. 229). In a special issue discussing both aspects of big data—made and found—Jensen and Helles (2013, para. 1) describe data generally as "[d]ata are widely understood as minimal units of information about the world, waiting to be found and collected by scholars and other analysts". As to the *making* aspect, they point out that data are indeed made by 'multiple social agents', ranging from communicators, service providers, commercial stakeholders and government authorities to international regulators and of course communication researchers. Moreover, data are being made in any context (political, institutional, private) and any time. However, the processes involved to generate data are often "opaque and certainly under-documented in the published research" (Jensen and Helles, 2013, para. 2).

Thus, the association of data with something clean and scientifically pure, that can be processed with data analysis tools to produce truth, must be revised, such as the assumption that there was an "a priori existence of data 'out there', waiting to be simply recovered and turned into insight" (Vis, 2013, para. 5). Instead, data are and have always been co-produced or made by different actors, as knowledge and insights are the offspring of their specific epistemic communities and knowledge generating apparatuses (Knorr-Cetina, 1999). Whilst the aforementioned opaqueness regarding the details of the data production processes has also always been there—and in the past these problems were 'justified' or at least brought to accountability through the varying scientific routines and standards inscribed in the different disciplines—it does not mean that this circumstance is problem free. In fact, one can easily argue that with the explosion of data quantities, the problems regarding information on data production details have increased proportionately. Two reasons can be given for this: First of all, with big data we are facing the so-called GIGO problem (Garbage In, Garbage Out; see Karpf, 2012) on an immense scale. Public data do not come in a clean and ready-made form; they can indeed have "deep, systematic flaws which too often goes ignored" (Karpf, 2012, p. 648). Hence, our data sets are often contaminated (at best), contradicting any traditional standard of academic research, hence potentially leading to errors of interpretation. And still, as Markham (2013) points out, data is a term so frequently used bearing the potential of adding "instant credibility to that which it describes" (Markham, 2013, para. 2).

It is in fact this notion that makes it so easy to argue for an inherit truth in data, seeing them as "discrete objects that can be located in time and space" (Markham, 2013, para. 2), inviting maybe even some nostalgic ideas in the spirit of Positivism, only now it would be positivism 2.0, that is without the strong believe in science. In fact, in a positivism 2.0 notion, in which all truth is put into the data that are out there, social media consequently are serving as our sensors that collect our experiences and thus take up the role of the exclusive source of all authoritative knowledge. Hence, using Comte's argument that the physical world operates according to gravity and other absolute laws and thus does society (Macionis, 2012), can be turned into its 2.0 version, stating that the *world operates according to big data and other absolute laws, and so does society.*

The second problem is that big data has the potential to profoundly change the way we conduct research. Whereas changes *per se* are not something that one would want to reject, they should, however, at least come with some critical consideration as to the impact those changes will have. boyd and Crawford (2012) discuss the epistemological as well as research ethical implications of big data and summarise that "Big Data reframes key questions about the constitution of knowledge, the processes of research, how we should engage with information, and the nature and the categorization of reality" (boyd and Crawford, 2012, p. 665). Moreover, if we believed in the notion that the detection of patterns suffice in our future research—that is following the suggestion that big numbers will produce some relevant results—we are also in a way giving up the actual *raison d'être* of not just audience research but social sciences research in general, that is to gain understanding about social interaction and social knowledge. Insights into social knowledge are integral with critical insights into context and the effects of interpretation. Couldry (2013) warns in this respect that "'big data' advocates' claims about what *counts as* social knowledge affect all of us interested in producing social knowledge". boyd and Crawford (2012, p. 671) note that there is an inherent problem with big data that are being modelled, but then are lacking context because context is "hard to interpret at scale and even harder to maintain when data are reduced to fit into a model". And we need context to interpret and to explain the 'big picture' that for example social network graphs depict. Those graphs can merely depict a network, and do not explain the actual relationships behind the nodes and ties. As Boellstorff (2013) states by drawing on Geertz's notion of interpretation at the centre of data analysis: "big data is never ontologically prior to interpretation [. . .] and interpretation takes place within horizons of culture that are embedded in contexts of power". Couldry (2013) relates the big data discourse to the anthropological concept of myth and discusses in detail current popular ideas on the relevance and irrelevance of 'sense-free' numbers, which at some point always reveal some valuable pattern: "The result is to undercut the rationale of not just qualitative methods of analysis, but also of the interpretative models—the hermeneutics, if you like—that for decades have driven *large-scale survey research*" (Couldry, 2013). And by giving in to this "datafied" form of big data language, which disregards the individual voice by substituting meaning of action with meaning-free action patterns and predictions, we might be building social landscapes of "'dead souls': human entities that have financial value [. . .], but are not alive, not at least in the sense we know human beings to be alive" (Couldry, 2013, citing Gogol, 2008).

BIG DATA METHODS IN AUDIENCE STUDIES

There are critical voices who claim that big data includes only data-driven research. However, particularly when it comes to audience research and the social sciences in general, the traditional and dominant drivers are research questions and hypotheses (see e.g. Karpf, 2012). The critical voices often correctly point to the trend that the mere ability to access large data sets—such as Twitter feeds—already justify any research project. Schroeder and Meyer (2012) summarise this criticism in a more colloquial tone: "Is the tail of the availability of big data and computational methods wagging the dog of good research questions?"

Theory- and hypothesis-driven research certainly cannot nor should not be replaced. However, one needs to acknowledge that those large data sets of social media usage are also of interest for audience researchers, given that they provide a glimpse into society and social mechanisms that one could hardly dream of in the "Pre-Internet" age (Welker and Kloß, 2013). In fact, a variety of tools already exists which permit relatively fast and easy access to large datasets on social media usage. One increasingly popular category of these tools is the so-called API (Application Programming Interface), which describes a group of different instruments or algorithms through which (structured) data provided by the operators of social media can be accessed. Thus, for example all photos of a certain group with their descriptions, and other information, can be downloaded with the public Flickr API (Manovich, 2011). Given that Twitter is one of the few social media applications (among the most popular ones) that still considers its content public, it goes without saying that the Twitter API was an instant success (see e.g. Kwak, et al., 2010; Tumasjan, et al., 2010; Lee and Chien, 2013; Lewis, Hermida and Zamith, 2013; Vergeer, Hermans and Cunha, 2013).

Regarding concrete areas of big data research, Welker and Kloß (2013) mention ad hoc evaluation, predictive analysis, opinion mining and behaviour pattern recognition (see also Bruns and Liang, 2012; Bruns 2013). The individually applied methods such as content analyses, or observations, are usually non-reactive (the latter refers to the evaluation of data tracks or log file analyses; Welker and Kloß, 2013). The authors emphasize though that big data research not only covers the entire spectrum of passive data collection instruments but also reaches from the public to the most personal realm of the individual social media user (Welker and Kloß, 2013). Other areas of application, in particular regarding the newly developed field computational social sciences (Lazer, et al., 2009), are automatic information extraction and data analysis, social network analysis, geo data analysis, modelling of complex systems and simulation models of social systems (Cioffi-Revilla, 2010).

However—as already mentioned—traditional audience research methods hardly work with big data. First, the *per definitionem* large data records demand a computer-based handling that go beyond regular statistical programmes such as SPSS (and that are run on conventional computers). Those conducting research with large data sets are actually forced to deal from the outset with technical questions and challenges—starting with the data collection, processing and data curation and ending with the analyses' and results' presentations and visualisations. Given the aforementioned four methodical challenges (volume, velocity, variety, veracity) mainly manual techniques and approaches are simply not feasible. Furthermore, predictive analytics play an increasingly relevant role for market analyses, electoral research, or management studies.[5]

From less a tool perspective, but still relating to audience research and social sciences' methods, Karpf (2012) states in connection to internet research in general that traditional *ceteris paribus* assumptions do not hold in dynamic and ephemeral online environments. Because of the rapidly changing online environment, traditional time-series studies are "diluted", and he concludes that "[w]e can look for statistically significant findings in the large datasets, but only while embracing *ceteris paribus* assumptions that are clearly unsupportable" (Karpf, 2012, p. 647).

CRITICALLY CONCLUDING

Despite or perhaps because big data is a hot topic in all social and academic areas, there are nevertheless substantial differences in the discussions. Pragmatic approaches to capture the main challenges of big data and find technical solutions are often found in information and computer sciences fields. Predominantly utopian and profoundly promising discussions, on the other hand, are situated in commercial market research and popular management literature. Audience researchers and social scientists however are primarily concerned with big data as research apparatus: Questions about the benefits, challenges, risks, and generally affordances for research and epistemological paradigms are in the centre of their attention[6]. The critical points relate to three main areas (as also depicted in Figure 14.2): *philosophy of science, methodological discussions* and *ethics*.

The criticism stemming from a *philosophy of science* approach raises important questions concerning the epistemological consequences of big data. With the introduction of computational procedures to research, it also must be considered to what extent the applied algorithms affect our research processes and results: "Big Data of reframes key questions about the constitution of knowledge, the processes of research, how incoming goods should engage with information, and the nature and the categorization of reality" (boyd and Crawford, 2012, p. 665). That is epistemologically it should be asked to what extent the instruments form or affect our results.

According to some proponents of big data, large numbers speak for themselves (Anderson, 2008; Mayer-Schönberger and Cukier, 2013). This again would mean that the actual algorithms, software programmes, methods or the sampling strategies are hardly relevant. Manovich (2011) and boyd and Crawford (2012) dispute this vehemently:

> Twitter data has serious methodological challenges that are rarely addressed by those who embrace it. When researchers approach a data set, they need to understand—and publicly account for—not only the limits of the data set, but also the limits of which questions they can ask of a data set and what interpretations are appropriate.
> (boyd and Crawford, 2012, pp. 669–670)

The criticism relating to methodological discourses focuses on two main aspects: first, the evident necessity to extend the traditional methods and instruments, which often integrates the need to integrate not only software tools into the research process but also powerful computing hardware. It also should be mentioned that in the opinion of some researchers, the instrument/tool problem could be solved by engaging more in large, multidisciplinary and international collaborations. In this context the terms *e-science* or *e-research* are often mentioned: "e-Research is the use of advanced information and communication technologies (ICTs) to enable new forms of collaborative research that involves access to distributed research resources (datasets, methods, compute cycles)" (Ackland, 2009, p. 486). Ackland in fact pleads for a stronger involvement of social sciences' research in e-research collaborations, because this way, researchers could access new data sets generated by different/new sampling methods and could have access to new instruments for the analysis of big data. Here, it is, however, important to note critically that those new instruments often do not offer access to entire data histories/records (e.g. Google Ngram Viewer or Twitter Analytics). This makes absolute sense from an entrepreneurial perspective: Given that big data is also viewed as the new oil of the internet, its economic value is not to be ignored, which in turn means that it usually cannot be in the interest of for-profit enterprises to make their data freely accessible for everybody.

The method-oriented discussions also increasingly come with a criticism of an exclusively quantitative approach to big data. Thus, Snijders, Matzat and Reips (2012), boyd and Crawford (2012), Fielding (2007), Lewis, Hermida and Zamith (2013), and Manovich (2011) all underscore the relevance of qualitative data in big data research. This holds true in particular for the numerously accomplished network analyses, in which important information was lacking: "A crucial problem is that we do not know much about the underlying empirical micro-processes that lead to the emergence of these typical network characteristics of Big Data" (Snijders, Matzat and Reips, 2012, p. 2). boyd and Crawford (2012) refer to the problem of data sampling (see also Mahrt and Scharkow, 2013) by claiming that "[b]igger data are not always better data" (boyd and Crawford, p. 668). As to the challenge of correctly contextualizing both data and research results they summarize: "Taken out of context, Big Data loses its meaning" (boyd and Crawford, p. 670).

Regarding the ethical discussions, Schmidt (2013) speaks of a nightmare for data protection. Internet research often walks a tightrope between ethical viability and technological/methodological feasibility (Fraas, Meier and Pentzold, 2012; Welker and Kloß, 2013; see Figure 14.2). The actual watering down of the concept or definition of public versus private, represented through concepts such as public, half-public and private communication can be regarded as a profound and tricky problem (Schmidt, 2013). This problem is also relevant to research with big data. It should go without saying, however, that the fundamental ethical principles of research also account for internet research projects with big data. For example big data projects that are using Twitter corpora do not legally have to worry about privacy issues, because Twitter is considered public data. However, ethically they should consider what kind of data they are using and for what means:

> Very little is understood about the ethical implications underpinning the Big Data phenomenon. Should someone be included as a part of a large aggregate of data? What if someone's 'public' blog post is taken out of context and analyzed in a way that the author never imagined? What does it mean for someone to be spotlighted or to be analyzed without knowing it? Who is responsible for making certain that individuals and communities are not hurt by the research process? What does informed consent look like?
> (boyd and Crawford, 2012, p. 672)

Finally, going back to the questions posed in the very beginning of this chapter, big data will not bridge the traditional gap between the different concepts of audience as they are defined by academia and industry. If anything, this gap might even widen, considering the different motivations behind the concepts (see also Baym, 2013). So what does big data mean for contemporary and future audience research? Apart from creating the highly valuable 'extra mileage' of stimulating long awaited discussions in audience research about their core concepts and methods, big audience data "can reduce uncertainty, facilitate more effective predicting of audience behavior and consequently enable more effective strategic decision-making" (Napoli, 2011, p. 51). Big data research certainly goes beyond mere methodological advancements, but claiming that big data also brings a change of audiences would certainly go too far. This notion, of changing audience behaviours, indeed has come up quite some time before we adapted the term *big data*, such as in studies on produsage (Bruns, 2008), cultures of connectivity (van Dijk, 2013) or the participatory internet (Jenkins, 2006). However, by taking up Karpf's (2013) notion of the dynamically changing media environment, that is online environment and media usage including media affordances, there will be an ongoing necessity to discuss concepts of agency in relation to big data—and neo-linguistic expressions such as "data-ism" (Brooks, 2013) or "datafication" (Couldry, 2013)—without getting lost in data-driven research altogether.

NOTES

1. This chapter is based on prior work of the author, see Zeller (2014).
2. Big data is discussed here as a concept, hence the use of the singular form.
3. The first two paradigms of scientific research are usually referred to as heliocentric (also known as experimental science such as after Ptolemy) and geocentric (also known as theoretical science, such as after Kepler and Newton) world views. The third paradigm is called computational science and describes the usage of computer simulations for scientific insights (Hey, Tansley and Tolle, 2009; see also Harris, 2012).

4. The terms *internet research* and *online research* are used here interchangeably.
5. See in this connection the field of business intelligence, for example Chen, Chiang and Storey (2012) or Klein, Tran-Gia and Hartmann (2013).
6. See also some recent critical discussions in more broadly received/consumed publications, such as Harford (2014), Marcus and Davis (2014) and Lazer, et al. (2014).

REFERENCES

Ackland, R., 2009. Social network services as data sources and platforms for e-researching social networks. *Social Science Computer Review*, 27(4), pp. 481–492.
Anderson, C., 2008. The end of theory: the data deluge makes the scientific method obsolete [online]. *Wired Magazine*. Available at: <http://www.wired.com/science/discoveries/magazine/16–07/pb_theory>.
Barton, D., 2012. Making advanced analytics work for you. *Harvard Business Review*, 90(10), pp. 78–83.
Baym, N. K., 2013. Data not seen: the uses and shortcomings of social media metrics. *First Monday*, 18(10).
Boellstorff, T., 2013. Making big data, in theory. *First Monday* [e-journal] 18(10). Available at: <http://journals.uic.edu/ojs/index.php/fm/article/view/4869>.
Bollier, D., 2010. *The promise and peril of big data*. Washington, DC: The Aspen Institute.
boyd, D. and Crawford, K., 2012. Critical questions for big data. *Information, Communication & Society* 15(5), pp. 662–679.
Brooks, D., 2013. The philosophy of data. *The New York Times* [online]. Available at: <http://www.nytimes.com/2013/02/05/opinion/brooks-the-philosophy-of-data.html>.
Bruns, A., 2008. *Blogs, Wikipedia, Second Life, and beyond: from production to produsage*. Digital Formations, 45. New York: Peter Lang.
Bruns, A., 2013. Faster than the speed of print: reconciling "big data" social media analysis and academic scholarship. *First Monday* [e-journal] 18(10). Available at: <http://journals.uic.edu/ojs/index.php/fm/article/view/4879>.
Bruns, A. and Liang, Y. E., 2012. Tools and methods for capturing Twitter data during natural disasters. *FirstMonday* [e-journal] 17(4). Available at: <http://firstmonday.org/article/view/3937/3193>.
Burgelman, L., 2013. Attention, big data enthusiasts: here's what you shouldn't ignore [online]. *Wired Magazine*. Available at: <http://www.wired.com/insights/2013/02/attention-big-data-enthusiasts-heres-what-you-shouldnt-ignore/>.
Chen, H., Chiang, R. H. and Storey, V. C., 2012. Business intelligence and analytics: from big data to big impact. *MIS Quarterly* 36(4), pp. 1165–1188.
Cioffi Revilla, C., 2010. Computational social science. *Wiley Interdisciplinary Reviews: Computational Statistics* 2(3), pp. 259–271.
Couldry, N., 2013. A necessary disenchantment: myth, agency and injustice in a digital world. Inaugural lecture. *London School of Economics and Political Science*, pp. 1–16.
Davenport, T.H. and Patil, D.J., 2012. Data scientist: The sexiest job of the 21st century. *Harvard Business Review*, 90(10), pp. 70–77.
Diebold, F., 2012. *On the origin(s) and development of the term "big data."* PIER Working Paper. Philadelphia: University of Philadelphia. Available at: <http://ssrn.com/abstract=2152421>.
Fielding, N., 2007. Grid computing and qualitative social science. *Social Science Computer Review* 26(3), pp. 301–316.

Fischer, F., Fuchs, J., Mansmann, F. and Keim, D., 2013. BANKSAFE: Visual analytics for big data in large-scale computer networks. *Information Visualization.*
Flew, T., Spurgeon, C., Daniels, A. and Swift, A., 2012. The promise of computational journalism. *Journalism Practice* 6(2), pp. 157–171.
Fox, P. and Hendler, J., 2011. Changing the equation on scientific data visualization. *Science* 331(6018), pp. 705–708.
Fraas, C., Meier, S. and Pentzold, C., 2012. *Online-Kommunikation. Grundlagen, Praxisfelder und Methoden.* Wien: Oldenbourg Verlag.
Gogol, N., 2008. *Dead Souls.* Penguin Classics.
Greenwald, G. and MacAskill, E., 2013. NSA Prism program taps in to user data of Apple, Google and others. *The Guardian* [online]. Available at: <http://www.alleanzaperinternet.it/wp-content/uploads/2013/06/guardian.pdf>.
Halevi, G. and Moed, H., 2012. The evolution of big data as a research and scientific topic. *Research Trends* 30, pp. 3–6
Harford, T., 2014. Big data: are we making a big mistake? *Financial Times Magazine* [online]. Available at: <http://www.ft.com/intl/cms/s/2/21a6e7d8-b479-11e3-a09a-00144feabdc0.html#axzz2xS1VXiUc>.
Harris, R. 2012. ICSU and the challenges of big data in science. *Research Trends* 30, pp. 11–12.
Hey, A.J.G., Tansley, S. and Tolle, K., eds., 2009. *The fourth paradigm.* Redmond, Washington: Microsoft Press.
Jenkins, H., 2006. *Convergence culture: where old and new media collide.* New York: New York University Press.
Jensen, K.B., 2014. Audiences, audiences everywhere—measured, interpreted and imagined. In G. Patriarche, H. Bilandzic, J. Linaa Jensen and J. Jursic, eds. 2014. *Audience Research Methodologies.* New York: Routledge, pp. 227–239.
Jensen, K.B. and Helles, R., 2013. Making data—Big data and beyond: Introduction to the special issue. *First Monday* [e-journal] 18(10). Available at: <http://firstmonday.org/article/view/4860/3748>.
Karpf, D., 2012. Social science research methods in internet time. *Information, Communication & Society* 15(5), pp. 639–661.
Klein, D., Tran-Gia, P. & Hartmann, M., 2013. Big data. *Informatik-Spektrum* 36(3), pp. 319–323.
Knorr-Cetina, K., 1999. *Epistemic cultures: how the sciences make knowledge.* Cambridge: Harvard University Press.
Kwak, H., Lee, C., Park, H. and Moon, S., 2010. What is Twitter, a social network or a news media? In *Proceedings of the 19th international conference on World Wide Web.* Raleigh: ACM. pp. 590–600.
Lazer, D., Pentland, A., Adamic, L., Aral, S., Barabasi, A. L., Brewer, D., Christakis, N., Contractor, N., Fowler, J., Gutmann, M., Jebara, T., King, G., Macy, M., Roy, D. and Alstyne, M. van, 2009. Computational social science. *Science* 323(5915), pp. 721–723.
Lazer, D., Kennedy, R., King, G., and Vespignani, A. 2014. The parable of Google flu: traps in big data analysis. *Science* 343(6176), pp. 1203–1205.
Lee, C.-H. and Chien, T.-F., 2013. Leveraging microblogging big data with a modified density-based clustering approach for event awareness and topic ranking. *Journal of Information Science* 39(4), pp. 523–543.
Leetaru, K.H., 2011. Culturomics 2.0: forecasting large-scale human behavior using global news media tone in time and space. *First Monday* [e-journal] 16(9). Available at: <http://firstmonday.org/ojs/index.php/fm/article/view/3663/3040>.
Lewis, S.C., Hermida, A. and Zamith, R., 2013. Content analysis in an era of big data: a hybrid approach to computational and manual methods. *Journal of Broadcasting & Electronic Media,* 57(1), pp. 34–52.
Mahrt, M. and Scharkow, M., 2013. The value of big data in digital media research. *Journal of Broadcasting & Electronic Media* 57(1), pp. 20–33.

Macionis, J. J. (2012). *Sociology 14th Edition*. Boston: Pearson
Manovich, L., 2011. Trending: the promises and the challenges of big social data. *Debates in the digital humanities*, pp. 1–17. Available at: <http://www.manovich.net/DOCS/Manovich_trending_paper.pdf>.
Manyika, J., Chui, M., Brown, B., Bughin, J., Dobbs, R., Roxburgh, C. and Byers, A., 2011. *Big data: the next frontier for innovation, competition, and productivity*. New York: McKinsey & Company.
Marcus, G. and Davis, E., 2014. Eight (no, nine!) problems with big data. *The New York Times* [online]. Available at: <http://www.nytimes.com/2014/04/07/opinion/eight-no-nine-problems-with-big-data.html?ref=opinion&_r=1>.
Markham, A.N., 2013. Undermining "data": a critical examination of a core term in scientific inquiry. *First Monday* [e-journal] 18(10). Available at: <http://firstmonday.org/article/view/4868/3749>.
Mayer-Schönberger, V. and Cukier, K., 2013. *Big data. A revolution that will transform how we live, work and think*, London: John Murray.
Michel, J. B., Shen, K. S., Presser Aiden, A., Veres, A., Gray, M. K., The Google Books Team, Pickett, J. P., Hoiberg, D., Clancy, D., Norvig, P., Orwant, J., Pinker, S., Nowak, M. A. and Lieberman Aiden, E., 2011. Quantitative analysis of culture using millions of digitized books. *Science* 331(6014), pp. 176–182.
Napoli, P., 2011. *Audience evolution: new technologies and the transformation of media audiences*. New York: Columbia University Press.
Park, H. W. and Leydesdorff, L., 2013. Decomposing social and semantic networks in emerging "big data" research. *Journal of Informetrics* 7(3), pp. 756–765.
Schmidt, J.-H., 2013. *Social media*. Wiesbaden: VS Verlag.
Schroeder, R. and Meyer, E., 2012. Digital research and big data. Poster. *Digital Research 2012*. Available at: <http://digital-research.oerc.ox.ac.uk>.
Snijders, C., Matzat, U. and Reips, U.-D., 2012. "Big data": big gaps of knowledge in the field of internet science. *International Journal of Internet Science* 7(1), pp. 1–5.
Tumasjan, A., Sprenger, T. O., Sandner, P. G. and Welpe, I. M., 2010. Predicting elections with Twitter: what 140 characters reveal about political sentiment. In: *Fourth International AAAI Conference on weblogs and social media*, George Washington University, Washington, DC, 23–26 May.
van Dijk, J., 2013. *Culture of connectivity. A critical history of social media*. Oxford: Oxford University Press.
Vergeer, M., Hermans, L. and Cunha, C., 2013. Web campaigning in the 2009 European Parliament elections: a cross-national comparative analysis. *New Media & Society* 15(1), pp. 128–148.
Vis, F., 2013. A critical reflection on big data: considering APIs, researchers and tools as data makers. *First Monday* [e-journal] 18(10). Available at: <http://firstmonday.org/ojs/index.php/fm/article/view/4878>.
Welker, M. and Matzat, U., 2009. Online-Forschung: Entwicklungslinien, Defizite und Potentiale. In: H. Schoen, N. Jackob, & T. Zerback, eds. *Sozialforschung im Internet. Methodologie und Praxis der Online-Befragung*. Wiesbaden: VS Verlag, pp. 33–48.
Welker, M. and Kloß, A., 2013. Soziale Medien als Gegenstand und Instrument sozialwissenschaftlicher Forschung. In: C. König, M. Stahl, E. Wiegand, eds., 2013. *Soziale Medien*. Wiesbaden: VS Verlag.
Zeller, F., 2014. Online-Forschung und Big Data. In: B. Batinic, N. Jackob, J. Schmidt, M. Taddicken and M. Welker, eds. 2014. *Handbuch Online-Forschung*. Reihe Neue Schriften zur Online-Forschung, Band 12. Köln: Herbert von Halem Verlag.
Zikopoulos, P., Eaton, C., DeRoos, D., Deutsch, T. and Lapis, G., 2012. *Understanding big data: analytics for enterprise class Hadoop and streaming data*, New York: McGraw-Hill.

Contributors

Piermarco Aroldi, Ph.D., is Associate Professor of Sociology of Cultural and Communicative Processes at Università Cattolica del Sacro Cuore of Milano and Piacenza, Italy, where he teaches Sociology of Cultural and Communicative Processes and Media and Children's Cultures. He is Director of OssCom, Research Centre on Media and Communications.

His research interests are about media and educations, media cultures and children's cultures, media consumption in the everyday life and in a generational perspective and technologies, communications and social media in health care, nutrition and risks. He is member of the COST Action IS0906—"Transforming Audiences, Transforming Societies", EU Kids Online and Net Children Go Mobile Networks.

Joke Bauwens is Professor of Media Sociology at the Department of Media and Communication Studies, Free University of Brussels, Belgium (Vrije Universiteit Brussel [VUB]). In 2003 she joined the VUB-research group SMIT, aka iMinds-SMIT, where she guides research in the field of Digital Cultures and Arts. Drawing on media-sociological, media-theoretical and media-philosophical approaches, her research interests and expertise cover the social and moral consequences of digital and virtual media cultures. She has published on young people and the internet, virtuality and morality and the digitization of culture.

Joke Beyl is a doctoral student and teaching assistant at the Department of Communication Studies, Free University of Brussels, Belgium (Vrije Universiteit Brussel [VUB]). Her doctoral study is directed at understanding how authority of cultural producers, literary writers in specific, is constructed in a digital culture. Since 2007 Joke Beyl is affiliated to the research centre iMinds-SMIT (Vrije Universiteit Brussel), where she has been conducting research on cultural institutions and their relationships with their audiences in a digital culture. Her interests are situated in the field of blog studies, narrative analysis, self-representation and interaction in a digital culture, questions of authority and social relations in media and cultural fields.

Maria José Brites has a Ph.D. and a master's degree in communication sciences—journalism and media studies (Faculty of Social and Human Sciences—University of Lisbon [FCSH]) and a diploma in advanced studies in journalism and media studies (FCSH-UNL). Currently, she is Lecturer at Lusophone University of Porto, Portugal, and Researcher at Media and Journalism Research Center (CIMJ)–FCSH-UNL. She coordinates (in Portugal) an European research project called "Radioactive Europe: Promoting Engagement, Informal Learning and Employability of at Risk and Excluded People across Europe through Internet Radio and Social Media" (531245-LLP-2012-UK-KA3-KA3MP). She also worked as journalist for several years, mostly in print media.

Cédric Courtois is a researcher at the iMinds (www.iMinds.be) research group for Media and ICT (Information and Communication Technology), at Ghent University, Belgium. His research interests span digital media consumption, online 'prosuming,' and youth and new media. Moreover, he has a special interest in methodological innovation, especially in the field of mixed-method media research. Recently, he finished his dissertation titled "The Triple Articulation of Audiovisual Media Technologies in the Age of Convergence", which explores the consequences of convergent media for audiovisual audiences.

Alexander Dhoest is Associate Professor in Communication Studies at the University of Antwerp (Belgium). In 2002 he got his Ph.D. in social sciences at the K.U. Leuven, working on the construction of national identity in Flemish television drama. Since then, he has specialised in qualitative audience research, looking in particular at the relationship between TV viewing and social (including national, ethnic and sexual) identities. He also has a continued interest in television, including issues of national identity and quality in TV drama.

Katleen Gabriels is a doctoral researcher at the Vrije Universiteit Brussel (VUB), Belgium. Her PhD, funded by the Flemish Research Foundation (FWO Project 'Living virtual lives'), seeks to conjoin a strong grounding in moral philosophy with actual empirical studies of online moral practices and ethical reflection in three-dimensional social virtual worlds. Her research interests are situated within moral philosophy, philosophy of technology, ethics of technology (such as computer and Information and Communication Technology ethics) and media ethics. Katleen is part of the Department of Philosophy and Moral Sciences. She is also a member of iMinds-SMIT (Studies on Media, Information and Telecommunication) and the Centre for Ethics and Humanism (EtHu), both at VUB. She holds master's degrees in Germanic Philology (Catholic University of Leuven, Belgium) and Moral Philosophy (Ghent University, Belgium).

Ingunn Hagen is Professor in the Department of Psychology, Norwegian University of Science and Technology (NTNU), Trondheim, Norway. Professor Hagen's main research interests include media and communication psychology, and recently topics such as health, happiness, Yoga, and Mindfulness. Professor Hagen's research also includes more traditional media and communication psychology research fields such as audience reception studies, political communication, consumption of popular culture, young people and new media, and recently children and consumption. For example she has done research on media audiences and the role of media and Information and Communication Technologies in people's lives. She has also been involved in research on consuming children and the commercialization of childhood. In addition, she has competence and interest in topics such as sociocultural, positive and discursive psychology, organizational communication and qualitative research methodology. She has published articles in a number of books and journals, both in English and Norwegian (http://www2.svt.ntnu.no/ansatte/ansatt.aspx?id=295).

Craig Hight is Associate Professor in Screen and Media Studies at the University of Waikato, New Zealand. His research has been based within documentary theory, addressing aspects of the production, construction and reception of documentary hybrids (in particular mockumentary). His most recent book was on television mockumentary series, titled *Television Mockumentary: Reflexivity, Satire and a Call for Play* (2010). His current research focuses on the relationships between digital media technologies and documentary practice, especially the variety of factors shaping online documentary cultures.

Taisto Hujanen, Dr.Soc.Sc., is Professor of Electronic Media in the School of Communication, Media and Theatre, University of Tampere, Finland. Most recently published work is a co-edited book *Intermediality and Media* Change (2012). Currently introducing and supervising a research project on "Broadcasting in the Post-Broadcast Era: Policy, Technology, and Content Production, funded by the Academy of Finland" (for 2013–2017). Main research interests include strategic development and governance of public service media, media change and discursive transformation of broadcast media.

Ana Jorge is Guest Assistant Professor at University NOVA of Lisbon. She holds a Ph.D. in Communication Sciences from the same University, with a thesis on young audiences and fans of celebrity culture. Currently member of European projects EU Kids Online (Safer Internet Programme) and RadioActive Europe (Lifelong Learning Programme), she has participated in an international project dedicated to digital inclusion and participation, and national projects about the representation of gender in lifestyle magazines and press. She has worked as communication officer in companies and agencies, and on science communication projects. Her research interests include audience studies, children and media, media education and consumption.

Seppo Kangaspunta, Dr.Soc.Sc., is Senior Lecturer of Television Journalism in the School of Communication, Media and Theatre, University of Tampere, Finland. Recently published works include a book (in Finnish, 2013) about digital television and the transformation to multimedia and an edited book (in Finnish, 2011) about changes in interpretations of the community. Main research interests include digitalisation of television, media practices and media use in cross-media context.

Christian Kobbernagel is Assistant Professor who is teaching communication theory and quantitative methodology in Communication Studies at Department of Communication, Business and Information Technologies at Roskilde University, Denmark. His area of interest is methodological innovation to enable cross-fertilizing research using quantitative and qualitative methods in combination. He has conducted quantitative research in various fields such as film audience studies, news consumption, museum audience reception and young peoples' media use in everyday life—some of which has a special focus on theory and analysis in latent variable modelling.

Dafna Lemish, Ph.D. (Ohio State University, 1982) is Professor of Communication, Interim-Dean of the College of Mass Communication and Media Arts at Southern Illinois University Carbondale and founding editor of the *Journal of Children and Media*. She is the author and editor of numerous books and articles on children, media and gender representations including most recently: *The Routledge International Handbook on Children, Adolescents and Media* (2013) and *Screening Gender on Children's Television: The Views of Producers Around the World* (2010). She is a Fellow of the International Communication Association (ICA), the first recipient of the Teresa Award for the Advancement of Feminist Scholarship and the inaugural recipient of the Senior Researcher Award of Children, Adolescents and Media Division of the association.

Barbara Lewandowska-Tomaszczyk is Professor Ordinarius of English Language and Linguistics at the University of Lodz, Poland. Her research interests are primarily in semantics and pragmatics of natural language, corpus linguistics and their applications in online audience research, translation studies, lexicography and discourse analysis. She has published a number of books and papers in those areas and organized numerous international conferences and seminars. Over the years Professor Lewandowska-Tomaszczyk has been invited to read papers at international conferences and to lecture and conduct seminars at European and American universities. She has coordinated numerous international programmes and supervised a number of dissertations and research activities. She is editor-in-chief of the series Lodz Studies in Language, published at Peter Lang (Frankfurt a. Main). Professor Lewandowska-Tomaszczyk's current research focuses on three projects, which look at event structure and time concepts, the conceptualization of emotions and computer-mediated communication, as well as in cross-linguistic and translational perspectives.

Yuwei Lin is Course Leader for B.A. (Hons) Media and Communications in the School of Film and Media at the University for the Creative Arts, UK. She was awarded a Ph.D. in sociology by the University of York in 2005. Her research interests centre on the socio-technical dynamics within and across open innovation systems, including Free/Libre Open Source Software (FLOSS), Open Data, Amateur/Citizen Science, and Participatory/Social Media. In addition to her teaching and research, Yuwei also advocates for free/open-source software, open data, digital rights and encouraging girls to participate in science and technology. Prior to being appointed to her current post, Yuwei was Lecturer in the School of Arts and Media at the University of Salford (2009–2013), Research Associate in the School of Social Sciences at the University of Manchester (2006–2009) and Postdoctoral Research Fellow in the Business School at the Vrije Universiteit Amsterdam (2005–2006).

David Mathieu, Ph.D., is currently Assistant Professor at the Department of Communication, Business and Information Technologies at Roskilde University, Denmark, where he lectures and researches in audience and reception studies, as well as in the area of methodologies. Mathieu completed his Bachelor and Master Degrees at Laval University (Québec, Canada) and was awarded his Ph.D. in 2013 at Roskilde University (Denmark) based on a thesis in which he developed a contextual approach to news reception at the intersection of culture, language and cognition. His interests include not only audience but also discourse, language and cognition, news production and consumption, as well as the interplay between qualitative and quantitative research. His current work focuses on the changing nature of audience on social media, trying to understand audience meanings at the intersection of old and new media.

Galit Nimrod, Ph.D., is Associate Professor at the Department of Communication Studies and a research fellow at the Center for Multidisciplinary Research in Aging at Ben-Gurion University of the Negev, Israel. She holds a Ph.D. in Communication and Journalism from the Hebrew University of Jerusalem, and she was a Fulbright postdoctoral scholar in the Gerontology Center and the Department of Leisure and Recreation Studies at the University of Georgia, US. Dr. Nimrod studies psychological and sociological aspects of leisure and media use among populations with special needs such as older adults and people with disabilities. Within this area, she focuses on several subjects, including leisure and later life transitions (such as retirement, widowhood and health decline), innovation in leisure and new media as leisure activity and their functions for individuals and various social groups.

Brian O'Neill is Head of the School of Media at Dublin Institute of Technology, Ireland. His research interests include media literacy research, policymaking and public interest issues in media and communications. He has written widely on media technologies and media literacy for academic journals as well as for organisations such as UNICEF and the Broadcasting Commission of Ireland. He is a member of the Management Committee of COST Action IS0906 ("Transforming Audiences, Transforming Societies") and is Chair of the Audience Section of the International Association for Media and Communication Research (IAMCR). Brian O'Neill is also a member of the Management Group of EU Kids Online and leads the work package on "Policy and Recommendations".

Cristina Ponte, Ph.D. and Habilitation on Media and Journalism Studies, Associate Professor at the Faculty of Social and Human Sciences (FCSH) / NOVA, New University of Lisbon, Portugal. Her research examines media, journalism and society; children, youth and media; media and generations, with a focus on the family; digital inclusion. Coordinating the Portuguese team in the EU Kids Online Project since 2006, she has a wide experience on leading international and large teams of researchers, including the Working Group on Social Integration in the COST Action "Transforming Audiences, Transforming Societies" (2010–2014), and the funded projects "Digital Inclusion and Participation" (2009–2011), and "Children and Young People in the News" (2005–2007). The author of ten books and several articles in Portuguese and English, and a former vice-chair of the Audience and Reception Section of ECREA (2008–2012), she is currently vice-chair of the European Communication Research and Education Association Temporary Working Group on Children, Youth and Media.

Seija Ridell works as a professor in the School of Communication, Media and Theatre at the University of Tampere, Finland. Her areas of expertise include news narratology, social semiotic theory of genre, cultural audience research, web studies and theories of publicness. Ridell's most recent research revolves around medium theory and technology-mediated modes of (inter)action in diverse public and semi-public spatial contexts.

Kim Christian Schrøder is Professor of Communication at the Department of Communication, Business and Information Technologies at Roskilde

University, Denmark. His co-authored and co-edited books in English include *Audience Transformations: Shifting Audience Positions in Late Modernity* (2014), *Museum Communication and Social Media: The Connected Museum* (2013), *Digital Content Creation* (2010), *Researching Audiences* (2003), *Media Cultures* (1992) and *The Language of Advertising* (1985). His interests comprise the theoretical, methodological and analytical aspects of audience uses and experiences of media in everyday life, with particular reference to the challenges of methodological pluralism. His recent work explores different methods for mapping news consumption.

Andra Siibak, Ph.D., is Senior Research Fellow of Media Studies at the Institute of Social Sciences at the University of Tartu, Estonia. Her present research interests include young people's social media use, people's perceptions conceptualisations of privacy in networked publics and intergenerational relations in new media. She is principal investigator of the research project "Conceptualisations and Experiences with Public and Private in Technologically Saturated Society" financed by the Estonian Research Council and engaged in the project "Generations and Intergenerational Relations in the Emerging Information Society". In COST IS0906 "Transforming Audiences, Transforming Societies", she is a task force leader within working group three and co-leader of the cross-working group initiative "Generations and Media".

Christine W. Trültzsch-Wijnen is Professor for Media Education and E-learning at the University of Education Salzburg, Austria. She studied media and communication as well as music and holds a Ph.D. in communication from the University of Salzburg. From 2010 to 2014 she was post-doctoral research assistant at the Department of Education at the University of Vienna. Her work focuses on audience research, young people and the internet, media socialisation, media literacy, international comparisons of media education as well as methods and methodologies of qualitative research. She is member of the advisory board of Saferin-ternet.at, chair of the section media education of the Austrian Association of Research and Development in Education, vice chair of the section media education of the German Association of Journalism and Communication Research and Austrian Country Representative of the Young Scholars Network of European Communication Research and Education Association.

Sascha Trültzsch-Wijnen received his Magister Artium (Master of Arts) in Sociology and Media and Communication Studies after studying at Martin-Luther-University Halle-Wittenberg, Germany. As a research assistant, from 2004 to 2007, he worked in the Project Programme of East-German Television–The Family Series founded by the German Research Foundation and completed his doctoral thesis: "Contextualised Media Analysis—A Discourse-analytical Method Sensitive to Ideological Components in

Entertaining Television Shows". In 2008, he received his PhD (Dr. Phil.). Since 2009, his post-doctoral work has been at the Department of Communication Studies of the University of Salzburg, Austria. In COST IS0906 "Transforming Audiences, Transforming Societies", he is a task force leader within working group four. He currently works on social web usage and privacy, television history, media analysis and audience studies.

Nicoletta Vittadini is Associate Professor of Sociology of Culture and Communication at the Università Cattolica del Sacro Cuore in Milan, Italy. She is a senior researcher at OssCom (Research Centre on Media and Communication) and is Director of the Master in Digital Communications Specialist. Her research interests concern digital media and everyday life, social media theory, youth digital cultures and migrants. She is also interested in research methodologies relating to digital and social media. She is member of the research group who carried out national projects on "Media and Generations in the Italian Society" (2006–2009) and "Online Social Relations and Identity: Italian Experience in Social Network Sites" (2011–2013). She is a member of the COST Action IS0906, "Transforming Audiences, Transforming Societies", where she co-leaded the cross-working group on media and generations and (in 2012) she became a member of the DIMRCL (Developing & Investigating Methodologies for Researching Connected Learning) network of the MacArthur Foundation.

Frauke Zeller is Assistant Professor in the School of Professional Communication at Ryerson University in Toronto (Ontario), Canada. She received her Ph.D. (Dr. Phil.) from Kassel University, Germany, in 2005 in English Linguistics and Computational Philology. From 2005 to 2011, she was a researcher and lecturer at Ilmenau University of Technology, Germany, working in the Institute of Media and Communication Studies. She finished her Habilitation (highest academic degree in Germany) in 2011, using mixed methods to analyse online communities. Frauke Zeller was awarded with a range of major research grants, among them a Marie Curie Fellowship (2011–2013), which is one of Europe's most distinguished individual research grants. It enabled her to conduct research on big data and multimodal communication analyses tools. She worked as a Marie Curie Fellow at the renowned Centre for Digital Humanities at University College London (Great Britain). She is also involved in several international research projects, notably as member of the steering group and chair in the EU COST Action "Transforming Audiences, Transforming Societies". Her research interests include organizational communication, Human-Computer Interaction/Human-Robot Interaction, digital communication, and method development for digital research analyses.

Index

Abbas 180–2
ability 37, 64, 67, 71, 75, 147, 151, 182–3, 266, 271
accessibility 153
active subject 45, 50, 56–7
actuality 2, 15–16, 18, 24
adolescents 40
adults 6, 147, 153, 159–60, 162, 185, 225
affordances 1–2, 64–8, 70–2, 75–7, 117, 125, 195, 201, 210, 244, 254, 261, 266, 273
Agar 14, 18–21
age 5, 13, 33, 38, 59, 99, 145–7, 149–50, 153, 163–4, 169, 172–3, 176, 181, 189, 195–8, 205, 219, 226, 229, 254
ageism 147–9, 154–5
agency 3, 48, 62, 68, 70–2, 75–6, 88, 127, 148, 195, 199–201, 203–5, 210, 239, 261, 275
agentic power 200, 203
Agosto 180–2
Atkinson 14, 21, 31
audiencehood 3–4, 7, 62, 67, 70–2, 76, 215, 246, 249–52; contemporary 4, 76; model of 71, 76
audiencing 216, 238, 250
authorities 25, 110, 114, 161, 172, 218, 220
autoethnography 2–3, 29–34, 41
avatars 2, 13, 17–21, 23

Bakardjieva 13, 15–17, 245
Baker 177, 181, 184–6
Baltes 146, 151, 153–4
Bauman 117, 161, 164, 205
Baumer 177, 185–6
Baym 15, 18, 176, 262, 275
Beneito-Montagut 14–17, 24

Bennett 107–8, 198, 211
Berry 31, 64, 69–70
Big Brother 89, 222, 224
big data 7, 261–4, 266–76
Big Five 178, 187, 189
Boellstorff 15–16, 18–21, 24, 271
Bourdieu 106–9, 178, 183, 187–8, 198, 211
boyd 102, 176–7, 179, 201–2, 206, 208, 250, 262–3, 268, 270–1, 273–5
broadcast media 219, 249
Brooks 261–2, 275
Bruns 110, 262, 272, 275
Buckingham 74, 81, 103, 149, 161, 196–7, 199
bullying 148, 160–1, 165–70, 172–3; online 166–7
Burgelman 265
Burgess 73

Calvert 148–9, 180–1
catalyst 47, 55–6, 152
Chang 31–2
changing media environment 145, 275
charismatic authority 107–8
childhood 146–52, 154–5
children 5, 34, 145–55, 159–66, 168–70, 172–3, 181, 185, 197, 208, 224–5, 227–8, 237; online 165
Chomsky 86, 89–91, 92, 95–7
city 19, 204, 237, 239–40, 242, 245–52, 254–5; contemporary cities 240, 244, 246, 248, 252–3
class 30, 33, 40, 85, 106, 108–9, 149, 162–3, 179, 195–6, 202
CMC *see* computer-mediated communication
codes 39, 62–3, 65, 67, 77, 110, 115–16, 236, 239

Index

cognition 51, 70; cognitive 3, 51, 56–7, 59, 82, 84, 87, 146–7, 149, 151, 179, 197–8
cohesiveness 87, 100, 102–3
collapsed contexts 102
commentator 85, 89–90, 92–3, 95–6, 98, 100, 102–3
commenting readers 114, 116
communication 17, 33, 62–3, 65, 75, 82, 96, 99, 111–12, 116–18, 125–6, 176, 182, 198, 206, 220, 227, 236, 239, 243, 246–7; acts 80, 82, 103; technologies 176, 236, 243, 274; interaction patterns 80, 82
community 16, 18, 21, 57, 83, 85, 112, 183, 216–17, 275; online 102
comparative research 5, 123–4, 127, 130, 139, 141, 145, 153, 160, 169, 173
complexity 3, 5–6, 20, 23, 29, 32, 38, 42, 72, 265
comprehension 49–51, 56–7
computer-mediated communication (CMC) 4, 80, 85, 112, 118; computer-mediated interaction 4, 80–1, 103
conceptual models 70, 151
conscientiousness 178, 189
consistencies 206–7, 243
constraint 74, 47, 75, 148, 152, 154, 195, 199–200, 210
consumer 74, 107, 136, 217–18, 220, 226, 230, 265
context 2–3, 6, 9, 20–4, 31, 37, 40, 44–5, 47–50, 52–3, 55–9, 69–72, 82, 84–5, 110, 112, 115, 117–18, 127, 146, 160–1, 163–4, 166–7, 173, 216–19, 227–8, 230–2, 269, 271, 274–5; contextual factors 55, 72, 146, 164; contextual inquiry 44–5; of media use 29, 54; personal 114, 116–17; social 16, 32, 57–8, 103, 111, 196–7, 199, 205
continuum 18, 160, 198, 231
convergence 9, 34, 106, 113, 215, 218, 221, 232; convergent media 9, 200
corpus 80, 83–90, 92–6, 97–102, 275
Couldry 110, 126–8, 140, 233, 237, 240–1, 261, 271, 275
Crawford 262–3, 268, 270–1, 273–5
creative practices 62, 66–7

Creese 111–12
cross-cultural 100, 130, 165; comparative research 130
cross-media 9, 225, 227, 229–32, 234; context 216, 229–31; environment 6, 215; use 215
cultural consumers 107, 109
cultural contexts 32, 56, 68, 93, 181, 184, 196, 201, 216
cultural identity 39–40, 118
cultural producers 106–7, 109, 114, 117–18
cultural software 64, 68
cultural specificities 130, 164
culture 5, 13, 32–3, 49, 51, 63, 67, 76, 83–5, 101, 111, 123, 125, 127–30, 133, 149, 151, 160, 164–5, 172, 179, 187, 201–3, 231, 271, 275, 278; online 74, 162
culturomics 268–9
cyberbullying 166–7

Denzin 29–30
dialogue 116, 118, 130, 204
diary 19, 33, 36, 109
digital culture 114, 234
digital ecology 3, 62, 68–9, 77
digitalisation 217–18, 220–1, 223, 225, 227–9, 236, 239, 247
digital media 70, 72, 77, 103, 160, 200–1, 231
digital natives 197–8, 227
digital switchover 216, 220–3, 227–9
digital technologies 15, 106–7, 110, 118, 197, 199, 202, 220, 252
digital television 6, 215, 218–23, 225, 229–30, 233
digital video 62, 109, 234
Dijck 122
disclosure 31–2, 191
discourse(s) 4, 44, 51, 57, 59, 63, 80, 82, 84–5, 89, 98–100, 109, 112, 159–61, 163, 172, 217–18, 225, 261, 267; markers 90, 93, 96, 98, 100
domestication 7, 128, 179, 223, 226, 240, 242–3, 253–4
double articulation 240, 242–3, 254
dropping out 183
Drotner 160, 236–7, 250

Eichhorn 20–2, 25
elites 4, 106, 109–10, 117
eliteness 106–7, 110, 114, 117

elite identities 107–9, 114–15, 117; *see also* identity
elite studies 106, 109, 114, 117
Ellison 176, 178–82, 184–7, 208
emotionality 96, 98–9
empowerment 68, 72, 74, 152
engagement 3, 63, 65, 69–70, 76, 181, 199–201, 204–5, 250, 269
enhanced television 221–2, 228
essentialist 82, 238
ethics 162, 273
ethnicity 40, 85, 149, 181, 195–6
ethnography 2, 14, 17–19, 22–3, 31–2, 111–12
EU Kids Online 163, 165, 181
everyday life 32, 34, 37, 45, 52, 56–7, 59, 125–6, 163–4, 188, 195, 197, 226
expectations 21–2, 148, 186, 218, 221–2, 224
extraversion 178, 189

Facebook 13, 24, 36, 64–5, 69, 74, 76–7, 162, 167, 169–72, 179, 181–7, 204–9, 227
Facebook non-users 183–6
face-to-face 19–21, 195, 236
families 33–4, 54–5, 72, 83, 85, 90, 100–1, 133, 137, 149, 151, 153, 161, 164–5, 172, 178–80, 182, 187–8, 198, 216, 221, 223–9
Fetveit 232–3
Fielding 268, 274
fieldwork 21–2, 25, 164
first articulation 243–4, 254
Fiske 33, 196, 238
focus groups 5, 49, 52, 54, 166, 173
frequent users 185–6
friends 49, 55, 69, 74, 90, 151, 162, 166–71, 178–82, 184–6, 198, 202, 207–10, 222, 224, 226–7
friendship groups 180, 182
friends of friends 169, 171, 178

Gane 239, 253
Gangadharbatla 182
gender 5, 30, 33, 38, 40, 45, 85, 87, 90, 100, 149–50, 163, 171, 173, 195–8, 202, 205
Georgakopoulou 112
girls 54, 86–7, 99–100, 166, 168–71, 184, 205
Godbey 152–3

Google 65–6, 74, 76, 229, 264, 269
Görzig 163, 165
Graham 247, 252
Graney 153
grey zones 5, 159, 172
groups 6, 23, 31–3, 50–2, 55, 66, 81, 84–5, 88, 98, 102–3, 129, 134–5, 140–1, 146–7, 150, 153–5, 164–5, 167, 169, 171, 178, 184, 195–6, 198, 202–4, 207, 209, 220, 272; cohesiveness 87, 102–3; groups of users 3, 66–7, 76, 198; identity 4, 80, 100–4, 102, 113; social groups 81, 196, 199, 202–3; *see also* identity
Gubrium 30, 52, 57, 59

habitus 6, 183, 188–9, 196, 198
Haddon 145, 159, 163, 165, 179, 240, 243, 254
Hagen 160–2
Halevi 261, 263
Hammersley 14, 21, 31, 33, 45
Hargittai 180–1, 197–9
harm 153, 163, 165
Harrison 109, 184, 187
Hartmann 243–4, 254, 264–5, 276
Hasebrink 125–6, 176–7
Hepburn 46–8, 57, 59
Hepp 123–5, 127–8, 140
Herkman 216, 224, 226
Herring 85
Hine 14, 16, 22, 25
Hirsch 179, 223, 237
Holstein 30, 52, 57
homogenous groups 150, 154–5
households 179, 188, 199, 218, 220, 222–3, 229, 237, 241–4
humanities 63, 67, 261, 263
hybrid ethnographies 2, 13, 16–22, 24
hybridisation 15–16
hybrid light news consumer 132, 136

ICTs (Information and Communication Technologies) 35, 150, 176, 187, 197, 236–7, 243–4, 274
identification 40, 55, 81, 98, 102, 154, 227
identity(ies) 2, 4, 6, 13–14, 16, 34, 39–41, 48–9, 55, 80–5, 88, 101–2, 107, 109, 111, 113–14, 117–18, 170, 178, 195, 204, 209–11, 215–16, 229–31, 233; elite 107–9, 114–15, 117; group

4, 80, 100–4, 102, 113; literary 115–16; online 80; sexual 40
identity of television 219
impression management 187
independence 83, 85, 151–2
individuals 81, 85, 141, 146–7, 151–2, 154, 159, 161, 185, 197, 200–4, 275
individual users 68, 76, 90, 92, 272
Information and Communication Technologies *see* ICTs
infrastructure 25, 72, 74, 77, 239, 252
interactive social media 106, 265
interactive television 221
interactivity 199, 218, 221–2, 229, 231
interconnectivity value 86–7, 90–2, 95–7, 102
intermediality 6, 215–16, 218–19, 227, 233–4
intermedial redefinition 215, 217–18, 232
intermedial user practices 6, 217–18, 224, 228, 230, 233
intermedia project 215, 232
internet research 160, 267, 272, 274
internet usage 198; patterns 165, 198
internet users 82, 102, 162, 197; uses 159, 197
interview 3, 18, 29, 36–7, 39–40, 44–52, 54–9, 113, 162, 166, 172, 183, 186, 204–5, 211, 216, 218, 223, 226; context 37–8; in-depth 19, 30, 37, 204; method 49–50, 52, 55–6, 59; models 55; participatory 3, 45, 52–3, 56–8; performative 3, 48, 50–1, 56–8; process 30, 53; research 44, 47, 58–9; semi-structured 44–6; situation 47–8, 51, 59; statements 55–6; traditional 45, 47–8, 50, 56–8; traditional interview process 57, 59
ISFOL 187
Ito 177, 191, 200–1, 203, 251

Jansson 202, 237, 241
Jenkins 48, 75, 83, 110, 162, 167, 196, 229–30, 262, 275
Jensen 44, 49, 227, 269
Jers 179–80
Joinson 180
journalism 52, 54, 231

Kalmus 176–7, 180–1, 183–4, 186
Kangaspunta 217, 220–2, 234
Karpf 270–3, 275
Kendall 13, 15–16, 22
keyness 87, 94
keywords 85, 87, 93–4
Kidd 106, 109
Kirwil 165
Kitchin 62–3, 68, 77, 247
Kleiber 148, 152, 154
Klein 264–5, 276
Kloß 272, 274
knowledge production 50, 55–7
Krämer 177–8, 180
Kvale 44, 46, 59

Lampe 178–81, 184–7
language 4, 39–40, 48, 50, 57, 66, 73, 82–5, 90, 93, 95, 103, 106, 111–12; data 82, 84; users 87–8
large data sets 261, 263–4, 266, 268, 271–2
late adopters 220, 224, 226, 234
Lazer 272, 276
Leander 15, 17, 25
leisure 152, 154–5, 202
Lenhart 166, 180–1
Leung 179–80
lexis 88
Leydesdorff 263–4
life span 146, 154
lifestyles 133, 150, 202–3, 210, 231
life transitions 154–5
lifeworld 24, 44–5, 56, 58
light news consumers 132, 136–7, 139
Lincoln 29–30, 153
linguistic ethnography 4, 106, 110–12, 114, 117–18
literacies 62, 64, 71–2, 127, 197–8; media literacy 6, 64, 72, 149, 176, 183, 188–9, 226; software literacies 3, 70–2, 75; *see also* media; software
literary identity *see* identity
literary self-representation 117
literary writers 107–9, 114–16
Livingstone 44–5, 70, 72, 110, 127, 129–30, 148, 153, 155, 159, 163–6, 176, 180–1, 195–6, 198–200, 203, 211, 237
Lupton 162–3

Madden 177, 181, 185–6
Manovich 62–5, 67–70, 73, 76–7, 262, 268, 272–4
marginalisation 149
Markham 15, 270
mass media 39, 69, 221, 242, 244–6, 248–9, 251; audiencehood 246, 251; reception 246
Matzat 263, 267, 274
McCarthy 237, 241, 245–6, 248–9
McKim 15, 17, 25
media 5–6, 9, 31, 33–5, 38–42, 52–3, 55, 63–4, 66–7, 69–70, 110, 112, 123–7, 133–4, 136, 138, 145–6, 148–55, 159–62, 177, 188, 200–1, 215–16, 226–7, 229–30, 232–4, 236–8, 240–5, 248–9, 254; analysis 228; change 219, 232; choices 35, 138, 179; city 255; consumption 52–3, 55, 107, 126, 177, 196, 200, 223, 249; contents 38, 48, 149, 154–5, 229; cultures 52, 127, 140, 161; discourses 51, 159; ecologies 76; education 188; effects 148, 155; ethnography 196, 240; forms 77, 215–16, 232; generations 160, 226; identities 6, 81–2, 215–16, 234; industries 118, 146, 229; life 126; literacy 6, 64, 72, 149, 176, 183, 188–9, 226; logics 124; mobile 135, 139, 148, 236, 246, 251; morality 160; networked 65, 68, 71, 227; news 125, 127–31, 133–6, 140; online 136–9; panics 160; personalised 240, 245–6 power 124; practices 55, 76, 126, 216, 229, 233; processes 70; products 146; reception 44, 50, 55, 237–8, 242; refusal 183; relationships 216–17, 227, 229–30, 233; repertoires 9, 125–6; research 30, 34, 41, 160; systems 130, 200; technologies 218, 226–7, 242–4, 251, 254; usage 3, 29–31, 35–6, 38, 41, 45, 55, 177, 184, 188, 243, 275; users 216, 228–31
mediation 126, 163, 215–16, 232–3; processes 215, 233
mediatisation 54, 123–5, 128
mediator 226–7
medium relationship 6, 226, 233–4
metaphor 86, 88–9, 217, 241, 248–9
Miller 15–18
mobile communication 237
mobile devices 70, 73, 176, 249–50
modalities 6, 227, 233–4
modes 15, 29, 31, 50, 201, 205, 238
Moed 261, 263
moral compass 159, 168
moral economy 179, 188
morality 15, 17, 23, 159–64, 172–3
Morley 38, 179, 196, 236–7, 241–2, 244
Moscovici 217
motivations 9, 71, 74, 177, 180, 197, 199, 275
motives 23, 116, 177, 179–81, 187
movies 39–40, 172
Moyser 109
multiple self-positionings 15, 19

Napoli 228–9, 269, 275
narratives 47, 110, 112–13, 115–17, 154; analysis 115–16; content 114–18; personal 113
Naughton 180–2
Navarrete 18, 25
negotiation 57, 81, 83, 159, 161, 166–7, 169, 172–3, 196, 253
networked audiences 6, 195
networked media *see* media
networks 8, 63, 97, 112–13, 125, 179, 182, 202–3, 207–10, 269, 271
neuroticism 178, 189
new media: environment 196, 199; hype 218, 221; technologies 227–8, 241
news comprehension 49, 51
news consumption 4–5, 123–8, 131, 135, 138–40, 267
news diet 131, 134–5
news media *see* media
new technologies 9, 107, 160, 183, 187, 202, 220–1, 228, 230, 247
Nicholls 106, 109
non-representation 7, 239, 247–8
non-usage 177, 187–8
non-users 5–6, 181, 183–8
norms 18, 160–2, 164–5, 168–9, 172–3, 176, 203, 231

occupations 106, 108, 116–17
Ólafsson 165, 176, 180

old age 146, 148–9
older adults 5, 145, 147–55, 227
older audiences 150
older people 220
old media 1, 196, 199
online behaviour 161, 169, 195, 268
online bullying *see* bullying
online communication 80–2, 96, 102, 177, 182
online communities *see* community
online culture *see* culture
online identities *see* identities
online interactions 14, 81
online media *see* media
online news 134–5
online performances 195, 205
online risks 161–2, 172
online video *see* video
open source software 118
opponents 81, 92, 99, 101
Orgad 14–17, 20–1, 159–60, 173

Page 112–13
Papacharissi 201, 203, 205, 208
parental mediation 165
parents 5, 40, 146, 153, 159, 161–2, 164–5, 167, 170, 172–3, 199, 225, 227
Park 128, 181, 263–4
Parsons 108
participant observation 24–5, 32, 151
participatory interview *see* interview
participatory model 45, 55
participatory process 53–4
peers 54–5, 72, 153, 159, 161–2, 164, 166, 171–3, 177, 181–2, 188; peer cultures 161, 171
performance 3, 7, 48–51, 57–8, 68–70, 76–7, 112, 116, 186, 207, 238, 242, 250; of software 69
performative ambiguity 48
performative interview *see* interview
performative model 45
personal context *see* context
personal experiences 112–13, 116
personalised media *see* media
personal narratives *see* narratives
plurality 196, 198–9
politics 50, 83, 85, 124, 128, 149, 259
pornography 148, 165–6
Portwood-Stacer 183, 185–7
Porvoo 222–4, 226
positioning 58, 159–61, 168, 170, 172, 187, 246

Potter 46–8, 57, 59
power 109–10, 160, 162, 200, 203, 210, 238–9, 248, 250, 252–4, 271; of agency 6, 200, 203, 210, 212; dynamics 238–9, 252, 254; power-relatedness 6, 236, 239–40, 245, 248, 253–4; relationships 4, 106, 117
privacy 97, 114, 153, 171, 180, 185, 188, 241; paradox 180
programming code 64, 66, 68
proliferation 3, 73–4, 107, 236, 239, 244, 246–7
proper distance 20, 160, 168
public space 222, 249, 251
Putnam 106, 178–9

q elicitation cards 130
q factor analysis 129, 131, 135
q grid 129
q methodology 4, 123, 128–30, 135, 140
q sort 128, 140; q sorting 131
q task 136
qualitative: analysis 4, 90, 93, 96, 98, 124, 129; approach 123, 216–7; data 128, 130, 159, 164, 183, 274; media 30, 33; methods 80, 82, 113–4, 129, 271; research 29–31, 36–8, 44, 46, 48, 76, 124, 130, 183, 188, 195, 268; study 6, 128, 177, 204
qualitative and quantitative methods 80, 82, 103, 129, 130,
quantitative: analysis 4, 37, 93, 98, 100, 124; approach 123, 274; data 129–30, 269, 93; methods 80, 82, 113, 129; research 29, 36, 46, 268; studies 188; tools 4, 80
quasi-researcher 45, 54, 56–7
question–answer model 45–6, 53, 59

race 33–4, 83, 85, 196, 202
Rampton 112
Rantanen 33
readers 32, 41, 108–9, 113, 115–16, 119, 140–1, 210
reception 1, 9, 45, 49–50, 58, 218, 245, 251, 253; analysis 49–50
recipients 3, 45, 49–51, 57, 110, 178, 187; recipient factors 179, 183
Reed-Danahay 31–2

reflexivity 13, 15, 31, 34, 54, 56, 58, 203, 205
reform 219–21, 228
relationship(s) 15–17, 19–20, 23, 25, 52–3, 58–9, 69, 106, 111, 116, 150, 153–4, 166–8, 170, 173, 176, 178–9, 200, 202, 206, 210, 220, 227–8, 233, 245, 268; factors 178, 181, 187
remediation 215
repertoire 128–9, 133, 136–7, 229
Ribak 147–8, 153
Riessman 115
risk perception 5
risks 81, 148, 159, 162–5, 169, 172–3, 176, 188, 233, 261–2, 273
routines 126, 202–4, 242–3, 245, 253–4
Runnel 180–1, 183–4

safety 169
Scannell 242
Schmidt 110, 114, 176–7, 274
Schupp 178
Second Life 2, 13–14, 18–25
segmentation 102, 150
self 2, 13, 19, 23, 32, 39, 41, 81–2, 113, 116–18, 201–3, 206, 210, 236, 242, 246; self-disclosure 31, 36, 42; self-expression 186, 205, 210; self-performances 201–2, 210; self-positioning 15, 19; self-presentation 89, 176, 178, 185–7, 201–3; self-reflection 30–3; self-representation 116–17, 178, 202, 205
semi-structured interview *see* interview
seniors 150, 152, 155
set-top boxes 220, 223, 228–9
sexual identity *see* identity
Silverman 44, 49, 52
Silverstone 7, 160, 168, 179, 188, 237, 240–4, 253–4
Singer 148
Skains 108
skills 3, 58, 71, 74, 149, 163, 165, 188, 198
Slater 14–18, 24–5
Smith 13, 16–17, 177, 184, 241
SNS (social networking sites) 166, 173, 176–89, 195, 197–201, 203–5, 207, 211; usage 176–7, 181, 188–9; users 180, 183, 185, 196, 200, 204, 210
social capital 178–9, 181, 187
social context *see* context
social groups *see* group
social life 16, 111, 239, 242, 252–3
social media 4, 6, 63, 82, 107–10, 112–13, 117–18, 122, 131, 133, 135, 137–40, 162, 177, 227, 261–2, 264–5, 268–70, 272, 278; applications 272; context 64, 69, 107, 118; platforms 63, 65–6, 71, 76; usage 177, 180, 189, 261–2, 265, 268–9, 272
social networking 64, 179–81
social networking sites *see* SNS
social networks 8, 73, 75, 195, 201, 209, 231–2
social positions 6, 179, 195–6, 198, 203, 210
social virtual worlds 14–15
socio-technical actors 6, 195
software 3, 25, 62–72, 74–7, 83, 253; applications 63–7, 70–1; culture 3, 62, 66–8, 70, 73–6; contemporary software culture 65, 74; interfaces 63, 67; literacies 3, 70–2, 75; studies 3, 62–4, 67; tools 64, 67, 71, 73, 75, 274; users 66
spatial contexts 237–8, 242, 245, 248
spatial turn 240–2
Staksrud 164–5, 176, 180
Star 239
Steinfield 178–81, 187
stereotypes 148
stories 31–2, 110, 112–13, 119
strangers 25, 46, 160, 162, 169–73, 179, 251
strong ties 178, 181
subcultures 196, 202–3
switchover 215, 217–20, 224
Syntax 87

Tansley 264, 276
target-oriented audiencing 216, 231
teachers 72, 159, 161–2, 164
techno eliteness 109–10, 114, 117–18
techno elites 109–10, 117–18
teens 162, 185
terrestrial television 216, 218
Thaddicken 179–80
Thrift 239, 247, 252–3
Tolle 262, 264, 276

traditional interview *see* interview
traditional interview process *see* interview
transnational 127, 140, 189
triple articulation 244–5, 253–4
trust 2, 19–20, 24, 168
TTR (Type/Token Ratio) 90, 92
Tufecki 184–6
Turkle 14–17
Turner 81, 83
typologies 128, 140, 198–9, 226–7

UGC *see* user-generated content
urban infrastructures 239, 247, 252, 254
urban mass media audiencehood 7, 236, 249
urban space 7, 239, 246–9, 252
urban triple articulation 7, 240, 248, 254
Urrichio 217, 219
user-generated content (UGC) 3, 124–5, 199
user types 131, 135, 198

validity 45–8, 56, 58, 130, 195
Valkenburg 176–7, 181, 197–8, 211
van Dijck 65, 68, 76, 107
van Dijk 44, 49, 197, 211, 275
variable 38, 48, 128, 146, 196, 198–9, 205, 210
variety 264–6, 272
velocity 264–6, 272
veracity 264, 266, 272

video 71, 73, 75–6, 166, 223, 225, 265; online 3, 73
virtual experiences 15, 17, 19, 21–3
virtuality 2, 14–18, 24, 241
virtual spaces 14, 16–18, 20, 23, 168, 250
virtual worlds 2, 15–16, 24, 82, 110, 241
visualisation 90, 95–7
Vitak 182, 184–6
volume 263–4, 266, 272
vulnerability 147–8, 155, 173

Wagstaffe 109
Ward 30
weak ties 178–82
weblogs 4, 113, 116–18
Welker 267, 272, 274
well-being 150, 152–5, 176
worthwhileness 125, 134–6, 140
writers 31, 41, 108, 114–16, 118

younger generations 226–8, 230–1, 233
younger people 148, 176
young non-users 184, 186
young people 5–6, 54–5, 154, 159–66, 171–2, 176–7, 180–1, 183, 188–9, 197–9, 227, 237, 251
youngsters 54, 161–3, 165, 170, 172
youth cultures 161, 170, 172
youths 5, 52–5, 171
YouTube 63–5, 69, 73, 75, 229

Ziehe 203–4